WITHDRAWN

Highl

D0391035

WITHDRAWN
HIGHLINE COLLEGE LIBRARY
line College Library

Reef Life

A Guide to Tropical Marine Life

Brandon Cole
Text by Scott Michael

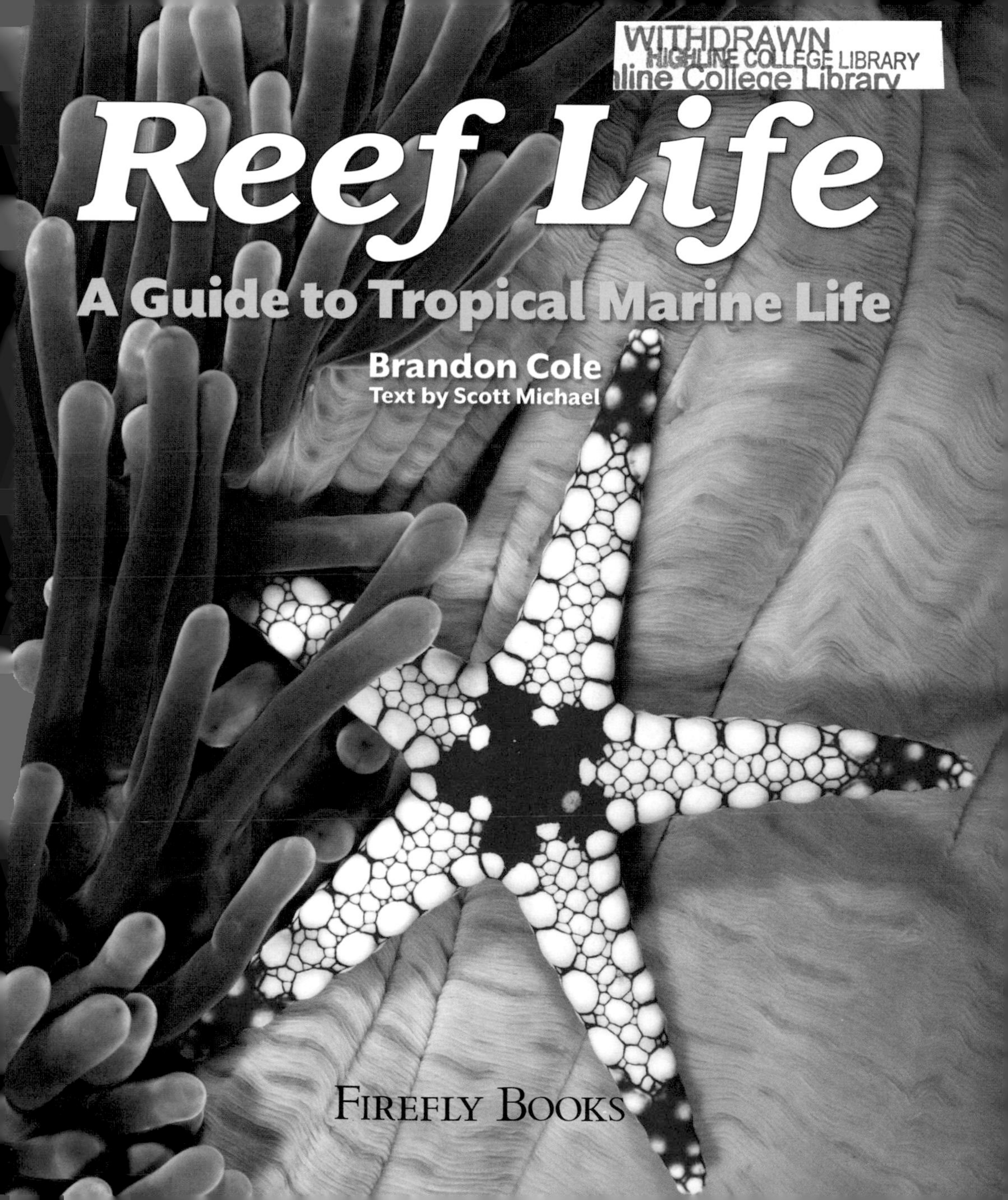

FIREFLY BOOKS

A FIREFLY BOOK

Published by Firefly Books Ltd. 2013

Copyright © 2013 Firefly Books Ltd.
Photographs copyright © Brandon Cole 2013, except as noted on page 616
Text copyright © Scott Michael 2013

All rights reserved. No part of this publication may be reproduced,
stored in a retrieval system, or transmitted in any form or by any means,
electronic, mechanical, photocopying, recording or otherwise, without
the prior written permission of the Publisher.

First printing

Publisher Cataloging-in-Publication Data (U.S.)
Cole, Brandon.
Reef life : a guide to tropical marine life /
Brandon Cole; and Scott Michael.
[616] p. : col. photos. ; cm.
Includes index.
Summary: A comprehensive guidebook for divers,
naturalists and students, featuring photographs of
800 species of tropical ocean life.
ISBN-13: 978-1-77085-190-0 (pbk.)
1. Coral reef animals. I. Michael, Scott. II. Title.
591.90942 dc23 QL125.C654 2013

**Library and Archives Canada Cataloguing in
Publication**
Cole, Brandon
Reef life : a guide to tropical marine life /
Brandon Cole, Scott Michael.
Includes index.
ISBN 978-1-77085-190-0
1. Marine biology--Tropics. I. Michael, Scott W. II.
Title.
QH95.59.C64 2013 578.770913 C2012-
907584-1

Published in the United States by
Firefly Books (U.S.) Inc.
P.O. Box 1338, Ellicott Station
Buffalo, New York 14205

Published in Canada by
Firefly Books Ltd.
50 Staples Avenue, Unit 1
Richmond Hill, Ontario L4B 0A7

Cover and interior design: Hartley Millson
ID design: Gareth Lind
Editing and index: Gillian Watts

Printed in China

LEGEND
⊕ Location
⊙ Habitat
↕ Water depth
↔ Length

*With heartfelt thanks to family and friends, above and
below the waves*
—BC

*To my mother, Donna Michael, for her love and enduring
support of my piscine obsession*
—SM

Contents

Preface

In all things of nature there is something of the marvelous.
—Aristotle

This book presents selected work from a "life aquatic" career spanning twenty years. After earning a bachelor's degree in marine biology from the University of California at Santa Barbara and working as an underwater researcher with the US National Park Service and the Australian Institute of Marine Science, I pursued a PhD for a month, then succumbed to the lure of underwater photography. I left the lab and now spend up to six months each year exploring one of the planet's last frontiers — the world beneath the waves.

Since I had no formal training in the studio or the darkroom, the transition from scientist to artist was a clumsy one. I admit to making far more miserable pictures than memorable ones, breaking more than one camera, and, even after two decades, still being baffled by the complexity of the craft. It's the critters, large and small, that have kept me going through it all.

In recording the oceans' majesty I have traveled the globe, logging millions of air miles and more than 15,000 hours underwater. I count among my favorite scuba-diving locales the coral reefs of Indonesia, the "Enchanted Isles" of the Galápagos, and the current-swept chilly waters off British Columbia. Paradoxically I live in landlocked Spokane, Washington, with my wife, Melissa, an artist and frequent diving companion.

In the ocean I am continually experiencing new manifestations of the marvelous: the contagious thirst for life shown by a group of frolicking wild dolphins; a kelp forest wrapped in silence, yet noisy with color and motion;

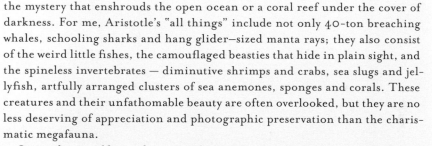

the mystery that enshrouds the open ocean or a coral reef under the cover of darkness. For me, Aristotle's "all things" include not only 40-ton breaching whales, schooling sharks and hang glider–sized manta rays; they also consist of the weird little fishes, the camouflaged beasties that hide in plain sight, and the spineless invertebrates — diminutive shrimps and crabs, sea slugs and jellyfish, artfully arranged clusters of sea anemones, sponges and corals. These creatures and their unfathomable beauty are often overlooked, but they are no less deserving of appreciation and photographic preservation than the charismatic megafauna.

I consider myself most fortunate that my day job allows me to work underwater, witness to the reef's denizens as they go about their daily lives. Though the rush of encountering big animals is undeniable, I'm also happy to spend hours observing the smaller creatures, such as attitudinal 5-centimeter (2-inch) blennies — frantically active fish whose bulging eyes rotate independently — and the mimic octopus, a most engaging cephalopod — a chameleon actor that tries to dupe me with one ingenious disguise after another. I'm sure my laughter at its antics can clearly be heard drifting on the current. Also heard, I hope, is my sincere wish that an appreciation and respect for the wildlife and habitat be foremost in the minds of those who visit the great ocean and those who live along its shores. It's all about enjoying nature — but not at her expense.

—*Brandon Cole, July 2012*

Chapter 1

Tropical Marine Ecosystems

Biodiversity — this is probably the most frequently used term to describe a coral reef. The moment neophyte snorkelers stick their heads under the water's surface, they are awestruck by the spectacular colors displayed by the reef's inhabitants, as well as the great variety of shapes, sizes and behaviors.

Like a calcareous city, stony corals make up the foundation of tropical reefs, and their skeletons provide a framework on which many sedentary animals attach and grow. This includes sponges of different shapes and colors, lattice-like sea fans and gaudy soft corals. Space is a limited resource on the reef, and while corals may look rather benign, they actually engage in chemical and physical warfare to hold on to and expand their "turf." Sea slugs, snails, octopuses, cuttlefishes, shrimps, crabs, urchins, sea stars and other "spineless creatures" utilize the reef for shelter and as a living buffet at which to nourish themselves, while many other invertebrates and fish occupy the sand and rubble plains that border the reef itself. Fishes reach their apex of diversity in this tropical marine ecosystem. Among the branches of the stony corals you can find some of the smallest fish species known, the pygmy gobies, while swimming off the reef face you might see the planet's largest fish, the whale shark.

While there are terrestrial biomes that host comparable species numbers (for example, the rainforests of South America or Papua New Guinea), there is no other ecosystem where you will encounter the "in-your-face" diversity that awaits on the coral reef. On a single small patch of reef you can see hundreds of species, not to mention all the animal varieties you cannot see that conceal themselves deep in reef interstices or under the fringing soft substrate of sand or mud.

But the coral reef is not the only intriguing tropical marine ecosystem. Mangroves and seagrass beds, for example, are important nursery and feeding grounds for reef-dwelling species. There is also the open ocean habitat that

Top
A scuba diver videos a 10 m (33 ft) whale shark (*Rhincodon typus*). Galápagos Islands.

Bottom
A humpback whale mother and her two-month-old calf (*Megaptera novaeangliae*). Hawaiian Islands.

borders seaward reef slopes and walls. While the open ocean may seem "diversity-challenged" when compared to the reef itself, it has its own fascinating community of animals adapted to life in a more nutritionally impoverished environment. Many larger animals that visit inshore tropical environments such as coral reefs also ply the open oceans as they move from breeding to feeding grounds and back again.

In the pages that follow, you will get a glimpse into the ecology and behavior of the animals that inhabit tropical marine ecosystems, especially the most charismatic group of reef creatures — the bony fishes. We have also included a helpful pictorial survey of many of the species, large and small, that you are likely to encounter beneath the waves.

The Coral Reef

Approximately 93,000 species of plants and animals have been reported from coral reefs. This number could easily increase by a factor of ten as we further explore reef habitats, especially deep reefs. Around 30 percent of described marine fish species are found on or around coral reefs, even though this ecosystem is limited to about one-sixth of the world's coastlines. In fact, it is estimated that coral reefs are home to over a quarter of all the ocean's species. It is this amazing biodiversity that has captivated naturalists for centuries and is responsible for luring tens of thousands of divers annually to coral reefs around the world.

So what is a coral reef, anyway? The primary constituents of the reef are the stony corals. These animals belong to the order Scleractinia. Those species that are reef-building varieties are known as hermatypic corals (as opposed to ahermatypic forms). Stony corals are colonial animals that consist of numerous genetically identical, anemone-like creatures called polyps, each of which is encased in calcium carbonate armor (known as a corallite). When a coral colony dies, coral larvae (planula) settle onto its skeleton, attach themselves and begin to grow and reproduce to form a living veneer on the "bones" of their predecessors. Over millions of years, these accumulations of skeletons and the living corals that cover them have formed coral reefs around the world.

But corals are not the only structural component of tropical reefs. A plant group is equally important in reef formation. Coralline algae belong to the

Healthy hard coral growth, here a species of branching coral (*Acropora*). Lyretail anthias (*Pseudanthias squamipinnis*) and reticulated dascyllus (*Dascyllus reticulatus*) school in the current, feeding on plankton. Fiji.

Close-up view of tentacles of the feeding polyps of a stony (hard) coral colony (*Galaxea fascicularis*). Indonesia.

red algae phylum Rhodophyta; like stony corals, they extract calcium carbonate from the surrounding seawater and incorporate it into their cell walls. Coralline algae consolidate reef structure, acting to cement together dead coral skeletons and rubble. You may be surprised to learn that some coral reefs are dominated not by coral but by encrusting coralline algae.

Conditions for Reef Development

So why are coral reefs limited to only one-sixth of the world's coastlines? It's because they require specific environmental conditions in order to develop. Most coral reefs are found where water temperatures range from 25° to 29°C (77° to 84°F), although some reef-building corals can withstand temperatures

A Verco's nudibranch (*Tambja verconis*) crawls across coralline algae searching for the bryozoan upon which it feeds. New Zealand.

as low as 12.8°C (55°F) and as high as 40°C (104°F) for short periods of time. When water temperatures get too high (or too low — a less frequent problem), corals expel their zooxanthellae, which are unicellular algae in the genus *Symbiodinium* that live in the coral's tissue. This phenomenon is known as bleaching. Zooxanthellae are critical to the health of reef-building corals, many soft corals, sea anemones and their relatives. As much as 90 percent of the organic material these algae manufacture by photosynthesis is transferred to the host coral tissue. The plant partners are also responsible for helping to remove metabolic waste from their host. If these algal cells are expelled by the polyps, the host is likely to perish soon after.

Water depth and clarity are also important to ensure that coral polyps and their algae partners get enough light. Most reef-building corals grow at depths of less than 100 meters (325 feet), and reef development is relatively sparse deeper than 70 meters (230 feet). Luminance at greater depths does not allow vigorous coral growth, and water turbidity (which reduces light penetration) will have an impact on corals. Most reefs are found in clear-water environs, although certain corals do well in (and even prefer) more nutrient-rich murky conditions.

Sedimentation will retard coral growth in turbid inshore habitats. As a result, coral reefs are not found where there is substantial river runoff. While most stony corals will be smothered by sediment (it negatively affects both feeding and respiration), some species of large-polyped stony corals are adept at shedding sediment. For example, stony corals in the genus *Scolymia* can transport sediment and sand grains to the edge of the oral disc by means of strands of mucus and cilliary action. They will also distend the center of the disc to move inert materials away from the mouth region or, in some cases, ingest

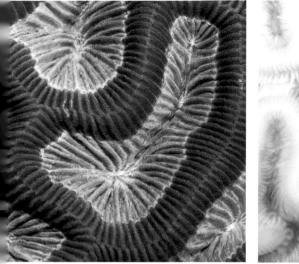

Close-up view of healthy brain coral (*Colpophyllia natans*). Dominica.

Bleaching in boulder brain coral (*Colpophyllia natans*). The polyps have expelled their zooxanthellae symbiotic algae, probably as a result of being stressed by very warm water. This coral may die soon. Dominica.

the sediment and regurgitate it in the form of mucus-bound "pseudofeces." Other large-polyped stony corals able to shed sediment include members of the genera *Alveopora*, *Catalaphyllia*, *Cynarina*, *Goniopora*, *Fungia*, *Heliofungia*, *Herpolitha*, *Polyphyllia* and *Trachyphyllia*; however, these are not usually reef-building species.

Water movement is yet another important ingredient for healthy reef development. Currents act to keep corals from being covered by sediment and bring nutrient-bearing phytoplankton and zooplankton, which certain corals catch in their extended polyps. Salinity also affects coral: reefs occur within a relatively narrow range of between 32 and 42 parts per thousand (ppt). This, along with the associated sedimentation, prevents reef building in areas with lots of freshwater river discharge. And corals also need a consolidated substrate on which to grow; soft substrates will not support reef development.

Because of these specific environmental requirements, coral reefs are limited in distribution to the latitudes between approximately 30° north and 30° south of the equator, with the most well-developed reefs occurring in the tropical Indo-Pacific. Over 90 percent of the world's reefs are found in this region.

A busy, vibrant coral reef showcasing many species of stony and soft corals, with a cloud of lyretail anthias (*Pseudanthias squamipinnis*) swarming above. Fiji.

Algae

Algae comprise the primary plant or plant-like organisms found on coral reefs. Those most often found on reefs are green algaes (Chlorophyta), brown algaes (Phaeophyta), red algaes (Rhodophyta), diatoms (Chrysophyta) and dinoflagellates (Dinoflagellata). Cyanobacteria, commonly known as blue-green or slime algae, are also abundant.

Algae can be classified into two groups based on their physical structure: microalgae and macroalgae. The microalgae are made up of either a single cell or a string of cells. Boring algae, which grow under the surface of live and dead stony corals, fire corals and some soft corals, are microalgae. If you were to split a hard coral in two, you would see green bands in the skeleton — filamentous algae growing in the inert skeleton's pores. In dead stony corals, boring algae can be red or green algae or cyanobacteria, while only green filamentous algae occur in live corals. Boring algae are common in reef substrates and are an important food source for parrotfishes, which extract them from dead corals with their beak-like teeth.

Our old friends the zooxanthellae are dinoflagellates in the genus *Symbiodinium*. These microalgae live symbiotically in the tissues of many stony and soft corals, sea anemones, zoanthids, tridacnid clams and some other invertebrates.

Macroalgae usually have a solid body and look more like complex vascular plants. The *Caulerpa* species and bubble algae (*Valonia* spp.) are examples of green macroalgae that have cells with multiple nuclei and no walls dividing the cells; these are known as siphonous algae. *Sargassum*, *Padina* and *Dictyota* are all large, fleshy brown macroalgae that are important food for browsing plant-eaters such as sea chubs (*Kyphosus* spp.) and the black durgon triggerfish (*Melichthys niger*). They are also notorious for overgrowing coral in some locations. Fleshy red macroalgae are an apparent favorite with many herbivores such as tangs and rabbitfishes. When such algae appear on the reef, these fish quickly crop them back. The coralline algae, which are also red algae, are important in the development of reefs. They come in encrusting, laminar and articulated forms. Coralline algae are eaten by Moorish idols, puffers and certain triggers.

Some algae produce chemical deterrents (e.g., terpenoids) to discourage hungry herbivores. For example, *Halimeda* contains a strong chemical deterrent known as halimedatrial. At least 23 compounds have been isolated from algae (mostly from green algae) and cyanobacteria that significantly reduce feeding by herbivores.

Mermaid's fan green algae (*Udotea* sp.). Chemical deterrents keep most fish from eating many *Udotea* and *Halimeda*. Indonesia.

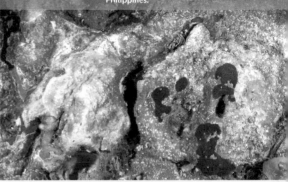

An encrusting red coralline algae growing over rocks and coral. Philippines.

Sea lettuce (*Ulva* sp.), a green macroalgae eaten by many fish and invertebrates. Widespread tropical and temperate Pacific.

Scroll algae (*Padina* sp.), a brown macroalgae. Genus members are found worldwide.

Sea grapes (*Caulerpa* sp.), a type of green algae, among coral on a shallow reef. Hawaii.

A mysterious filamentous red algae, or perhaps a cyanobacteria. Indonesia.

A scuba diver swims around a coral pinnacle, called a "bommie" in Australia. Great Barrier Reef.

Coral Reef Types

Coral reefs take different forms, in part as a function of where they occur. One of the most common types is fringing reefs, which develop along the coastlines of continents or islands. The ocean side of a fringing reef can be bordered by a lagoon or by open ocean. Platform reefs (also known as patch reefs or coral "bommies") grow on solid submerged structures. The tops of these reefs sometimes reach the sea surface, where sand may accumulate and form a coral cay. Platform reefs vary widely in shape and size: they can be up to 20 kilometers (32 miles) wide and may even contain a shallow central lagoon.

Bank reefs are similar to platform reefs but usually occur farther out on the continental shelf and never reach the water's surface; in fact, the tops of most tend to be in rather deep water (40 meters/132 feet). There are also barrier reefs, which are well-known to most divers because of the renowned Great Barrier

Schoolmasters (*Lutjanus apodus*), a type of snapper, in front of a colorful Caribbean fringing reef. Belize.

Reef off the coast of eastern Australia. Barrier reefs usually develop parallel to a coastline and are separated from the landmass by a lagoon that can be quite expansive and even harbor other types of reef structures. Barrier reefs sometimes develop along the edge of the continental shelf, with the reef's seaward edge plummeting into the deep. Finally there are atolls, which are basically reef rings with a large central lagoon. Channels cutting through the reef connect lagoon and open ocean; they are typically replete with corals and zooplankton-feeding fishes because of the huge amounts of water and associated food that flow through them.

Coral Reef Zones

Corals reefs can be broken down into a number of different zones. Environmental conditions vary from one zone to another, and as a result there are differences in the plants and animals you will find inhabiting them. The primary reef zones are the lagoon, back reef, reef flat, reef face and reef slope.

The lagoon is an area enclosed by a barrier reef or an atoll ring. It is usually better protected from surge and

An aerial view of barrier coral reefs, part of Australia's Great Barrier Reef.

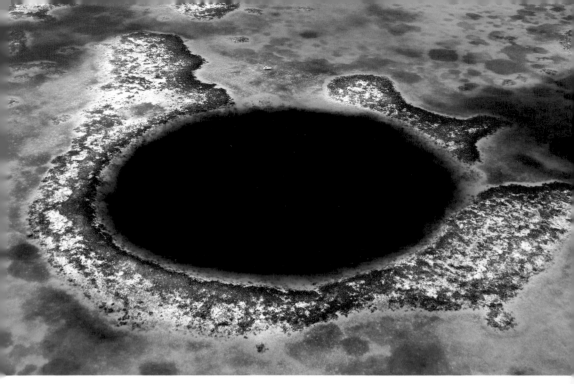

The Blue Hole, a collapsed cavern now submerged, is 145 m (480 ft) deep and 300 m (1,000 ft) across. This world-famous dive site is on Lighthouse Atoll, off Belize.

turbulent water movement than the outer reef zones and thus tends to support more fragile, highly branched coral forms. There may also be seagrass beds in the lagoon, adjacent mangrove areas, vast open sandy expanses and patch reefs. If a lagoon is bordered by a barrier reef you will find a back-reef zone. It too is well protected from violent water movement and tends to be home to tracts of beautiful delicate stony corals and soft coral.

The reef flat is the part of a barrier reef that extends from the back reef to the reef face. It can be just a few to several hundred meters wide. This zone is affected by tidal flux, and at low tide (especially during spring tides) portions may be partially exposed or pools may be temporarily isolated from the lagoon and oceanic waters. Corals living here must be resilient to changes in environmental parameters such as temperature and salinity. There is often more reef pavement (where there are no live corals) that provides growing substrate for

An aerial view of Hardy Reef, a coral reef in the Whitsunday Islands. Australia.

algae. During the tidal influx, groups of herbivorous fishes move onto the reef flat and feed on these algae. The coral heads and tide-pools of the reef flat may serve as a nursery for certain reef fishes. On some reef flats, the edge on the open-ocean side may have a reef crest. This zone can be exposed to punishing wave action and consequently is home to few stony corals. Instead it tends to be a growing surface for coralline algae. Only fishes that enjoy turbulent conditions live here; this includes a number of surgeonfishes that feed on the growing algae. The reef crest may be totally exposed at extreme low tides.

The reef face (also called the shallow fore reef) and slope (or deep fore reef) are the two zones where divers spend most of their time. The reef face starts at the edge of the reef flat (or crest) and extends to a depth of approximately 20 meters (65 feet). Often exposed to strong currents and clear water, this zone showcases the greatest biodiversity you will find on most coral reefs — which is why divers choose to hang out here! Depending on the reef, soft corals may predominate in the shallow portions of the reef face, while in other locations, varied fields of stony corals cover much of the substrate. There are also pockets of sandy substrate or sandy grooves between stony spurs where animals that prefer a soft-bottomed habitat reside. The angle of the reef face can vary dramatically; in some cases there is a gentle slope, while on other reefs a precipitous wall plummets into the depths. These reef walls are often honeycombed with caves, crevices and overhangs that are not only fun to explore but are home to a very different animal fauna. The reef face exhibits relatively limited variation in environmental conditions. It is frequented by numerous plankton-feeding animals, such as sponges, soft corals, sea fans, crinoids, anthias and fusiliers, that rely on the currents sweeping through to bring them life-giving plankton. The many stony corals also provide sanctuary and food for myriad fish species.

The reef slope zone begins where the reef face ends. In most cases it consists of a sand or rubble slope with scattered coral heads or patch reefs. The latter can be composed of not only stony and soft corals but also sponges, some of which can be massive. These prominent structures are the focal point of fish activity. Corals on the reef slope tend to be sheet-like, a growth form better able

A scuba diver swims along a colorful wall covered with soft corals (*Dendronephthya* and *Chironephthya* spp.) and branching cup corals (*Tubastraea micrantha*) amid lyretail anthias (*Pseudanthias squamipinnis*), 25 m (80 ft) deep. Fiji.

to capture the diffuse light rays. As one travels deeper, coral coverage decreases (there are more soft than stony species) and the fish fauna begins to change. At great depths (more than 100 meters/325 feet) you find fewer algae and coral-eaters (because the growth of both is relatively sparse) and more zooplankton-feeders, such as anthias and chromis damsels. In some locations, clouds of these planktivorous fishes hang over the slope. There are also unique sponge-feeding fishes. Large predatory fishes lurk in these deep reef areas too, and some (for example, tiger sharks) move into the shallows at night to feed. On certain deep slopes there are great escarpments, the result of past geological activity. In some cases these form walls that provide growing substrate for sponges and other encrusting creatures and hiding places for a variety of motile animals.

Artificial Reefs

For hundreds of years humans have been creating artificial reefs. Even ancient peoples realized that fishes are attracted to foreign objects placed in their environment. In the past few decades intense efforts have been made to fund and create artificial reefs (ARs). Their primary functions are to provide habitat for adult fishes and to increase recruitment and facilitate survival of young reef-associated animals. In many cases they are created to benefit both recreational fishermen and scuba divers. For example, in the Florida Keys, divers will find numerous ships that have been intentionally sunk to provide both homes for marine life and fascinating dive sites.

Some of the most interesting ARs were not at all intended to benefit divers or fishes. During the Second World War, many Japanese ships were destroyed and sunk in Micronesia. These now serve as valuable habitat for vibrant communities of reef fauna in places such as Truk (also called Chuuk) Lagoon, luring divers from around the world. Airplanes, tanks, ships and similar war detritus function as reef structures near many islands scattered throughout the Western Pacific. Likewise, the submerged legs and crossbeams of the support framework of offshore oil and gas platforms can provide places of refuge, feeding grounds and solid settlement substrate for a wide range of fishes and invertebrates in

Sponges and corals encrust the submerged pilings of the Salt Pier in Bonaire, now a vibrant artificial reef. The large sponge is a yellow tube sponge (*Aplysina fistularis*).

Artificial Reefs

1 Spanish flag snapper (*Lutjanus carponotatus*) schooling under the Navy Pier, an excellent artificial reef in Western Australia.

2 The windlass on the deck of the sunken *La Salvatierra* ferry near La Paz, Baja, Mexico. Many fish species are schooling around this shipwreck in the Sea of Cortez.

3 A shorthead fangblenny (*Petroscirtes breviceps*) peeking out of discarded pipe — now covered with tunicate (*Botryllus* sp.) — turning garbage into its home under a pier. Indonesia.

4 With time this metal hull will be colonized by invertebrates and attract fish looking for shelter. Cozumel.

5 A diver swims along the cup coral–covered exterior of the wheelhouse of the US Coast Guard cutter *Duane*, a 100 m (327 ft) long shipwreck in the Florida Keys.

6 This huge (1.3 m/4 ft) giant trevally (*Caranx ignobilis*) was visiting the SS *Yongala* shipwreck to be cleaned. Australia.

7 Snappers (family Lutjanidae) and sweetlips (family Haemulidae) under the mast of SS *Yongala*, which is covered with sponges, cup corals and oysters. *Yongala* is one of the top shipwreck dives in the world. Australia.

A loggerhead sea turtle (*Caretta caretta*) eating sponges growing on the invertebrate-covered legs of an oil rig in the Gulf of Mexico.

Inset: Beneath the waves, some oil platforms deliver premier artificial reefs for scuba diving. Southern California.

what are often barren reaches of ocean. In the Gulf of Mexico, divers head out to the rigs to see schools of fish, colorful encrusting life and even sea turtles, sharks and game-fish. Besides recreation, artificial reefs are also being created for commercial production of aquatic organisms, habitat restoration, biodiversity conservation projects and research.

In the past, the primary constituents of ARs were discarded materials (e.g., cars, tires, barges, pipes, concrete blocks, rock, etc.), but more recently, materials have been designed specifically for AR construction. A non-profit group called the Reef Ball Foundation manufactures hollow concrete structures called Reef Balls. Ranging in size from 30 centimeters (1 foot) to more than 2 meters (6.6 feet), weighing up to more than 4,000 kilograms (8,800 pounds), and perforated with numerous holes, they provide both a growing substrate for sessile invertebrates and shelter sites for motile reef creatures. At the time of writing, half a million Reef Balls have been deployed in more than 70 different countries.

Another fascinating technology being used to created artificial reefs is Biorock™, licensed to the Global Coral Reef Alliance. Reefs are created out of metal and wire mesh formed into domes and tunnels and then wired to a low-voltage direct current provided by solar panels, windmills or tidal and wave generators. The current flowing through the structure causes minerals in the seawater to precipitate out onto the steel frame, resulting in the formation of a limestone layer. Scientists then attach small sprigs of salvaged coral, which quickly become cemented into place by the accumulating limestone. These transplants grow two to six times faster than normal. Coral larvae drifting by find this fertile substrate ideal, and they settle down to sprout with vigor. Biorock "reefs" are being used in more than 20 different countries to help build up degraded coastal reef habitat.

Artificial reefs are rapidly colonized by marine fauna. Opportunistic fish species are the first to show up. Certain fishes will reach maximum population size on an AR in only several months, utilizing the habitat for shelter, feeding, spawning and orientation. Algae and invertebrates (including encrusting sponges, corals and bivalves) follow in short order. In some cases the density and biomass of marine fauna may be higher on artificial reefs than natural ones. For example, in a comparison of natural reefs and an artificial one off St. John, US Virgin Islands, the latter had a concentration of fishes 11 times higher than that of the natural reef areas. One reason is because ARs can be more complex, with more growing surfaces and hiding places than found on some natural reefs. Also, ARs can be placed close to other desirable habitat (in the study mentioned above, the AR was near a seagrass bed).

But such richness is not always the case. Comparisons made between the ichthyofauna around oil-rig platform supports and the Flower Garden coral reef in the Gulf of Mexico demonstrated that while oil rigs support a diverse ichthyofauna, the number of species as well as the number of individuals was greater on the natural reef. The ARs were more attractive to roving pelagic species and mid-water schooling fishes, as well as site-attached species. Complexity may be the key here, as an oil rig's superstructure is not as complex as natural coral reef habitat in this region.

An artificial reef project in Pemuteran Bay, on the island of Bali, Indonesia. The metal Biorock™ structure is energized by a low-voltage electrical current flowing through it. This causes minerals in the seawater to precipitate onto the steel frame, forming a limestone layer. Scientists then attach small pieces of coral to the structure, and the corals quickly become cemented in place by the accumulating limestone. As a technique to aid coral-reef restoration, projects such as this hold promise in global efforts to reverse reef degradation and restore habitat. The project, begun in 2000, is partially supported by the sale of tags to divers. Indonesia.

Some of the most productive and accessible artificial reefs are those created by pier pilings. These structures often occur next to sand plains that are devoid of much structure, and thus are a magnet for a host of refuge-seeking creatures. The pilings provide substrate for the growth of sponges and corals — especially those that don't mind some shade, like the beautiful orange cup corals (*Tubastrea* spp.). In turn, these sessile invertebrates provide sanctuary and a food source for a variety of invertebrates and fishes. The protection that pier pilings provide is often utilized by seahorses and frogfishes, two groups of charismatic critters sought out by aquanauts. Butterflyfishes, angelfishes, filefishes and boxfishes feed on the pier's sessile invertebrate veneer, while larger piscivores, such as lionfishes, trumpetfishes and groupers, sneak around the pilings looking for unwary victims. The bottom is often littered with manmade materials such as bottles, metal pipes, cans and car tires, as well as waterlogged terrestrial plant material. What may seem like unsightly trash to us can be a valuable refuge for octopus, crabs, scorpionfish, damsels, blennies and many other opportunists.

Mangrove Forests

First impressions can be deceiving. The mangrove forest — those scraggly "bushes" at ocean's edge — may seem to the casual observer nothing more than a smelly swamp, the domain of unpleasantries such as mosquitoes and snakes. Though it does indeed harbor such underappreciated wildlife — plus many more life forms that you might actually want to meet — the mangrove forest is one of the most productive habitats on the planet and a critical part of tropical marine ecosystems. Many of the brightly colored fishes we admire on the coral reef owe their lives to mangrove habitat.

Mangrove forests are found throughout the tropics, except for the Central Pacific. They occur on approximately 60 percent of tropical coastlines, with the majority in Southeast Asia. Mangroves grow in intertidal areas, most often

Top
Mangroves near a river mouth along the coast of Belize.

Bottom
Mangroves (*Rhizophora* sp.) at low tide, their buttress-like aerial prop roots exposed. Florida.

in bays, protected lagoons and estuaries. Rather than referring to only one particular type of plant, the term *mangrove* summarizes a botanical community comprising around 70 species, many of which are in the genus *Rhizophora*. This community thrives in an environment much too harsh for most woody plants. Mangroves must overcome withering heat, oxygen-deprived substrate, and of course salt water, deadly to most plants. The trees that make up mangrove forests are variable in size and shape. In suboptimal conditions they are often low-growing and shrub-like, but in more favorable environments mangrove trees can form a dense canopy more than 10 m (33 ft) high.

The secret is in the roots. As mangroves usually grow in anoxic mud, extracting oxygen and essential nutrients from the soil as most plants do is not an option. Mangroves cope thanks to their "snorkel roots" (pneumatophores), which extend above the substrate, thereby allowing oxygen uptake. Arched, buttress-like roots above the waterline, called aerial prop roots, also aid in respiration and provide key structural support for the plant. Intertwined with the scaffold-like root systems of neighboring trees, they form a thick network of vegetation that effectively traps sediments generated by coastal erosion and runoff. This greatly limits the amount of harmful sediment flushing out to sea, which may smother nearby coral reefs. Mangroves also protect in the shoreward direction, acting as breakwaters. They are effective natural buffers that help shield the coastline and coastal communities from punishing waves and winds produced by tropical storms. Studies have shown that the presence of healthy mangroves can reduce property damage and the human death toll during hurricanes.

The elaborate root systems below the water create a botanical labyrinth in which juvenile fishes can shelter from predators until they are large enough to head out to the reef. They're all there: snappers and angelfish, baitfish and flatfish. Some adult reef fish swim into the mangroves to reproduce, giving the next generation a jump-start on survival. Parents that choose to procreate on nearby coral reefs may very well see their offspring end up in mangroves too, drifting there as larvae on the current. This is excellent habitat for settling out from the plankton and metamorphosing from larvae to juvenile fish, the life-cycle stage known as recruitment. Mangrove forests serve as vital nursery grounds for hundreds of species, including elasmobranchs such as lemon sharks (*Negaprion brevirostris*) in Bimini, Bahamas, and golden cownose rays (*Rhinoptera steindachneri*) in the Galápagos. And one must not forget the armies

A saltwater crocodile (*Crocodylus porosus*) in the mangroves. Palau.

of invertebrates found there in abundance — lobsters and snails, crabs and shrimps — or the birds and marine reptiles, including — yes — snakes.

While most mangroves grow in relatively silty areas with limited underwater visibility, there are some in clear water that are worth traveling across the world to explore. Perhaps the most spectacular are in Raja Ampat, on Indonesia's eastern fringe. There you can swim through serpentine channels to view beautiful sponges and fiery soft corals sprouting from prop roots. Schools of orbicular cardinalfish (*Sphaeramia orbicularis*) lurk in the shadows while rivers of baitfish stream past, pursued by predators-in-training such as young barracuda and jacks. Just under a surface shimmering green and blue as it reflects the overhanging forest, the banded archerfish (*Toxotes jaculatrix*) awaits. With a well-aimed squirt of water into the leaves above, it shoots down the unsuspecting insect prey on which it feeds. And if you're really lucky, you might even encounter a saltwater crocodile (*Crocodylus porosus*).

These remarkable tangles of life are under attack. Critical mangrove habitat is being razed to make room for luxury hotels, golf courses, sprawling oceanfront residences, industrial complexes, airports and mariculture facilities such as shrimp ponds. An estimated 30 to 50 percent of the world's mangrove forests have disappeared in the past half-century. Such losses place an additional burden on already pressured coral-reef ecosystems.

5

6

1 Juvenile golden cownose rays (*Rhinoptera steindachneri*) in mangrove channels. Galápagos Islands.

2 Schoolmasters (*Lutjanus apodus*), grunts (*Haemulon* spp.) and chubs (*Kyphosus* sp.) congregate around mangrove prop roots. Bahamas.

3 Red mangroves (*Rhizophora mangle*) in a split view showing the root system. Bahamas.

4 Marine biologist Dr. Tristan Guttridge, of the Bimini Biological Field Station, uses a PIT tag reader to scan a baby lemon shark (*Negaprion brevirostris*) captured in the mangroves. Bahamas.

5 Juvenile fish schooling over a cushion sea star (*Oreaster reticulatus*) in the mangroves. Bahamas.

6 A Bimini boa (*Epicrates striatus fosteri*) in a red mangrove (*Rhizophora mangle*). Bimini, Bahamas.

1 The fiddler crab (*Uca vocans*), 3 cm (1.2 in) wide, lives in burrows in the sand in mangrove areas. The male has one giant claw. Indonesia.

2 An upsidedown jellyfish (*Cassiopea* sp.) pulses through a shallow channel in a maze of mangroves. Bahamas.

3 Pollution of our oceans — including critical mangrove habitats — is a growing global problem. Bahamas.

4 Banded archerfish (*Toxotes jaculatrix*) and their reflections. This fish swims just beneath the surface in the mangroves. When it sees a bug on an overhanging branch above, it squirts out a jet of water to knock the bug off into the water. Indonesia.

5 One red mangrove (*Rhizophora mangle*) plant growing where once many thrived before development of a big resort. Bahamas.

An "over-and-under" view of a coral reef and mangroves, both important marine habitats. Raja Ampat, Indonesia.

Symbiosis

Among the most fascinating features of tropical reef ecosystems are the many symbiotic relationships that occur between organisms. From the corals that use unicellular algae as a solar-powered energy source to the hitchhiking remoras that clean sharks of parasites and share their dinner scraps, the coral reef is a place where partnerships have developed to benefit one or both of the participating species. These relationships are referred to as symbiosis.

The word *symbiosis* is derived from Greek and literally means "living with." It was first used in reference to interactions between living organisms in 1877. In later years the term was refined to refer only to interactions between "unlike" organisms (i.e., not members of the same or similar species). The organisms involved in symbiotic interactions are known as symbionts, so the term applies to both anemonefish and the anemones they live in. A passive participant is known as a host; in the example just mentioned, the anemone plays that role.

There are different types of symbiotic relationships, and the cost or benefit to the symbionts varies. We often refer to the "fitness" of an organism in relation to the type of symbiotic relationship(s) in which it is involved. We are not talking about the species' muscle tone but rather its ability to reproduce and contribute its genes to future generations. With that in mind, the different types of symbiosis can be broken down into three general categories: parasitism, commensalism and mutualism. Let's look at each of these in more detail.

Parasitism

In a parasitic relationship, one partner harms the other; the species that harms the host is known as the parasite. In general the parasite increases its own population size — its fitness — at the expense of the fitness of the host population. In many cases this involves the parasitic species' feeding off the host. Examples are the copepod crustaceans (genus *Pandarus*) and gnathiid isopods that attach

---

Top

Spinecheek anemonefish (*Premnas biaculeatus*) and bulb tentacle sea anemone (*Entacmaea quadricolor*). Indonesia.

Bottom

This close-up detail of mushroom coral (*Fungia fungites*) shows its tentacled polyps retracted. Through photosynthesis, zooxanthellae algae in the coral's tissues help nourish the coral, an example of symbiosis. Indonesia.

This Xenia swimming crab (*Caphyra* sp.) lives in a parasitic symbiosis association with *Xenia* soft corals. Indonesia.

to and feed on the body tissues of sharks and rays. Parasites can be divided into endoparasites — those that live inside their host — and ectoparasites — those that live on the outside of the host. Both copepod and gnathiid isopods are ectoparasites, while certain nematode worms that live within the alimentary tract of fishes are endoparasites.

While parasites can harm their hosts and usually influence their overall fitness negatively, in many cases they are not lethal, nor do they cause irreparable damage. After all, it is more advantageous for the parasite if the host on which it is feeding continues to survive so the parasite itself doesn't perish or have to find another food source. In the case of copepods, they are not uncommon on elasmobranchs and do relatively little harm to their hosts.

Fire urchin snails *(Luetzenia asthenosomae)* on a fire sea urchin *(Asthenosoma varium)* — an example of parasitism, a symbiotic relationship in which one party (the snail) benefits while the other (the urchin) is harmed. Indonesia.

Fishes are not the only reef organisms infected with parasites. Xenia crabs (*Caphyra* sp.) are parasites on soft corals. They live among corals in the genus *Xenia* and feed on the polyps in a leisurely manner, at a rate that allows the coral colony to survive, which ensures the crab a long-term food source and place of refuge. How does this differ from predation? In the case of predation, the predator is larger than its prey, while the opposite is usually true in the parasite–host relationship. Also, predators normally kill and eat their prey outright, while parasites kill their host slowly or, as noted above, are not lethal to the host at all. While the Xenia crab does not kill the soft coral, however, its chewing on the polyps does negatively affect its reproductive fitness.

Commensalism

In a commensal relationship, one organism benefits while the other partner is neither harmed nor helped. The term *commensalism* (from "at table together") was originally used to refer to feeding relationships between two species. While there are examples involving feeding, the term now encompasses a much broader meaning. Commensal relationships can be divided into inquilinism, endoecism, epizoism and phoresis.

Inquilinism is an association in which the host serves as a source of protection. One example is the hairy squat lobster (*Lauriea siagiani*), which seeks refuge between the ridges of barrel sponges. The host sponge is not harmed by the crustacean, nor does it benefit from the squat lobster's presence. Shrimps in the genus *Periclimenes* engage in inquilinism with crinoids, sea stars, urchins and cucumbers. The emperor shrimp (*P. imperator*) is often found "surfing" along on sea cucumbers or sea slugs, feeding on detritus and fecal matter. Coleman's shrimp (*P. colemani*) live on venomous sea urchins in the genus *Asthenosoma*. An adult pair of these gorgeous crustaceans clear off a section of the urchin

A yellowlined roboastra nudibranch (*Roboastra luteolineata*) sea slug, with emperor shrimp (*Periclimenes imperator*). An example of inquilinism, a type of commensal symbiosis, with the small shrimp benefiting by gaining protection (the nudibranch's bad taste keeps many predators at bay) while the nudibranch host is neither helped nor harmed. Indonesia.

by snipping off its spines, tube feet and pedicellariae, then spend their lives on this little bit of echinoderm real estate. They derive some protection from the surrounding venom-laden urchin spines, and their presence neither helps nor harms their host. Other hitchhikers include Brooke's urchin shrimp (*Allopontonia brooki*), urchin bumblebee shrimp (*Gnathophylloides mineri*) and purple urchin shrimp (*Stegopontonia commensalis*).

Endoecism is a relationship in which one species lives in a burrow constructed by another. Some dart gobies (*Ptereleotris* spp.) share burrows built by pistol shrimps (*Alpheus* spp.), and certain juvenile surgeonfishes live with orange-spotted sleeper gobies (*Valenciennea puellaris*). The burrow-maker is not harmed by the freeloader, and the latter certainly benefits.

Epizoism is a commensal relationship in which one species uses another as a surface on which to live. It differs from endoecism in that the epizoistic symbiont relies on the other species as a place to grow and live, not simply to hide. It may thus gain access to currents that bring food and help disperse its gametes. Examples of epizoism include the wing oysters (*Pteria* spp.) attached to the branches of gorgonians, and Christmas tree worms (*Spirobranchus* spp.) living on stony corals.

Finally, phoresis is a symbiotic pairing in which the host provides a means of transport for its associate. An example of this is the remoras and shark-suckers that ride on sharks, rays and other large fishes. (Their host may also provide them with a source of the parasitic crustaceans that some remoras and sharksuckers eat, shifting this association from commensalistic to mutualistic.) The relationship between barnacles and the whales or sea turtles on which they live is also phoresistic.

Mutualism

In a mutualistic relationship, both or all the organisms involved benefit — that is, there is an increase in fitness. These are among the most intriguing of symbiotic relationships because the participants have co-evolved to come together so both parties gain an advantage. Sea anemones, especially large tropical species, are a great place to find mutualistic relationships. Most have symbiotic algae known as zooxanthellae (genus *Symbiodinium*) that live in their tissues. The anemone provides a place for the algae to live, while the products of the algae's photosynthesis provide nutrients for the anemone.

While the zooxanthellae–anemone relationship is very important, the best-known examples of mutualism involve sea anemones (at least 10 different species) and anemonefishes, also called clownfishes. Sea anemones have stinging cells for defense and for capturing small prey items. While most animals avoid the stinging tentacles, anemonefishes are always found living with sea anemones. The anemone provides the fish with a place to take refuge and deposit its eggs (near the base of the anemone), while the fish provides its host with many benefits. Ammonia excreted by the fish is used by the anemone and its

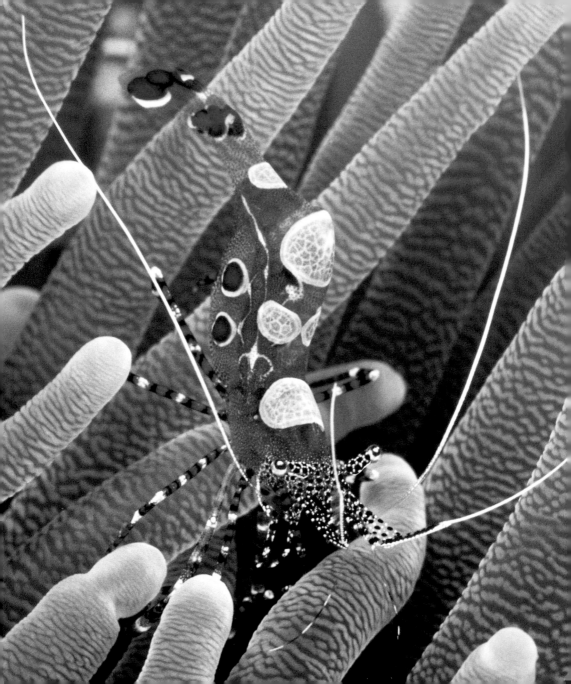

associated zooxanthellae, and the fish's movement within the anemone's tentacles helps circulate fresh, oxygen-rich seawater among the host's tentacles and body folds. All of this increases the anemone's rate of growth and reproduction (i.e., its fitness). Anemonefishes also vigorously defend their hosts from butterflyfishes and other potential predators.

In addition to anemonefish symbionts, anemones harbor species of small shrimp (most from the genus *Periclimenes*) that seek protection among the tentacles. As with the anemone-associated fishes, the nitrogen produced by the shrimp may provide nutrients for the anemone's zooxanthellae, but the benefits provided by crustaceans likely do not equal those of their piscine counterparts. The shrimps do benefit other creatures in their community, however. Fishes will stop next to the anemone to be cleaned by these grooming crustaceans. The shrimps remove necrotic tissue and the larvae of parasites (isopods) from their clients. This type of cleaning relationship is also observed between certain fishes (namely wrasses) and a variety of fish clients.

A similar mutualistic relationship exists between *Dascyllus* damsels and the stony coral colonies that they live within. The coral offers a hiding place for the fish, while the activity and the nitrogen the fish excretes increase the coral's growth rate and reproductive fitness (increased growth means more coral polyps, which leads to more reproductive cells being produced). There are other scleractinian symbionts that not only supply their host with nutrients but also provide protection. Guard crabs (*Trapezia* spp.), which are always associated with stony coral colonies, will attack crown-of-thorns sea stars that attempt to eat the host coral.

One of the less obvious forms of mutualism occurs between surgeonfishes and protozoa. Ciliated protozoa living in the guts of surgeonfishes help break down the algal material that collects in the alimentary tract. Their activity helps the surgeonfish process food and utilize algal nutrients the fish would not otherwise have access to, while the fish provides a place for these microorganisms to live and reproduce. A win-win situation!

A spotted cleaner shrimp (*Periclimenes yucatanicus*) gains protection from predators by staying close to this sea anemone's stinging tentacles. Dominica.

Commensalism

1 The Christmas tree worm (*Spirobranchus giganteus*), an example of epizoic commensal symbiosis. This polychaete is 3 cm (1.2 in) tall and retracts into its hole when disturbed. Dominica.

2 Emperor shrimp (*Periclimenes imperator*) on a synaptid sea cucumber, above — an example of inquilinism, a commensal symbiotic relationship. Indonesia.

3 Coleman's shrimp (*Periclimenes colemani*) live among the spines of the venomous fire sea urchin (*Asthenosoma varium*). Indonesia.

4 A barnacle-covered gray whale (*Eschrichtius robustus*) spy-hopping. Baja, Mexico.

5 A manta ray (*Manta birostris*) with remoras attached to its underside. Baja, Mexico.

6 Caribbean reef shark (*Carcharhinus perezi*). Note the sharksucker (*Echeneis naucrates*) clinging to the shark's underside. Bahamas.

Mutualism

1 Clark's anemonefish (*Amphiprion clarkii*), a common "clownfish" species, in a bulb tentacle sea anemone (*Entacmaea quadricolor*). Indonesia.

2 A giant hermit crab (*Petrochirus californiensis*) with stinging sea anemones attached to its shell. This is a clever example of phoresistic commensalism transitioning to mutualism: the stinging anemones help protect the crab while the crab provides both a means of transportation for the anemones and likely also food, because of its messy eating habits. Galápagos Islands.

3 Reticulated dascyllus fish (*Dascyllus reticulatus*) shelter within coral. They also help the coral because nitrogen excreted by the fish as waste is used by the zooxanthellae algae that live in the coral. Indonesia.

4 A juvenile jack (family Carangidae) following overtop a striped puffer (*Arothron manilensis*). Perhaps the smaller fish gains protection by being close to the larger one, which has toxic flesh and is thus not on the average predator's menu. Indonesia.

5 A six-week-old humpback whale (*Megaptera novaeangliae*) calf with dozens of remoras following along. Some consider this to be an example of phoresistic commensalism shifted to mutualism. Tonga.

Chapter 2

Coral Reef Communities

Many divers get excited about finding some unusual fish species they have never encountered before. In fact, more and more underwater explorers are keeping fish "life lists" similar to those amassed by birdwatchers. Like birders, these divers travel throughout the tropics, exploring different reef zones and habitats and hoping to observe or photograph fishes and invertebrates they have yet to meet.

While the greatest piscine diversity is to be found on coral reefs, the fish communities they support differ from one location to another. For example, some places are home to more unique species than other places. A species known only from a specific region is referred to as being endemic to that location. Endemism is most often influenced by physical boundaries that prevent species dispersal (in the larval or the adult stage) to adjacent regions. For example, the Atlantic Ocean basin prevents most reef-bound fishes from swimming to or their young being carried from the Caribbean to Africa's west coast. Currents may also stop the eggs or larvae of a species from being carried from one island group to an adjacent group, or large river deltas may prohibit fish from immigrating from one location along the coast to another. An example of the latter would be the Amazon Delta, which has prompted the evolution of unique reef-fish communities in Brazil that are related to but different from those in the Caribbean.

Changes in the geography of continents have also shaped the distribution of coral-reef fish species. For example, before the isthmus of Panama formed, immigration occurred back and forth between the Western Atlantic and the Eastern Pacific. But when the landmasses shifted and an impassable barrier formed, the two oceans became isolated. Formerly contiguous fish populations were cut off from each other to evolve independently. Over time, one species became two, a process known as speciation. An interesting example is the very closely related geminate, or sister, species that formed in the two regions, such as the gray angelfish (*Pomacanthus arcuatus*) in the tropical Western Atlantic and the Cortez angelfish (*P. zonipectus*) in the Eastern Pacific.

Scuba divers in a small boat explore the South Pacific's coral-reef kingdom in Fiji.

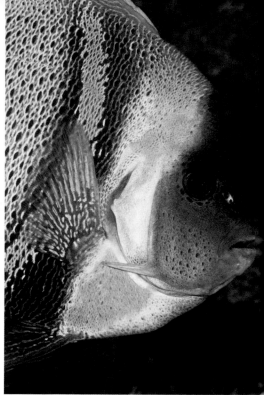

Gray angelfish (*Pomacanthus arcuatus*), a curious and commonly seen resident of Caribbean reefs. Note the sharp cheek spine, characteristic of all angelfish, which helps protect it from predators. Belize.

Cortez angelfish (*Pomacanthus zonipectus*), the Pacific Ocean's "sister species" to the Caribbean's gray angelfish. Baja, Mexico.

Certain fish groups are more likely to exhibit endemism than others. These are usually smaller species with reproductive modes that limit dispersal of their progeny. For example, reef fishes that lay their eggs on the seafloor and/or have shorter larval stages are less likely to disperse over great distances than those with planktonic eggs and longer larval duration. The Banggai cardinalfish (*Pterapogon kauderni*) is the ultimate example of a fish with very limited dispersal of its young. As a result, it has an extremely limited distribution. The adult male broods both the eggs and larvae in his mouth; when he finally releases them, they are fully developed miniatures of their parents. There is no pelagic life stage, so this species lived only around Banggai Island, off

Splendid toadfish (*Sanopus splendidus*), endemic to the island of Cozumel off Mexico's Yucatan Peninsula.

eastern Sulawesi, Indonesia, until a population was artificially established (by fish collectors) farther north, in Lembeh Strait. There are few cases of endemism in sharks, jacks or other fishes that are able to swim great distances. The only sharks that exhibit some degree of endemism are those that are tied to coral reefs and are not extremely strong swimmers, such as the epaulette sharks (*Hemiscyllium* spp.).

In this chapter you will find a brief survey of many of the world's regions that support coral-reef fish communities, with specific information on coral and fish diversity and endemism. We start with the most expansive and species-rich area, the tropical Indo-Pacific, and end up closer to home, in the tropical Western Atlantic.

Banggai cardinalfish (*Pterapogon kauderni*) aggregating around a sea anemone (*Heteractis magnifica*). Lembeh Strait, Indonesia.

The Indo-Pacific is an expansive biogeographical region that consists of the tropical Indian, Western Pacific and Central Pacific Oceans. It extends from the eastern coast of Africa east to the Hawaiian Islands. The boundaries from north to south are approximately the Red Sea and southern Japan to Madagascar and New Caledonia. This region includes the epicenter of biodiversity known as the "Coral Triangle," an area that includes Malaysia, the Philippines, Indonesia, Papua New Guinea and the Solomon Islands. The number of species in this region exceeds that seen in any other tropical area, with 76 percent (more than 600 species) of all known stony coral species occurring here. The number of reef fishes recorded in this area exceeds 2,500 species. Through extensive surveys,

Yellowmask angelfish (*Pomacanthus xanthometopon*). Maldives.

Dr. Gerald Allen has found that, while it occupies only 3 percent of the surface area of the tropical Indo–West and Central Pacific, the heart of the Coral Triangle contains 52 percent of its total species.

To better understand the various coral-reef fish communities in the Indo-Pacific, we have broken the region down into more manageable bites that consist of island groups.

Diagonal-banded sweetlips (*Plectorhinchus lineatus*) form a tightly packed school against a shallow bommie on Australia's Great Barrier Reef.

Hawaiian Islands

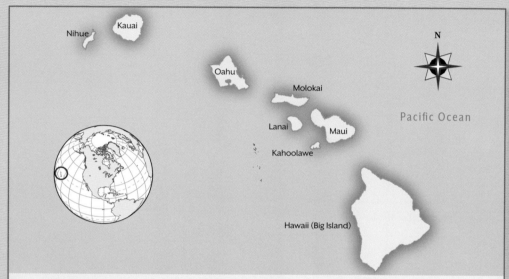

In the minds of many, the Hawaiian Islands are synonymous with tropical paradise. The eight principal islands are characterized by spectacular volcanic peaks, lush rainforests and white or black sand beaches. Because of their proximity to the North American mainland they attract many scuba divers. The topography beneath the waves is as dramatic as above, although the structure and level of development displayed by Hawaiian coral reefs differ from most other areas of the South Pacific. This is due in part to lower winter water temperatures, which preclude vigorous coral growth. Lava boulders and limestone rock formed by coralline algae are the primary structural components of Hawaiian reefs, although in some areas stony corals are abundant. Fringing reefs are most common in the southeastern portion of the chain, while barrier reefs and atolls are found in the leeward, or northwestern, portion of the archipelago. The Hawaiian Islands have a unique ichthyofauna. In fact, of the 600-plus inshore fishes reported, around 23 percent are endemic. This is the highest rate of endemism found in any warm-water marine region, and a major draw for serious fish-watchers.

1 Snorkelers exploring the fringing coral reef at Hanauma Bay, Oahu, Hawaii.

2 Potter's angelfish (*Centropyge potteri*), also called the russet angelfish, is endemic to the Hawaiian Islands and Johnston Island.

3 Giant frogfish (*Antennarius commersoni*), widespread in the tropical Indo-Pacific region.

4 Day octopus (*Octopus cyanea*), a common cephalopod denizen of the tropical coral reef in Hawaii.

French Polynesia

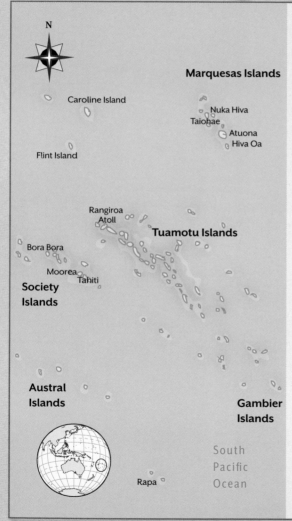

N

Marquesas Islands

Caroline Island

Nuka Hiva
Taiohae
Atuona
Hiva Oa

Flint Island

Rangiroa
Atoll
Tuamotu Islands

Bora Bora

Moorea
Tahiti
**Society
Islands**

**Austral
Islands**

**Gambier
Islands**

South
Pacific
Ocean

Rapa

French Polynesia consists of 130 islands (84 are atolls) with a total landmass of about 4,000 square kilometers (1,544 square miles) scattered over an area of ocean covering 2,500,000 million kilometers (970,000 square miles). The islands vary greatly in size and shape, from high islands with jagged mountainous peaks to low atolls. French Polynesia is made up of five archipelagos: the Society Islands (Tahiti, Moorea and Bora Bora), the Austral Islands, the Tuamotus, the Gambiers and the Marquesas Islands. This area boasts fascinating fish life, including numerous species found nowhere else. It is also one of the best areas on the planet for viewing sharks — Rangiroa Atoll is a shark-lovers' paradise. In total, 1,024 species of fishes are known from French Polynesia; 94 percent (966 species) are reef-associated and 60 coastal species are endemic. Stony coral diversity is low in French Polynesia when compared to areas in the Western Pacific: 168 species in 51 genera have been recorded.

1　Freckled hawkfish (*Paracirrhites forsteri*). French Polynesia.

2　Gray reef shark (*Carcharhinus amblyrhynchos*).

3　Humphead wrasse (*Cheilinus undulatus*), also called Napoleon or Maori wrasse.

4　Tahiti butterfly fish (*Chaetodon trichrous*), endemic to French Polynesia.

Fiji Islands

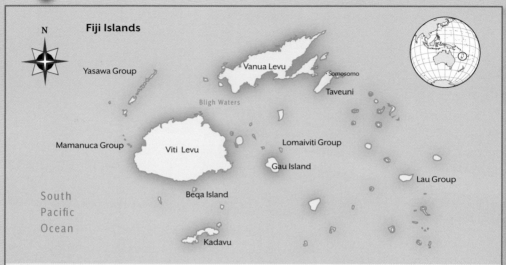

Fiji is a very popular South Pacific destination for North American divers because of its proximity and underwater beauty. This nation comprises 322 islands, most of which are surrounded by fringing and/or barrier reefs. Some of the top sites include Kadavu's Great Astrolabe Reef, Beqa Lagoon and its shark-filled barrier reef, the Somosomo Strait's Rainbow Reef, and the Bligh Waters, between the main islands of Viti Levu and Vanua Levu. Sheer walls and coral pinnacles are punctuated with caves, ledges and swim-throughs that are positively overgrown with sea fans and multicolored soft corals (*Chrionephthya*, *Dendronephthya* and *Scleronephthya* spp.). They are so impressive it's no surprise that Fiji's nickname is "the soft coral capital of the world." Approximately 250 species of stony corals (representing 45 different genera) and around 1,200 inshore fishes, including a handful of endemics (about 10 species), occur around the Fiji Islands.

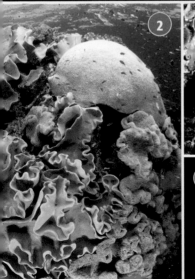

1 A fringing coral reef around an island in Fiji.

2 Coral reefs support diverse coral and fish populations. Among the species pictured here are mushroom leather corals (*Sarcophyton* spp.), anthias fish (*Pseudanthias* spp.) and a brain coral.

3 Spotted unicornfish (*Naso brevirostris*).

4 Barber's anemonefish (*Amphiprion barberi*), endemic to Fiji, Tonga and American Samoa.

Philippines

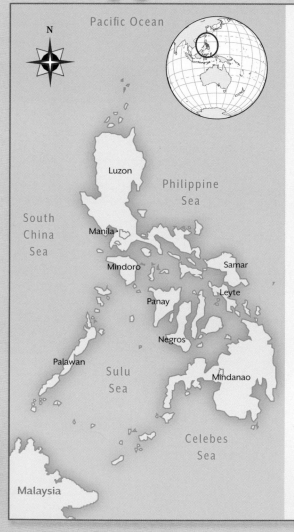

The Philippines Republic is part of the Coral Triangle, and it has unmatched coral reefs and overall species numbers. Like any region with incredible biodiversity, the Philippines boasts a wide variety of marine habitats: estuaries, mangrove swamps, seagrass beds, nutrient-rich coastal reefs and "clean" oceanic reefs. Coral numbers are high here, with more than 410 recorded species of scleractinians. These reefs, and those in northern Indonesia, support the world's richest coral-reef fish communities, with an astonishing 2,500 inshore species (not all are reef-associated). Endemism is not as common in many Western Pacific island groups because of the proximity of other islands, which facilitates transport of larvae from one region to the next. Thus many of the species seen in the Philippines will also be found in Indonesia. However, 31 species of reef fishes are endemic to the Philippines, most of which are smaller species that exhibit limited dispersal of their young, such as cardinalfishes, blennies, dragonets and gobies.

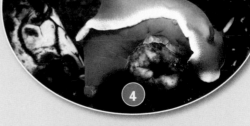

1 Philippines blenny (*Ecsenius dilemma*), endemic to the Philippines.

2 Crabs (possibly *Procellanella picta*) well camouflaged in a soft coral tree (*Dendronephthya* sp.).

3 Painted frogfish (*Antennarius pictus*) — this is a juvenile, 2 cm (0.8 in) long.

4 Robe hem hypselodoris nudibranch (*Hypselodoris apolegma*), a member of the *H. bullocki* complex. Philippines.

Micronesia

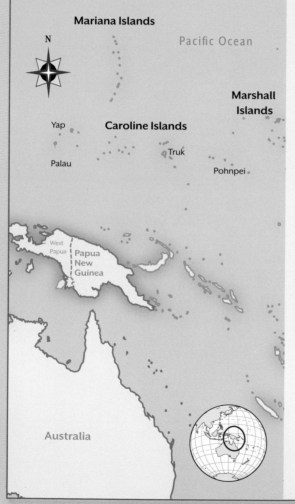

Micronesia consists of three major island chains: the Caroline, Mariana and Marshall Islands. The Carolines consist of five high islands, 43 atolls or low islands, and numerous sunken atolls and bank reefs. They include such well-known dive destinations as Truk, with its Second World War shipwrecks, Yap, Pohnpei and Palau (or Belau). Palau is the most species-rich area in Micronesia, reporting some 1,400 inshore fishes. A study calculated that 96 percent of all reef fishes occurring in Micronesia, and 35 percent of all those from the entire Indo-Pacific, are found around Palau. There is a wide range of marine habitats, including seagrass beds, mangroves, mud basins, deep algal beds, estuaries, tidal channels and areas exposed to upwellings. There are even marine lakes filled with harmless sea jellies. Palau is renowned for its Rock Islands, a maze of mushroom-shaped limestone islets, and also reef walls that plummet vertically into the abyss (for example, the Ngemelis Wall). Many areas are prone to very strong currents that attract myriad planktivores, as well as large predators. Stony coral diversity is also mind-boggling around Palau, with an estimated 425 species in 78 genera. An estimated 500 species of sponges are found in the various habitats, as well as 185 species of opisthobranchs.

1 Aerial view of the Rock Islands, a proposed World Heritage Site in Palau.

2 Harlequin shrimp (*Hymenocera elegans*) feed on sea stars. Here the 5 cm (2 in) long predator has already cut off two of the star's arms.

3 Shepard's angelfish (*Centropyge shepardi*), endemic to Micronesia and southern Japan.

4 Clown triggerfish (*Balistoides conspicillum*), a popular fish in the aquarium trade.

Indonesian Archipelago

I ndonesia is a diver's utopia. Just about every imaginable type of diving in the full gamut of marine habitats is possible here, from classic coral-reef walls to "muck diving," which involves searching for rare, often cryptic species in soft-bottomed habitats. There are approximately 18,585 islands in the Indonesian archipelago, and the coastlines of many support rich coral environments. Most reefs are of the fringing variety and attract many different types of invertebrates and fishes because of the nutrient-rich coastal waters. There are also oceanic islands bathed by clean seawater and exposed to strong currents; their reefs are home to many small-polyped stony corals, fields of soft corals and living clouds of planktivorous fishes. Coral diversity is very high, with more than 500 species of zooxanthellae-bearing stony corals reported. Along with the Philippines, Indonesian waters showcase the richest reef-fish communities on the planet. An estimated 2,200 fish species (in more than 113 families) are thought to occur in the archipelago, with around 70 known endemics — more in absolute total numbers than any other area.

A stunning jewel in Indonesia's crown is West Papua (formerly Irian Jaya). The Bird's Head Peninsula, which includes the Raja Ampat Islands, the Fakfak-Kaimana Coast and Cenderawasih Bay, has recently been extensively surveyed. This relatively small area boasts one of the richest reef-fish faunas on earth, with 1,511 species in 451 genera and 111 families. Piscine endemism is relatively high, with 33 species in 14 families. Researchers have also counted a stunning 574 species of stony corals, 699 mollusks and 42 reef-associated mantis shrimp — and this is just the tip of the iceberg when it comes to non-coral invertebrates. It is the most biologically diverse area in the Coral Triangle.

1   The amazing view from atop Padar Island, Komodo National Park. This part of central Indonesia is home to countless superb reefs. The dive boat *Seven Seas* can be seen in the bay below.

2   A pair of longfin bannerfish (*Heniochus acuminatus*) swim alongside a steep wall covered in soft corals, sponges and crinoids. Bali.

3   Damsels and anthias fish (also called fairy basslets) gather around a sponge on which crinoids (feather stars) have perched. Raja Ampat Islands.

Papua New Guinea & the Solomon Islands

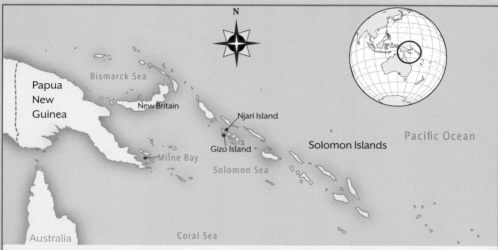

Papua New Guinea (PNG) is the world's second-largest island. Tropical seas wash its entire coastline but only about one-sixth is bordered by coral reefs. One reason for this is the large amount of sediment-filled freshwater coughed out by many rivers. Another reason is the large amount of tectonic activity — including volcanoes and plate uplifting and buckling — that has occurred here over the millennia. Extensive luxuriant reefs occur along the southeast coast, where biodiversity is high. More than 67 genera of scleractinian corals totaling 500-plus species have been recorded in PNG waters. At least 1,500 fish live on these reefs, but currently only 12 endemics are known.

Located just east of PNG, the Solomon Islands comprise 922 islands, islets and reefs strewn over 27,556 square kilometers (8,267 square miles). It is best known by divers for dramatic fore-reef drop-offs and sunken war relics. Like PNG, these islands are also relatively impoverished in terms of extensive reef development. All the reefs here are of the fringing type, emerging from rocky coastlines or limestone benches. The Solomons have rich stony coral communities (494 species) and at least 1,150 species of reef fishes. Njari Island and Gizo support the most diverse reef-fish communities, with species counts surpassed only by the Raja Ampat Islands. Second World War wreckage is commonplace in some areas. On a single dive you can explore a sunken Japanese Zero as well as observe a great variety of shrimpgobies on an adjacent sand slope. Because of the proximity of other island groups, there is little endemism in the Solomons.

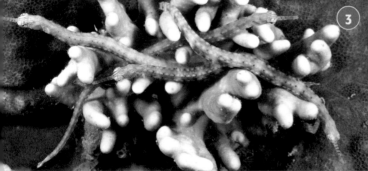

1 The very dangerous reef stonefish (*Synanceia verrucosa*). This is one of the most venomous fish in the world — a puncture from its fin spines can be fatal.

2 Sea whip corals (*Ellisella* sp.) sway in the current, 25 m (82 ft) deep.

3 Pipefish (*Corythoichthys* sp.) sleeping in a small coral head at night (possibly reeftop pipefish, *C. haematopterus*, or *C. intestinalis*).

4 The Vanderloos angelfish (*Chaetodontoplus vanderloosi*) has a very narrow distribution; it is endemic to the Milne Bay region in Papua New Guinea.

Great Barrier Reef

T he Great Barrier Reef (GBR) is the longest coral formation on Earth, extending for more than 2,300 kilometers (1,426 miles) along Australia's northeastern border. Its size is mirrored by its fame, for this is indisputably one of the world's most popular tropical diving destinations. Close-up encounters with huge potato grouper (*Epinephelus tukula*) are nearly guaranteed, and during the austral winter, dwarf minke whales (*Balaenoptera acutorostrata*) hang around the terraced coral gardens. Few other places present an opportunity to photograph anemonefish and cetaceans on the same dive! Stony coral diversity is moderate here, ranging from 244 species in the Capricorn Group (at the southern end of the GBR) to 324 in the northern portion. Approximately 1,300 fish species have been reported from the GBR, with distinct differences in ichthyofauna occurring over its tremendous length. For example, approximately 24 percent of the species found in the Capricorn-Bunker Group (southern GBR) do not occur at Lizard Island (northern GBR). In addition, fewer fishes (860 species) are reported from the southern GBR, which also has a small subtropical-temperate element.

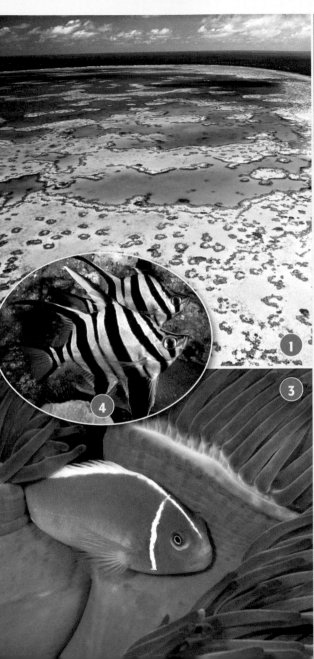

1 Aerial view of coral reefs along Australia's Great Barrier Reef.

2 Scuba allows exploration of the coral kingdom beneath the waves.

3 Pink anemonefish (*Amphiprion perideraion*) live in symbiotic association with magnificent sea anemones (*Heteractis magnifica*).

4 The old wife (*Enoplosus armatus*) can grow to 25 cm (10 in) long. Endemic to Australia, it is found in southern Queensland, subtropical to cool temperate southern Australia and west to southwestern Australia.

Western Thailand & Andaman Sea

Myanma (Burma)

Andaman Islands

Andaman Sea

Surin Islands

Similan Islands

Thailand

Phuket   Phi Ph

Nicobar Islands

Bay of Bengal

N

This region is located in the northeastern Indian Ocean. Thailand is a popular scuba destination with some beautiful reefs and world-class diving, even after the deadly tsunami of 2004. That said, the tsunami did have a profound impact on some of Thailand's coastal reefs. At certain sites, reefs were scoured clean of coral, while the retreating wave left debris (coral fragments, rubble and detached mangroves) at the edges of the reef margins. These debris fields now harbor relatively rich fish communities. Surveys done post-tsunami have shown that reef fish communities were greatly disturbed in severely affected areas (more than 50 percent of coral coverage destroyed), but some reef areas were affected lightly or not at all, and fishes thrive there in pre-tsunami numbers.

Phuket, Phi Phi and the Surin Island group are well-known Thai dive locations. Richelieu Rock, a submerged coral pinnacle that is part of Surin National Park, is a favorite. It acts as a magnet for marine life large and small and is a great place to observe the mating ritual of Pharaoh cuttlefish (*Sepia pharaonis*). Another underwater paradise is the Similan Islands. They consist of nine granitic islands, washed with clear water, that have dramatically different dive profiles from the east to the west. The more remote Andaman Islands, which are actually part of India, support vibrant stands of soft corals and swirling schools of fish. In total, Andaman Sea reefs host at least 353 stony coral species and nearly 900 reef-associated fishes.

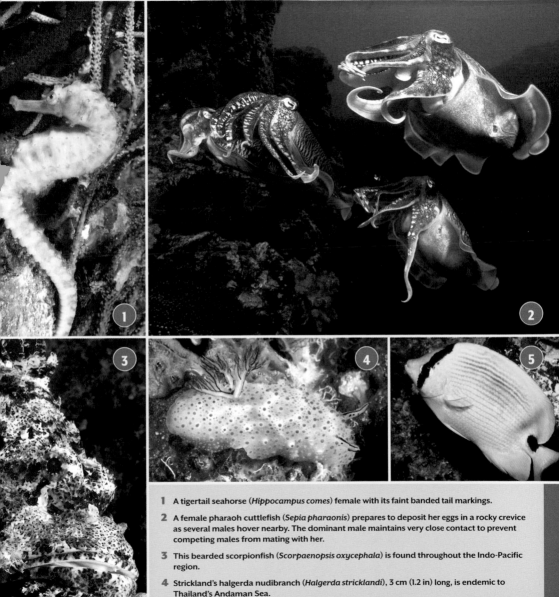

1 A tigertail seahorse (*Hippocampus comes*) female with its faint banded tail markings.

2 A female pharaoh cuttlefish (*Sepia pharaonis*) prepares to deposit her eggs in a rocky crevice as several males hover nearby. The dominant male maintains very close contact to prevent competing males from mating with her.

3 This bearded scorpionfish (*Scorpaenopsis oxycephala*) is found throughout the Indo-Pacific region.

4 Strickland's halgerda nudibranch (*Halgerda stricklandi*), 3 cm (1.2 in) long, is endemic to Thailand's Andaman Sea.

5 The Andaman butterflyfish (*Chaetodon andamanensis*) is endemic to the eastern Andaman Sea, the Maldives and northern Sumatra.

Maldives

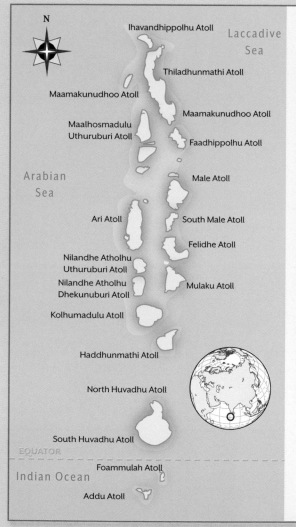

N

Ihavandhippolhu Atoll

Laccadive Sea

Thiladhunmathi Atoll

Maamakunudhoo Atoll

Maamakunudhoo Atoll

Maalhosmadulu Uthuruburi Atoll

Faadhippolhu Atoll

Arabian Sea

Male Atoll

Ari Atoll

South Male Atoll

Felidhe Atoll

Nilandhe Atholhu Uthuruburi Atoll

Nilandhe Atholhu Dhekunuburi Atoll

Mulaku Atoll

Kolhumadulu Atoll

Haddhunmathi Atoll

North Huvadhu Atoll

South Huvadhu Atoll

EQUATOR

Foammulah Atoll

Indian Ocean

Addu Atoll

The 26 coral atolls in the Maldives chain support some of the densest fish communities in the world. Though species diversity does not equal that of the Western Pacific, the immense numbers of fish are truly remarkable. The Maldives, scattered in the oceanic blue to the southwest of India's tip, are surrounded by water 2,000 to 4,000 meters (6,500 to 13,000 feet) deep. The central lagoons can be as deep as 84 meters (273 feet). Approximately 60 genera and 237 scleractinian corals are found on these reefs, and more than 700 species of reef fish. Relatively few endemics occur here. Reef manta rays (*Manta alfredi*) are regular visitors at cleaning stations year-round and come together seasonally to form feeding aggregations 20 to 50 strong. Experienced local guides know where and when to find whale sharks (*Rhincodon typus*) too. Yet another attractive feature for fish-watchers and underwater photographers is that some reef fishes that are normally shy elsewhere are often surprisingly easy to approach in the Maldives. This is likely due to a lack of spearfishing. Fish numbers are especially high in the *kandus* (channels) that cut through the atolls into the lagoons. Huge amounts of water and plankton funnel through these channels with the tides, and in localized areas, colorful soft corals, sea fans and huge trees of *Tubastraea micrantha* coral are abundant.

1 Longfin batfish (*Platax teira*), masked bannerfish (*Heniochus monoceros*), oriental sweetlips (*Plectorhinchus vittatus*) and soldierfish (*Myripristis* sp.) congregate under a ledge.

2 A reef outcropping overgrown with colorful soft corals, which thrive in current-swept channels.

3 Reef manta rays (*Manta alfredi*) and a scuba diver crossing flight paths.

4 Whale shark (*Rhincodon typus*) and snorkelers.

5 The Maldives anemonefish (*Amphiprion nigripes*), endemic to the Maldives and Sri Lanka.

Red Sea

The Red Sea has been a favorite of European aquanauts for decades. Clear water, beautiful reefs and numerous fish species bring divers back year after year. It is part of the Great East African Rift and is approximately 2,300 kilometers (1,429 miles) long, with a maximum depth of 2,000 meters (6,500 feet). Surrounded by desert, the Red Sea loses about 2 meters (6.5 feet) of water each year to evaporation. With very little rain to replenish what is lost, water instead flows into the Red Sea from the Gulf of Aden. As a result, the salinity of the Red Sea varies from 36.5 ppt at its southern end to 40.5 ppt in the Gulf of Suez, at its northern tip. The southern Red Sea has 115 species of stony corals but few coral reefs; its substrate is comprised primarily of soft-bottom habitats. The central waters have higher diversity, with 150 stony coral species, while 139 species have been reported from the northern Red Sea. Around 1,250 fish species have been reported, with about 900 of these associated with coral reefs or adjacent habitats such as seagrass beds. One thing that makes the Red Sea so unique is the high proportion of endemic species: 13 percent (about 114 species) of the Red Sea's reef-fish ichthyofauna is found nowhere else. Many of the Red Sea's fringing reefs have an interesting feature known as a "Sargassum zone," a portion of the reef flat that supports rich growth of the brown macroalgae *Sargassum*.

1   Schooling lyretail anthias fish (*Pseudanthias squamipinnis*) around the wreck of the *Numidia*, a Scottish ship built in 1901. The hull is 137 m long by 16 m wide (450 ft by 52.5 ft).

2   Bicolor parrotfish (*Cetoscarus bicolor*).

3   Bluespotted ribbontail ray (*Taeniura lymma*).

4   Yellowbar angelfish (*Pomacanthus maculosus*), found in the Red Sea, with limited distribution in the western Indian Ocean.

5   The Red Sea anthias (*Pseudanthias taeniatus*), also called striped anthias, is endemic to the Red Sea. Seen here are a male (left) and female (right).

S ome divers have the good fortune to be able to explore the subtropical/trop-ical Eastern Pacific. Unique reef-fish fauna and high-voltage diving with larger marine animals in the offshore island groups make this area very special. As a general rule these are rocky reefs, as coral development is extremely limited because of wide-ranging water temperatures, fluctuations in salinity and the large tides that prevail in the Eastern Pacific. The region's best-developed coral reefs occur off Panama's coast, but they are small and occur only in shallow waters to about 10 meters (33 feet). Sporadic coral outcroppings and modest coral reefs are also found on some of the islands (e.g., the Galá-pagos) and near the southern end of the Baja Mexico peninsula. Instead of coral kingdoms, it's boulder-strewn slopes, craggy rock pinnacles and seamounts that provide the majority of suitable habitat for this region's reef fishes.

The Eastern Pacific claims a relatively small number of tropical reef fishes, partly because of deep-water upwellings and cold currents that originate in temperate areas. There are also few islands to provide "stepping stones" that would enable fish larvae to emigrate from one area to another. In addition, current patterns don't facilitate the transportation of larvae from the Central and Western Pacific. Fish diversity is also limited by the paucity of habitats and microhabitats present when there are no extensive coral reefs.

Many fish families that have undergone tremendous speciation on coral reefs in the

A California sea lion (*Zalophus californianus*) playing with a sea star. Sea of Cortez, Baja.

Scalloped hammerhead sharks (*Sphyrna lewini*). Galápagos Islands.

Pacific creolefish (*Paranthias colonus*) swimming above stony coral mounds. Galápagos Islands.

Indo-Pacific are poorly represented on Eastern Pacific reefs. For example, only four species of angelfish are known from this region, while there are 27 species in Micronesia alone. However, two families that are more specious in the Eastern Pacific than in most other regions are the weedy blennies (Labrisomidae: 37 species, all endemic) and the tube blennies (Chaenopsidae: 33 species, all endemic). All told, 84 percent of all the shore fishes in the Eastern Pacific are endemic to the region. Such numbers are celebrated as extraordinary among the ranks of hardcore fish-watchers.

In diving circles their names are legend: Galápagos, Cocos Island, Las Revillagigedos. These offshore islands represent the pinnacle of "big animal" diving in the Eastern Pacific. They attract a guild of experienced recreational scuba divers intent on encounters with sharks, giant mantas, walls of jacks, gamefish, sea lions and even a penguin for good measure.

A Galápagos penguin (*Spheniscus mendiculus*) flies through equatorial waters in the Galápagos Islands.

Galápagos Archipelago

Darwin
Wolf
Pinta
Canal de Pinta
Roca Redonda
Marchena
Genovesa
Canal de Marchena
Banks Bay
Santiago
Bartolomé Island
Fernandina
Canal de San Salvador
Bahia Isabel
Santa Cruz
N
Isabela
Canal de Santa Fé
San Cristobal
Floreana
Espanola
Pacific Ocean

The Galápagos archipelago consists of 13 main islands located 1,046 kilometers (650 miles) west of Ecuador. The islands, which are volcanic in origin, have rocky shorelines, sand and coral gravel beaches, and mangrove swamps. Large, barnacle-covered boulders strewn over the seafloor and steep rock walls are prominent features of the underwater landscape, while the drop-offs are often permeated with caves, deep crevices and ledges. Although they are limited in coverage, there are also some patchy coral reefs, with 14 species of reef-building corals reported in addition to abundant bushes of black coral.

Seven major oceanic currents, both cold and warm, influence the Galápagos Islands. The temperature from one side of an island to the other can vary by as much as 11°C (20°F). These unusual conditions are partially responsible for the unique assemblage of fishes. Fish diversity in this National Park and World Heritage Site is higher than around other islands in the Eastern Pacific. There are approximately 300 fish species, with about 75 percent representing inshore forms and the rest pelagic; 17 percent (50 species) are endemic, meaning that 50 of the fishes have been reported only to this archipelago. Two unique species are the Galápagos blue-banded goby (*Lythrypnus gilberti*) and the Galápagos puffer (*Sphoeroides angusticeps*). Divers must divide their time between searching for these reef rarities and fending off friendly Galápagos sea lions (*Zalophus wollebaeki*) and cheeky Galápagos sharks (*Carcharhinus galapagensis*) — not to mention remembering to breathe when a whale shark passes overhead, right after a squadron of scalloped hammerhead sharks (*Sphyrna lewini*).

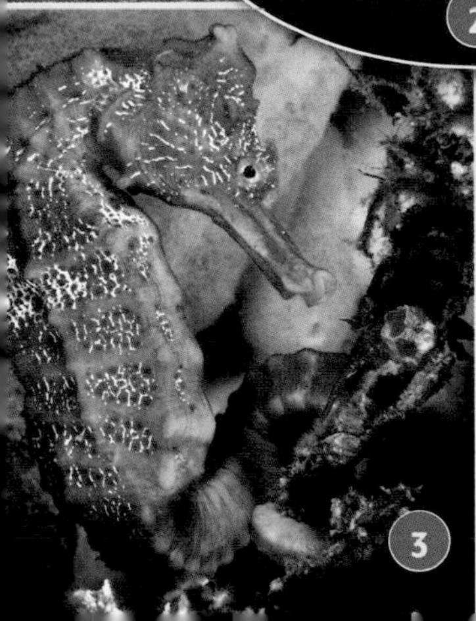

1 A scenic view of
  Pinnacle Rock and the
  surrounding volcanic
  landscape from
  Bartolomé Island.

2 Spotted eagle rays
  (*Aetobatus narinari*).

3 Pacific seahorse
  (*Hippocampus ingens*).

4 Galápagos garden
  eels (*Taenioconger
  klausewitzi*), an
  endemic species.

Cocos Island

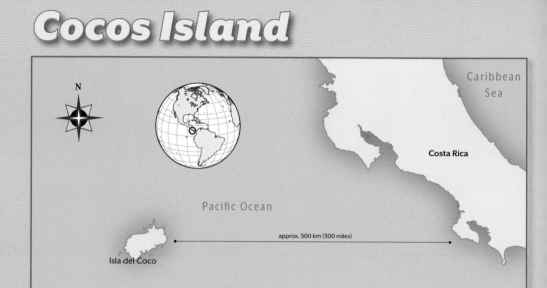

N

Caribbean
Sea

Costa Rica

Pacific Ocean

approx. 500 km (300 miles)

Isla del Coco

Whereas much of the Galápagos above the tideline is dry, with desert-like scraggly vegetation, or volcanic slag, with none at all, Costa Rica's Cocos Island is a verdant oasis with thick jungle and sheeting waterfalls. Underwater, kinship is obvious, for the nickname of Isla del Coco is "Island of the Sharks." Famous for waves of hammerheads streaming through the blue, it also delivers roving packs of whitetip reef sharks (*Triaenodon obesus*) and marbled stingrays (*Taeniura meyeni*). At least 11 species of stony corals are found on the reef, but no "true" coral reefs are present. In some areas the substrate has been sculptured by the boring activities of longspine sea urchins (*Diadema* spp.), which can occur at incredible densities. More than 120 species of inshore fishes have been reported at Cocos, a number likely to grow with further exploration, as 800 species have been counted along the mainland, 500 kilometers (300 miles) to the east. Over 80 percent of Cocos fishes are Panamic in origin, while less than 5 percent are endemic. Many species of wide-ranging jacks (family Carangidae) swarm around Cocos, with the schools of bigeye (*Caranx sexfasciatus*) thronging together in amazing numbers. It pays to stay alert when diving at Cocos — yellowfin tuna (*Thunnus albacares*) and billfish (family Istiophoridae) have been known to materialize without warning.

1 **Long-finned bigeyes** (*Cookeolus japonicus*). Also known as the bulleye glasseye, this fish favors deep, cool water below the thermocline.

2 **Whitetip reef sharks** (*Triaenodon obesus*) prowling the reef at night.

3 A **giant hawkfish** (*Cirrhitus rivulatus*) poses for a portrait in front of cup corals.

4 A **scalloped hammerhead shark** (*Sphyrna lewini*) swims among a cloud of creole-fish, an ominous tattoo on a blue background.

Revillagigedo Islands

Baja Pennisula

Mexico

La Paz

Cabo Pulmo Marine Park

Cabo San Lucas

Islas Marias

N

Roco Partida

San Benedicto

Socorro

Clarion

Pacific Ocean

The northernmost of the big three island groups is the Revillagigedos, which consist of four small volcanic islands: Socorro, San Benedicto, Clarion and Roca Partida. The so-called "Mexican Galápagos" are approximately 400 kilometers (250 miles) southwest of Cabo San Lucas, Mexico. About 120 fish species live around these islands, including 10 endemics. The one that seems to attract the most attention — from both underwater photographers and the hang glider–sized manta rays (*Manta birostris*) in need of cleaning services — is the Clarion angelfish (*Holacanthus clarionensis*). Though not members of the endemic club, the mantas, silky sharks (*Carcharhinus falciformis*) and Panamic green moray eels (*Gymnothorax castaneus*) do a fine job of keeping divers from missing the lack of true coral reefs. To get a peek at those, divers should visit Cabo Pulmo before returning home to north of the border. Pulmo, on the eastern side of the Baja Peninsula near the city of La Paz, has a lovely "real" stony coral reef with good *Pocillopora* species coverage and loads of fish life. It proudly bears the distinction of being mainland North America's only true coral reef in the Pacific Ocean.

1 Hard corals (*Pocillopora eydouxi*) at Cabo Pulmo, mainland North America's only true coral reef in the Pacific Ocean.

2 A woman peers through a reef split decorated with sea fans (*Pacifigorgia* sp.) and gorgonians at Cabo Pulmo, Sea of Cortez.

3 Trumpetfish (*Aulostomus chinensis*) and endemic Clarion angelfish (*Holacanthus clarionensis*) at 80 feet deep. Roca Partida.

4 A diver encounters a Panamic green moray eel (*Gymnothorax castaneus*).

Numerous locations in the tropical Western Atlantic support extensive stony coral reef communities, many of which are a draw to North American scuba divers. These areas include Bermuda, the south Florida coast, parts of the Gulf of Mexico, the Central American coastline, Brazil, the Caribbean and the Bahamas. While isolated stony corals are found as far north as North Carolina, cool winter seawater temperatures prevent the development of coral reefs farther north than southern Florida. Bermuda, which is washed by the warm Gulf Stream, is an exception. Coral reefs occur as far south as the Brazilian coast, although distribution is limited by excessive amounts of sediment discharged from the Amazon and Orinoco Rivers. The most common reef type in the tropical Western Atlantic is the fringing reef, though there are also barrier reefs, bank reefs and atolls. Unfortunately, the face of Western Atlantic reefs has changed much in recent decades because of overfishing, coral diseases, massive bleaching events and the die-off of *Diadema* sea urchins. As a result, some reefs are now dominated by macroalgae, with live coral coverage decreased by 50 percent. The Caribbean has far fewer species of stony corals (less than 75) than the Indo-Pacific (more than 500 species), but those present display numerous growth forms.

There are approximately 1,500 species of shore fishes in the tropical Western Atlantic, about 1,020 of which associate with coral reefs. The greatest diversity of reef fishes is found in the western Caribbean (around 750 species), while the lowest number of species occurs on reefs around Florida, Bermuda and Brazil. Overall, the most abundant families on tropical Western Atlantic reefs are the surgeonfishes and parrotfishes, followed by grunts, snappers, angelfishes, triggerfishes and groupers. Most reef-fish assemblages around the Caribbean are relatively homogeneous. That is, the cores of communities consist of the same ubiquitous species. Generally speaking, endemism is low because there are lots of islands that act as stepping stones for dispersal and few barriers to prevent dispersal or immigration. Although the northern limit of many tropical fish species is Palm Beach, Florida, the Gulf Stream may carry larvae and juveniles as far north as New England — although most don't survive the colder winter months.

"Diviner than the dolphin is nothing yet created," quoth the poet Oppian 1,800 years ago. Perhaps he was inspired by these Atlantic spotted dolphins (*Stenella frontalis*) in the Bahamas.

Florida

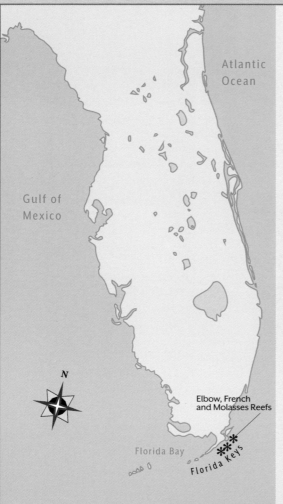

Atlantic
Ocean

Gulf of
Mexico

N

Elbow, French
and Molasses Reefs

Florida Bay

Florida Keys

The Florida Keys are North America's only extensive coral reefs. They consist of patch and bank reefs that are bathed by the warm Florida Current, a "tributary" of the Gulf Stream. Some of the best-known sites are the Elbow, French and Molasses Reefs. A fleet of shipwrecks turned into artificial reefs helps to make Florida a very popular scuba destination. Mangroves and seagrass beds provide vital nursery areas for reef fishes. More than 500 species of inshore fishes are reported from the Florida coast. The blue dartfish (*Ptereleotris calliurus*) is the only species known to be endemic.

Great barracuda (*Sphyraena barracuda*) congregate around the radar tower of the sunken *Duane* shipwreck, now a stunning artificial reef in the Florida Keys.

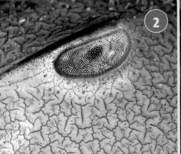

1 Bluestriped grunts (*Haemulon sciurus*) on a shallow reef in the Florida Keys.

2 The eye of a horseshoe crab (*Limulus polyphemus*).

3 Porkfish (*Anisotremus virginicus*) under a reef ledge.

4 Looking out from the invertebrate-covered wheelhouse of the US Coast Guard cutter *Duane*, a 100 m (327 ft) long shipwreck in the Florida Keys.

5 The blue hamlet (*Hypoplectrus gemma*) was long thought to be endemic to Florida and the Bahamas, but it is now known from parts of Mexico. However, its distribution is still limited compared to the other hamlets.

Bahamas

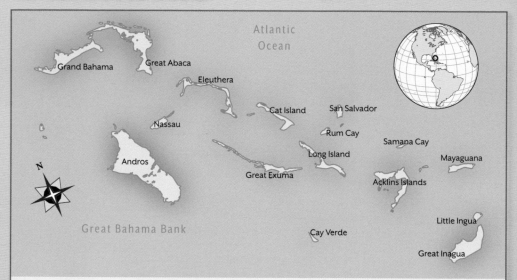

Atlantic Ocean

Grand Bahama
Great Abaca
Eleuthera
Cat Island
San Salvador
Nassau
Rum Cay
Samana Cay
Andros
Long Island
Mayaguana
Great Exuma
Acklins Islands
N
Little Ingua
Great Bahama Bank
Cay Verde
Great Inagua

The Bahamas was one of the first areas to offer organized shark-diving and is one of a very few locations in the world where you can consistently see tiger sharks (*Galeocerdo cuvier*) and great hammerhead sharks (*Sphyrna mokarran*). Add swimming with wild dolphins to the day's agenda and it's obvious why the Bahamas are synonymous with "charismatic megafauna." Thirteen major islands and 700 small islands and cays form this nation, whose coral reefs are primarily fringing in nature. An estimated 500 to 600 fish species frequent the inshore waters, including Nassau groupers (*Epinephelus striatus*), a species overfished in much of the Atlantic. Huge spawning assemblages of dozens to more than 100,000 individuals still occur at traditional Bahamian spawning sites in the winter months.

1 Atlantic spotted dolphins (*Stenella frontalis*) race over White Sand Ridge north of Grand Bahama Island.

2 Great hammerhead shark (*Sphyrna mokarran*).

3 Tiger shark (*Galeocerdo cuvier*) and an enthralled scuba diver at the renowned Tiger Beach dive site.

Central Caribbean Sea

The main island group in the central Caribbean is the Greater Antilles, which consists of Cuba, the Dominican Republic and Haiti (Hispaniola), Jamaica, the Cayman Islands and Puerto Rico. Cuba has two barrier reefs and a unique environment where coral reefs are surrounded by a muddy substrate. Pristine offshore reefs in the Archipiélago Jardines de la Reina bolster Cuba's wide variety of habitats; they are home to 912 species of fishes at last count, including big predatory species such as black and goliath groupers.

The Cayman Islands are low limestone platforms renowned for their precipitous outer reef walls that fall off to great depths. In the nearby Cayman Trench, the bottom is some 6,000 meters (19,500 feet) below. In contrast to the famous deep-wall dives with their large, colorful sponges, Stingray City is a shallow lagoon site on Grand Cayman where snorkelers and divers interact with dozens of food-conditioned southern stingrays (*Dasyatis americana*). In total, 381 fishes (with one endemic, a weedy blenny) have been reported from the Cayman Islands. Most of the usual suspects widely encountered around other small Antillean islands are here, including strong contingents of gobies and groupers.

1 A secretary blenny
(*Acanthemblemaria maria*)
peeks out of a hole in coral.

2 Chain moray eel (*Echidna
catenata*), Cayman Islands.

3 Balloonfish (*Diodon
holocanthus*).

4 A yellowline arrow crab
(*Stenorhynchus seticornis*) in
front of a giant sea anemone
(*Condylactis gigantea*).

Eastern Caribbean Sea

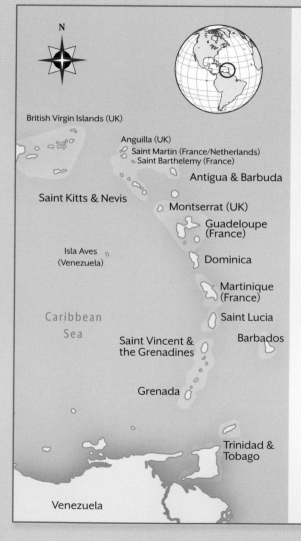

British Virgin Islands (UK)

Anguilla (UK)
Saint Martin (France/Netherlands)
Saint Barthelemy (France)

Antigua & Barbuda

Saint Kitts & Nevis

Montserrat (UK)

Guadeloupe
(France)

Isla Aves
(Venezuela)

Dominica

Martinique
(France)

Caribbean
Sea

Saint Lucia

Barbados

Saint Vincent &
the Grenadines

Grenada

Trinidad &
Tobago

Venezuela

The eastern Caribbean region comprises primarily the Lesser Antilles, an island arc that forms the eastern boundary of the Caribbean Sea and includes the British Virgin Islands, the US Virgin Islands, Anguilla, Antigua and Barbuda, Guadeloupe, Dominica, Martinique, St. Lucia, Barbados, St. Vincent and the Grenadines, and Trinidad and Tobago. These consist of many low coralline islands (e.g., the US Virgin Islands) surrounded by extensive fringing reefs, but there are also high islands (e.g., St. Vincent and Barbados) with limited marine shelf and reef development. Some islands boast seagrass beds and mangrove forests. Sponge gardens on Dominica's steep reef slopes are a riot of color, and just offshore, pods of sperm whales (*Physeter macrocephalus*) socialize. Reef-fish communities in the eastern Caribbean exhibit low to moderate diversity, with 300 to 400 species on average. Coral diversity is also moderate; for example, 57 species of scleractinians have been reported from the US Virgin Islands.

1 A colorful reef with rich invertebrate growth, including crinoids and many sponge species.

2 Creole wrasse (*Clepticus parrae*) feeding en masse in late afternoon.

3 The village of Soufrière, adjacent to the best dive sites on Dominica.

4 Azure vase sponge (*Callyspongia plicifera*) and golden crinoid (*Davidaster rubiginosa*).

5 A curious sperm whale calf (*Physeter macrocephalus*) swims closer to investigate. (Photo taken under permit.)

Southern Caribbean Sea

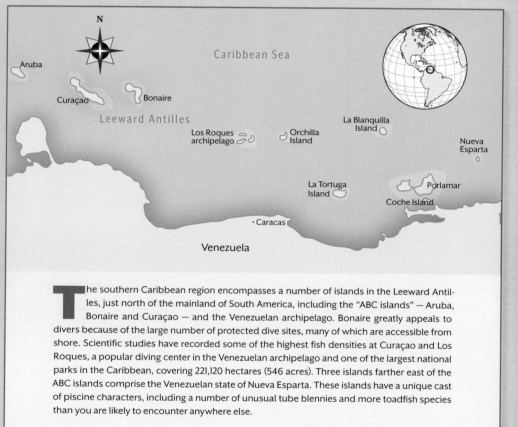

The southern Caribbean region encompasses a number of islands in the Leeward Antilles, just north of the mainland of South America, including the "ABC islands" — Aruba, Bonaire and Curaçao — and the Venezuelan archipelago. Bonaire greatly appeals to divers because of the large number of protected dive sites, many of which are accessible from shore. Scientific studies have recorded some of the highest fish densities at Curaçao and Los Roques, a popular diving center in the Venezuelan archipelago and one of the largest national parks in the Caribbean, covering 221,120 hectares (546 acres). Three islands farther east of the ABC islands comprise the Venezuelan state of Nueva Esparta. These islands have a unique cast of piscine characters, including a number of unusual tube blennies and more toadfish species than you are likely to encounter anywhere else.

1 A moman snorkeling in Boca Slagbaai, Bonaire.

2 Spotted moray eel (*Gymnothorax moringa*).

3 A hawksbill sea turtle (*Eretmochelys imbricata*) rests at the base of a resplendent reef.

4 Longlure frogfish (*Antennarius multiocellatus*). Note the smaller brown male next to the large yellow female. Bonaire.

Western Caribbean Sea

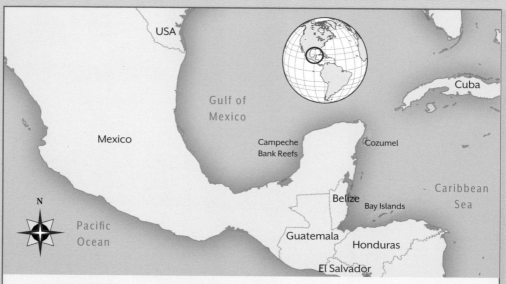

The Mexican coastline has some extensive areas of coral reef development. In the southwest Gulf of Mexico, the Campeche Bank Reefs lie offshore on a wide carbonate shelf. Along the Yucatan Peninsula, fringing reefs are common. The warm, clear waters of the Mexican Caribbean are where most divers vacation, with Cozumel being the scuba epicenter. Swift currents whisk one along sponge-covered reef ridges, under which the keen-eyed may spot the endemic coral toadfish (*Sanopus splendidus*). The extensive barrier reef and atoll system located off the coast of Belize is one of the world's longest at approximately 240 kilometers (386 miles). Numerous reef zones and habitats, including lagoons and mangroves, contribute to greater biodiversity than in the rest of this region.

Heavy freshwater runoff limits coral reefs along the Central American coastline. But offshore, in the Bay Islands of Honduras, cleaner water nourishes shallow fringing reefs that drop sharply to about 75 meters (244 feet). Belize and the Bay Islands share a fantastic phenomenon that involves the largest known fish. Whale sharks (*Rhincodon typus*) visit both areas in the spring (March to April) and late summer (August to September). These congregations are linked to massive spawning aggregations of a variety of reef fishes, especially larger snapper species.

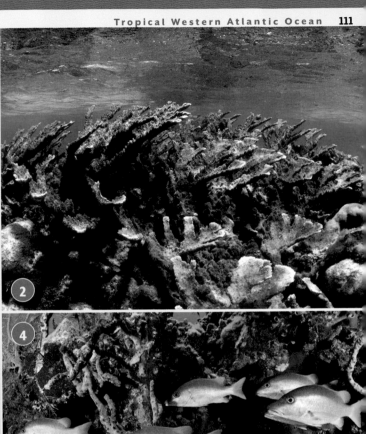

1 Queen angelfish (*Holacanthus ciliaris*), widespread throughout the Caribbean Sea.

2 Elkhorn coral (*Acropora palmata*) is disappearing throughout much of the Caribbean. Healthy stands can be found here in the Hol Chan Marine Reserve in Belize.

3 Diver exploring a fissure in the complex three-dimensional reef structure off Cozumel.

4 Schoolmasters (*Lutjanus apodus*), a type of snapper, call a Belizean reef home.

5 A bottlenose dolphin (*Tursiops truncatus*) greets the photographer in warm waters off Honduras.

Lion Invasion!

The invasion of lionfish (*Pterois volitans*) will have profound ramifications on the health of the Western Atlantic reef communities.

I n 1993, divers along the Florida coast made an unexpected discovery — lionfish. Since that time, at least two species of Indo-Pacific lionfish (*Pterois russellii* and *P. volitans*) have been reported from New York down to the southern Caribbean and Gulf of Mexico. In fact, populations have reached plague proportions in many places. In the Bahamas more than 390 lionfish per hectare have been recorded, a density greatly exceeding the norm in their natural range in the Indo-Pacific. How did they end up in the Atlantic? Apparently this alien invasion is the result of accidental and/or intentional releases by unscrupulous marine aquarists.

While you might think that spotting a lionfish on a Bahamian coral reef would be cool, it certainly isn't for the local critter community. Lionfish are causing big problems for smaller reef fishes and crustaceans that are evolutionarily unfamiliar with these stealthy scorpaenids. As a result, lionfishes are very successfully slurping up nearly any crustacean or small fish that they can ingest. Field biologists are finding that in areas where *Pterois* are common, populations of certain small fish species (e.g., grammas, cardinalfishes, wrasses) are decreasing. In one day a single lionfish may eat more than 50 fish. Lionfishes are also likely to put strong competitive pressure on other piscivores, which may decrease their abundance. Some divers have made a concentrated effort to kill as many invading lions as possible, even noting that they are quite tasty on the barbecue or as ceviche! But their culling efforts may be for naught, as the *Pterois* have apparently established a strong fin-hold as the newest permanent members of the Western Atlantic ichthyofauna.

Chapter 3

Ray-Finned Fishes

T he class Actinopterygii, often referred to as ray-finned or bony fishes, includes more than 24,000 species. They make up over half of all known living vertebrates, and many new species are discovered and described every year. The class is very diverse, with members ranging from tiny gobies to the immense ocean sunfish. The bony fishes we encounter on coral reefs belong to the infraclass Teleostei, which are often referred to as modern ray-finned fishes. There are approximately 23,000 species in this group — over 96 percent of all living fishes.

Teleosts possess highly protrusible jaws that enable them to suck up their prey rather than simply grasp it. They have bony vertebrae and gill arches and paired fins with bony spines and/or flexible rays; most have a homoceral tail, meaning that the upper and lower lobes are symmetrical. Many teleosts have small cycloid or ctenoid scales that are light and flexible, which allows them to be quicker and more maneuverable. Some, like the eels and coral catfishes, have no scales. Many have a buoyancy-control device known as a swim bladder that also functions in sound production in some species. The teleosts are found in a great variety of ecosystems and habitats. They are important as a protein source for people around the world and delight aquanauts with their many colors, forms and fascinating behaviors.

Food Habits

While the coral reef may look like a veritable smorgasbord for a hungry fish, many marine organisms possess anatomical or behavioral features that make them a less than attractive lunch. As a result, most reef fishes have evolved to take advantage of specific types of food. In some cases a species may have a very specialized diet, such as the tailspot butterflyfish (*Chaetodon ocellicaudus*), which feeds only on soft corals, while others have a more catholic bill of fare; many puffers and triggers include a variety of invertebrate prey as well as plant material in their diet. Coral-reef fishes can be classified into several different dietary categories: detritivores, herbivores, carnivores and omnivores.

The tailspot butterflyfish (*Chaetodon ocellicaudus*) feeds exclusively on soft corals. Tropical Western and Central Pacific Ocean.

Detritivores

Detritivores feed on decomposing organic particles, which includes animal and plant remains, waste products and the bacteria and other microorganisms associated with them. Some fishes ingest this material selectively while others consume it incidentally, along with algae or encrusting invertebrates. At least three fish families feed heavily on detritus in what scientists call the epilithic algal matrix. These are the surgeonfishes, damselfishes and blennies.

While many surgeonfishes (Acanthuridae) feed on algae, some species specialize in detritus. For example, most members of the genus *Ctenochaetus* ingest detritus, bacteria, diatoms and large amounts of sediment. When feeding, they press their jaws against the substrate and then throw the lower jaw upward. This effectively brushes particulate matter off rock and dead corals and out of turf algae. Some damselfishes (Pomacentridae) also rely on detritus as a major food source. It was once thought they fed primarily on algae and small invertebrates living in the algae that the damsels farm in their territories. More recent

Pacific double-saddle butterflyfish (*Chaetodon ulietensis*) mass together to feed on coral polyps. Fiji.

studies suggest that detritus in the algal mat makes up the bulk of territorial pomacentrid diets.

Coral mucus can also be classified as detritus. It is loaded with energy-rich wax esters and triglycerides, providing a valuable source of energy. The best-known "mucus munchers" are butterflyfish. Obligatory coral-feeders, such as the ornate butterflyfish (*Chaetodon ornatissimus*), rely heavily on mucus. The shortbodied blenny (*Exallias brevis*) and other reef fish also ingest large quantities of coral mucus along with the polyps.

Fish feces is a waste product utilized by many detritivores (feeding on fecal material is known as coprophagy). Fecal pellets contain macronutrients such as carbon, nitrogen, protein, carbohydrates and lipids. They also contain micro- and nano-nutrients important for growth, such as phosphorus, silicon, copper, iron, manganese, zinc, nickel and chromium. Detritivores and herbivores have digestive equipment that allows them to extract further nutrients from fecal material. In the case of herbivores, whose diets are low in nitrogen, they use carnivore feces as a source of this important nutrient. Herbivorous members of the angelfish, chub, parrotfish, rabbitfish, surgeonfish and triggerfish families occasionally ingest fish feces.

Top
The Panamic fanged blenny (*Ophioblennius steindachneri*) is a detritivore that eats decomposing organic particles, algae and encrusting invertebrates — the epilithic algae mix. Baja, Mexico.

Bottom
Blue tangs (*Acanthurus coeruleus*) and doctorfish (*A. chirurgus*) are herbivores. Here they travel in a school along the reef edge at dusk. Belize.

Herbivores

Algae are inconspicuous in the majority of reef habitats. The main factor affecting their abundance is herbivore numbers (fish and sea urchins). For example, on shallow fore-reef slopes where herbivores are abundant, all the algae are consumed except coralline algae, the "roots" of filamentous forms, and macroalgae with chemical or structural defenses (e.g., *Halimeda*). Herbivores take an estimated 40,000 to 156,000 bites per square meter per day in this reef zone! Therefore it is not surprising that in the absence of herbivores, algae grow like mad. In reef habitats where algae-eating fish are scarce, macroalgae are common, which can be a real problem for sessile invertebrates like corals. Some suggest that modern reefs would not exist in their present form if it were not for herbivores. These fishes (and urchins) stop the competitively superior macroalgae from overgrowing corals. On portions of the Great Barrier Reef, some believe, pinnate batfish (*Platax pinnatus*) may be the only hope for reefs being smothered by *Sargassum* macroalgae. This batfish is one of the only fishes known to feed heavily on this macroalga, which is carpeting some nearshore reef areas.

All herbivores are diurnal and, in contrast to many carnivores, consume large quantities of food, feeding continuously throughout the day. For example, a surgeonfish may feed for seven hours a day, nipping at the substrate more than a thousand times per hour. The Cortez damselfish (*Stegastes rectifraenum*) consumes nearly one-seventh its weight in algae per day. Herbivores consume large quantities of food because algae do not contain a lot of digestible nutrients.

Carnivores

Carnivorous fish feed on animal prey. Reef fish consume members of every animal phylum found on or near coral reefs, from the lowly sponges to our mammal relatives the bats (yes, there is a snapper that regularly feeds on bats!). Fish capture and handle their quarry in different ways depending on the prey item and their anatomy. For example, fish that eat sessile invertebrates may do so by scraping their prey off hard substrate using comb-like dentition (e.g.,

The dagger-like teeth of a lemon shark (*Negaprion brevirostris*) ensure that slippery prey does not escape from this cartilaginous carnivore's maw. Bahamas.

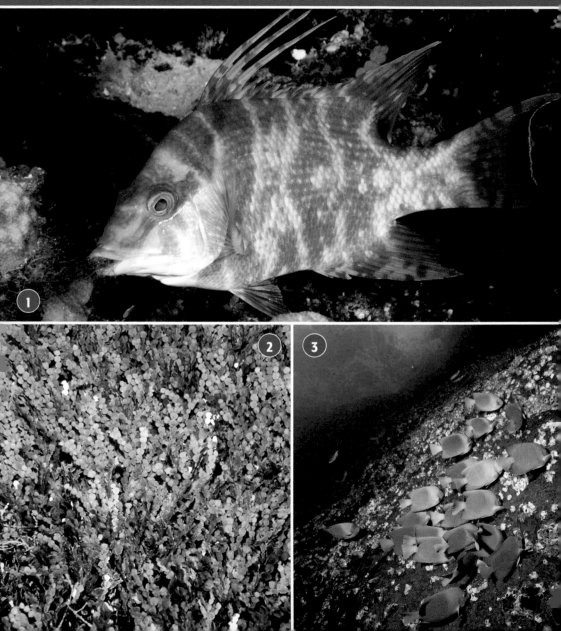

1 A hogfish (*Lachnolaimus maximus*) feeding on algae. Belize.

2 This green macroalga with distinctive disc-shaped segments (*Halimeda* sp., possibly *H. micronesica*) has calcium carbonate in its tissues, making it inedible for many herbivores. Kiribati, Central Pacific Ocean.

3 Clarion angelfish (*Holacanthus clarionensis*), feeding on algae growing on a rock. Baja, Mexico.

4 This close-up shows the special fused teeth used by parrotfishes (*Scarus* sp.) to scrape coral. Fiji.

5 A coral head with parrotfish bite marks. Most parrotfish are herbivores that scrape algae from coral.

angelfishes) or fused, beak-like teeth (e.g., puffers). Other fish rip small pieces of flesh or body parts from prey items (e.g., butterflyfishes), ingest their victims whole (e.g., groupers) or tear or break them into bite-sized morsels (e.g., wrasses). Many carnivores change eating habits as they grow. This is usually a function of physical limitations — their ability to capture and ingest larger prey — and differences in habitat usage between size classes. For example, juvenile coral groupers (*Plectropomus* spp.) focus on smaller invertebrates while the adults' diet consists almost entirely of fish prey.

The frequency of food intake also varies among species. Those fishes whose diet consists of sessile invertebrates feed often and throughout the day. For example, French angelfish (*Pomacanthus paru*) dine mainly on sponges, taking an average of three bites per minute. Like herbivores, this species eats several small meals during the day rather than one large meal. In contrast, fish-eaters consume relatively few meals during a day on the reef. The variegated lizardfish (*Synodus variegatus*), for instance, eats an average of two fish per day, approximately 12 percent of its total body weight.

A group of highly specialized carnivores, the zooplanktivores, make their living by picking off tiny planktonic animals. The primary target is usually crustaceans (i.e., copepods), but opportunism may rule the day. For example, fusiliers and chromis damselfish, both of which prefer planktonic crustaceans, will swim down-current of spawning surgeonfishes and wrasses to feast on their released eggs. While most zooplankton-feeding fishes are active during the day, nocturnal zooplankton-feeders do exist (some soldier and cardinalfishes). They tend to consume larger plankton that swarm near the seafloor.

Omnivores

Omnivores are species that consume both plants and animals. They make up the second most specious guild in coral-reef fish communities. The amount of each food group they eat depends on the species and the age of the fish and may vary by location. The trend among most omnivorous reef fishes is to include more animal prey in their diet as juveniles. There is more nitrogen, which is necessary for growth, in animal prey than in plant material.

A grouper (*Epinephelus* sp.) eating a mantis shrimp. This species is a gulper that usually ingests its victim whole. Indonesia.

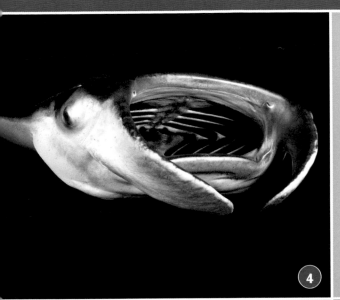

4

1 A slingjaw wrasse (*Epibulus insidiator*), intermediate phase, extends its mouth (hence the name) to suck up prey. Maldives.

2 King angelfish (*Holacanthus passer*) feeding on jellyfish. Galápagos Islands.

3 Fusiliers schooling over an Indonesian reef; these zooplanktivores are probably scissortail fusiliers (*Caesio caerulaurea*) and ruddy fusiliers (*Pterocaesio pisang*). In the foreground are leather corals (*Sinularia* and *Sarcophyton* spp.).

4 A manta ray (*Manta birostris*), mouth open, feeds on plankton at night. Note the gill rakers, which strain out the plankton, and its throat behind. Hawaii.

5 A yellow morph Pacific trumpetfish (*Aulostomus chinensis*) moves closely alongside a leather bass (*Dermatolepis dermatolepis*). This is likely a clever hunting strategy: the trumpetfish hides behind the larger fish as it moves about the reef looking for prey. Baja, Mexico

5

1 The longlure frogfish (*Antennarius multiocellatus*), also known as an anglerfish, is a clever, patient carnivore that lures prey near with its filament (called an esca), then gulps it down. Dominica.

2 A school of striped eel catfish (*Plotosus lineatus*) feeding by digging in the sand. Their diet consists primarily of benthic crustaceans and mollusks on or just under the sand. Indonesia.

3 Whitetip reef sharks (*Triaenodon obesus*) feeding at night. Cocos Island, Costa Rica.

4 Striped marlin (*Tetrapturus audax*) feeding on Pacific sardines (*Sardinops sagax*). Baja, Mexico.

5 A Spanish hogfish (*Bodianus rufus*) eating a sea urchin. This clever carnivore breaks open the sea urchin by rasping it against coral to avoid biting down on its sharp spines. Caribbean Sea.

Antipredation Behavior: Staying Off the Menu

There's an arms race taking place on the coral reef. Predators evolve anatomical and behavioral adaptations to exploit a certain set of prey species. In response, prey organisms parry the offensive tactics of their enemies by developing new defenses. Sponges have developed spicules and toxins, while corals have evolved spiny sclerites, calcareous armor, stinging cells and noxious compounds. Some crustaceans take advantage of the defenses of other invertebrates, living among their spines or stinging tentacles, and others hide in soft substrate or reef crevices. Sea stars and urchins are armed with sharp spines and tough exoskeletons to thwart the attacks of predators. But invertebrates are not the only reef residents to develop strategies to dissuade hungry fishes. Many of the reef's piscine residents are potential prey for their carnivorous kin, and therefore also participants in this "arms race."

Avoiding Detection

A very common way that reef fishes evade predators is avoiding being detected. There are several ways to do this. A fish might employ crypsis so that a predator overlooks it, or it may take shelter in a hole or crevice when its predators are most active.

Camouflage, or crypsis, can take one of two forms: either a fish matches its surroundings so that it goes totally undetected (eucrypsis) or it takes on the appearance and actions of something inedible (masquerade). Examples of eucrypsis include the many fish species that rest on the substrate and assume a color pattern that enables them to blend in with their surroundings. The flatfishes are an excellent example of fishes that are able to hide in plain sight. They normally exhibit colors similar to the benthos and are able to lighten or darken their coloration depending on the hue of the bottom they are resting on. Other species that demonstrate eucrypsis include the scorpionfishes, flatheads, some dragonets and certain gobies.

Top
A peacock flounder (*Bothus lunatus*), well camouflaged on a sandy bottom. Dominica.

Bottom
A bearded scorpionfish (*Scorpaenopsis oxycephala*) well camouflaged against a reef covered with coralline algae. Thailand.

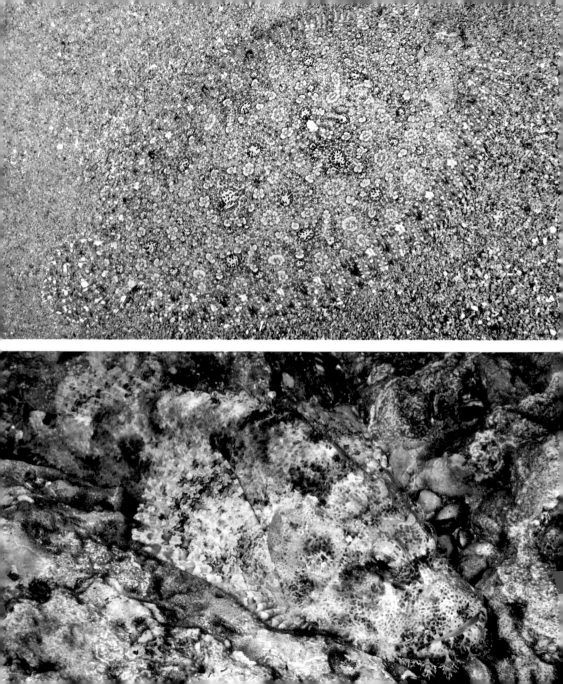

Fishes that engage in masquerade to avoid predators might resemble seagrass, macroalgae, leaf litter or invertebrates. The halimeda ghost pipefish (*Solenostomus halimeda*), for example, looks like *Halimeda* algae fronds, sometimes complete with pink spots that resemble epiphytic coralline algae; other ghost pipefish resemble the arms of feather stars (crinoids) or soft coral branches. The pygmy seahorse (*Hippocampus bargibanti*) showcases a stunning example of masquerade. This minute creature has small nodules on its body that look like the contracted polyps of the sea fan (*Muricella* spp.) that it clings to. Many frogfish expertly mimic sponges; this superb disguise enables an otherwise defenseless fish to effectively avoid predators and ambush unwary prey. The leaf scorpionfish (*Taenianotus triacanthus*) and the cockatoo waspfish (*Ablabys taenianotus*) look — and act — like pieces of benthic debris, swaying from side to side like plant material being affected by the surge. Likewise, the juvenile dragon wrasse (*Novaculichthys taeniurus*) mimics algae, floating just above the substrate, while a young orbiculate batfish (*Platax orbicularis*) resembles a fallen leaf as it hangs near the water's surface.

Another way a prey species can avoid detection is to hide or take refuge. Some fishes seek shelter in caves and crevices during the day, when visually oriented predators are most active, while others slip into reef interstices at dusk to avoid the crepuscular and nocturnally active piscivores. Other fishes bury themselves in soft substrate. Some can actually "swim" under the sand; the snake eels and razorfishes, for example, are able to move from one location to another beneath the substrate.

Parrotfishes, and some wrasses, may avoid being located by predators that hunt after dark by producing excessive amounts of mucus, which envelops their bodies. This slimy cocoon acts as a barrier to prevent the emission of sensory cues (e.g., olfactory stimuli) that attract piscivores such as moray eels. Some of these fishes are more likely to secrete a mucus cocoon if injured or stressed — situations when more olfactory attractants are likely to be discharged.

Deterring Attackers
Once detected, a fish may avoid being eaten by thwarting the predator's attack. Reef fishes employ a number of different strategies to discourage piscivores

This pygmy seahorse (*Hippocampus bargibanti*) is well camouflaged on its host sea fan (*Muricella* sp.). Indonesia.

1 The halimeda ghost pipefish
(*Solenostomus halimeda*) hangs around
clumps of *Halimeda* algae, in which it is
well camouflaged. Maldives.

2 The filamentous skin appendages of
the hairy frogfish (*Antennarius striatus*)
help to camouflage this 15 cm (6 in)
fish, making it look like a ball of algae.
Indonesia.

3 A painted frogfish (*Antennarius pictus*),
well hidden against a sponge. Indonesia.

4 A double-ended pipefish (*Syngnathoides
biaculeatus*), well camouflaged among
seagrasses. Indonesia.

5 The cockatoo waspfish (*Ablabys
taenianotus*) looks like the leaf behind it
and mimics it by flopping back and forth
in the surge. Papua New Guinea.

6 An eight-banded butterflyfish
(*Chaetodon octofasciatus*) sheltering
in a coral head at night for protection.
Indonesia.

from ingesting them. Some fishes do not even attempt to hide from predators but instead deter them with spines, distasteful secretions and venom.

Certain fishes boldly advertise the fact that they taste bad, are venomous or are simply spiny. Most predatory fish learn very quickly. If a predator survives an attempt to eat a harmful species exhibiting bright colors, it likely will learn to associate the striking chromatic attire of the undesirable prey species with a bad dining experience. Other predators may even learn by social facilitation; in other words, observing one of these unpleasant predatory events will teach them that they should avoid that particular prey species. An example of a fish that displays aposematic, or warning, coloration, is the mandarin dragonet (*Synchiropus splendidus*), which produces copious amounts of distasteful slime.

Members of the scorpionfish family are spectacular advertisers.

A mandarinfish (*Synchiropus splendidus*), also known as a mandarin dragonet. Its bright colors and bold patterns are an example of aposematic coloration — a warning to potential predators that this small fish tastes very bad because of the slime it produces. Indonesia.

For example, the devilfishes (*Inimicus* spp.) typically sport cryptic colors to prevent both their prey and potential predators from detecting them. But if one of these highly venomous fishes is located and harassed, it throws its large, fan-like pectoral fins forward and down, revealing brightly colored inner surfaces. This broadcasts a very effective warning to a potential predator. The related

A parrotfish (*Scarus* sp.) sleeping in its mucus cocoon. It blows this mucus web around itself at night to help mask its scent and deter predators. Indonesia.

Pacific creolefish (*Paranthias colonus*) in the Galápagos Islands.

Sleek unicornfish (*Naso hexacanthus*). Indonesia.

humpbacked scorpionfishes (*Scorpaenopsis* spp.) have similar pectoral fins, and they also show a "flash flight" response. If threatened they will dart away, displaying the bright inner pectoral surfaces as they flee. The sudden flash of color as it dashes away may distract or put off the pursuing predator. After swimming a short distance they settle back on the bottom and freeze.

Speed and Agility

Swimming faster than one's pursuer and outmaneuvering the enemy are additional ways to avoid being eaten. Zooplanktivores often rely on speed to get back to the reef if attacked. Among these fishes, species with a fusiform body and lunate tail feed farther from the reef. Because they are built for speed, they are able to retreat back to safety more rapidly than their less speedy cohorts. Some reef fishes that rely on speed include anthias, creolefish (*Paranthias* spp.), tilefishes, fusiliers, certain damselfishes (e.g., *Lepidozygus* spp.), Creole wrasse (*Clepticus parrae*), the dart gobies (*Ptereleotris* spp.) and unicornfishes (*Naso* spp.).

Venom and Poison

There are several fish families whose members possess venomous dorsal, pelvic and anal fin spines that prevent many would-be predators from succeeding. The coral catfishes, scorpionfishes and rabbitfishes all own such formidable weaponry. Some holocentrids, such as the giant squirrelfish (*Sargocentron spiniferum*), have venomous cheek spines, while the stingrays have a barbed spine on the tail covered by a toxic sheath.

The fangblennies (genus *Meiacanthus*) are gifted with a pair of large grooved, venomous canines in the lower jaw, perfect for biting the inside of a predator's mouth if the blenny is ingested whole. The noxious nip usually results in the piscivore's spitting out the fang-bearing blenny, followed by head quivering, flaring of the gill covers and yawning. In most cases the blenny is no worse for wear after the experience. But the incident is so disagreeable for the predatory fish that it typically avoids these blennies — and any other fish that looks like them — from that point on. This defensive mechanism is so effective that fangblennies are usually observed hanging out in the open, above the reef.

Puffers and porcupinefishes accumulate a deadly neurotoxin (tetraodotoxin) in their skin and/or internal organs, especially the liver and sex organs. Other toxic fishes best left off the menu include the yellowmouth moray (*Gymnothorax nudivomer*), which exudes impressive amounts of poisonous slime; soapfishes, which are coated with toxic body slime known as grammistin; the shadow goby (*Yongeichthys nebulosus*); and trunkfishes.

1 This reef stonefish (*Synanceia verrucosa*), bottom center, is well camouflaged by an overgrowth of algae. One of the most venomous fish in the world, a puncture from one of its fin spines can be fatal. Australia.

2 The sabre squirrelfish (*Sargocentron spiniferum*), also known as the giant squirrelfish, has a long cheek spine that is venomous. Australia.

3 The spiny devilfish (*Inimicus didactylus*) is also called the bearded ghoul. This dangerous fish erects venomous spines and flares its fins as a warning to would-be predators. Indonesia.

4 The blue-spotted puffer (*Arothron caeruleopunctatus*), which reaches up to 70 cm (27.5 in), has toxic flesh. Australia.

5 A common lionfish (*Pterois volitans*) advertising its venomous spines. Indonesia.

Spines, Armor and Teeth

Sharp fin spines are another trick to effectively decrease palatability. In trigger and filefishes, the strong dorsal spine comes complete with a locking mechanism. If it is erected in a tight spot on the reef, the fish is almost impossible to extract. Some species have spines, formed from modified scales, on parts of or all over the body. Enter the pinecone fishes, which have a spine on each of their large scales. And stout, sharp cheek spines help to keep dozens of species of angelfish out of trouble. Surgeonfishes have spines on the sides of the caudal peduncle; if threatened, these fish will flail their spines the way a skilled surgeon wields a scalpel, hence their common name.

Another defensive option is to wear armor. Seahorses, pipefishes and trunkfishes are encased in rigid bony plating. In the case of the boxfishes, the "box" has holes for the eyes, mouth, gills, anus, fins and caudal peduncle. Many of the scorpionfishes, helmet gurnards and sea robins have bony plates and sharp spines that protect the head.

A few reef-fish families have long, sharp teeth that are used to bite would-be predators, as well as to catch their prey. For example, moray eels will not hesitate to bite any fish that attempts to eat them.

Some fishes will increase their girth to prevent predators from ingesting them. Members of the frogfish, filefish, pufferfish and porcupinefish families are all known to inflate. They do this by swallowing mouthfuls of seawater. Porcupinefishes

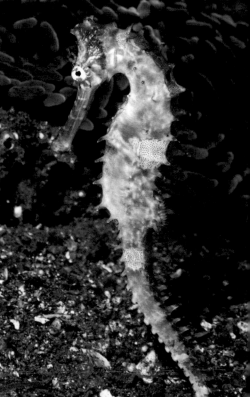

The thorny seahorse (*Hippocampus histrix*) has spiny armor-like plating that helps protect this slow-swimming fish. Indonesia.

A balloonfish (*Diodon holocanthus*) inflated, with defensive spines erect. Baja, Mexico.

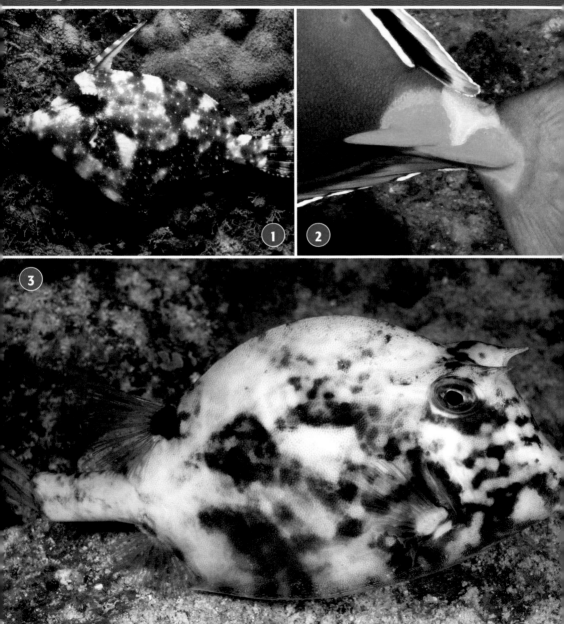

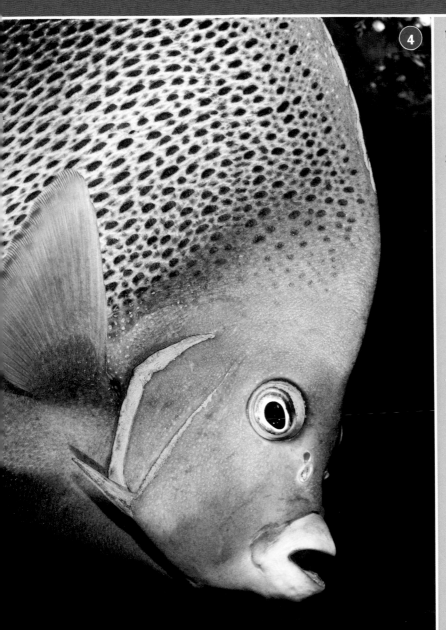

4

1 A pygmy filefish (*Monacanthus setifer*) at night. While it sleeps, the sharp dorsal spine is erected for protection and the fish changes color and presses up against a rock to hide. Dominica.

2 This close-up shows the spines on the caudal peduncle (at the base of the tail) of an orangespine unicornfish (*Naso lituratus*). These sharp recurved spines provide a defense against predators. Australia.

3 The scrawled cowfish (*Lactophrys quadricornis*) is a member of the boxfish family Ostraciidae. It has full body armor — almost like a shell — under its skin, as well as spines above the eyes. This fish is well protected, even out in the open! Belize.

4 Note the sharp cheek spine on this semicircle angelfish (*Pomacanthus semicirculatus*), which helps protect this fish from predators. Fiji.

augment this defensive behavior with long, sharp body spines, which are erected during inflation so that they look like a nail-studded basketball. The spiny boxfishes also have body spines, but they are usually shorter and are erect at all times.

Schooling and Shoaling

One way a fish may avoid becoming a meal is to live in a group. Such groups can be classified as schools (or polarized schools), shoals (non-polarized schools) or aggregations. A school is made up of individuals of similar size that usually maintain an equal inter-individual distance and move synchronously with one another. In some schooling species the movements are so well coordinated that the group looks like a single large organism. Herrings, sprats and sardines are examples of fish species that normally occur in true schools. Some fishes may form temporary schools when moving from one location to another or when feeding away from the reef.

A shoal, in contrast, is a group of fish whose members do not maintain equal distance from each other or engage in coordinated movements. For example, most of the reef-dwelling anthias and many chromis species form shoals. Many damselfishes do not aggregate when feeding near the substrate, but they do form shoals when they move into the water column to feed. This is because they are more vulnerable to predators when they leave the reef. In both schools and shoals there is social attraction between individual members.

An aggregation is a gathering of fish brought together by an environmental stimulus, not by social attraction. For example, a food source or a cave may attract an aggregation of one or more species whose individuals are different sizes. Members of this type of group usually mill around the mutually attractive stimulus and do not carry out coordinated movements. A number of fishes form mixed-species feeding aggregations, others will aggregate around a cleaning station, and nocturnal species regularly form aggregations under overhangs or in caves.

Top
Striped marlin (*Tetrapturus audax*) feeding on Pacific sardines (*Sardinops sagax*). Baja, Mexico.

Bottom
Black striped salema fish (*Xenocys jessiae*). Galápagos Islands.

The term *aggregation* is widely used for groups of fishes that converge at a particular location to spawn. However, by definition, that is not truly an aggregation (remember, the term is defined as individuals brought together by something other than attraction to members of their own kind). It has been suggested that "breeding/spawning assemblage" may be a more appropriate, less confusing term for these reproductive groups. Many grouper species, such as the Nassau grouper (*Epinephelus striatus*), form immense spawning assemblages that can consist of thousands of individuals.

How does living in a group decrease the chance a fish will be eaten? The "dilution of risk" theory predicts an inverse correlation between the size of the group and an individual's risk of predation. Basically, there's safety in numbers. Being one of many statistically reduces the likelihood of an individual's being captured. Another benefit is that there is more sensory equipment available to detect an approaching predator. If one individual senses potential danger it will warn the other group members by the way it behaves or by releasing pheromones. Some species, such as squirrelfishes, will even produce auditory signals to warn members of their own kind.

Another theory that attempts to explain the advantage of schooling behavior is "collective mimicry." This suggests that a school of fish looks like a larger organism, something a predator would not attack and might even avoid. However, the data available on the feeding behavior of fishes do not support this theory. For example, there are many predators that do not avoid — and even readily attack — schools or shoals of fish.

Probably the greatest benefit gained by individuals that school or shoal is the "confusion effect." Most predators have difficulty attacking more than one prey item at a time. When it encounters numerous targets, the hunter has difficulty selecting and pursuing a specific prey item. Schooling fishes usually move closer together and are more cohesive when initially approached, which brings more individuals into the predator's visual field. School members tend to be similar in size and shape and display like color patterns, all factors that aid in confounding an attacker. Studies have shown that aberrant individuals in a group are more likely to be eaten than those that blend in with the rest of

A striped marlin (*Tetrapturus audax*) and a California sea lion (*Zalophus californianus*) swim below a baitball of Pacific mackerel (*Scomber japonicus*). Baja, Mexico.

1 A shoal of purple anthias — probably magenta slender anthias (*Luzonichthys waitei*) — swarming in the current. A crinoid, or feather star, clings to the coral (*Acropora* sp.) at the top of the reef, 3 m (10 ft) deep. Fiji.

2 Blackbar soldierfish (*Myripristis jacobus*) aggregating in a cave during the day. Dominica.

3 Many species of fish shoal over a seamount into a large aggregation. They include rainbow runners (*Elagatis bipinnulatus*), sleek unicornfish (*Naso hexacanthus*) and giant trevally (*Caranx ignobilis*). Indonesia.

4 A Bryde's whale (*Balaenoptera brydei*) races in to feed on a small school of Pacific sardines (*Sardinops sagax*). The 12 m (40 ft) long baleen whale's huge mouth is wide open and its throat pleats billow out like a blimp.

5 Fish in a school of bigeye scad (*Selar crumenophthalmus*) flee from a cormorant (*Phalacrocorax* sp.) feeding on them. Baja, Mexico.

the school. Straggling school members are also more likely to be attacked.

Chromatic characteristics can also increase a predator's confusion. For example, many schooling species are silver in color, producing sudden flashes of light when they change position in the sunlit shallows. Others are barred or have lines that make it difficult for predators to tell one fish from another. When attacked by a predator, schooling species often engage in evasive maneuvers. These include the "fountain effect," when members of the school split, swim around the predator and regroup behind it, and "flash expansion," when the school members suddenly dash in all directions.

Other advantages to forming groups include increasing the hydrodynamic efficiency of the individual (this applies primarily to schooling species) and swamping the defenses of territorial herbivores.

Fishes are able to move in a coordinated fashion in a school or a shoal in part because of a line of pores along the side the body known as the acoustic-lateralis system, or lateral line. Water is a non-compressible medium; as a result, anytime something moves in the water, it produces pressure waves. With their lateral lines, fish can feel the changes in water pressure produced when schoolmates alter their course. This, along with visual cues, allows a group of schooling fish to change direction almost simultaneously.

Mimicry

Some fishes have evolved to resemble other fishes or invertebrates to dissuade predators from feeding on them. The species assuming the false identity is known as the mimic, while the organism being imitated is called the model. Obviously the two species must be sympatric, in both geographical range and their distribution on the reef. Also, the mimic must be less common than the model so that a predator is more likely to encounter the model and learn to avoid both. Several types of mimicry function to reduce predation: Batesian mimicry, Müllerian mimicry and social mimicry.

Batesian Mimicry

Batesian mimicry is when a "non-nasty" creature resembles a "nasty" one. A nasty organism is defined as one that tastes bad, is venomous or sports sharp spines. Most of the mimicry observed in coral-reef fishes falls into this category.

Reef fishes may mimic invertebrates or other fishes. One group of invertebrates that serves as models is the flatworms. Reef fishes rarely eat these worms, because of their distasteful or toxic qualities. Not only are the pinnate batfish (*Platax pinnatus*) and clown sweetlips (*Plectorhinchus chaetodonoides*) brightly colored like flatworms, they also swim like them. A small pinnate batfish will lie on its side and undulate its fins, while the sweetlips will swim with its head down, sculling with large pectoral fins and wagging its body. Another group of flatworm imposters consists of several tiny flatfishes that cunningly resemble, in both color and form, these noxious invertebrates.

Batesian mimics also resemble unpalatable fish. For example, a grouper called the false scorpionfish (*Centrogenys vaigiensis*) and an undescribed species of cardinalfish in the genus *Fowleri* both look like select *Scorpaenodes* and *Parascorpaena* venomous scorpionfishes. The cardinalfish often shares the same shelter sites as the similar-looking Guam scorpionfish (*Scorpaenodes guamensis*). One of the most fascinating mimetic relationships exists between the

Batesian mimicry: a juvenile pinnate batfish (*Platax pinnatus*), top, and a juvenile many-spotted sweetlips (*Plectorhinchus chaetodonoides*), bottom. Their swimming styles and bright colors are believed to mimic toxic flatworms, which may help to protect these small fish from predators. Indonesia.

Batesian mimicry: the mimic filefish (*Paraluteres prionurus*), top, looks like the saddled toby (*Canthigaster valentini*), bottom, an 8 cm (3 in) long poisonous fish also known as Valentini's sharpnose puffer. Indonesia.

comet (*Calloplesiops altivelis*) and the whitemouth moray (*Gymnothorax meleagris*). When threatened, the comet moves partially into a hole, leaving its expanded tail in full view. The body and tail are brown with white spots and there is a distinct eyespot on the edge of the comet's dorsal fin. When it assumes this posture, the posterior part of the comet's body bears a striking resemblance to the head of a moray, which typically is seen with only its head sticking out of the reef.

A number of harmless blennies look and act like the fang-blennies (*Meiacanthus* spp.). Many of these mimic blennies — for example, the Red Sea mimic blenny (*Ecsenius gravieri*) — are amazing imitations of the species they model. Certain surgeonfish may resemble pygmy angelfish, which are often avoided by predators because of their sharp pre-opercular spines. The young Indian Ocean mimic surgeonfish (*Acanthurus tristis*) is almost an exact chromatic replica of Eibl's angelfish (*C. eibli*). And the mimic filefish (*Paraluteres prionurus*) gains protection by brilliantly copying the poison-fleshed saddled toby (*Canthigaster valentini*).

Müllerian Mimicry

In Müllerian mimicry, one nasty creature looks like another. If a piscivore has a bad experience with one of these species, it will learn to avoid them both. This type of mimicry is rare in the coral-reef environment. There are, however, some blennies with venomous fangs that resemble one another. These include the striped fangblenny (*Meiacanthus grammistes*), yellowlined fangblenny (*M. lineatus*), shorthead sabretooth blenny (*Petroscirtes breviceps*) and yellow sabretooth blenny (*P. fallax*).

Cleaner Mimics

Cleaner fishes are rarely eaten by other fish because of the valuable function they serve in the reef community. It is not surprising that a handful of fish species derive some degree of protection by mimicking cleaner fishes. Species such as Springer's dottyback (*Pseudochromis springeri*), the cleaner mimic (*Aspidontus taeniatus*) and the bluestriped scale-eating blenny (*Plagiotremus rhinorhynchus*) fall into this category. The aforementioned blennies are also aggressive mimics of the bluestreak cleaner wrasse

A comet (*Calloplesiops altivelis*), top, guarding its eggs (above it). The spot on its dorsal fin is a "false eye" that confuses predators by giving this small fish the appearance of a whitemouth moray eel (*Gymnothorax meleagris*), bottom. Indonesia and Fiji.

Cephalopods are often considered the most intelligent of the invertebrate clan. Behavioral studies have shown that many cephalopods learn quickly, have complex ways of communicating and exhibit extensive behavioral repertoires. But two octopuses seem to possess special abilities that make others in the clan look positively dim. These are the mimic octopus (*Thaumoctopus mimicus*) and the wunderpus, or ornate octopus (*Wunderpus photogenicus*). These two long-armed species have been given much press in the past decade, appearing on TV documentaries, in dive magazines and all over the Internet. The reason for their sudden rise to stardom is their apparent mimicking behavior. It is thought that these animals take on the shape of other animals.

Like many sand-dwelling octopuses, when threatened, both species will usually slither into a nearby burrow in the sand. But if a mimic octopus finds itself too far away from its "den" or if the threat persists as it approaches its burrow, it may start acting in a very non-octopus-like way! The mimic octopus will alter its body shape, change how it holds its arms and engage in other unusual behaviors such as undulating its tentacles. The color may also intensify. In some cases it will continue to engage in this unusual behavior until the threat is gone. In other cases it will "strike a pose" and then retreat into its refuge.

In the late 1990s, some diving naturalists came to the conclusion that when this octopus engages in such behavior, it is attempting to resemble other animals. There is no doubt that the animal is different from many other cephalopods, adopting a variety of different postures that, at least to the human eye, make it seem to resemble some of the animals that share its environment. But is the mimic octopus really, truly mimicking a flounder, a sea snake, a lionfish, a crinoid, a sea anemone, a stingray? (It has been reported to mimic as many as 15 different sympatric sea creatures!)

A number of naturalists and scientists are convinced that this cephalopod does mimic other animals. Some have also concluded that at least *T. mimicus* takes on the appearance and behavior of at least three different noxious animals: a sea snake, a lionfish and a flatfish (they suggest a banded sole, *Zebrias* spp.). All three of these species either have venom (the first two) or are toxic (the sole). Scientists further suggest that it may also mimic the stinging sand anemone (*Megalactis* spp.) and possibly a pelagic jelly.

A mimic octopus (*Thaumoctopus mimicus*) mimicking a venomous common lionfish (*Pterois volitans*), inset. Indonesia.

Wunderpus, or ornate octopus (*Wunderpus photogenicus*). Indonesia.

Mimicry or Imagination?

Skeptics suggest that this may simply be a case of human observers' reading too much into the behavior of a very unusual cephalopod, and that this fabulous story represents our imaginations getting the best of us. A few individuals (including some prominent scientific sorts) are convinced that the mimic octopus is not trying to look like anything in particular but may simply be engaging in a form of deimatic behavior. Such displays help an animal blend in with its environment or serve as a threat to dissuade potential predators. Deimatic

displays include changes in color and splaying, flaring or contorting the arms. We see these behaviors in the mimic octopus and the similar wunderpus. For example, it is not uncommon that if you threaten one of these animals it will widen its arms and often curl the tips inward (many have suggested that they are actually mimicking a crinoid with this behavior).

It may be that these octopuses are not trying to mimic any organism in particular but that their sudden change of appearance may act to confound a predator's search image. Many fish develop a specific search image when they hunt. For example, an individual triggerfish may look specifically for one or two types of prey when foraging. When it comes across something that matches a specific search image, it attacks. By morphing from one shape to another, the mimic octopus might confuse the predator's search image. It would not even have to imitate a specific organism; by simply changing form it could throw off a potential predator.

One of the mimic octopuses apparent models is a flatfish. When it swims over the bottom, the mimic octopus often flattens its body and head and lets its arms trail behind as it glides over the substrate. But are these octopuses attempting to mimic a flatfish or is that just an effective way for a long-armed octopus to swim over the substrate?

Why would these octopuses engage in this type of mimicry to begin with? The most obvious reason for mimicking harmful animals is to dissuade potential predators from attacking (Batesian mimicry). If the mimic octopus (and the wunderpus) are venomous, then they may be engaging in Müllerian mimicry, in which harmful animals adopt similar color patterns to communicate to potential enemies that they should not be messed with. If a jack has a bad experience with a lionfish, its venomous spines jabbing into the sides of its mouth, resulting in a painful wound, it may avoid attacking the similar-looking mimic octopus. If enough venomous or toxic animals "spread the news" that they are unpalatable, predators will learn to avoid all of them more quickly.

The bold color patterns of the mimic and the wunderpus have caused some cephalopod experts to suggest that these animals are venomous. This type of chromatic advertising (known as aposematic coloration) is effective at warning potential predators that an animal is not palatable or that there may be severe consequences if they try to eat it (such as a venomous bite). Of course, the potential models — the banded sea snake and many

A mimic octopus (*Thaumoctopus mimicus*) looking remarkably like a mantis shrimp. Indonesia.

lionfishes — exhibit aposematic coloration.

It appears that one crustacean the mimic octopus will eat is the spanner crab (*Ranina ranina*). These are large, heavily armored and armed crabs that ambush passing fish and could inflict serious damage on this finely built octopus. It may be that the mimic octopus is more venomous than many of its relatives (the saliva of most octopuses contains some venom). Like the blue-ringed octopuses (genus *Hapalochlaena*), the mimic could use a virulent venom to rapidly dispatch the crab before the crab inflicts injury on its captor.

(*Labroides dimidiatus*), biting off pieces of fin or scales when a fish approaches them, expecting to have parasites removed.

Social Mimicry

There is safety in numbers. An individual that swims alone, or that appears different from the crowd, will likely be more vulnerable to predation. In order to take advantage of the dilution of risk that occurs when living in groups, some reef fishes adopt the coloration of and associate with schooling or shoaling species. For example, around Christmas Island, in the Line Islands, the peach anthias (*Pseudanthias dispar*) adopts the color pattern of the more abundant Bartlett's anthias (*P. bartlettorum*); both species naturally occur in shoals. The Midas blenny (*Ecsenius midas*) is a solitary species that also mimics the color pattern of and lives within groups of Bartlett's anthias. In other regions the Midas blenny mimics and lives among groups of lyretail anthias (*Pseudanthias squamipinnis*).

The cleaner mimic blenny, or false cleanerfish (*Aspidontus taeniatus*), top, is an aggressive mimic of the bluestreak cleaner wrasse (*Labroides dimidiatus*), bottom, here seen cleaning an oriental sweetlips (*Plectorhinchus vittatus*). Maldives.

Orange anemonefish (*Amphiprion sandaracinos*) and porcelain crab (*Neopetrolisthes maculatus*), roommates in the same sea anemone. Indonesia.

Reef Fish and Invertebrates

Many fish species associate with invertebrates, taking advantage of the defenses that these animals possess. A classic example of such a relationship occurs between anemonefishes and certain sea anemones. Sea anemones have stinging capsules, known as nematocysts, that they use for defense and to capture their prey; in fact, some sea anemones will actually catch and ingest small fishes. Anemonefishes, however, have evolved behavioral and physiological characteristics that allow them to seek protection among the tentacles of these virulent invertebrates. When young anemonefish settle out of the plankton, they will locate an anemone to live in. Some scientists believe that sea anemones release chemicals that help juvenile anemonefishes find them. Whereas some fish slowly get used to their anemone by making brief contact with its tentacles (often known as "acclimation"), others swim among the host's tentacles right away without being stung.

How do these fish avoid being stung and eaten? Although scientists are not sure of the exact mechanism involved in protecting anemonefish, they agree that it has something to do with the fish's mucus. Researchers have suggested that the anemonefish rubs the mucus of the anemone on itself during

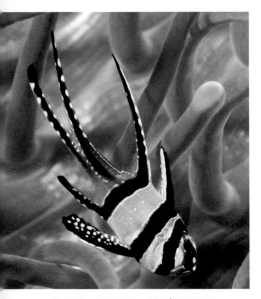

A juvenile Banggai cardinalfish (*Pterapogon kauderni*) shelters among the tentacles of sea anemone. Indonesia.

the "acclimation" period, and that once covered by anemone mucus the fish is "chemically camouflaged." Another theory is that the composition of the fish's mucus actually changes when it contacts the anemone, so that it no longer triggers nematocyst discharge. Both ideas may be true.

In providing sanctuary for the anemonefish, the anemone also benefits from this relationship: the presence of these fish actually increases the rate of host growth and asexual reproduction. Zooxanthellae algae living in the anemone's tissues use the ammonium excreted by resident anemonefishes as a nutrient source. Studies show that sea anemones with anemonefish regenerate tentacles more rapidly than those without fish, and that these tentacles contain more zooxanthellae. The movement of the anemonefish among the tentacles also stimulates the host to open, facilitating the circulation of oxygen-rich water among its tentacles and skin folds as well as wafting away debris from the sea anemone's oral disc. As greater surface area is exposed to the sun, the anemone's zooxanthellae engage in more photosynthesis. Larger anemonefishes also help defend their anemone partner from predators; in some areas, sea anemones are quickly consumed by large butterflyfishes if the anemonefishes are removed.

The Banggai cardinalfish (*Apogon kauderni*) from Indonesia also associates with stinging cnidarians. This species is not specially protected from nematocysts, however, and may bear scars from being stung. The bluehead wrasse (*Thalassoma bifasciatum*) often takes refuge in the giant anemone (*Condylactis gigantea*), carefully maneuvering between its tentacles or lying on the nematocyst-free oral disc; this is particularly true for juveniles and initial-phase individuals. The diamond blenny (*Malacoctenus boehlkei*) is another inhabitant of the Atlantic that usually lives at the base and under the tentacles of the giant anemone. This

Macro photo of the tentacles of a bulb tentacle sea anemone (*Entacmaea quadricolor*), which are armed with nematocyst stinging cells. Indonesia.

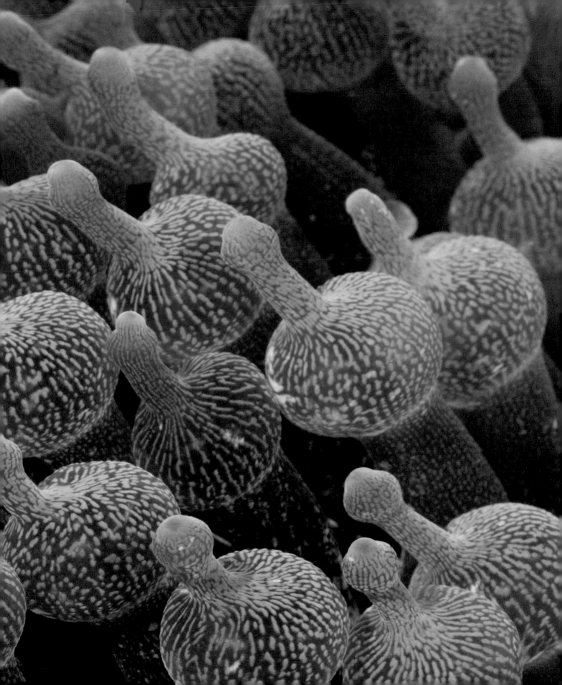

species does acclimate to the host's tentacles in a similar manner to anemone-fishes; the process can take several minutes to hours. Some hawkfishes, such as the coral hawkfish (*Cirrhitichthys oxycephalus*) and the dwarf hawkfish (*C. falco*), will rest among the tentacles of the magnificent sea anemone (*Heteractis magnifica*).

Stony corals are obvious hiding places for numerous fish species. Some, like the bluegreen chromis (*Chromis viridis*) and the reticulated dascyllus (*Dascyllus reticulatus*), hang above small-polyped stony corals, seeking shelter between the branches when threatened. Other species rarely, if ever, leave the interstices between stony coral branches. The mushroom coral pipefish (*Siokunichthys nigrolineatus*) associates with long-tentacled mushroom corals (*Heliofungia actiniformis*). This specialized pipefish looks like a white worm and usually lives in groups among the anemone-like tentacles of these unusual large-polyped stony corals. Gobies (e.g., *Pleurosicya micheli*) live on the grape-like vesicles of bubble coral (*Plerogyra sinuosa*).

Perhaps the most fascinating invertebrate–fish association occurs between certain gobies and pistol or snapping shrimp (*Alpheus* spp.). This relationship between crustacean and goby is mutualistic in nature, as it benefits both partners. The shrimp, which is thought to have poor vision, constructs a burrow in the sand adjacent to the reef. While the shrimp goes about maintaining the burrow, its goby burrow-mate acts as sentinel, ready to warn the crustacean of impending danger. They communicate via touch. The shrimp places an antenna on the vigilant fish's tail, and as soon as the goby detects a potential threat it wags its tail, alerting the shrimp to danger.

Echinoderms also serve as a refuge for certain reef fishes. For example, pearlfishes live in the alimentary tract of sea cucumbers, entering through the anal opening. The long spines of Diadema sea urchins are used as a sanctuary by certain clingfishes, juvenile leather bass (*Dermatolepis dermatolepis*), many cardinalfishes and the greenbanded goby (*Gobiosoma multifasciatum*). Urchins of the genus *Astropyga*, nicknamed "fire urchins" because of their painful sting, provide a home for juvenile emperor snappers (*Lutjanus sebae*) and certain cardinalfishes such as tubed siphonfish (*Siphamia tubifer*). Cardinals also shelter among the venomous spines of the much loathed crown-of-thorns sea star (*Acanthaster planci*). Feather stars (also called crinoids) harbor dozens of freeloader

Tubed siphonfish (*Siphamia tubifer*). These cardinalfish shelter among the spines of an *Astropyga radiata* sea urchin for protection. Indonesia.

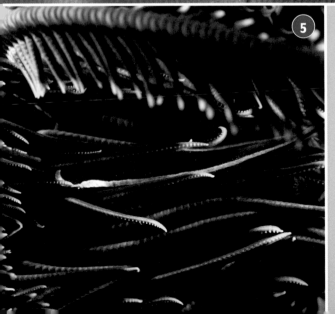

4

5

1 Mushroom coral pipefish (*Siokunichthys nigrolineatus*), which grow to 8 cm (3 in) long, associate with long-tentacled mushroom corals (*Heliofungia actiniformis*). Philippines

2 A blacksaddle snake eel (*Ophichthus cephalozona*) protruding from the sand with a cleaner shrimp on its head. This magnificent anemone shrimp (*Ancylomenes magnificus*; previously *Periclimenes magnificus*) uses the snake eel's head as a cleaning station to service other fish! Indonesia.

3 This flagtail shrimpgoby (*Amblyeleotris yanoi*) and shrimp (*Alpheus randalli*) live together in a burrow on a sand slope. The shrimp maintains their home, cleaning out the burrow, and the shrimpgoby acts as sentinel, guarding the shrimp. Indonesia.

4 A stonycoral ghost goby (*Pleurosicya micheli*) on bubble coral (*Plerogyra sinuosa*). Indonesia.

5 The crinoid clingfish (*Discotrema crinophila*), only 3 cm (1.2 in) long, lives in association with crinoids (feather stars). Look closely to find it, as it is well camouflaged. Indonesia.

crustacean species but also certain highly specialized fish. The ornate ghost pipefish (*Solenostomus paradoxus*) brilliantly resembles its echinoderm hideout to avoid the eyes of hungry predators. Crinoid clingfish (*Discotrema crinophila*) derive sanctuary and find food among the arms of their feather-star hosts.

Cleaner Fishes

A small guild of specialized reef fishes known as cleaners or parasite-pickers showcases a rather unusual feeding strategy that involves removing parasites, diseased and dying tissue, scales and slime from other fishes. Marine biologist William Longley was the first to describe cleaning behavior on coral reefs. However, he was unaware of the significance of the relationship between the fishes he observed. In 1918 he reported the following about the neon cleaner goby:

> The tiny, blue-striped *Elacatinus oceanops* may be seen at almost any time creeping over the bodies of larger fishes such as grunts and groupers. Its jerky movement seems a source of minor irritation commonly borne with indifference or an air of hopeless resignation, even when the little fellows stop almost within their host's capacious jaws. The severance of relations between the two usually occur in stereotyped fashion: the larger grows restless and with a characteristic movement halfway between jump and shrug rids itself of its visitor, which then goes back to its accustomed station near the coral heads, or rests upon their vertical faces.

Two decades later, Longley and other underwater naturalists would discover what was really happening between cleaners and their clients. As scientists began donning scuba gear, which enabled them to observe the more intimate lives of fishes in the field, they found a remarkable cast of characters that inspect and pick at other fishes. And they discovered that, rather than submitting to these attentions with "hopeless resignation," some of the fishes being groomed actually sought out and solicited these special cleaner fish.

Behavioral ecologists have now researched cleaning in greater detail and published a plethora of papers on their findings. But there are still many

An oriental sweetlips (*Plectorhinchus vittatus*) being cleaned by two bluestreak cleaner wrasses (*Labroides dimidiatus*), "full-time," or obligatory, cleaners. Maldives.

questions and controversies concerning this unique form of symbiosis, referred to as "one of the most remarkable classes of ecological interactions between taxonomically unrelated organisms."

Cleaner Categories

Cleaner fishes are classified into two major categories. The first, facultative cleaners, do not rely heavily on this feeding strategy to acquire nutrients. For example, juvenile hogfishes (genus *Bodianus*) set up cleaning stations and pick parasites off fish clients on a part-time basis. The majority of cleaner species fall into the facultative category. Many only parasite-pick during the juvenile stage of their life cycle, such as angelfishes in the genera *Holacanthus*

Surgeonfish (*Prionurus laticlavius*) congregate at a cleaner station.
Juvenile Cortez hogfish (*Bodianus diplotaenia*) act as the cleaner fish.
Galápagos Islands.

A 1.2 m (4 ft) long goliath grouper (*Epinephelus itajara*) being cleaned
by cleaner gobies — neon gobies (*Elactinus oceanops*). Florida Keys
National Marine Sanctuary.

and *Pomacanthus*, which readily clean when young but not as adults.

The second category comprises obligatory cleaners. These fishes depend almost entirely on cleaning for most, if not all, of their lives after settling from the plankton. The best-known of these full-time parasite-pickers are the cleaner wrasses (genus *Labroides*). Unlike the hogfishes mentioned above, the *Labroides* species clean throughout their lives. That said, a few species are obligatory cleaners as juveniles but undergo a shift in diet as they mature. As an example, the young fourline cleaner wrasse (*Larabicus quadrilineatus*) is an obligatory cleaner, but with age it switches from ectoparasites and fish slime to a diet almost exclusively of stony coral polyps.

Most obligatory cleaners devote considerable time to removing parasites from their clients. For example, cleaner gobies may clean up to 108 fish per hour, removing an average of 0.5 parasite per inspection event. The bluestreak cleaner wrasse (*Labroides dimidiatus*) inspects more than 2,000 fish in one day, consuming up to 1,200 parasites!

What Do Cleaners Eat?

Although diets vary between species, the main prey of most cleaners are parasitic crustaceans (copepods and isopods). These parasites attach to and feed on the body fluids and tissue of their hosts. For the bluestreak cleaner wrasse, juvenile gnathiid isopods are the dominant prey item. These common parasites tend to be larger in size (0.3 to 2.7 mm) and thus more conspicuous to cleaners than some other ecto-parasites. Flukes are also eaten by some cleaners such as the longfin bannerfish (*Heniochus acuminatus*), a facultative cleaner that consumes flukes known as monogenetic trematodes.

Other cleaners ingest large quantities of mucus and some scales from their clients. Hawaiian cleaner wrasses (*Labroides phthirophagus*) ingest up to 2 milliliters of host mucus per hour of cleaning. Mucus is an important food source for cleaners because it is rich in nutrients such as nitrogen and carbon. Feeding on another fish's slime is called mucophagy, and in some cases it may be a form of parasitism. This leads some to suggest that the cleaner–client relationship is not mutualistic but exploitative. Not all fishes that engage in mucophagy are cleaners. For example, the saber-toothed blennies (genera *Aspidontus* and *Plagiotremus*) also feed, at least in part, on the slime and scales of other fish.

A sabre squirrelfish (*Sargocentron spiniferum*) waiting to be cleaned by a bluestreak cleaner wrasse (*Labroides dimidiatus*) at a cleaning station under a table coral. To signal its desire to be cleaned, the fish often angles itself upward or downward, "posing." Australia.

While parasites, slime and scales are the most important nutritive items, some cleaners also pick at dead or dying tissue on the host fish. Wounded fishes often seek out cleaning services because, by removing necrotic tissue, cleaners facilitate the healing process.

Creole wrasse (*Clepticus parrae*) signaling cleaner fishes — in this case, juvenile Spanish hogfish (*Bodianus rufus*) — by head and tail standing. Bonaire.

Cleaner Ecology and Behavior

Some cleaner fish maintain specific sites that their clients visit when in need of cleaning. These "cleaning stations" are often conspicuous coral heads or promontories on the reef that are easy for clients to locate, and they may be in operation at a specific location for months or even years (*Gobiosoma* gobies may maintain the same cleaning stations for two years or more). Cleaning stations are typically centers of activity with a high diversity and concentration of fishes. Large groups of fish often queue up to wait their turn to be cleaned. In one study, up to 20 potential hosts were observed posing around a cleaning station at the same time.

Other species known to staff cleaning stations include juvenile angelfishes, barberfish (*Johnrandallia nigirostris*), many cleaner wrasses (*Labroides* spp.) and the yellow-cheek wrasse (*Halichoeres cyanocephalus*). More than one cleaner may inhabit the same station and service hosts together. For example, groups of more than 20 banded cleaner gobies (*Gobiosoma digueti*) may simultaneously clean larger hosts such as the Panamic green moray (*Gymnothorax castaneus*) or dog snapper (*Lutjanus novemfasciatus*). Likewise, groups of barberfish will clean schools of goatfish, chubs and scalloped hammerhead sharks (*Sphyrna lewini*).

Different species of cleaners might also work together. In the Caribbean, several species of *Gobiosoma* gobies may reside at the same station and simultaneously clean the same client. These gobies will also clean alongside juvenile bluehead wrasse (*Thalassoma bifasciatum*), Spanish hogfish (*Bodianus rufus*) and the cleaning shrimp *Periclimenes pedersoni*. One study documented that cleaner gobies occupying a cleaning station with juvenile bluehead wrasses had an advantage over those that did not. Because these wrasses swim up into the water column

Surgeonfish acting as "cleaners," although they are not full-time cleaning specialists. When these herbivores see a nice algae patch on a sea turtle's shell, they start grazing. One might say they are opportunistic facultative herbivorous cleaners, targeting the algae and not the usual parasites, mucus, or skin. Hawaii.

and are more highly visible to potential clients, they are likely to attract more hosts to a cleaning station than the smaller, sedentary gobies.

Rather than establishing specific stations, some cleaners roam freely over the reef or even catch a ride on their clients. The wandering cleaner wrasse (*Diprocanthus xanthurus*) is one species that makes house calls! It moves over the reef, visiting hosts within its home range. It tends to clean territorial fishes (e.g., damselfishes) that do not go to cleaning stations. The disk fishes (family Echeneidae) are hitchhiking cleaners. A modified dorsal fin allows them to adhere to their hosts, which include sharks, rays, billfishes, snappers, angelfishes, boxfishes, puffers, cetaceans and turtles. The disk fishes vary in their dietary preferences, but some, such as the remora (*Remora remora*), feed heavily on ectoparasites. The remora scrapes copepods off its host with its elongated lower jaw.

Some cleaner fishes actively solicit business by engaging in conspicuous swimming displays. For example, cleaner wrasses swim in a circle with their tails flared and lifted slightly. This is known as the "undulating dance display." The yellowcheek wrasse engages in seesaw swimming, moving forward as it bobs up and down. Cleaner gobies often swim in a zigzag pattern when soliciting clients, while juvenile French (*Pomacanthus paru*) and gray angelfish (*P. arcuatus*) perform exaggerated lateral body movements that may serve to attract clients. These swimming displays may also signal predators about the cleaning services they provide so they don't get eaten.

When a fish wants to be cleaned, it may adopt a specific pose to signal its desire. Some parrotfishes will hang motionless with their head slightly upward. To invite a cleaner's attention, the Creole wrasse (*Clepticus parrae*) performs a head- or tail-stand. Host fishes, even piscivorous species, will allow cleaners to enter their gill or mouth cavities in order to rid them of irritating parasites or scraps of food. Not all hosts pose when being cleaned, but this behavior appears to facilitate the cleaner's efforts.

Some host species change color prior to being cleaned. The Mexican goatfish (*Mulloidichthys dentatus*) shifts from white to a dark copper body color when being inspected by barberfish. The sleek unicornfish (*Naso hexacanthus*) changes from dark brown to light blue, while the bar jack (*Caranx ruber*) alters from silver to a deep bronze. These color changes may advertise a host's desire to be serviced and/or make ectoparasites easier for the cleaner to see.

Fish apparently seek out cleaners in part because the tactile stimulation feels good (perhaps it's the marine equivalent of a backrub or foot massage). Cleaner wrasses will gently drag their pelvic fins over the fish's body as they inspect it. This behavior reinforces the posing behavior of the "cleanee" and is referred to as stabilizing the host. Studies show that cleaners will stabilize clients even when they are not interested in feeding. This may ensure that visiting clients are kept "happy" and will return to the cleaning station in the future.

Irritation caused by external parasites may also motivate a fish to seek out cleaning services, although fish totally free of parasites will often invite cleaning. During some cleaning bouts the host fish may shudder or jerk as if irritated by

A busy cleaning station, with many different species of fish hanging around waiting to be cleaned. Barberfish (*Johnrandallia nigrirostris*) are the primary cleaners here. Baja, Mexico.

Cleaner Ecology and Behavior

1   Two remoras (*Remora* sp.) on the back of a manta ray (*Manta birostris*). Baja, Mexico.

2   This close-up of a whitefin sharksucker (*Echeneis neucratoides*) shows its sucker-like modified dorsal fin. Belize.

3   A reef manta ray (*Manta alfredi*) being cleaned by many juvenile bluntheaded wrasses (*Thalassoma amblycephalum*). Maldives.

4   A steephead parrotfish (*Chlorurus microrhinos*) being cleaned by bluestreak cleaner wrasses (*Labroides dimidiatus*) at a cleaning station. To signal its desire to be cleaned, the parrotfish often angles itself upward, "posing." Australia.

Cleaner Crustaceans

Crustaceans, specifically shrimps, also clean parasites and necrotic tissue off reef fishes. They typically occupy cleaning stations that may consist of a reef crevice or a cave (e.g., *Lysmata debelius*). Others associate with sea anemones or large-polyped stony corals. Some pistol shrimps (*Alpheus* spp.) provide regular cleaning services to gobies with whom they share their burrows.

Cleaner shrimps attract potential clients by whipping their antennae or antennules back and forth, by swinging their chelae and/or by rocking from side to side. As the fish approaches, the cleaner "dances" and then climbs onto the fish if it poses by remaining stationary (it sometimes also erects its fins or flares its gill covers). Once onboard, the shrimp will begin picking at the fish's body surface with its chelae (claws).

In addition to ingesting bits of dead tissue, many cleaner shrimps will also graze on the fish's body slime. At least one species, Pederson's cleaner shrimp (*Periclimenes pedersoni*), removes parasites — juvenile cymothoid isopods, in this case — for consumption. Further study is required to learn whether other cleaner shrimps also prey on parasites. As the industrious crustaceans go about their business, probing under gill covers and even between the teeth, their piscine clients seems to enjoy the tactile stimulation provided by strokes of the antennae and antennules.

A goldsnouted red shrimp (*Rhynchocinetes typus*), a cleaner shrimp, giving the photographer a manicure! Galápagos Islands.

A banded coral shrimp (*Stenopus hispidus*), a cleaner shrimp, attends to a spotted moray eel (*Gymnothorax moringa*). Bonaire.

the cleaner. This may be caused by the cleaner jerking an embedded ectoparasite, scale or necrotic tissue from the client fish. When a host fish wants to terminate the cleaning behavior, it will perform specific body, fin or mouth movements, swim away or chase off the cleaner (usually if the cleaner picks at a sensitive area or nips too aggressively). When the client is ready for the cleaner to exit its mouth or gills, it will snap its jaws shut (e.g., groupers) or shake its head (e.g., morays).

Cleaners service a wide variety of fish species from sharks to porcupinefish. In the tropical Atlantic, cleaner gobies groom more than 50 species of fish in 20 different families representing the gamut of ecotypes from small bottom-dwellers, such as the redlip blenny (*Ophioblennius atlanticus*), to active pelagic species, such as bar jacks and great barracudas (*Sphyraena barracuda*). There are even cleaners that regularly remove parasites from sharks and rays. Adult king angelfish (*Holacanthus passer*) feed on parasitic *Pandarus* copepods that infest scalloped hammerhead sharks (*Sphyrna lewini*) in the Eastern Pacific. Clarion angelfish (*Holacanthus clarionensis*) clean giant manta rays (*Manta birostris*) in Mexico's Socorro Islands. And reef mantas (*Manta alfredi*) are commonly serviced by various wrasses throughout the Indo-Pacific. One of the largest bony fishes, the ocean sunfish (*Mola mola*), is regularly cleaned by schooling bannerfishes (*Heniochus diphreutes*) off the island of Bali, Indonesia (*Mola mola* is reportedly one of the most parasite-ridden fishes in the sea).

Cleaner fishes appear to enjoy some immunity from predation. But lizardfishes, trumpetfishes, hamlets, larger hawkfishes, jacks and snappers have been known to "go bad" and feed on a cleaner species from time to time. They are more likely to eat a facultative cleaner than an obligatory one.

Reef-Fish Sex

Two of the most time- and energy-consuming activities for marine fish are finding food and procreating. Reproduction is calorically expensive and potentially dangerous. Courting reef fishes often drop their guard, becoming more susceptible to being eaten by neighborhood predators. For example, group-spawning surgeonfish rushing into the water column to release their

---

Barred hamlets (*Hypoplectrus puella*) just before spawning (releasing gametes). These fish are broadcast (pelagic) spawners and simultaneous hermaphrodites that exhibit egg trading. Bonaire.

A male squarespot anthias (*Pseudanthias pleurotaenia*), top (Fiji), and a female, bottom (Australia). This protogynous reef fish exhibits a form of synchronous hermaphroditism in which females transform into males.

gametes are sometimes fed on by black-tipped reef sharks (*Carcharhinus melanopterus*).

Reef fishes can be classified into several categories based on their patterns of sexual development. There are gonochorists, simultaneous hermaphrodites, and sequential hermaphrodites (either protogynous or protandric). Although all members of a family usually display the same pattern of sexuality, a few groups (e.g., moray eels) practice all three sexual strategies. Gonochoristic species are genetically predetermined to be either female or male and do not change sex. At least some members of the following groups fall into this category: sharks, rays, certain moray eels, jawfishes, snappers, goatfishes, butterflyfishes, triggerfishes, filefishes, trunkfishes and porcupinefishes.

In simultaneous hermaphrodites, mature individuals possess functional reproductive organs of both sexes and can reproduce as both male and female during a single spawning bout. Many simultaneous hermaphrodites do not release all their eggs at once but instead expel them in several batches during the spawning period, which usually lasts for several hours. This is known as "egg

False clown anemonefish (*Amphiprion ocellaris*) guarding and caring for eggs (the orange cluster at the anemone's base). The large, dominant fish in the group is a female, which has transformed from a smaller male — a process known as protandric hermaphrodism. Indonesia.

parceling." Many of the simultaneous hermaphrodites (e.g., hamlets, dwarf seabasses) alternate sexual roles. In the spawning period, each individual will release eggs and then sperm (or vice versa), which is referred to as "egg trading." Individuals that act solely as female or male rather than both are not playing by the rules; they will be discriminated against by potential mates in the future! Dwarf seabasses also engage in "egg advertisement." During courtship, individuals advertise the fact that they have ripe eggs, usually by directing their swollen abdomen toward a potential partner. One benefit to this hermaphroditic strategy is that an individual can mate with any other member of its own kind it happens to encounter. These fishes have not been reported to fertilize their own eggs in the wild. In fact, to prevent self-fertilization from accidentally occurring, the eggs and sperm are delivered through different ducts in front of the anus.

Synchronous hermaphrodites cannot function as both sexes simultaneously but instead transform from one sex to another. Protogyny is the most common form of synchronous hermaphroditism — when females transform into males. Examples of protogynous reef fishes include some hawkfishes, most groupers, anthias, some dottybacks, sea breams, angelfishes, sand perches, many damselfishes, most if not all wrasses, parrotfishes and some gobies. Protandric hermaphrodites transform from males to females. This type of hermaphroditism is relatively rare, with the best-known example being the anemonefishes. Many anemonefishes live in groups in which the most dominant — and in some species the largest — individual is a female. The individual just beneath her in the pecking order is male and all the rest of the group members are asexual (i.e., neither sex). If the female should die, the male changes into a female and the most dominant asexual individual transforms into a functional male, taking up the now vacant secondary spot.

It was once thought that when a synchronous hermaphrodite changed from one sex to another, the new gender was permanent (i.e., it couldn't change back). But a number of species can actually revert to their original sex, depending on the social situation. For example, coral gobies (*Gobiodon* spp.) are capable of changing sex in both directions. They are obligate coral dwellers that form

---

Mandarinfish (*Synchiropus splendidus*), 5 cm (2 in) long, prepare to spawn, rising out of the coral at dusk. Indonesia.

monogamous pairs, but if one of the pair members is lost, a goby from a neighboring coral head might join the now mateless individual. One of the gobies then changes sex so that the new pair can reproduce. Other species, such as some dottybacks (Pseudochromidae), swallowtail angelfishes (*Genicanthus* spp.) and fairy wrasses (*Cirrhilabrus* spp.), can engage in "both ways" sex change.

Reproductive Strategies

When it comes to procreation, reef fishes follow many different strategies to disperse their progeny. There are live-bearers, demersal spawners, egg-scatterers, pelagic spawners and benthic broadcasters. The last two groups produce buoyant eggs, while demersal spawners and egg-scatterers produce eggs that sink to or are deposited on the seafloor.

In the live-bearers the eggs are fertilized within the body and retained until the young are fully developed. Many sharks and rays, some cusk eels and certain species of labrisomid blennies display this reproductive mode. These fish produce relatively few offspring, which may or may not, depending on the species, enter the plankton. In live-bearing sharks and rays the young are miniatures of the adults and ready to fend for themselves at birth.

The majority of reef fish are pelagic spawners. They release planktonic eggs into the water column, where they hatch and the fry develop in the plankton, away from the reef. This strategy reduces predation on the young by getting them away from the many planktivorous predators near the reef. It also acts to disperse the offspring between reef systems, which helps reduce competition between adults and offspring and minimizes inbreeding. On average, pelagic spawners are typically three times the length of demersal spawners. Because of their larger size they are less likely to be eaten when they make their spawning ascents into open water or migrate to optimal mating sites. Benthic broadcasters also produce pelagic eggs but release them from the ocean bottom. This group comprises morays, congers and garden eels.

A number of reef fishes lay demersal eggs. Dermesal spawners deposit their eggs at a specific site and often care for them. Egg-scatterers broadcast eggs indiscriminately, like the pelagic spawners, but instead of floating, the eggs sink to the bottom. Few fish practice egg-scattering (some pufferfishes do), while there are a number of demersal spawners. Members of the latter group are typically smaller species that occupy a limited home range, and many of

Gray reef sharks (*Carcharhinus amblyrhynchos*), an example of a gonochoristic species, genetically hardwired to be either male or female for life. It is a live-bearing viviparous shark species that gives birth to a litter of up to six pups, miniature versions of the adults ready to fend for themselves at birth. Australia.

them guard their eggs against egg predators. Demersal spawners typically lay their eggs in a small, secluded area such as in a crevice or shell or under some rubble, so that they are easier to defend. In most of these species, when the eggs hatch, the fry swim up and enter the plankton. Some triggerfishes make depressions in the sand in which they deposit their eggs. The females vigorously defend this nest for 12 to 24 hours, after which time the eggs hatch and the female blows the fry out of the sand and into the water column.

Reproductive Strategies

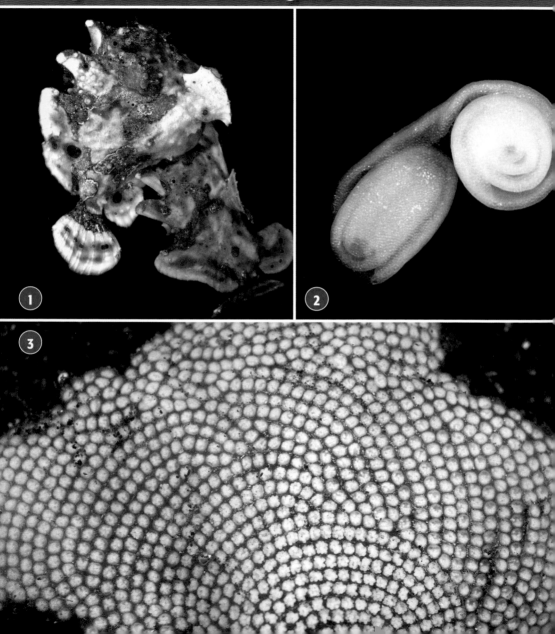

1

2

3

1 Warty frogfish (*Antennarius maculatus*). The large female, left, and small male, right, leave the reef and swim up into the water column, pressed together, a split second before spawning (releasing gametes). An example of pelagic broadcast spawning. Indonesia.

2 A frogfish egg mass resembles a buoyant raft. Frogfish are pelagic spawners that broadcast their eggs in the water column. The female frogfish produces an egg raft that is permeated with tens of thousands of eggs. In a few days the floating raft begins to degrade, the eggs hatch, and the larvae become part of the plankton for one to several months. Indonesia.

3 This goby egg mass on the bottom is an example of demersal spawning as opposed to pelagic or broadcast spawning. Indonesia.

4 Chubs in a spawning aggregation; either Cortez sea chubs (*Kyphosus elegans*) or blue-bronze chubs (*K. analogus*), these are pelagic spawners. Galápagos Islands.

5 This common ghost goby (*Pleurosicya mossambica*) has deposited eggs on a tunicate — an example of a demersal spawner. Indonesia.

Parental Care in Reef Fishes

Some reef fishes show varying degrees of care for their fertilized eggs. For example, there are damselfishes that guard their demersal eggs, warding off potential egg predators and even attacking fishes several times larger than they are. Other egg-defending species include the dottybacks, longfins, grammas, certain gobies, a number of triggerfishes and certain filefishes.

Several fish families orally incubate their eggs. After the egg mass is fertilized, the male scoops it into his mouth, holding it there until the eggs hatch. He periodically aerates them by spitting out the egg mass and rapidly sucking it back in. The assessors, jawfishes and cardinalfishes are all mouth-brooders.

Rather than brooding eggs in their mouth, some fish carry the next generation in special pouches or underneath or on the side of the body. For example, in seahorses the male incubates the fertilized eggs in a brood pouch located on the abdomen. Upon hatching, the young seahorses are expelled from the pouch and swim away under their own power. In some pipefishes the ova are embedded in a spongy matrix under the male's abdomen. Ghost pipefish

A male yellowhead jawfish (*Opistognathus aurifrons*) incubates eggs in its mouth. Bonaire.

females hold the eggs in a special pelvic fin "pocket." Although they do not possess a brood pouch, in several frogfish species the eggs are attached to the side of the male's body or the male wraps its body around the eggs to protect them.

Mr. Mom. A male lined seahorse (*Hippocampus erectus*) giving birth. Look closely to see the baby seahorses being expelled from his pouch and swimming away on their own, albeit a little clumsily at first. Florida.

Tarpon

Megalops atlanticus
Family Megalopidae (tarpon)

- Eastern and Western Atlantic; Eastern Pacific
- Coastal reefs; bays, lagoons, estuaries and rivers; adults sometimes near coral reefs
- 1–30 m (3.3–98 ft)
- 2.5 m (8.2 ft), 161 kg (355 lb)

Solitary or in groups. Swim bladder attaches to esophagus, enabling use of atmospheric oxygen, which they gulp at water's surface (juveniles obligatory air-breathers). Mainly piscivorous, targeting mid-water species (e.g., mullet, needlefish, sardines) but also crustaceans. Preyed upon by sharks (favorite of great hammerhead), dolphins and alligators. "Tarpon Alley" is famous dive site off Grand Cayman. Spawn annually, with females producing up to 120,000 eggs per spawn.

Viper Moray Eel

Enchelycore nigricans
Family Muraenidae (moray eels)

- Bermuda and Florida, south to Brazil; also in tropical Eastern Atlantic
- Coastal and outer coral and rocky reefs; lagoon patch reefs, reef faces, slopes
- 1–30 m (3.3–98 ft)
- 87 cm (34 in)

Solitary species. While not uncommon, very secretive and rarely seen by divers during the day; comes out to hunt after dark. Thought to feed on crustaceans and fishes. Similar to chestnut moray (*Enchelycore carychoa*), but this species has white spots around pores on the jaws.

- ⊕ Réunion Islands and Comoros (Indian Ocean), east to Hawaiian Islands, north to southern Japan and Korea and south to New Caledonia
- ☉ Coastal and outer coral and rocky reefs; reef faces, slopes
- ↧ 5–50 m (16–163 ft)   ↔ 80 cm (31 in)

Dragon Moray Eel
Enchelycore pardalis
Family Muraenidae (moray eels)

Most often seen on rocky reefs such as off Osezaki and Izu, Japan, where it occurs singly in reef crevices. Fish-eater that is sometimes cleaned by cleaner shrimp. Amount of orange on head and body varies between individuals. Not a shy eel; easy to approach.

- ⊕ South Florida to Bermuda to southern Brazil, east to St. Paul's Rocks and Ascension Island
- ☉ Coastal rocky and coral reefs; lagoons, reef faces
- ↧ 1–12 m (3.3–39 ft)   ↔ 71 cm (28 in)

Chain Moray Eel
Echidna catenata
Family Muraenidae (moray eels)

Solitary. Crustacean-feeding species with pebble-like teeth adapted to crush exoskeletons. Most hunting occurs after dark. Will chase crabs out of the water onto shore and then slither back into sea. Secretive species that is often shy; during the day only its head is seen sticking out from a crevice. White to yellowish overall, with a network of brown to gray saddles and marbling.

Snowflake Moray Eel

Echidna nebulosa
Family Muraenidae (moray eels)

⊕ East Africa and Red Sea, east to Panama, north to Ryukyu Islands and south to Lord Howe Island

⊙ Coastal and outer coral and rocky reefs; lagoons, reef flats, reef faces

↧ 1–10 m (3.3–33 ft) ↔ 75 cm (30 in)

Solitary. Will hunt in shallow water during both day and night (more often the latter). Feeds mainly on crabs but also eats mantis shrimps and fishes. Changes sex from female to male. Sexes similar in color, but in males teeth more pointed and some teeth are serrated, while in females (and juveniles) teeth more cone-like and lack serrations.

Zebra Moray Eel

Gymnomuraena zebra
Family Muraenidae (moray eels)

⊕ East Africa and Red Sea, east to Panama, north to Ryukyu Islands and south to Society Islands

⊙ Coastal coral and rock reefs; lagoon patch reefs, reef flats, reef faces, slopes

↧ 1–39 m (3.3–127 ft) ↔ 1.5 m (4.9 ft)

Solitary. A very docile, secretive moray that is usually seen with its head sticking out from a hole. Sometimes makes daytime and nighttime forays when looking for its favorite food: crabs. Also eats urchins and snails. Molar-like teeth used to crush prey's armor. Changes sex from female to male.

- 🌐 East Africa and Indian Ocean islands (e.g., Maldives, Seychelles)
- ☉ Outer coral and rocky reefs; reef flats; reef faces, slopes
- ↧ 4–25 m (13–81 ft)
- ↦ 75 cm (30 in)

Masked Moray Eel
Gymnothorax breedeni
Family Muraenidae (moray eels)

Solitary. Feeds on fishes. Often shares daytime haunts with shoals of anthias, which hang around the eel's head. Also in association with boxer shrimp (*Stenopus* spp.) and cleaner shrimp (*Lysmata* spp.). Most aggressive moray; regularly bites a hand resting near its hideout. Identified by black marking from rear of eye to corner of mouth.

- 🌐 Gulf of California south to Panama, including offshore islands (e.g., Galapagos)
- ☉ Coastal rocky reefs; rocky walls and boulder bottoms
- ↧ 3–37 m (10–120 ft)
- ↦ 102 cm (40 in)

Fine-spotted Moray Eel
Gymnothorax dovii
Family Muraenidae (moray eels)

Solitary. During day, hides with only its head sticking from a crevice. At night actively hunts cephalopods, crustaceans and fishes. Similar to Panamic green moray (*G. castaneus*), but *G. dovii* has many small white spots on body and dorsal fin.

Honeycomb Moray Eel

Gymnothorax favagineus
Family Muraenidae (moray eels)

⊕ Red Sea, south to east coast of Africa and east to Western Pacific
⊙ Coastal and outer coral reefs; lagoons, reef flats, reef faces, slopes
↕ 1–50 m (3.3–163 ft)   ↔ 1.8 m (5.9 ft); may be up to 3 m (9.8 ft)

This big, beautiful moray is a solitary species. Feeds on fishes and octopuses. Those that are fed by divers can be aggressive. Otherwise not a threat and can be easily approached. Similar to blackspotted moray (*G. isingteena*), which has spots equal to or smaller than the eyes.

Fimbriated Moray Eel

Gymnothorax fimbriatus
Family Muraenidae (moray eels)

⊕ Mauritius to Society Islands, north to southern Japan and south to northeast Australia
⊙ Coastal reefs; lagoons, reef faces, slopes
↕ 7–50 m (23–163 ft)   ↔ 80 cm (31 in)

Solitary. Juveniles secretive and rarely observed; adults seen with head protruding from hole or moving over reef at night. Often at shrimp cleaning stations. Feeds mainly on fishes but also crabs and shrimp. Protogynous hermaphrodite. Gray, with scattered black spots of varying shapes and sizes on body and head. Younger individuals have yellow head.

Green Moray Eel
Gymnothorax funebris
Family Muraenidae (moray eels)

- New Jersey and Bermuda, south to Brazil
- Coastal and outer coral reefs; reef faces, slopes
- 3–30 m (10–98 ft)
- 2.3 m (7.5 ft)

Solitary. Eats fishes and crabs, usually at night. Strongly site-attached, remaining at same location for many years. This monstrous eel should be respected by divers — hand-feeding is foolhardy, as this eel is capable of doing extreme tissue damage with its large teeth and powerful jaws.

Gray Moray Eel
Gymnothorax griseus
Family Muraenidae (moray eels)

- Red Sea, but also ranges to South Africa and Mauritius
- Coastal and outer coral reefs; reef flats, reef faces, slopes
- 1–14 m (3.3–46 ft)
- 65 cm (26 in)

Solitary, pairs or small groups. Usually in coral crevices but sometimes out and about hunting during the day. Feeds on crustaceans and fishes; often followed by opportunistic predators such as groupers, soapfishes and goatfishes as it probes in burrow entrances, between coral branches and into reef crevices. Easy to approach.

Giant Moray Eel

Gymnothorax javanicus

Family Muraenidae (moray eels)

🌐 Red Sea, east to Marquesas and Pitcairn Islands, north to southern Japan and south to New Caledonia and southern Great Barrier Reef

⊙ Coastal and outer coral and rocky reefs; lagoon patch reefs, reef faces, slopes

↧ 3–46 m (11–152 ft) ↔ 3 m (10 ft)

Solitary species that will fight for preferred hiding spots, biting and jaw-locking with one another. Eats fishes (including other morays), octopuses and crustaceans. Common participant at Western Pacific shark feeds. On rare occasions food-conditioned individuals will bite divers, sometimes inflicting severe wounds. Large blotch around gill opening.

Whitemouth Moray Eel

Gymnothorax meleagris

Family Muraenidae (moray eels)

🌐 East African coast to Galapagos Islands

⊙ Coastal and outer coral and rocky reefs; lagoon patch reefs, reef flats, reef faces, slopes

↧ 1–36 m (3.3–119 ft) ↔ 1.2 m (3.9 ft)

Solitary eel that feeds on crustaceans and fishes. Unique in having a white mouth lining, but comes in several different color forms; can be golden to chocolate brown. One form is white with dark reticulated color pattern. Serves as the model for the comet, which mimics this species. Easy for divers to approach.

⊕ Southern Florida and Bermuda, south to Brazil and east across Atlantic to St. Paul Rocks, Ascension, St. Helena and Cape Verde Islands

⊙ Coastal and outer reefs; lagoon patch reefs, reef faces

↕ 1–15 m (3.3–50 ft)　　　　　　　↔ 60 cm (24 in)

Goldentail Moray Eel
Gymnothorax miliaris
Family Muraenidae (moray eels)

Solitary. Remains partially hidden during the day. May occupy same patch reef or coral head for many days or even months, leaving at night to feed in surrounding environs and returning to home refuge at dawn. Feeds mainly on crabs, with fishes being secondary in the diet. Ubiquitous in the Caribbean and easy to approach and photograph.

⊕ South Carolina and Bermuda, south to Brazil and east to Ascension and St. Helena Islands

⊙ Coastal and outer reefs; seagrass, pier pilings, lagoon patch reefs, reef faces, slopes

↕ 1–190 m (3.3–618 ft)　　　　　　↔ 1.2 m (3.9 ft)

Spotted Moray Eel
Gymnothorax moringa
Family Muraenidae (moray eels)

Solitary. During the day, encountered with only its head protruding from a reef crevice, although will sometimes forage during the day. Most actively hunts after dark, consuming fish, crabs, spiny lobster and octopuses. Sometimes groomed by cleaner shrimps. Easily differentiated from other morays in the Caribbean by its dark brown spots on white background. Common at many Caribbean dive sites.

White-eyed Moray Eel

Gymnothorax thrysoidea
Family Muraenidae (moray eels)

⊕ West Thailand to Tuamotus, north to Ryukyu Islands and south to Tonga
⊙ Coastal and outer coral reefs; silty lagoons, outcrops on sand, mud slopes
↕ 1–7 m (3.3–23 ft)   ↔ 65 cm (26 in)

Often in pairs or even groups (sometimes even with other morays mixed in!). During the day takes refuge in reef crevices and manmade debris (e.g., car tires). Feeds on crustaceans (especially crabs), octopuses and fishes. Gray head with white iris. Usually allows close approach.

Jewel Moray Eel

Muraena lentiginosa
Family Muraenidae (moray eels)

⊕ Gulf of California south to Peru, also offshore islands
⊙ Coastal and offshore rocky reefs; rocky reef walls, boulder substrates, sometimes among macroalgae
↕ 2–25 m (7–81 ft)   ↔ 60 cm (24 in)

Solitary. Spends days undercover but moves over reef at night hunting for food. Main diet crustaceans and fishes. Recognized by yellow or cream spots on head, dorsal fin and body. Easy to approach, although if feels threatened will retreat into hiding place.

East Africa to Tuamotus, north to southern Japan and south to New Caledonia

Coastal reef slopes and protected lagoons

1–57 m (3.3–185 ft)   ↔ 1.2 m (47 in)

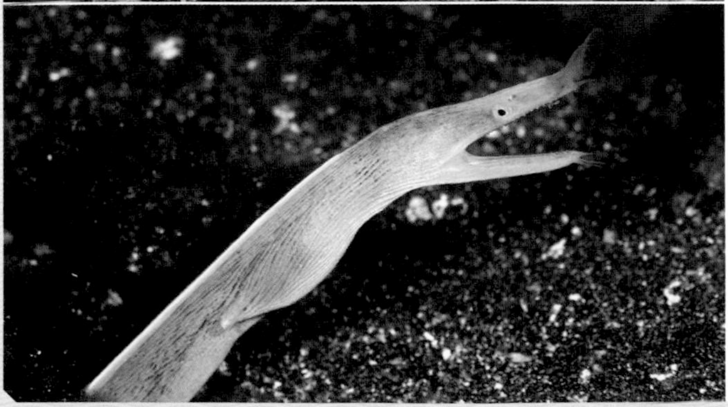

Ribbon Eel

Rhinomuraena quaesita

Family Muraenidae (moray eels)

Usually found singly, although sometimes more than one will occupy the same home. Burrows in sand or mud or among coral rubble. Tail produces copious mucus to help keep tunnel walls intact. Feeds on small fishes. Three colors, related to age and sex: juveniles are black, males are blue, females are yellow. Protandric hermaphrodite. Usually indifferent toward divers.

Ray-Finned Fishes

Reptilian Snake Eel

Brachysomophis henshawi
Family Ophichthidae (snake eels)

🌐 Arabian Sea, east to Hawaii, north to southern Japan and south to Coral Sea
⊙ Coastal mud and sand slopes near reefs
↧ 1–30 m (3.3–98 ft)   ↔ 106 cm (42 in)

Evil-looking solitary creature that spends most of its time either completely buried or with only its head protruding from the sand/mud. Similar to the crocodile eel (*Brachysomophis crocodilinus*) and stargazer snake eel (*B. cirrocheilos*). *B. henshawi* has a depression behind the eyes lacking in the other two. Easy to approach.

Sharptail Snake Eel

Myrichthys breviceps
Family Ophichthidae (snake eels)

🌐 South Florida and Bermuda, south to Brazil
⊙ Coastal coral reefs and sand bottoms; lagoons, reef flats, slopes
↧ 3–185 m (10–601 ft)   ↔ 102 cm (40 in)

Solitary. Forages on rubble flats and in seagrass beds during day and night. Primary food is crabs. As it probes rubble interstices, sometimes followed by opportunistic predators such as groupers, soapfishes and bar jacks. Slips tail-first into holes so only its head is protruding.

- 🌐 Gulf of California, south to Peru; also some offshore islands
- ◉ Coastal rocky reefs; sand and mixed sand and rocks
- ↧ 2–60 m (7–195 ft)   ↔ 75 cm (30 in)

Tiger Snake Eel
Myrichthys tigrinus
Family Ophichthidae (snake eels)

Solitary. Slithers over reef, probing cracks and crevices with snout in search of prey; hunts during both day and night. Feeds on crustaceans and small fishes. Will also enter burrows to find pistol shrimp. Buries itself under sand. Similar magnificent snake eel (*Myrichthys magnificus*) found throughout most of the Indo-Pacific.

- 🌐 South Africa to Indonesia, including Maldives
- ◉ Sand or mud flats and slopes, often near coastal coral reefs
- ↧ 1.5–20 m (5–66 ft)   ↔ 75 cm (30 in)

Napoleon Snake Eel
Ophichthus bonaparti
Family Ophichthidae (snake eels)

Solitary. During day, head seen protruding from sand. At night may leave sand refuge to hunt. Thought to feed on cuttlefish, crabs, cardinalfishes and soles. This gorgeous creature is easy to approach as long as you move toward it slowly.

Ray-Finned Fishes

Spotted Snake Eel

Ophichthus ophis
Family Ophichthidae (snake eels)

⊕ South Florida and Bermuda, south to Brazil and east to Eastern Atlantic
⊙ Coastal reef flats and slopes
↧ 1–15 m (3.3–49 ft)   ↔ 1.4 m (54 in)

Solitary. During the day buries itself under substrate, often with only head exposed. At night emerges to hunt crustaceans and fish prey. Like other snake eels, can "swim" under the sand and change positions. When buried with only head exposed, easy to approach.

Spotted Garden Eel

Heteroconger hassi
Family Congridae (garden eels)

⊕ Red Sea to Line Islands, north to Ryukyu Islands and south to New Caledonia and Tonga
⊙ Sandy slopes exposed to moderate or strong currents; often adjacent to coral
↧ 7–45 m (23–149 ft)   ↔ 35 cm (13.7 in)

Occurs in colonies that emerge from the sand and pick off zooplankton swept past by ocean currents. Predators include lizardfishes, emperor snappers and razorfishes. Most are quick to pull into burrows when approached by divers, but rare individuals (the dumb ones) will allow close approach. The closely related freckled garden eel (*Heteroconger lentiginosus*) is similar, but *H. hassi* has three large black spots on body.

⊕ Bermuda, south Florida and Bahamas to Lesser Antilles
⊙ Sand flats and slopes adjacent to coral reefs
↓ 4–60 m (13–195 ft)   ↔ 51 cm (20 in)

Brown Garden Eel
Heteroconger longissimus
Family Congridae (garden eels)

Lives in colonies. In some locations adult males and females burrow near one another; in other locations adults of both sexes are randomly spaced in colony. Rarely leaves burrow and at night will plug entrance with sand. Extends from burrow into the water column to pick off zooplankton (especially copepods) swept by in ocean currents. Feeds continuously throughout the day.

⊕ Indonesia (Bali and Flores), Mabul and Papua New Guinea
⊙ Sand slopes near coral reefs
↓ 8–35 m (26–116 ft)   ↔ 40 cm (15.7 in)

Taylor's Garden Eel
Heteroconger taylori
Family Congridae (garden eels)

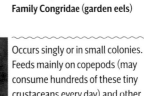

Occurs singly or in small colonies. Feeds mainly on copepods (may consume hundreds of these tiny crustaceans every day) and other zooplankton. At dusk retracts into hole until sun rises again. Relatively easy to approach for a garden eel. Base color cream to yellow, with black spots (lacks three large black markings found on *H. hassi*).

Striped Eel Catfish

Plotosus lineatus

Family Plotosidae (eel catfishes)

⊕ Red Sea to Samoa, north to South Korea and south to Lord Howe Island
☉ Coastal rocky and coral reefs; lagoons, reef flats, reef faces, slopes
↧ 1–45 m (3.3–146 ft)   ↔ 32 cm (13 in)

Juveniles occur in large "rolling" schools that grub in soft substrate. Each group consists of the young of a single brood. Release an attractant that keeps the group cohesive. As they grow, color becomes duller and they begin to live a solitary lifestyle. When spawning, males dig hole in substrate where females deposit eggs; males defend eggs. Spines have toxic venom that can cause very painful wounds.

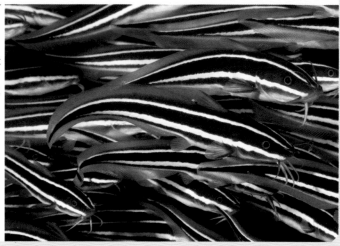

Milkfish

Chanos chanos

Family Chanidae (milkfish)

⊕ East Africa and Red Sea, east to Galapagos, north to Japan and south to Victoria, Australia
☉ Coastal bays, estuaries, reef lagoons, slopes; found in fresh and salt water
↧ 1–30 m (3.3–98 ft)   ↔ 1.8 m (5.9 ft)

Adults form small to large shoals. Feeds on cyanobacteria, algae, bottom-dwelling invertebrates, fish eggs and larvae. Spawns at reef edge at night on a lunar cycle (populations near equator spawn year-round). Young fish live in mangrove habitats or estuaries, returning to reef habitats with age. Live at least 15 years. Important food fish.

- ⊕ East Africa and Red Sea, east to French Polynesia, north to southern Japan and south to Great Barrier Reef
- ⊙ Coastal and outer coral reefs; mangroves, lagoon patch reefs, reef flats, feef faces, slopes
- ↧ 2–135 m (7–439 ft)   ↔ 32 cm (9.8 in)

Slender Lizardfish
Saurida gracilis
Family Synodontidae (lizardfishes)

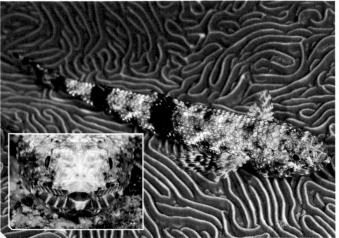

Solitary. Rests on substrate or partially buries itself under sand to enhance camouflage. Dashes from seafloor to grab passing fishes. One of a few species that will eat cleaner wrasses. Similar clouded lizardfish (*Saurida nebulosa*) has shorter pectoral fins (they do not extend past pelvic fin base).

- ⊕ North Carolina, Bermuda and northern Gulf of Mexico, south to Brazil and the Guianas
- ⊙ Coastal and outer reefs; lagoons, reef faces, slopes
- ↧ 3–320 m (10–1,040 ft)   ↔ 45 cm (18 in)

Sand Diver
Synodus intermedius
Family Synodontidae (lizardfishes)

Solitary. Voracious predator that rests on seafloor waiting for unsuspecting prey to come near. Feeds on smaller fish species, squids and crustaceans. Sometimes rests near cleaning stations of anemone shrimp to take advantage of crustaceans' grooming services and to pick off other fishes that come to be cleaned.

Blackblotch Lizardfish

Synodus jaculum
Family Synodontidae (lizardfishes)

⊕ East Africa to Marquesas and Society Islands, north to Izu Island and south to southeast Australia
⊙ Coastal reefs; sand and rubble flats and slopes adjacent to reef
↧ 2–100 m (7–325 ft)   ↔ 14 cm (5.5 in)

Solitary or in pairs or loose groups. Sits on or buries itself just under sand. Will also scull in water column when attacking schools of small fishes. Main diet is fish but also eats some crustaceans. Recognized by black band around base of tail.

Calico Lizardfish

Synodus lacertinus
Family Synodontidae (lizardfishes)

⊕ Southern California south to Chile, including offshore islands (e.g., Malpelo, Galapagos)
⊙ Coastal rocky reefs; boulder, gravel or sand bottoms
↧ 1–156 m (3.3–507 ft)   ↔ 20 cm (7.9 in)

Solitary ambush predator that rests on bottom waiting for unwary crustaceans and fishes. At night buries itself under sand. Easy to approach and photograph. Several color forms, including white with bright red markings, white with pink mottling and yellowish with reddish brown markings.

- ⊕ Red Sea to Hawaiian, Marquesas and Ducie Islands, north to Ryukyu Islands and south to Lord Howe Island
- ⊙ Coastal and outer coral and rocky reefs; lagoons, reef faces, slopes
- ↓ 3–60 m (10–195 ft) ↔ 27 cm (10.5 in)

Reef Lizardfish
Synodus variegatus
Family Synodontidae (lizardfishes)

Usually solitary, but sometimes individuals rest next to or on top of one another, usually on hard substrate. Diet mainly small fishes; catches new prey item every 35 minutes during the day. Has six blotchy saddles, red or brown on lighter background. Easy to approach and photograph.

- ⊕ Circumglobal
- ⊙ Coastal coral and rocky reefs; lagoons, slopes
- ↓ 1–400 m (3.3–1,300 ft) ↔ 33 cm (13 in)

Snakefish
Trachinocephalus myops
Family Synodontidae (lizardfishes)

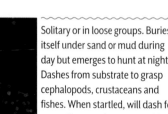

Solitary or in loose groups. Buries itself under sand or mud during day but emerges to hunt at night. Dashes from substrate to grasp cephalopods, crustaceans and fishes. When startled, will dash for some distance, then stop suddenly and bury itself. Very short snout and pale blue stripes.

Splendid (Coral) Toadfish

Sanopus splendidus
Family Batrachoididae (toadfishes)

⊕ Cozumel, Mexico
⊙ Outer reefs; reef faces, slopes
↧ 4–25 m (22–81 ft)   ↔ 20 cm (8 in)

Solitary. Secretive during the day. Tends to be site-specific (enabling savvy dive-masters to return to same area and find this fish for interested divers). Hides in reef cracks and crevices at base of reef. Hunts fishes, snails and worms after dark. Rarely strays too far from a shelter site. This attractive toadfish has zebra stripes on its head and bright yellow to yellowish orange fin margins. Endemic to Cozumel, Mexico.

Giant Frogfish

Antennarius commerson
Family Antennariidae (frogfishes)

⊕ Southern Africa and Red Sea to tropical Eastern Pacific, north to southern Japan and south to Lord Howe Island
⊙ Coastal and outer coral and rocky reefs; lagoons, reef faces, slopes; usually associates with large sponges
↧ 1–50 m (3.3–163 ft)   ↔ 30 cm (12 in)

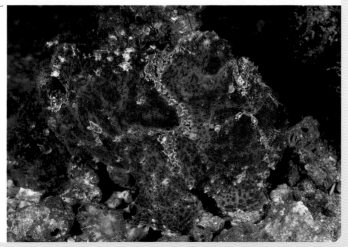

Usually solitary, but males begin visiting females just prior to spawning. This, the largest of the frogfishes, will eat any fish it can swallow whole, including porcupinefishes. Tends to be site-specific, staying in same general location for months or even years.

Mauritius to Solomon Islands, north to Ryukyu Islands and south to Great Barrier Reef

Coastal coral reefs; lagoon patch reefs, reef faces, slopes

1–15 m (3.3–50 ft)   10 cm (3.9 in)

Warty Frogfish
Antennarius maculatus
Family Antennariidae (frogfishes)

Solitary or in pairs (most often the latter just prior to spawning). Often found among sponges and macroalgae. Recognized by large warts on skin and lure like a fish. Exhibits various colors (yellow, red, white, black, etc.). Often with "scabby" patches and saddles on body. Juveniles may mimic flatworms: a sinusoidal wave travels down the dorsal fin as they move along the bottom. Juvenile in inset photo.

Bermuda, south to Brazil; also Ascension Island in Eastern Atlantic

Coastal and outer reefs; pier pilings, lagoon patch reefs, reef faces, slopes

1–61 m (3.3–198 ft)   20 cm (7.9 in)

Longlure Frogfish
Antennarius multiocellatus
Family Antennariidae (frogfishes)

Solitary or in pairs or small groups (the latter during spawning period). Will eat any fish it can swallow whole, including venomous scorpionfishes. Uses modified first dorsal spine to lure prey. Blends in very well with surroundings. Easy to approach and photograph if you can find it! Comes in a variety of different colors and can also change color; often takes on hue of favorite sponge perch.

Painted Frogfish
Antennarius pictus
Family Antennariidae (frogfishes)

⊕ Mozambique to Hawaiian Islands, north to southern Japan and south to New South Wales, Australia
⊙ Rocky and coastal coral reefs; lagoons, reef flats, reef faces, slopes
↕ 1–73 m (3.3–240 ft)   ↔ 10 cm (3.9 in)

Solitary or pairs (prior to mating). Associates with sponges, coral rubble, macroalgae or live corals during day but will move on sand and mud at night. Feeds on crustaceans and fishes. Abdomen will swell the day before spawning, which occurs with male in attendance. Comes in many colors.

Bloody Frogfish
Antennarius sanguineus
Family Antennariidae (frogfishes)

⊕ Gulf of California to Chile, including Galapagos Islands
⊙ Coastal and outer rocky reefs
↕ 1–40 m (3.3–132 ft)   ↔ 14 cm (5.5 in)

Solitary or in pairs. Secretive species that hides in crevices and caves, often hanging upside down at cave ceilings. Feeds on small crustaceans and fishes. Just prior to spawning, female (which is larger than male) will swell with eggs. Color highly variable, including pink, orange, brown or red overall with blotches.

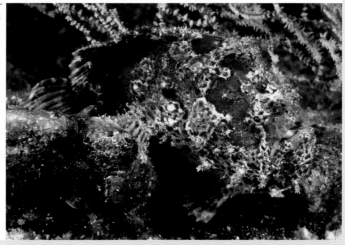

- ⊕ Widespread: Western Atlantic, Eastern Atlantic and Indo-Pacific
- ⊙ Coastal rocky and coral reefs; most often on sand or mud bottoms, sometimes among micro- or macroalgae
- ↨ 7–218 m (23–709 ft)
- ↔ 22 cm (8.6 in)

Striated Frogfish
Antennarius striatus
Family Antennariidae (frogfishes)

Solitary or in pairs or small groups (the latter two social units most often during reproductive period). Feeds on crustaceans and fishes. Wormlike lure emits scent to attract prey. Female's abdomen swells hours before spawning, at which time one or more males will attempt to spawn with her. Some individuals sport long skin appendages (known as "hairy frogfish"). Usually has dark stripes and streaks on body and fins.

- ⊕ Offshore islands (Galapagos) and coast of Peru
- ⊙ Coastal and insular sand and mud slopes, sometimes near rocky reefs
- ↨ 3–76 m (10–247 ft)
- ↔ 24 cm (9.4 in)

Red-lipped Batfish
Ogcocephalus darwini
Family Ogcocephalidae (batfishes)

Solitary. Perches on seafloor or hops along on paired fins. Plucks small invertebrates off substrate. Has a small lure under rostrum, but not sure of the function. Easy to approach and photograph. Similar rosy-lipped batfish (*Ogcocephalus porrectes*), endemic to Cocos Island, differs in having white hairs around jaws.

Shortnose Batfish

Ogcocephalus nasutus
Family Ogcocephalidae (batfishes)

- Florida, south to Amazon River mouth
- Coastal seagrass beds, sand/rubble flats, slopes
- 1–275 m (3.3–894 ft)
- 38 cm (15 in)

Solitary. Has modified pectoral fins that are like legs with feet, which it uses to hop along bottom. Has "rod with lure" (modified first dorsal spine) between tip of snout and mouth, thought to be used to attract prey but diet would not indicate that: feeds on crabs, snails and small bivalves. Preyed upon by sharks.

Fringelip Mullet

Crenimugil crenilabis
Family Mugilidae (mullets)

- East Africa and Red Sea, east to Line Islands, north to Japan and south to Australia
- Coastal reefs; lagoons, reef flats, reef faces
- 1–20 m (3.3–65 ft)
- 60 cm (7.9 in)

Schooling species. Descends to bottom to suck detritus and algae from sand surface. Spawns in larger groups after dark. Has narrow gray stripes on body that are lacking in related species; also lunate tail with dusky margins.

- ⊕ Circumtropical
- ⊙ Shallow sand flats in lagoons and inshore reef faces
- ↓ Near surface
- ↔ 1 m (2.9 ft)

Crocodile Needlefish or Houndfish

Tylosurus crocodilus
Family Belonidae (needlefishes)

Solitary or in schools (especially younger fishes). Feeds on small schooling fishes. Has been known to impale divers at night — including cases where eye socket was penetrated — and windsurfers and waders. Differentiated from others in genus by forked tail with longer lower lobe. Fed on by larger fishes and sea eagles.

- ⊕ Western and Eastern Australia
- ⊙ Coastal rocky reefs; under overhangs and in caves
- ↓ 20-250 m (65-813 ft)
- ↔ 22 cm (8.7 in)

Pineapple Fish

Cleidopus gloriamaris
Family Monocentridae (pinecone fishes)

Occurs singly or in pairs or groups, the latter often in large caves or other preferred daytime hiding places. Light organs — a patch of skin where bioluminescent bacterium grow — at corners of mouth. Feed on small plankton shrimps. Similar to pinecone fish (*Monocentris japonicus*) but in *M. japonicus* profile is much more rounded.

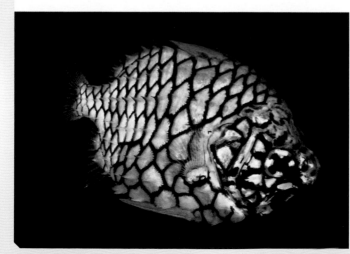

Splendid Soldierfish

Myripristis botche

Family Holocentridae
(squirrelfishes and soldierfishes)

- ⊕ East Africa to New Caledonia, north to Ryukyu Islands and south to Great Barrier Reef
- ⊙ Coastal reefs; deep lagoon patch reefs, reef faces, slopes; often on silty dead reefs
- ↧ 20–65 m (65–211 ft)
- ↔ 19 cm (7.5 in)

Solitary or in pairs or small groups. Stays hidden during day, moving out to feed at night. As in many nocturnal fishes, eyes large and so sensitive it can see tiny prey in moonlight. Red coloration also indicative of nocturnal life-style. Easy to approach and photograph. Body lighter than most others in genus; red median fins with black tips.

Blackbar Soldierfish

Myripristis jacobus

Family Holocentridae
(squirrelfishes and soldierfishes)

- ⊕ North Carolina, south to Brazil, including Gulf of Mexico; Eastern Atlantic
- ⊙ Coastal and outer reefs; pier pilings, wreckage, lagoon patch reefs, reef faces, slopes
- ↧ 5–50 m (17–163 ft)
- ↔ 20 cm (7.9 in)

Solitary or in loose groups. Typically occurs at mouths of caves or under ledges during the day. At night disperses over reef to feed on larger zooplankton (crustacean larvae). As sun begins to rise, moves back to daytime haunts. Only species in genus in the Caribbean.

🌐 East Africa to Hawaiian Islands, north to Japan and south to Lord Howe Island
☉ Coastal and outer coral and rocky reefs; lagoons, reef flats, reef faces, slopes
↧ 1–35 m (3.3–116 ft)   ↦ 19 cm (7.5 in)

Epaulette Soldierfish
Myripristis kuntee
Family Holocentridae
(**squirrelfishes and soldierfishes**)

Solitary or in groups in caves during the day. Disperses onto surrounding reef at night to feed on larger zooplankton. Large eyes help locate prey in minimal light (e.g., moonlight). Scales are smaller than in relatives; fins have white margins.

🌐 East Africa to Tuamotus, north to Ryukyu Islands and south to New Caledonia
☉ Coastal and outer coral reefs; lagoons, reef faces, slopes
↧ 4–25 m (13–81 ft)   ↦ 20 cm (7.9 in)

Violet Soldierfish
Myripristis violacea
Family Holocentridae
(**squirrelfishes and soldierfishes**)

Solitary. Feeds at night on zooplankton and bottom-dwelling invertebrates such as worms and crustaceans. Silver with violet hue; scales have dark margins; red band along rear edge of gill cover.

Ray-Finned Fishes

Whitetip Soldierfish

Myripristis vittata
Family Holocentridae
(squirrelfishes and soldierfishes)

- ⊕ East Africa to Marquesas and Tuamotu Islands, north to southern Japan and south to New Caledonia
- ⊙ Coastal and outer coral reefs; lagoons, reef faces, slopes
- ↧ 3–80 m (10–260 ft)
- ↔ 20 cm (7.9 in)

Solitary or in pairs or large aggregations. Often lives under overhangs and in caves with other species of soldierfish. May move from shelter during the day, but never far from a hiding place. At night moves over reef to feed on larger zooplankton. All red, with white-tipped fins.

Longspine Squirrelfish

Holocentrus rufus
Family Holocentridae
(squirrelfishes and soldierfishes)

- ⊕ Florida and Bermuda, south to Venezuela
- ⊙ Coastal and outer reefs; lagoon patch reefs, reef faces, slopes
- ↧ 1–125 m (3.3 to 406 ft)
- ↔ 28 cm (11 in)

Solitary. Found under overhangs and in caves during the day. At night hunts crabs, shrimps, snails and serpent stars. Uses swim bladder and associated muscles to create noises (grunts, clicks) to communicate with conspecifics. Dorsal fin has small white triangles near spine tips.

⊕ Red Sea to Marquesas and Ducie Islands, north to southern Japan and Hawaiian Islands and south to Lord Howe Island

⊙ Coastal coral reefs; patch reefs in seagrass meadows of sheltered lagoons, back reefs, reef flats, reef faces, slopes

↧ 2–46 m (7–150 ft)   ↦ 32 cm (12.6 in)

Spotfin Squirrelfish
Neoniphon samara
Family Holocentridae
(**squirrelfishes and soldierfishes**)

Solitary or in small aggregations. Hovers over branching corals or near home crevice. Disperses at dusk from diurnal haunt to hunt shrimps and crabs. Similar to clearfin squirrelfish (*Neoniphon argenteus*) but differs in having large black spot at front of dorsal fin. In related blackfin squirrelfish (*Neoniphon opercularis*), entire spiny dorsal fin is black.

⊕ Red Sea to Line, Marquesas and Tuamotu Islands, north to south Japan and Marcus Island and south to southern Great Barrier Reef

⊙ Coastal and outer coral reefs; lagoons, reef faces, slopes

↧ 4–40 m (13–130 ft)   ↦ 25 cm (9.8 in)

Silverspot Squirrelfish
Sargocentron caudimaculatum
Family Holocentridae
(**squirrelfishes and soldierfishes**)

Solitary or in groups. Often seen during the day near entrances of caves or crevices. Hunts on benthic invertebrates at night. Large spine on gill cover; rear of body and tail are white, turning red at night to match rest of body.

Sabre Squirrelfish

Sargocentron spiniferum
Family Holocentridae
(squirrelfishes and soldierfishes)

Solitary or in small groups. Usually at entrances of caves or crevices or under overhangs during the day. Moves onto reef at night to feed on crabs, mantis shrimps, slipper lobsters and fish. Large spine on cheek is venomous. Similar violet squirrelfish (*Sargocentron violaceum*) has blue-edged scales.

⊕ Red Sea and east Africa, east to Hawaiian Islands, north to southern Japan and south to New South Wales
⊙ Coastal and outer coral reefs; lagoons, reef faces, slopes
↨ 3–122 m (10–397 ft)   ↔ 45 cm (18 in)

Dusky Squirrelfish

Sargocentron vexillarius
Family Holocentridae
(squirrelfishes and soldierfishes)

Solitary; occasionally forms small groups. Takes refuge during the day; hunts crustacean larvae, crustaceans, snails and shrimps after dark. Anal fin and tail bordered in reddish brown; spots between dorsal spines.

⊕ Florida and Bermuda, south to Venezuela
⊙ Coastal and outer reefs; lagoon patch reefs, reef faces, slopes
↨ 1–20 m (3.3–65 ft)   ↔ 18 cm (7.1 in)

⊕ East Africa, north to Red Sea, east to French Polynesia, north to southern Japan and south to Lord Howe Island

⊙ Coastal sand and mud slopes

↨ 1–91 m (3.3–296 ft)   ↔ 7 cm (2.8 in)

Dragon Sea Moth
Eurypegasus draconis
Family Pegasidae (sea moths)

Solitary or in pairs (usually as adults). Feeds on crustaceans, worms, eggs and larvae off seafloor. Diurnal fish that stops crawling soon after sunset and is inactive until sun begins to rise. Forms long-term bonds. Spawns at dusk and is a broadcast spawner, releasing eggs into the water column. Females have a larger carapace than males.

⊕ East Africa to Fiji Islands, north to Japan and south to the New South Wales, Australia

⊙ Coastal coral reefs; sand flats, slopes, seagrass beds

↨ 1–25 m (3.3–81 ft)   ↔ 15 cm (5.9 in)

Robust Ghost Pipefish
Solenostomus cyanopterus
Family Solenostomidae (ghost pipefishes)

Solitary as juveniles and in pairs as adults. Feeds on crustaceans that swarm near bottom. Hangs vertically, with head directed toward the bottom, when mimicking plant material. Male smaller than female. Tail stalk very short. Comes in many colors, including green, brown and red; often looks as if coralline algae is growing on skin (as seen in seagrass). Several similar undescribed species.

Roughsnout Ghost Pipefish

Solenostomus paegnius
Family Solenostomidae

- ⊕ Indonesia to southern Japan
- ⊙ Coastal coral reefs; sand flats; slopes; often with algae or soft corals
- ↧ 4–20 m (3.3–81 ft)
- ↔ 12 cm (4.7 in)

Adults usually in pairs. Several bushy appendages on underside of snout; can also have long filamentous appendages on head, body and fins. Color variable, can be bright green, brown or pink. Has longer tail stock than robust ghost pipefish (*S. cyanopterus*).

Ornate Ghost Pipefish

Solenostomus paradoxus
Family Solenostomidae
(ghost pipefishes)

- ⊕ East Africa, north to northern Red Sea, south to New South Wales, Australia, and north to Japan
- ⊙ Coastal coral and rocky reefs; patch reefs in sheltered bays, reef faces, slopes, drop-offs
- ↧ 3–30 m (10–98 ft)
- ↔ 10 cm (3.9 in)

Juveniles occur singly, adults typically in pairs (on rare occasions forms small groups). Hangs vertically among arms of crinoids, branches of gorgonians and black coral. Eats small shrimps and swarming mysids. Forms long-term pair bonds. Female recognized by pelvic fins: joined together along anterior edge and united along rear margin. This species is recognized by incisions between tail rays.

- 🌐 Indonesia to Palau
- ⊙ Coastal coral reefs; lagoons, reef flats, reef faces, slopes
- ↕ 1–15 m (3.3–49 ft)   ↔ 17 cm (6.7 in)

Banded Messmate Pipefish

Corythoichthys sp.
Family Syngnathidae

Occurs singly or in small groups. Crawls about on seafloor feeding on small benthic invertebrates. Others in genus are haremic: male mates with numerous females. Stocky species with distinct bands encircling body; head tattooed with dark lines. Several similar species.

- 🌐 East Africa to Tonga, north to Ryukyu Islandss and south to Australia
- ⊙ Coastal coral reefs; lagoons, reef flats, reef faces, slopes
- ↕ 1–30 m (3.3–98 ft)   ↔ 15 cm (5.9 in)

Schultz's Pipefish

Corythoichthys schultzi
**Family Syngnathidae
(pipefishes and seahorses)**

Occurs singly, in pairs or (rarely) in small groups. Crawls about on rubble, sand or coral substrate. Hunts tiny crustaceans that it picks off seafloor. During spawning, female extrudes single flat layer of eggs into male's brood pouch. Orange to rusty brown spots on body, with no white flecks.

Ray-Finned Fishes

Ray-Finned Fishes

Ringed Pipefish

Dunckerocampus dactyliophorus
**Family Syngnathidae
(pipefishes and seahorses)**

⊕ Red Sea to Austral Islands, north to Izu Islands amd south to New Caledonia
⊙ Coastal coral reefs; patch reefs in nutrient-rich bays and lagoons, reef faces, slopes
↧ 1–56 (3.3–182 ft)   ↔ 20 cm (7.9 in)

Occurs singly, in pairs or in small groups, usually under overhangs or in caves. Unlike some reef-associated pipefishes, hovers over the bottom. Similar to orange-banded pipefish (*D. pessuliferus*), which has narrow, alternating black and orange bands, but maroon and white/cream instead.

Orange-banded Pipefish

Dunckerocampus pessuliferus
Family Syngnathidae

⊕ Northwestern Australia, Indonesia and Philippines
⊙ Coastal coral reefs; patch reefs on mud or sand slopes
↧ 15–35 (49–114 ft)   ↔ 16 cm (6.3 in)

Occurs singly or in pairs. Hovers over substrate, often near shrimp cleaning stations. Feeds on zooplankton near and off seafloor. Males incubates eggs in brood pouch on abdomen. Distinctive red tail with yellow spot, similar to many-banded pipefish (*D. multiannulatus*), which has red tail with white margins.

🌐 Red Sea to New Caledonia, north to southern Japan
☉ Near coastal reefs; bays, estuaries, lagoons, seagrass meadows
⬇ 1–42 (3.3–137 ft)　　　　　↔ 40 cm (16 in)

Stick Pipefish

Trachyrhamphus bicoarctatus
Family Syngnathidae
(pipefishes and seahorses)

Occurs singly or in pairs. Sits motionless on bottom looking like plant material, often with head raised. Uses tail end to grip seafloor. Feeds on zooplankton in water column as well as tiny invertebrates on substrate. Newly hatched larvae are planktonic, settling to the bottom when about 10 cm (3.9 in). Color varies.

🌐 Philippines, south to Great Barrier Reef and New Caledonia
☉ Coastal and outer coral reefs; reef faces and slopes
⬇ 16–60 m (52–195 ft)　　　　　↔ 5 cm (1.9 in)

Pygmy Seahorse

Hippocampus bargibanti
Family Syngnathidae
(pipefishes and seahorses)

Usually forms groups numbering up to 28 pairs. Probably monogamous. Found on gorgonians of genus *Muricella*. Individuals may stay on same fan for many months. Feeds on tiny zooplankton trapped in gorgonian's polyps or slime and maybe on tissue of host. Several similar-looking species. The closely related Denise's pygmy seahorse (*H. denise*) lacks bumps.

Denise's Pygmy Seahorse

Hippocampus denise
Family Syngnathidae

⊕ Indonesia to Vanuatu, north to southern Japan and south to New Caledonia
⊙ Coastal and outer coral reefs; reef faces and slopes
↧ 20–84 m (65–273 ft)   ↤ 1.5 cm (0.6 in)

Occurs singly or in groups. Found mainly on gorgonians in genus *Annella*, but also *Muricella*, *Acanthogorgia* and *Echinogorgia*. Smooth-bodied, lacking tubercles seen in *H. bargibanti*. One of the smallest bony fishes, reaching sexual maturity at the tiny size of only 1.33 cm (0.5 in).

Thorny Seahorse

Hippocampus histrix
Family Syngnathidae
(pipefishes and seahorses)

⊕ East Africa to Hawaiian and Society Islands, north to southern Japan and southwest to Papua New Guinea
⊙ Sheltered bays, estuaries, mangroves, seagrass beds, coral reefs
↧ 1–34 m (3.3–111 ft)   ↤ 17 cm (6.7 in)

Solitary species. Feeds on tiny crustaceans. Thorns extending from head and body and tail ridges. Usually cream or yellow but can also be red or orange; color may change depending on habitat. Red Sea Jayakar's seahorse (*H. jayakari*) is similar species.

- California south to Peru, including Cocos and Galapagos Islands
- Coastal rocky reefs; also open ocean; found clinging to seagrass, sponges, black corals and soft corals
- 1–20 m (3.3–65 ft)   ↔ 25 cm (9.8 in)

Pacific Seahorse

Hippocampus ingens
**Family Syngnathidae
(pipefishes and seahorses)**

Occurs singly or in pairs. Feeds on zooplankton and tiny benthic crustaceans. Does most moving around at night. When in open ocean, preyed upon by tuna. Gestation period around 15 days, with brood size about 400. Only seahorse species in Eastern Pacific.

- North Carolina, south to Brazil, including Gulf of Mexico
- Coastal reefs; seagrass beds, lagoon patch reefs, reef faces
- 1–15 m (3.3–49 ft)   ↔ 15 cm (5.9 in)

Longsnout Seahorse

Hippocampus reidi
**Family Syngnathidae
(pipefishes and seahorses)**

Solitary and in pairs. Often seen hanging on to branching sponges or gorgonians on pier pilings or in coral reef habitat. Color highly variable, including black, brown, orange, red and yellow, often with crusty areas to help blend with surroundings. Males and females form bond over breeding period. Males hold the eggs, which hatch and are expelled from his pouch in about two weeks; brood size from 200 to 1,600.

Ray-Finned Fishes

Common Seahorse
Hippocampus taeniopterus
Family Syngnathidae
(pipefishes and seahorses)

⊕ Eastern Indonesia, Papua New Guinea and northern Australia
⊙ Coastal coral reefs, mangroves, seagrass beds, mud slopes; often clings with tail to sponges and grasses
↕ 1–15 m (3.3–49 ft)   ↔ 22 cm (8.6 in)

Occurs singly or in pairs. Gives birth to 20–1,000 young per brood after 20–28 days' gestation. Body smooth, lacking spines; crown on head swept backwards. Color varies from black to yellow; often has tiny white and/or black spots.

Pacific Trumpetfish
Aulostomus chinensis
Family Aulostomidae
(trumpetfishes)

⊕ East Africa to Panama, north to Ryukyu Islands and south to Great Barrier Reef
⊙ Rocky and coral reefs; almost all reef habitats
↕ 5–122 m (16–397 ft)   ↔ 90 cm (35 in)

Usually solitary but may aggregate around suitable shelter sites. Will hang among gorgonians, sea fans and manmade debris (e.g., pipes, ropes). Feeds on wide range of fishes and shrimps. Will hunt by riding alongside other fishes (often herbivores or omnivores such as parrotfishes, angelfishes and puffers), using them as a moving blind. Spawns just before dusk, releasing pelagic eggs. Mostly gray to brown, but also a golden form.

- Florida and Bermuda, south to Brazil
- Coastal and outer rocky and coral reef; all reef habitats
- 1–25 m (3.3–81 ft) ↔ 1 m (39 in)

Atlantic Trumpetfish 229

Aulostomus maculatus
Family Aulostomidae
(trumpetfishes)

Solitary. Wily hunter that will hang vertically among gorgonian branches or barrel sponges to avoid detection by prey (small fishes). Relies on stealth, waiting until they get close enough before launching attack. Will also use larger fishes (e.g., parrotfishes) or roving schools of fish (e.g., blue tangs) as moving blinds to approach quarry. Color can change; includes blue-nosed phase and all-gold phase.

- East Africa, east to Panama
- Coastal and outer reefs
- 1–132 m (3.3–429 ft) ↔ 1.6 m (5.2 ft)

Reef Cornetfish

Fistularia commersonii
Family Fistulariidae (cornetfishes)

Solitary or in groups. Moves over sand bottoms and reef areas. Feeds on fishes, squids and crustaceans. Although does not engage in this behavior as often as trumpetfishes, on occasion will hunt by riding. Can change colors rapidly from plain to barred pattern.

Bluespotted Cornetfish

Fistularia tabacaria
Family Fistulariidae (cornetfishes)

- ⊕ Massachusetts and Bermuda, south to Brazil, including Gulf of Mexico; also Eastern Atlantic
- ⊙ Coastal and outer reefs; seagrass beds, lagoon patch reefs, reef faces, slopes
- ↧ 1.5–60 m (5–195 ft)
- ↤ 2 m (6.5 ft)

Solitary. Feeds on fishes. Series of blue spots along snout, head and front portion of body; also has long filament on tail. Can quickly alter coloration to blend in with surroundings. Shy and often difficult to approach, but an occasional individual may become curious and let down its guard.

Razorfish

Aeoliscus strigatus
Family Centriscidae (razorfishes)

- ⊕ Aldabra and Seychelles, east to New Caledonia, north to southern Japan and south to southeast Australia
- ⊙ Coastal reefs; reef faces, slopes
- ↧ 1–30 m (3.3–98 ft)
- ↤ 15 cm (5.9 in)

Most often in large schools but sometimes singly or in pairs. Sometimes shelters among spines of *Diadema* urchins (especially the young), seagrass or soft corals. Swims or hovers upside down, with head down. Schools swim synchronously, using pectoral fins to propel them forward. Feeds on swarming crustaceans (e.g., mysid shrimps). Similar to rigid shrimpfish (*Centriscus scutatus*), which has rigid rather than hinged dorsal spine.

- East Africa to Hawaiian, Marquesas and Tuamotu Islands, north to southern Japan and south to New Zealand
- Coastal sand flats and slopes
- 1–45 m (3.3–146 ft) — 38 cm (14.9 in)

Oriental Flying Gurnard

Dactyloptena orientalis
Family Dactylopteridae

Occurs singly. Has pelvic fin rays that are leg-like, employed to crawl along bottom and to probe sand and turn rubble when searching for food. Feeds on crustaceans, tiny bivalves and benthic fishes; most feeding apparently occurs after dark. Takes on orange hue at night. When startled, swims off with pectoral fins spread, which increases apparent size.

- Massachusetts and Bermuda, south to Argentina; also Eastern Atlantic
- Coastal sand flats and slopes adjacent to reefs; seagrass beds
- 1–12 m (3.3–39 ft) — 45 cm (17.7 cm)

Flying Gurnard

Dactylopterus volitans
Family Dactylopteridae
(flying gurnards)

Solitary. Crawls along bottom using modified pectoral and pelvic fin spines. Diet of crabs, shrimps and small bottom-dwelling fishes. When moving quickly, uses tail fin and throws open large pectoral fins, possibly to increase apparent size. Easier to get close to at night; during the day, may swim off when approached.

Ambon Scorpionfish

Pteroidichthys amboinensis

Family Scorpaenidae
(scorpionfishes)

🌐 Northern Australia, Papua New Guinea and Indonesia to southern Japan
☉ Coastal reefs; sand and mud flats, slopes
↧ 3–40 m (10–130 ft)　　　　　　　↦ 12 cm (4.7 in)

Solitary or in pairs. Rests on seafloor; moves by crutching along on pectoral fins. Sometimes hairy individuals in presence of filamentous algae. Feeds on small benthic crustaceans and fishes. Color variable, including brown, green, orange, yellow and lavender.

Lacy Scorpionfish

Rhinopias aphanes

Family Scorpaenidae
(scorpionfishes)

🌐 New Caledonia; Queensland, Australia; Papua New Guinea; Solomon Islands
☉ Coastal reefs; current-prone coral pinnacles with rich stony/soft corals
↧ 5–30 m (16–98 ft)　　　　　　　↦ 23 cm (9.1 in)

Solitary. Often associated with crinoids, which it may mimic. Snout longer and with narrower profile than other species; supra-orbital tentacles antler-like. Color highly variable but always has complicated lattice pattern of dark lines on head, body and fins.

⊕ Baja south to Chile; also Galapagos Islands
⊙ Coastal and insular rocky reefs; rocky, sand and rubble bottoms
↧ 5–157 m (16–510 ft)   ↔ 26 cm (10 in)

Player Scorpionfish

Scorpaena histrio
Family Scorpaenidae
(scorpionfishes)

Solitary. Sedentary, ambushing crustaceans and fishes that come within striking range. Similar to stone scorpionfish (*S. mystes*) but has fewer appendages on head (often none) and can have dark spot on side. Color variable, including brown, red and lavender.

⊕ New York and Bermuda, south to Brazil; Eastern Atlantic; also tropical Eastern Pacific (different subspecies)
⊙ Coral and rocky reefs; jetties, pier pilings, seagrass beds, reef faces, slopes
↧ 1–55 m (3.3–179 ft)   ↔ 36 cm (14.2 in)

Spotted Scorpionfish

Scorpaena plumieri
Family Scorpaenidae
(scorpionfishes)

Solitary. Capable ambush predator that waits patiently until crustaceans, octopuses or fish stumble into strike zone. Usually brown, gray or pink with lighter mottling and three dark bars on tail. Skin flaps on head and jaws (which help it blend with reef) and tentacles over eyes. Back sides of pectoral fins black with white spots; fin spines venomous and can result in painful injury if contacted.

Ray-Finned Fishes

Reef Scorpionfish

Scorpaenodes caribbaeus

Family Scorpaenidae (scorpionfishes)

⊕ Florida and Bahamas, to Panama and northern South America
⊙ Coastal coral reefs; lagoon patch reefs, tide pools, reef faces, slopes
↧ 1–50 m (3.3–163 ft)　　　　↔ 10 cm (3.9 in)

Solitary. Found on rubble, among sponges or resting upside down on ceilings of caves and overhangs. One of few scorpionfish that will drift in water column, just above substrate. Ambush predator that hunts crustaceans; may move about reef at night. Pectoral, dorsal and caudal fins are spotted.

Devil Scorpionfish

Scorpaenopsis diabolus

Family Scorpaenidae (scorpionfishes)

⊕ Red Sea to Hawaiian Islands, north to southern Japan and south to Great Barrier Reef and Tonga
⊙ Coastal and outer reefs; reef flats, crests, reef faces, slopes
↧ 2–70 m (7–231 ft)　　　　↔ 30 cm (12 in)

Solitary or in pairs. Found on rubble, on sand near reef edge or among seagrass or macroalgae. Fish-eater, consuming variety of fish that swim into striking range. When threatened, swims rapidly, exposing bright colors on underside of pectoral fins, then stops abruptly and blends with seafloor. Body color variable: gray, pink or orange mottled. Similar to flasher scorpionfish (*S. macrochir*).

⊕ Red Sea to Mariana Islands, north to Taiwan and south to Great Barrier Reef
⊙ Coastal and outer coral and rocky reefs; lagoon patch reefs, reef flats, reef faces, slopes
↕ 1–35 m (3.3–116 ft)   ↔ 36 cm (14 in)

Bearded (Tasseled) Scorpionfish

Scorpaenopsis oxycephala
Family Scorpaenidae (scorpionfishes)

Solitary. Cryptic scorpaenid that rarely moves. Relies on camouflage to ambush prey and stay hidden from predators; will hide in sponges or among soft corals. Feeds on fishes, crustaceans and squids. Similar to several other species, including Poss's scorpionfish (*S. possi*) and Papuan scorpionfish (*S. papuensis*), that can be difficult to differentiate from.

⊕ East Africa to Galapagos Islands, north to Ryukyu Islands and south to New South Wales, Australia
⊙ Coastal and outer rocky and coral reefs; lagoon patch reefs, reef faces, slopes
↕ 1–134 m (3.3–442 ft)   ↔ 10 cm (3.9 in)

Leaf Scorpionfish

Taenianotus triacanthus
Family Scorpaenidae (scorpionfishes)

Occurs singly or in pairs or small groups (possibly associated with spawning period). Looks and behaves like waterlogged vegetation; rocks from side to side. Feeds on crustaceans and fishes. Color highly variable: juveniles usually transparent or light colored; adults can be white, yellow, orange, maroon, black or pink. Microalgae can grow on skin, which is sloughed off along with cuticle (outer layer of skin) when leaf scorpionfish "sheds."

Twinspot Lionfish

Dendrochirus biocellatus
Family Scorpaenidae
(scorpionfishes)

⊕ Mauritius to Society Islands, north to Japan and south to Australia
⊙ Coastal and outer coral reefs; lagoon patch reefs, reef faces, slopes
↧ 1–40 m (3.3–132 ft)   ↔ 10 cm (3.9 in)

Occurs singly or in pairs. Cryptic species most often encountered after dark. Lives in reef crevices and caves during day; hunts shrimp and small fish at night. When stalking prey, snaps dorsal spines back and forth, possibly to distract or lure prey. Tends to hop along bottom. Recognized by mustache and twin spots on dorsal fin.

Zebra Lionfish

Dendrochirus zebra
Family Scorpaenidae
(scorpionfishes)

⊕ South Africa to Samoa, north to southern Japan and south to Lord Howe Island
⊙ Coastal and outer coral and rocky reefs; rocky shorelines, lagoon patch reefs, reef faces, slopes
↧ 1–35 m (3.3–114 ft)   ↔ 18 cm (7 in)

Solitary or in small groups. Home-ranging, not territorial. Males may fight, especially during spawning period, jabbing each other with dorsal spines. Meets females at rendezvous site in home range and spawns with one or more around sunset. Feeds on crustaceans and small fishes; most feeding takes place after dark. Pectoral fins fanlike, with dark stripes.

🌐 East Africa to Marquesas and Mangareva Islands, north to southern Japan and south to Great Barrier Reef and Austral Island

◎ Coastal and outer coral reefs; lagoons, reef flats, reef faces, slopes

↨ 1–50 m (3.3–165 ft)　　　　　↔ 20 cm (7.8 in)

Spotfin Lionfish

Pterois antennata

Family Scorpaenidae (scorpionfishes)

Solitary or forms groups in larger hiding places. During the day takes refuge in caves, under ledges and in crevices. Moves out of cover at night to hunt crustaceans and fishes, usually consuming several prey items per hunting trip. Identified by a few spots on pectoral fins, similar to Mombasa lionfish (*P. mombasa*), which has numerous large spots on these fins.

🌐 Western Australia and Malaysian peninsula to Pitcairn Island

◎ Coastal and outer coral reefs; lagoons, reef faces, slopes, shipwrecks

↨ 1–30 m (3.3–98 ft)　　　　　↔ 38 cm (15 in)

Common Lionfish

Pterois volitans

Family Scorpaenidae (scorpionfishes)

Occurs singly or in groups. Hunts crustaceans and fishes, usually after dark. Often hunts near substrate, using large pectoral fins to corner prey. Sometimes hunts cooperatively in groups, herding small fish. Will also follow foraging morays to feed on animals they flush from cover. One of a number of similar species that can be difficult to differentiate. Juvenile in inset photo.

Spiny Devilfish

Inimicus didactylus

Family Synanceiidae

(stonefishes and their relatives)

- ⊕ Thailand to Vanuatu, north to southeast China and Micronesia
- ⊙ Coastal sand, mud and mixed sand/rubble flats and slopes
- ↓ 5–40 m (17–132 ft)
- ↔ 18 cm (7 in)

Solitary; in pairs during spawning period. Walks along bottom on pectoral fin rays. Buries itself in substrate so only eyes and snout show — easy for a diver to kneel on. Males will fight over females with swollen abdomens, indicating readiness to spawn. When threatened, throws pectoral fins forward to show colorful inner surface. Color variable; usually brown or black overall but in some locations can be orange, yellow or pink.

Reef Stonefish

Synanceia verrucosa

Family Synanceiidae

(stonefishes and their relatives)

- ⊕ Red Sea to French Polynesia, north to southern Japan and south to New Caledonia
- ⊙ Rocky and coral reefs; lagoons, reef flats, reef faces, slopes
- ↓ 1–20 m (3.3–66 ft)
- ↔ 35 cm (14 in)

Solitary; rarely found in groups. Often rests near cleaning stations or other areas where prey fish aggregate. Ambush predator that seldom moves. Algae and sessile invertebrates grow on skin and may attract potential prey; sloughed off occasionally with skin cuticle. Can be pink after recent shedding. Most venomous coral-reef fish; few deaths reported.

⊕ Andaman Sea to Fiji, north to southern Japan and south to Australia
⊙ Coastal reefs and seagrass beds
↧ 1–20 m (3.3–66 ft)　　　　　↔ 15 cm (5.9 in)

Spiny Waspfish

Ablabys macracanthus
Family Tetrarogidae (waspfishes)

Solitary or in pairs. Often among seagrass or water-logged vegetation (leaves) but also on sand slopes. Algae grows on body surface. Feeds on small crustaceans that it snaps off the seafloor. Females move into male's home range in afternoon to spawn; pair swim in water column to release eggs. Very similar to cockatoo waspfish (*A. taenianotus*) but has 15 dorsal spines instead of 17. Usually brown or black; sometimes cream colored with pink patches.

⊕ Borneo to Yap, north to Philippines and south to New Caledonia
⊙ Coastal reefs, mangroves, seagrass beds
↧ 1–30 m (3.3–98 ft)　　　　　↔ 54 cm (21.3 in)

Crocodile Flathead

Cymbacephalus beauforti
Family Platycephalidae (flatheads)

Solitary. Large flathead that relies on ambush to capture prey; rests among soft corals, rubble or vegetation waiting for prey to come near. Feeds on crustaceans and fishes. Juveniles often jet black.

Spiny Flathead

Onigocia spinosa
Family Platycephalidae (flatheads)

- ⊕ Northern Australia, east to Indonesia and north to southern Japan
- ⊙ Coastal coral reefs; sand or mud flats and slopes
- ↧ 4–250 m (13–813 ft)
- ↔ 13 cm (5.1 in)

Solitary. Buries itself in substrate during day; emerges at night to hunt worms and small crustaceans. Most often encountered on night dives. Has two white bands, one mid-body and one at base of tail; overall color brown to red, often with white head.

Magenta Slender Anthias

Luzonichthys waitei
Family Serranidae (groupers)

- ⊕ Aldabra east to Fiji, north to Japan and south to Great Barrier Reef
- ⊙ Outer coral reefs; reef faces, steep walls, slopes
- ↧ 1–55 m (3.3–179 ft)
- ↔ 7 cm (2.8 in)

Shoaling species that forms large groups. Members of this genus more slight of body than other anthias and also have a split dorsal fin. Feeds on zooplankton. Pink with yellowish orange back and violet to yellow on tail margins.

- ⊕ Christmas Island (Indian Ocean) east to Line Islands, north to southern Japan and south to Great Barrier Reef
- ⊙ Coastal and outer reefs; reef faces, slopes
- ↧ 1–15 m (3.3–49 ft)
- ↔ 9.5 cm (3.7 in)

Redfin Anthias
Pseudanthias dispar
Family Serranidae (groupers)

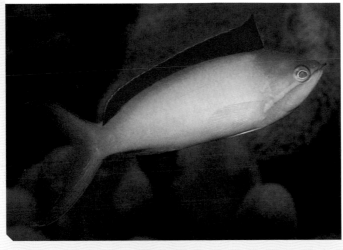

Shoaling species; groups composed mainly of females. Males display to females by spreading their red fins and intensifying body color. Feeds on zooplankton during day. Dashes to cover of coral when threatened and at night. Similar to flame anthias (*Pseudanthias ignitus*), an Indian Ocean species that has red borders on tail fin.

- ⊕ Philippines, south to Great Barrier Reef and east to Samoa
- ⊙ Coastal and outer coral reefs; reef faces, slopes
- ↧ 10–190 m (33–594 ft)
- ↔ 20 cm (7.8 in)

Squarespot Anthias
Pseudanthias pleurotaenia
Family Serranidae (groupers)

Shoaling species; orange females outnumber pink males in most groups. Protogynous hermaphrodite, like all other anthias. Males swim into water column with U-shaped trajectory; color intensifies during these displays. Most common on deep reef slopes, where pink spot glows. Male twinspot anthias (*P. bimaculatus*) lack square spot on body.

Redbar Anthias
Pseudanthias rubrizonatus
Family Serranidae (groupers)

⊕ Andaman Sea, east to Solomon Islands, north to Japan and south to Great Barrier Reef
⊙ Coastal and outer coral reefs; reef faces, slopes
↕ 10–58 m (33–189 ft) ↔ 10 cm (3.9 in)

Shoals found in areas prone to strong current. Feeds on zooplankton. Females outnumber more colorful males; latter are very aggressive, chasing one another as they fight to defend harem. Both sexes have reddish band in middle of side; male often has yellow on posterior portion of body.

Lyretail Anthias
Pseudanthias squamipinnis
Family Serranidae (groupers)

⊕ Red Sea to Fijian Islands, north to Japan and south to New South Wales, Australia
⊙ Coastal and outer reefs; reef faces, slopes
↕ 2–20 m (7–66 ft) ↔ 12 cm (4.7 in)

Forms huge shoals (sometimes in the thousands) consisting mostly of juveniles and females. Males defend a group of females. Females change sex: some individuals seen in shoal with start of male coloration. Rise into water column to feed on zooplankton. Sometimes joined by other zooplankton feeders. May be more than one species classified as *P. squamipinnis*.

🌐 Indonesia to Solomon Islands, north to southern Japan and south to Great Barrier Reef and New Caledonia

☉ Coastal and outer coral reefs; reef faces, slopes

↧ 2–40 m (7–130 ft)   ↔ 12 cm (4.7 in)

Purple Anthias

Pseudanthias tuka
Family Serranidae (groupers)

Shoaling species; groups consist mainly of females. Changes sex from female to male. Females have yellow line along back and yellow on tail. Males have dark blotch on rear of dorsal fin. Females of similar purple queen (*P. pascalus*) lack yellow markings, while males lack dark blotch on dorsal fin.

🌐 Indonesia to Fiji, north to southern Japan and south to Great Barrier Reef and New Caledonia

☉ Coastal and outer coral reefs; reef faces, slopes

↧ 15–70 m (50–230 ft)   ↔ 13 cm (5.1 in)

Hawk Anthias

Serranocirrhitus latus
Family Serranidae (groupers)

Occurs singly or in pairs or small groups. Usually hang at entrances of caves or under overhangs; at greater depths sometimes in groups hanging over coral colonies. Feeds on zooplankton. Originally classified as hawkfish and later recognized as anthias, hence its common name.

Ray-Finned Fishes

Pacific Mutton Hamlet

Alphestes immaculatus
Family Serranidae (groupers)

⊕ Gulf of California to Peru, including offshore islands
⊙ Coastal and insular rocky reefs; lagoons, reef faces, slopes
↕ 4–30 m (13–98 ft)   ↔ 25 cm (9.8 in)

Solitary. Often rests on bottom among macroalgae (*Padina, Sargassum*), under overhangs or in crevices during day. Active at night, hunting crustaceans and small fishes. Curious, keeping an eye on approaching divers but easily approached. Variegated coloration can include brown, green and red.

Slender Grouper

Anyperodon leucogrammicus
Family Serranidae (groupers)

⊕ Red Sea to Line Islands, north to Ryukyu Islands and south to New Caledonia
⊙ Coastal and outer coral reefs; lagoon patch reefs, reef faces, slopes
↕ 1–40 m (3.3–132 ft)   ↔ 65 cm (25.5 cm)

Solitary or in pairs or small groups (latter is rare). Secretive species that lurks in coral crevices and caves. Juvenile is aggressive mimic of a variety of wrasses (genus *Halichoeres*); uses disguise to sneak up on crustaceans and small fishes. Adults mainly eat fish but also cephalopods. Will dash out from cover to capture passing prey.

- ⊕ Red Sea to Pitcairn Islands, north to southern Japan and south to Lord Howe Island; introduced to Hawaiian Islands
- ⊙ Coastal and outer coral reefs; lagoon patch reefs, reef faces, slopes
- ↧ 1–40 m (3.3–132 ft)
- ↔ 42 cm (16.5 in)

Peacock Hind
Cephalopholis argus
Family Serranidae (groupers)

Haremic species; territory of male contains 1–6 females. Males court with each female sequentially and spawn at dusk. Feed on wide array of bony fishes; crustaceans minor part of diet. Hunts mainly at dusk. Also opportunistic, following foraging eels or octopuses. Bluespotted hind (*C. cyanostigma*) also has blue spots but lacks deep blue fin margins of *C. argus*.

- ⊕ North Carolina, south to Brazil, including Gulf of Mexico
- ⊙ Coastal and outer coral reefs; reef faces, slopes
- ↧ 2–170 m (7–553 ft)
- ↔ 35 cm (13.8 in)

Graysby
Cephalopholis cruentatus
Family Serranidae (groupers)

Solitary. Usually in coral-rich areas, where it rests waiting for unsuspecting prey. Feeds on crustaceans and variety of coral-reef fishes. Hunting activity reaches peak at dusk and dawn. Will follow foraging eels and pounce on prey items flushed out by eels . Individuals will defend "their" eels from members of own kind. Protogynous hermaphrodite and haremic; dominant male's territory will be home to several females.

Bluelined Hind

Cephalopholis formosa
Family Serranidae (groupers)

- ⊕ India and Maldives to northern Australia and north to southern Japan
- ⊙ Coastal and outer coral reefs; lagoon patch reefs; reef faces; often on dead silty reefs
- ↓ 1–15 m (3.3–49 ft)   ↔ 34 cm (13.4 in)

Solitary; may be haremic like others in genus, but data lacking. Diet crustaceans and fishes. Harlequin hind (*C. polleni*) also has blue to violet lines along body but base color is greenish yellow. Latter species found on deep reefs, usually more than 30 m (98 ft).

Coney or Yellow Hind

Cephalopholis fulva
Family Serranidae (groupers)

- ⊕ Bermuda and Florida, south to Brazil
- ⊙ Coastal and outer coral reefs; lagoons, back reefs, reef faces, slopes
- ↓ 3–45 m (10–146 ft)   ↔ 37 cm (14.6 in)

Solitary. Rests on substrate waiting for prey to move past or hovers in water column. Feeds on reef fishes and crustaceans; will even eat parasite-picking wrasses. Opportunistic and will follow foraging snake eels. Haremic: male defends a territory that usually contains several females. Color variable, including brown and white, red and bright yellow forms (latter more common at greater depths).

🌐 Red Sea to Line Islands, north to southern Japan and south to Lord Howe Island
◉ Coastal and outer reefs; lagoon patch reefs, reef faces, slopes
↧ 2–150 m (7–495 ft)   ↦ 41 cm (15.7 in)

Coral Hind
Cephalopholis miniata
Family Serranidae (groupers)

Solitary or in pairs (probably hare-mic, like *C. argus*). Fish-eater with preference for anthias; eats crustaceans to lesser degree. Tends to prefer areas with rich coral growth. Will follow hunting morays and octopuses. Similar saddled hind (*C. sexmaculata*) has 6–7 light bands and more scattered blue spots (usually found in caves or under overhangs). Juvenile coral hind has fewer spots.

🌐 East Africa to Vanuatu, north to southern Japan and south to New Caledonia
◉ Coastal and outer reefs; lagoons, reef faces, slopes
↧ 1–40 m (3.3–130 ft)   ↦ 70 cm (28 in)

Panther Grouper
Chromileptes altivelis
Family Serranidae (groupers)

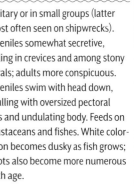

Solitary or in small groups (latter most often seen on shipwrecks). Juveniles somewhat secretive, hiding in crevices and among stony corals; adults more conspicuous. Juveniles swim with head down, sculling with oversized pectoral fins and undulating body. Feeds on crustaceans and fishes. White coloration becomes dusky as fish grows; spots also become more numerous with age.

Ray-Finned Fishes

Leather Bass

Dermatolepis dermatolepis
Family Serranidae (groupers)

- ⊕ Southern California, south to Ecuador; also offshore islands
- ☉ Coastal and insular rocky reefs; lagoons, reef faces, slopes
- ↓ 2–40 m (7–130 ft)
- ↦ 1 m (39 in)

Solitary or in small groups. Juveniles hide among spines of long-spined sea urchins. Very cunning predator: adults use herbivorous fishes as blind to approach unwary prey. Will even join groups of surgeonfishes that move about reef invading damsel territories; will also follow morays. Feeds on crustaceans, cephalopods and fishes.

Blacktip Grouper

Epinephelus fasciatus
Family Serranidae (groupers)

- ⊕ Red Sea to Marquesas and Pitcairn Islands, north to southern Japan and south to Lord Howe Island
- ☉ Coastal and outer coral reefs; lagoons, reef flats, reef faces, slopes
- ↓ 1–160 m (3.3–520 ft)
- ↦ 40 cm (15.7 in)

Solitary. Often reposes on seafloor. Feeds on octopuses, crustaceans and fishes. Often follows octopuses and morays as they probe rubble and reef crevices for food; will even rub against stationary eels to encourage them to move along. Color variable: light greenish gray to pale red, with or without body bars, which appear and disappear depending on fish's mood. May be more than one species represented by *E. fasciatus*.

- 🌐 East Africa and Red Sea, east to Samoa, north to Ryukyu Islands and south to Great Barrier Reef
- ⊙ Coastal and outer coral reefs; mangroves, lagoons, reef faces, slopes
- ↧ 1–60 m (3.3–195 ft) ↔ 90 cm (35.4 in)

Brown-marbled Grouper
Epinephelus fuscoguttatus
Family Serranidae (groupers)

Solitary. Often sits on open sand bottoms or hides in caves. Ambushes passing fishes, crustaceans and cephalopods. Forms large spawning groups; spawning occurs at full moon. A number of similar mottled groupers, but this one has small black saddle on base of tail.

- 🌐 North Carolina and Bermuda, south to Brazil, including Gulf of Mexico; also Eastern Atlantic and tropical Eastern Pacific
- ⊙ Coastal and outer reefs; seagrass beds, mangroves (especially young fish), reef faces, slopes, wreckage (i.e., artificial reefs)
- ↧ 1–100 m (3.3–325 ft) ↔ 2.5 m (8.2 ft)

Goliath Grouper
Epinephelus itajara
Family Serranidae (groupers)

Adults solitary and territorial. Has become scarce in many locations because of overfishing; however, numbers increasing because of protection. Feeds on variety of fishes, including rays, sharks and poisonous trunkfishes and porcupinefishes; also eats lobsters, octopuses and young sea turtles. Vocal fish: produces a booming sound to communicate with own kind. Will form spawning groups of 3–100 individuals. Usually easy to approach.

Giant Grouper
Epinephelus lanceolatus
Family Serranidae (groupers)

- ⊕ East Africa and Red Sea, east to Hawaiian Islands, north to southern Japan, south to New South Wales, Australia
- ⊙ Coastal and outer coral reefs; estuaries, lagoons, back reefs, reef faces, slopes
- ↧ 2–100 m (7–325 ft)
- ↔ 2.7 m (8.9 ft)

Usually solitary but may aggregate in some locations, especially around caves and ship wreckage. Voracious predator, eating larger crustaceans (crabs, lobsters), sharks, rays and bony fishes. Some larger individuals attract groups of golden trevally (*Gnathanodon speciosus*). May behave pugnaciously toward divers, especially where fed, but not dangerous. Also known as Queensland grouper.

Highfin Grouper
Epinephelus maculates
Family Serranidae (groupers)

- ⊕ Cocos-Keeling Islands to Samoa, north to southern Japan and south to Lord Howe Island
- ⊙ Coastal and outer coral reefs; lagoons, reef faces, slopes
- ↧ 2–100 m (7–325 ft)
- ↔ 62 cm (24 ft)

Solitary. Regularly rests on open sand or rubble bottoms. Feeds on octopuses, crustaceans and fishes. Juveniles have small black spots and white blotches; adults brownish with darker spots and white saddle in front of and in middle of dorsal fin.

- Red Sea, east to Tonga, north to southern Japan and south to New Caledonia
- Coastal and outer rocky and coral reefs; estuaries, mangroves, lagoons, reef faces, slopes
- 1–150 m (3.3–488 ft)   ↔ 2.3 m (7.6 ft)

Malabar Grouper
Epinephelus malabaricus
Family Serranidae (groupers)

Solitary. Large predator that feeds on cephalopods, crustaceans and fishes. During summer months forms spawning assemblages in reef channels. Dark spots and white patches. Often wary and difficult to approach unless in area where fed by divers. Targeted by live-fish trade.

- North Carolina and Bermuda, south to Brazil
- Coastal and outer reefs; seagrass beds, lagoon patch reefs, back reefs, reef faces, slopes
- 1–35 m (3.3–114 ft)   ↔ 1.2 m (3.9 ft)

Nassau Grouper
Epinephelus striatus
Family Serranidae (groupers)

Solitary or in groups. Ambush hunter that consumes variety of reef fishes and crustaceans. Forms larger breeding assemblages; individuals spawn just around sunset. Groups of males (3–25) will dash after ripe female as she ascends to release eggs in water column. Eggs hatch in about 24 hours, spending about 35–40 days in plankton before settling out on reef. May live 28 years. Black saddle on caudal peduncle.

Potato Grouper

Epinephelus tukula
Family Serranidae (groupers)

⊕ Eastern Africa and Red Sea, east to Great Barrier Reef and north to southern Japan
⊙ Coastal and outer coral reefs; lagoons, reef faces, slopes
↧ 5–150 m (16–163 ft)   ↔ 2.0 m (6.5 ft)

Solitary or in aggregations. Eats a variety of fishes (including sharks and rays) and also some crustaceans and cephalopods. Large grouper often attendant at shark feeds off Australian coast (e.g., Cod's Hole). Gray with large dark blotches. Sometimes referred to as "potato cod."

Indigo Hamlet

Hypoplectrus indigo
Family Serranidae (groupers)

⊕ Florida to throughout Caribbean
⊙ Coastal reefs; back reefs, reef faces, slopes
↧ 12–39 m (39–127 ft)   ↔ 14 cm (5.5 in)

Found singly and in pairs. Usually among soft corals and gorgonians. Feeds heavily on crustaceans (mainly shrimps) but also eats fishes; has predilection for blue chromis. Blue bars on body may make it less visible to chromis as it moves up into water column to attack them. Simultaneous hermaphrodite.

🌐 Florida and Bermuda, throughout Caribbean; also Gulf of Mexico
◉ Coastal and outer coral reefs; lagoon patch reefs, back reefs, reef faces, slopes
↧ 3–30 m (10 to 98 ft)　　　　　↔ 13 cm (5.1 ln.)

Barred Hamlet
Hypoplectrus puella
Family Serranidae (groupers)

Occurs singly or in pairs. Found among soft corals and gorgonians. Feeds on crustaceans and small fishes. Pairs often stay close together. Simultaneous hermaphrodites that trade off, being one sex and then the other during early evening spawning bouts. Individual that initiates spawning rises up into water column and displays to mate; pair then clasp bodies, rise and release gametes (initiator acts first as the female).

🌐 South Florida to Yucatan and south to Venezuela
◉ Outer reefs; lagoon patch reefs, reef faces, slopes
↧ 5–40 m (16–130 ft)　　　　　↔ 8 cm (3.1 in)

Peppermint Bass
Liopropoma rubre
Family Serranidae (groupers)

Solitary or in pairs. Very secretive; rarely seen by divers except when peeking from crevices or moving from one hiding place to another at dusk. Sometimes hangs upside down under overhangs and in caves. Feeds on small crustaceans and fishes. Spawns in pairs at dusk. Does not change sex.

Black Grouper

Mycteroperca bonaci
Family Serranidae (groupers)

🌐 New England (mainly young fish); Bermuda south to Brazil, including Gulf of Mexico
⊙ Coastal and outer coral reefs; seagrass beds, reef faces, slopes
↧ 6–33 m (20–107 ft)   ↔ 1.3 m (4.3 ft)

Solitary or in aggregations. Found hovering in the water column. Adults almost entirely piscivorous; young fish also ingest crustaceans. Protogynous hermaphrodite. Tends to segregate by sex, with almost all males found in deeper, offshore reefs. Thought to live more than 30 years. Biggest enemy is sharks, particularly great hammerhead. Populations have declined in some areas because of overfishing.

Tiger Grouper

Mycteroperca tigris
Family Serranidae (groupers)

🌐 South Florida and Bermuda to Brazil, including Gulf of Mexico
⊙ Coastal and outer coral reefs; reef faces, slopes
↧ 3–40 m (10–130 ft)   ↔ 100 cm (39.4 in)

Solitary or in aggregations. Hovers among soft corals, gorgonians and sponges. Ambushes reef fishes and occasional squid or octopus. Juvenile thought to mimic initial phase of bluehead wrasse; because these wrasses much more abundant, young grouper can sneak up on prey that do not view model (the wrasse) as threat. Forms large spawning groups in deeper water.

- ⊕ North Carolina and Bermuda to Brazil
- ☉ Coastal and outer reefs; reef faces, slopes
- ↧ 8–100 m (26–325 ft) ↔ 35 cm (13.7 in)

Creole-fish

Paranthias furcifer
Family Serranidae (groupers)

Occurs in shoals. Swims high in water column to capture passing zooplankton. Individuals may rest on pectoral fins on sand patches or hide among corals. Often parasitized by gnathiid isopods. Does not change sex and will cross-breed with coney (*Cephalopholis fulva*). Pacific Creolefish (*P. colonus*) is sister species from tropical Eastern Pacific; its young are bright yellow.

- ⊕ South Africa to Mangareva, north to Ryukyu Islands and south to New Caledonia and Rapa Island
- ☉ Coastal and outer reefs; lagoon patch reefs, reef faces, slopes
- ↧ 4–90 m (13–297 ft) ↔ 1.1 m (3.3 ft)

Black Saddled Coral Grouper

Plectropomus laevis
Family Serranidae (groupers)

Solitary. Usually in areas with rich coral growth. Voracious fish-eater; diet includes wide variety of bony fishes. Juveniles may mimic saddled toby (*Canthigaster valentini*), which is poisonous. Color changes; adults dark gray with light bars and spots on body.

Tobaccofish

Serranus tabacarius
Family Serranidae (groupers)

🌐 South Florida and Bermuda, south to Brazil
⊙ Coastal and outer coral reefs; seagrass, edges of reef faces, slopes
↓ 3–70 m (10–228 ft) ↔ 18 cm (7.1 in)

Solitary or in pairs. Moves just above seafloor during day. Feeds on crustaceans and small fishes. Simultaneous hermaphrodite. Courtship in mid to late afternoon; spawning ends with rush into water column and release of gametes. Pair returns to seafloor and swaps sexual roles (fish that just spawned as female now spawns as male, etc.). Larger individuals spawn more than smaller conspecifics.

Harlequin Bass

Serranus tigrinus
Family Serranidae (groupers)

🌐 Northern Florida and Bermuda, south to Venezuela
⊙ Coastal coral reefs; lagoon patch reefs, reef faces, slopes
↓ 3–36 m (7–117 ft) ↔ 10 cm (3.9 in)

Forms pair territories. Pairs hunt cooperatively for small reef fishes and crustaceans. Pair member may abandon mate to pair up with solitary larger neighbor (larger size equates to more eggs). Simultaneous hermaphrodite. Spawns in territory around sunset, with increased spawning activity just before and after full moon.

⊕ Red Sea to Pitcairn Islands, north to southern Japan and south to Lord Howe Island
⊙ Coastal and outer reefs; lagoon patch reefs, back reefs, reef faces, slopes
↧ 1–240 m (3.3–780 ft)   ↔ 90 cm (35 in)

Yellow-edged Lyretail Grouper
Variola louti
Family Serranidae (groupers)

Solitary. Patrols over reef in search of prey. Diet almost entirely fishes; crustaceans and cephalopods eaten occasionally. Will follow morays as eels search in reef crevices and among rubble. Juvenile white over much of body, with red and black on back and dark spot at base of tail. Lunate tail of adult has yellow rear margin.

⊕ India to Papua New Guinea, north to southern Japan and south to Lord Howe Island
⊙ Coastal coral reefs; lagoon patch reefs, reef faces, slopes
↧ 1–25 m (3.3–75 ft)   ↔ 25 cm (10 in)

Doublebanded Soapfish
Diploprion bifasciatum
Family Serranidae (groupers)

Solitary. Hovers in caves or at entrances of crevices during day. Moves onto reef to hunt at dusk, in search of crustaceans and small fishes. Spawns at dusk. Males form temporary spawning territories. Pair rises above bottom to release gametes. Protogynous hermaphrodite. Black color form with yellow fins from eastern Australia. Like other soapfishes, has toxic body slime.

Ray-Finned Fishes

Sixlined Soapfish
Grammistes sexlineatus
Family Serranidae (groupers)

⊕ Red Sea to Marquesas and Mangareva, north to southern Japan and south to New Caledonia
⊙ Coastal and outer reefs; lagoon patch reefs, reef flats, reef faces, slopes, outcroppings on muddy slopes; occasionally in estuaries
↕ 1–130 m (3.3–423 ft)   ↔ 30 cm (11.8 in)

Solitary. Takes refuge in holes and crevices and under ledges. At dusk leaves daytime hiding place to hunt crustaceans and small fishes. When launching an attack, will tip onto side and present quarry with view of back only; approaches slowly and rapidly shakes head from side to side. Young may mimic innocuous cardinalfish species, a possible case of aggressive mimicry. As fish grows, lines break up into rows of spots.

Spotted Soapfish
Pogonoperca punctata
Family Serranidae (groupers)

⊕ Comoros to Marquesas and Society Islands, north to southern Japan and south to New Caledonia
⊙ Outer coral reefs; reef faces, slopes
↕ 15–150 m (49–488 ft)   ↔ 35 cm (13.8 in)

Solitary. Hangs under ledges and in caves during day, moving out to hunt at dusk. Feeds on crustaceans and small fishes. Also known as leaflip soapfish because of appendage on lower jaw. Similar ocellated soapfish (*P. ocellata*) from Indian Ocean has black blotches on body that are lacking in *P. punctata*.

🌐 South Florida and Bermuda to Brazil, east to St. Paul Rocks, St. Helena and Eastern Atlantic
⊙ Coastal and outer rocky and coral reefs; lagoons, reef faces, slopes
↕ 1–55 m (3.3–179 ft)   ↔ 33 cm (13 in)

Greater Soapfish

Rypticus saponaceus
Family Serranidae (groupers)

Solitary. Mostly in hiding during day in crevices and caves; at night emerges to hunt crustaceans and small fishes. Will occasionally rest in open on seafloor during day. Sometimes follows sea snakes as they probe burrows and rubble interstices. Spawns at dusk.

🌐 Northwestern Australia, north to southern Japan
⊙ Coastal and outer coral reefs; lagoons, channels, reef flats, reef faces
↕ 1–15 m (3.3–49 ft)   ↔ 20 cm (7.9 in)

Firetail Dottyback

Labracinus cyclophthalmus
Family Pseudochromidae (dottybacks)

Solitary. Highly territorial. Feeds on variety of benthic invertebrates (including worms, crustaceans, snails, chitons, small sea urchins, serpent stars) as well as smaller fishes. Color variable: some individuals red with darker head, some have lines along body; also olive with bright pink spot on abdomen.

Splendid Dottyback

Manonichthys splendens
**Family Pseudochromidae
(dottybacks)**

⊕ Flores and Banda Sea, Indonesia
⊙ Coastal and outer coral reefs; lagoon patch reefs, reef faces, slopes
↕ 3–40 m (10–131 ft)   ↔ 13 cm (5.1 in)

Solitary. Feeds on worms and crustaceans. Dashes from one hiding place to another with large fins erected. Often associates with rich sponge growth. Thought to mimic yellowtail angelfish (*Chaetodontoplus mesoleucus*), which may be less desirable to eat because of stout cheek spines.

Royal Dottyback

Pictichromis paccagnellae
**Family Pseudochromidae
(dottybacks)**

⊕ Indonesia to northern Australia, east to Papua New Guinea and Solomon Islands
⊙ Coastal and outer coral reefs; steep reef slopes or drop-offs
↕ 1–70 m (3.3–231 ft)   ↔ 5 cm (2 in)

Solitary. Hovers outside cracks and crevices in reef walls, dashing into hiding if approached too closely. Very aggressive and territorial. Feeds on planktonic and benthic crustaceans. Lays an egg ball in crevice, where defended by male. Similar diadem dottyback (*P. diadema*) is yellow with magenta stripe down back. Two other similar species difficult to distinguish.

- Red Sea, east to Line Islands, north to southern Japan and south to Great Barrier Reef and Tonga
- Coastal and outer coral reefs; lagoons, reef faces, slopes
- 3–45 m (10–149 ft)
- 13 cm (5 in)

Comet
Calloplesiops altivelis
Family Plesiopidae (roundheads)

Solitary. Secretive, peering from cervices or caves. Preys on crustaceans and small fishes. Curls body to side and swims with head down as approaches prey. Lays eggs at top of crevice; egg mass (300–500 eggs) guarded by the male. When threatened, sticks tail out of crevice so it looks like head of whitemouth moray. Simllar comet, *C. argus*, has more, smaller spots.

- Bermuda and Bahamas, south to Venezuela
- Coastal and outer coral reefs; lagoon patch reefs, reef faces, slopes
- 1–76 m (3.3–247 ft)
- 8 cm (3 in)

Royal Gramma
Gramma loreto
Family Grammatidae (basslets)

Forms loose groups. Feeds on plankton in water column. Found under overhangs and among rich coral growth. Protogynous hermaphrodite. Male defends hole in reef to which he adds pieces of algae; female deposits eggs in this nest. Color shows geographical variation: in certain parts of range has more yellow on body. Replaced by similar Brazilian gramma (*G. brasiliensis*) in Brazil.

Yellowhead Jawfish

Opistognathus aurifrons
Family Opistognathidae (jawfishes)

🌐 South Florida and Bahamas, to Barbados and northern South America
⊙ Coastal coral reefs; lagoons, reef faces, slopes
↕ 3–50 m (10–163 ft) ↔ 10 cm (3.9 in)

Small to large colonies. Mostly one jawfish per burrow; pairs may share one for short period. Hovers over opening of burrow to capture passing zooplankton. Defends burrow from conspecifics and other small fishes that attempt to enter. At night closes burrow entrance with piece of rubble. Oral incubators: male holds egg ball in mouth until eggs hatch.

Banded Jawfish

Opistognathus macrognathus
Family Opistognathidae (jawfishes)

🌐 Florida, Gulf of Mexico and Bahamas, to northern South America
⊙ Coastal reefs; mixed sand/rubble flats, slopes
↕ 1–44 m (3.3–143 ft) ↔ 20 cm (4.7 in)

Solitary or in pairs or aggregations. Digs burrow with large jaws. Males move burrow closer to that of female during spawning season. Spawning peaks on day of full moon. Eggs develop in five days. Males larger than females. Does not hover in water column; instead peeks out of burrow opening. Feeds on benthic prey (including shrimps, isopods and small fishes) that come near burrow entrance.

⊕ Indonesia, Eastern Borneo and Philippines
☉ Coastal reefs; mixed sand/rubble flats, slopes
↧ 5–30 m (16–98 ft)   ↔ 12 cm (4.7 in)

Gold-specs Jawfish
Opistognathus randalli
Family Opistognathidae (jawfishes)

Solitary or in small colonies, but males strongly territorial. Burrow dweller that digs tunnels in sand. Spits mouthfuls of sand and rubble from abode. Usually seen with only head protruding from substrate, but if you remain still at a distance, will dash out occasionally to capture passing zooplankton. Sometimes males seen brooding eggs. When they hatch, larvae are spit into water column, where they begin planktonic life. Female has black spot on front of dorsal fin.

⊕ South Florida to Venezuela
☉ Coastal and outer coral reefs; lagoons, reef faces, slopes
↧ 3–25 m (10–81 ft)   ↔ 9.5 cm (3.7 in)

Redspotted Hawkfish
Amblycirrhitus pinos
Family Cirrhitidae (hawkfishes)

Solitary or in pairs. Usually found among sponges and coral growth. Feeds on zooplankton, small benthic crustaceans and worms. Haremic: male's territory includes one to several females. Male will spawn with one or more females at dusk. Only hawkfish in the Western Atlantic. Usually easy to approach.

Pixy Hawkfish

Cirrhitichthys falco
Family Cirrhitidae (hawkfishes)

⊕ Red Sea and southern Africa to Panama, north to Marianas Islands and south to New Caledonia
⊙ Coastal and outer coral reefs; lagoon coral heads, reef channels, reef faces, slopes
↕ 4–46 m (13–150 ft)   ↔ 7.0 cm (2.8 in)

Solitary and haremic. Rests on substrate (often live stony corals or at base of coral colonies) and easy to approach and photograph. Feeds on variety of small benthic invertebrates, mainly worms and small crustaceans. Male defends one to seven females. Sneaker males will attempt to steal females from harems of dominant males. Spawns daily.

Coral Hawkfish

Cirrhitichthys oxycephalus
Family Cirrhitidae (hawkfishes)

⊕ Red Sea and South Africa, to Panama and middle Gulf of California, north to Marianas and south to New Caledonia
⊙ Coral and rocky reefs; lagoon coral heads, reef channels, reef faces, slopes
↕ 1–40 m (3.3–132 ft)   ↔ 8.5 cm (3.3 in)

Haremic: male defends one to seven females. Spawns at dusk. Male nudges female and hops around her; pair then ascend in water column to release gametes. Sits on hard substrate; in some locations (Komodo) inhabits sea anemones. Feeds on crustaceans, worms and fish eggs.

🌐 Gulf of California, south to Colombia and most offshore islands
☉ Coastal and insular rocky reefs; boulder-strewn bottoms, reef walls
↧ 4–23 m (13–75 ft)   ↔ 52 cm (21 in)

Giant Hawkfish
Cirrhitus rivulatus
Family Cirrhitidae (hawkfishes)

Solitary. Feeds on crustaceans and fishes. Does most hunting after dark. Adults often perch in open on top of boulders. Juveniles more secretive, living in crevices and between rocks. Juveniles lack large spots of adults; banded instead.

🌐 East Africa and Red Sea, east to Panama
☉ Coastal and outer rocky and coral reefs; pinnacles, slopes
↧ 12–150 m (39–489 ft)   ↔ 13 cm (5.1 in)

Longnose Hawkfish
Oxycirrhites typus
Family Cirrhitidae (hawkfishes)

Usually in pairs, living on sea fans or gorgonians. Usually deeper than 25 m (81 ft). Feeds on crustaceans and small fishes. If prey too large to swallow whole, will bash it against rock to break into smaller-sized pieces. Spawns just before sunset.

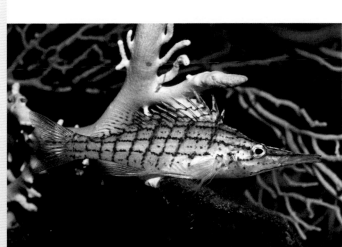

Arc-eye Hawkfish

Paracirrhites arcuatus
Family Cirrhitidae (hawkfishes)

⊕ East Africa to Hawaiian Islands, north to southern Japan and south to New Caledonia
⊙ Coastal and outer coral reefs; lagoon patch reefs, channels, reef faces, slopes
↧ 1–91 m (3.3–98 ft)   ↔ 14 cm (5.5 in)

Solitary and haremic. Perches on stony coral colonies, sheltering in coral at night. Feeds off seafloor and from water column, ingesting larger zooplanktons, crustaceans and small fishes. Male-dominated harems contain one to several females. Male vigorously defends harem; females non-territorial. Spawning occurs year-round, just before and after sunset.

Freckled Hawkfish

Paracirrhites forsteri
Family Cirrhitidae (hawkfishes)

⊕ Red Sea to Hawaiian, Line, Marquesas and Ducie Islands, north to southern Japan and south to Norfolk and Austral Islands
⊙ Coastal and outer coral reefs; lagoon patch reefs, reef faces, slopes
↧ 3–30 m (33–98 ft)   ↔ 22.5 cm (8.9 in)

Haremic, with one to three females living in male's territory. Has large mouth and thus can eat wide range of crustaceans and bony fishes. Sits on stony coral colonies much of the time, waiting for prey to pass by. Courtship and spawning occur just before and after sunset. Several different color forms but all with numerous spots on head.

⊕ Circumtropical
☉ Coastal and outer coral reefs; lagoon patch reefs, reef faces, slopes
↧ 1–20 m (3.3–66 ft)   ↔ 32 cm (13 in)

Glasseye
Heteropriacanthus cruentatus
Family Priacanthidae (bigeyes)

Nocturnal fish with large eyes, complete with reflective pigment layer on retina that allows better utilization of starlight or moonlight at night (also responsible for eye-shine). Occurs singly or in aggregations that hang out in caves or under overhangs during day and emerge to feed at dusk. Feeds on larger zooplankton and small fish. Usually red overall but will take on silver coloration when feeding above bottom.

⊕ Southern Africa and Red Sea to Marquesas Islands, north to southern Japan and south to northern Australia
☉ Coastal and outer coral reefs; lagoon pinnacles, reef faces, slopes
↧ 8–250 m (26–825 feet)   ↔ 40 cm (16 in)

Crescent-tail Bigeye
Priacanthus hamrur
Family Priacanthidae (bigeyes)

Solitary, although occasionally in large spawning assemblages. Hangs around crevices and cave entrances during day and hunts in water column at night. Feeds on larger zooplanktons, small fishes and benthic invertebrates. In some areas reproduces in the fall. Large eyes with tapetum lucidium: reflective layer on retina that helps it see in dark conditions and causes eye-shine. Has strongly lunate (crescent-shaped) tail; red overall or has light bands on body.

Flamefish

Apogon maculatus
Family Apogonidae (cardinalfishes)

⊕ New England and Bermuda, south to Venezuela, including Gulf of Mexico
⊙ Coastal and outer coral reefs; lagoon patch reefs, reef flats, reef faces, slopes; also seagrass and mangroves
↧ 1–127 m (3.3–413 ft)   ↔ 10.5 cm (4.1 in)

Solitary. Spends days in holes and crevices; moves out into open to feed at night. Feeds on zooplankton, benthic crustaceans and worms. Can be found hovering among spines of sea urchins. Male incubates 75–100 eggs in mouth until they hatch, at which time larvae enter plankton. Distinguished by black spot under second dorsal fin. Easy to approach.

Belted Cardinalfish

Apogon townsendi
Family Apogonidae (cardinalfishes)

⊕ South Florida and Bahamas, south to northern South America
⊙ Coastal and outer coral reefs; lagoon patch reefs, reef flats, reef faces, slopes
↧ 3–55 m (10–179 ft)   ↔ 6.5 cm (2.6 in)

Solitary. Hides in crevices and caves during day; sometimes aggregates in hideouts. Moves to nearby sand patches to feed at night. Feeds on swarming zooplankton. Will rise into water column to capture prey. Barred cardinalfish (*A. binotatus*) is similar species that has no bar on base of caudal fin, unlike *A. townsendi*.

🌐 Indonesia to Papua New Guinea, north to the Philippines and south to Great Barrier Reef
◉ Coastal and outer coral reefs; lagoon patch reefs, reef faces, slopes
↧ 4 to 35 m (13 to 115 ft)　　　　↔ 25 cm (9.8 in)

Tiger Cardinalfish

Cheilodipterus macrodon
Family Apogonidae (cardinalfishes)

Solitary. Hangs under ledges or in caves. Larger teeth and mouth betray predaceous habitats. Feeds mainly on small fishes, including blennies. Males often seen with eggs incubating in mouth. When they hatch, larvae are spit into water column and become pelagic for a time. Young individuals have yellow head and distinct spot before tail.

🌐 East Africa to Tonga, north to southern Japan and south to New Caledonia
◉ Coastal reefs; lagoons, reef faces, slopes
↧ 1–50 m (3.3–163 ft)　　　　↔ 14 cm (5.5 in)

Ringtailed Cardinalfish

Ostorhinchus aureus
Family Apogonidae (cardinalfishes)

Found in pairs or shoals. Occurs under overhangs as well as out in open during day but never strays far from cover when on its own. Males occasionally seen incubating eggs in mouth. Similar to flower cardinalfish (*O. fleurieu*), which has tail bar that is uniform in width, while it narrows in middle in *O. aureus*.

Split-banded Cardinalfish

Ostorhinchus compressus
Family Apogonidae (cardinalfishes)

⊕ Malaysia to Solomon Islands, north to Ryukyu Islands and south to Great Barrier Reef
⊙ Coastal and outer coral reefs; lagoon patch reefs, reef faces
↧ 1–20 m (3.3–66 ft)   ↔ 12 cm (4.7 in)

Adults form small to large groups; juveniles solitary. Hides among branching stony corals during day, leaving shelter to hunt at night. Feeds on zooplankton. Blue eyes and short white stripe on shoulder. Juvenile has area of yellow with black spot at tail base.

Yellowstriped Cardinalfish

Ostorhinchus cyanosoma
Family Apogonidae (cardinalfishes)

⊕ Indonesia, east to Fiji, north to southern Japan and south to Great Barrier Reef
⊙ Coastal and outer coral reefs; lagoon patch reefs, reef flats, reef faces, slopes
↧ 1–49 m (3.3–159 ft)   ↔ 8 cm (3.1 in)

Juveniles form groups; adults solitary or pairs. Occur in seagrass, among coral branches or tentacles (e.g., long-tentacled plate coral, *Heliofungia actiniformis*) or in spines of long-spined sea urchins. Feeds on zooplankton that live near seafloor. Male holds eggs in mouth, releasing larvae into water column after they hatch. Several similar species exhibit subtle differences in color and distribution.

⊕ Banggai Island and Lembeh Strait, Sulawesi, Indonesia
◉ Coastal coral reefs; sheltered bays, lagoons, reef faces
↧ 1–16 m (3.3–52 ft) ↔ 8 cm (3.1 in)

Banggai Cardinalfish
Pterapogon kauderni
Family Apogonidae (cardinalfishes)

Occurs singly or in pairs or aggregations. Found among spines of sea urchins (*Diadema*), in sea anemones (especially *Heteractis* spp.) and in seagrass meadows. In right microhabitat (large anemone) sometimes forms large groups. Spawns during day; female releases eggs, which male fertilizes and takes in mouth. After they hatch, male also holds young fish (up to 42) in mouth for up to 25 days before spitting them out.

⊕ Java to Papua New Guinea, north to the Ryukyu Islands and south to New Caledonia
◉ Coastal coral reefs; sheltered bays, lagoons, reef faces
↧ 1–10 m (3.3–33 ft) ↔ 8 cm (3.1 in)

Pajama Cardinalfish
Sphaeramia nematoptera
Family Apogonidae (cardinalfishes)

Adults occur in loose shoals, often among branching stony corals; juveniles solitary. Groups of adults disband at night to feed on small invertebrates near seafloor. Males brood eggs in mouth. Related polka-dot cardinalfish (*S. orbicularis*) is grayish silver with black spots; often found in mangroves and inshore habitats.

Chlupaty's Tilefish

Hoplolatilus chlupatyi
Family Malacanthidae (tilefishes)

⊕ Indonesia and Philippines
⊙ Sand and rubble fore-reef slopes
↓ 30–70 m (98–228 ft)　　　　↔ 13 cm (5.1 in)

Occurs singly or in small aggregations. Does not live in "home" burrow; instead uses burrows of other tilefish species that occupy same habitat. Capable of amazing color changes. Dorsal coloration can be salmon, orange, green, violet or blue. In as little as 15 seconds an individual may display 24 different colors! Most similar to juvenile bluehead tilefish (*H. starcki*), which are blue with yellow tail.

Blanquillo

Malacanthus latovitattus
Family Malacanthidae (tilefishes)

⊕ East Africa and Red Sea, east to Line Islands, north to southern Japan and south to New Caledonia
⊙ Outer coral reefs; reef faces, slopes
↓ 5–40 m (17–132 ft)　　　　↔ 35 cm (14 in)

Adults occur in pairs; juveniles solitary. Most often over sand/rubble slopes. Juveniles may mimic bluestreak cleaner wrasse. Moves in sinuous fashion, stopping occasionally to scan surroundings. Sometimes darts at prey near seafloor. Preys on small fishes and crustaceans.

⊕ South Carolina and Bermuda, to southern Brazil and east to Ascension Island
⊙ Outer coral reefs; sand and mixed sand/rubble slopes
↓ 2–50 m (7–163 ft)   ↔ 60 cm (24 in)

Sand Tilefish

Malacanthus plumieri
Family Malacanthidae (tilefishes)

Colony-forming but defends territory from conspecific intrusion. Digs burrow in sand and piles rubble around burrow to form large mounds up to 2 m (7 ft) wide) that serve as hiding place for many reef fishes. Feeds mainly on serpent stars, crustaceans and small fishes. Changes sex from female to male. Spawns year-round. In a single evening male may spawn with as many as six partners.

⊕ Circumtropical
⊙ Coastal habitats and open ocean (depending on host)
↓ 1–50 m (3.3–163 ft)   ↔ 1.1 m (3.6 ft)

Sharksucker

Echeneis naucrates
Family Echeneidae (discfishes)

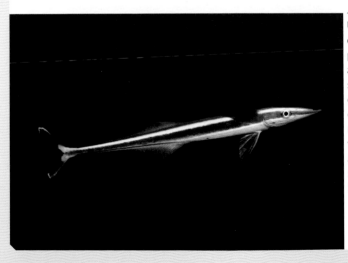

Usually solitary, although more than one may aggregate on host. Young prefer parrotfishes, trunkfishes and other smaller hosts; adults use sharks as host. Feeds on parasitic copepods and free-living crustaceans. Disc of a large suckerfish may measure up to 52 sq cm (8 sq in), which could exert a suction force of about 45.5 kg (100 lb). Often free-swimming; not as dependent on hosts as other disc fishes.

Gold-spotted Trevally

Carangoides fulvoguttatus
Family Carangidae (trevallies or jacks)

⊕ East Africa and Red Sea, east to Tonga, north to southern Japan and south to New Caledonia
⊙ Coastal and outer coral and rocky reefs; lagoons, reef faces, slopes
↕ 1–100 m (3.3–325 ft)   ↔ 1.2 m (3.9 ft)

Solitary or in schools. Feeds on crustaceans and fishes. Silver with gold or brassy spots and six faint bars on side. Orange-spotted trevally (*C. bajad*) can be silver with yellow on head and fins, have yellow spots or be yellow overall.

Giant Trevally

Caranx ignobilis
Family Carangidae (trevallies or jacks)

⊕ East Africa and Red Sea, east to Hawaiian Islands, north to southern Japan and south to Australia
⊙ Coral and rocky reefs; outer reef slopes
↕ 4–80 m (13–260 ft)   ↔ 1.6 m (5.4 ft)

Solitary. Feeds heavily on crustaceans, cephalopods and fishes, including schooling species (e.g., anchovies). Covers large distances, traveling as much as 5 km (3 mi) in a few months. Forms seasonal spawning groups during full moon; during this time males become much darker than females. Spawns in pairs. In some areas estuaries serve as nursery areas for young.

New England and Bermuda, south to Brazil, including Gulf of Mexico

Coastal and outer coral reefs; may enter brackish water and swim up rivers

1–140 m (3.3–455 ft)　　　101 cm (39.7 in)

Horse-eye Jack
Caranx latus
Family Carangidae (trevallies or jacks)

Occurs in small to large schools (sometimes mixes with other jack species). Adults found on offshore bank reefs; young fish found in coastal shallows. Feeds on variety of schooling fishes, crustaceans and other invertebrates. Will attack silverside prey among pier pilings (pilings apparently inhibit escape of prey species). Often approaches divers curiously.

East Africa and Red Sea, east to Panama, north to southern Japan and south to Australia

Coastal and outer coral and rocky reefs; usually reef faces, slopes

1–190 m (3.3–618 ft)　　　1 m (3.3 ft)

Bluefin Trevally
Caranx melampygus
Family Carangidae (trevallies or jacks)

Occurs singly or in roving schools. Moves over large home range. Feeds during day and at dusk in one area and takes refuge during night (sometimes in groups) in different part of reef. Über predator, feeding mainly on small reef fishes, but also eats some crustaceans and octopuses. Many different hunting tactics, including working cooperatively, driving schooling fishes into shallows before attacking.

Bar Jack
Carangoides ruber
Family Carangidae (trevallies or jacks)

🌐 New England and Bermuda, south to Venezuela, including Gulf of Mexico
◉ Coastal and outer coral reefs; lagoons, back reefs, reef faces, slopes
↧ 1–22 m (3.3–72 ft)　　　　↔ 60 cm (23.6 in)

Solitary or forms schools. Voracious predator that will attack small fishes and crustaceans. Opportunistic, following fishes that disturb substrate, such as stingrays and eels, attacking prey they expose. Young fish may clean other fishes of parasites; adults visit bluehead wrasse and Spanish hogfish cleaning stations. Take on bronze hue when being cleaned.

Bigeye Trevally
Caranx sexfasciatus
Family Carangidae (trevallies or jacks)

🌐 East Africa and Red Sea, east to Eastern Pacific, north to southern Japan and south to Australia
◉ Coastal and outer coral and rocky reefs; usually outer reef faces, slopes
↧ 2–50 m (7–163 ft)　　　　↔ 80 cm (32 in)

Occurs in schools, often consisting of hundreds or even thousands of individuals. Transient; groups do not remain in same place for long. At night individuals may disperse to feed. Diet of shrimp, mantis shrimp, small fishes and (in some locations) sea-skaters (marine insects). When spawning, pairs leave shoal, swimming side by side. Male becomes dark just before spawning.

⊕ Circumtropical
◉ Coastal and outer coral and rocky reefs; usually outer reef faces, slopes; also open ocean.
↧ 2–150 m (7–488 ft)   ↹ 1.8 m (5.9 ft)

Rainbow Runner
Elagatis bipinnulatus
Family Carangidae (trevallies or jacks)

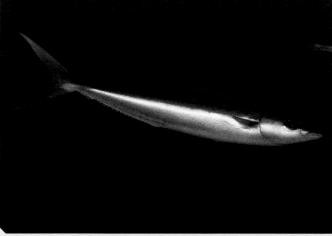

Solitary or in schools (sometimes large). Feeds on large zooplankton and small fishes. Sometimes associates with sharks, chafing against sides or tails of the larger predators. Group spawns, releasing pelagic eggs high in water column.

⊕ East Africa and Red Sea, east to Eastern Pacific, including Gulf of California
◉ Coastal and outer coral and rocky reefs; lagoons, reef faces, slopes
↧ 2–50 m (7–163 ft)   ↹ 1.2 m (3.9 ft)

Golden Trevally
Gnathanodon speciosus
Family Carangidae (trevallies or jacks)

Solitary or in schools (young fish almost always in schools). Engages in piloting behavior (especially young), swimming in front of other fishes such as sharks, manta rays and pufferfishes. Young may also associate with sea jellies. When hunting, schools descend to seafloor and work over sand or hard substrates with protrusible toothless jaws. Eats worms, crustaceans, mollusks and small fishes. Feeds during day. Juvenile shown here.

Yellowband Scad

Selar boops
Family Carangidae (trevallies or jacks)

- ⊕ Andaman Sea to Australia and north to Micronesia
- ⊙ Coastal and outer reefs; lagoons, reef faces, slopes
- ↧ 1–170 m (3.3–553 ft)
- ↔ 22 cm (8.8 in)

Shoaling species. Sometimes takes refuge in shallow water during day. Feeds mainly on small fishes (including schooling species) and invertebrates. In turn is eaten by sharks and jacks. Forms spawning groups. Yellow streak on flank not always present. Similar to bigeye scad (*S. crumenophthalmus*).

Snubnose Pompano

Trachinotus blochi
Family Carangidae (trevallies or jacks)

- ⊕ East Africa and Red Sea, east to Samoa, north to southern Japan and south to Australia
- ⊙ Coastal and outer reefs; bays, estuaries, reef faces, slopes
- ↧ 1–50 m (3.3–163 ft)
- ↔ 65 cm (26 in)

Young fish more likely to school; adults solitary. Feeds mainly on mollusks and crustaceans grubbed out of sand or mud bottoms. Dorsal, anal and caudal fins often yellow; large individuals may be golden yellow ventrally.

- New England and Bermuda, south to Brazil, including Gulf of Mexico
- Coastal inshore habitats, most often over sandy areas adjacent to reefs
- 1–30 m (3.3–98 ft)   ↔ 1.2 m (4 ft)

Permit
Trachinotus falcatus
Family Carangidae (trevallies or jacks)

Often forms small schools (10 individuals) but sometimes much larger groups, typically near reefs, wreckage or jetties. Adults feed mainly on mollusks, crustaceans and sea urchins rooted from sand and mud. Teeth on tongue and in pharynx to crush prey. Juveniles feed more on plankton. Lives more than 25 years. Sharks and barracuda are primary enemies.

- Ecuador and Peru, including Revillagigedo and Galapagos Islands
- Coastal and insular rocky reefs; steep walls and slopes
- 1–25 m (3.3–81 ft)   ↔ 30 cm (11.8 in)

Steel Pompano
Trachinotus stilbe
Family Carangidae (trevallies or jacks)

Schooling species, often in large schools. Most often near offshore islands. Prefers areas with strong current. Feeds on large zooplankton, sometimes near water's surface causing the sea surface to churn. White bar behind head.

Schoolmaster

Lutjanus apodus

Family Lutjanidae (snappers)

- ⊕ New England and Bermuda, south to Brazil, including Gulf of Mexico
- ⊙ Coastal and outer coral reefs; lagoons, mangroves, seagrass, reef faces, slopes
- ↧ 2–63 m (7–205 ft)
- ↔ 67 cm (26.4 in)

Found singly or in resting groups during day that disperse to feeding grounds at night. Hangs among gorgonians or stony coral stands. Sometimes enters river mouths with brackish conditions. Diet includes fishes, crustaceans, worms, snails and squid. Yellow fins; juveniles are barred. Wary but not difficult to approach if you move slowly.

Red Snapper

Lutjanus bohar

Family Lutjanidae (snappers)

- ⊕ East Africa and Red Sea to Marquesas and Tuamotu Islands, north to Ryukyu Islands and south to Lord Howe Island
- ⊙ Coastal and outer coral reefs; lagoons, reef channels, reef faces, slopes
- ↧ 1–180 m (3.3–585 ft)
- ↔ 90 cm (36 in)

Solitary. Takes refuge in caves or under overhangs. Juveniles aggressive mimics of certain chromis damsels. Feeds on bivalves, snails, cephalopods, crustaceans and fishes. In some areas spawn year-round (may peak at certain times of year). Adults red to pinkish gray overall with clear groove in front of eye.

- New England, south to Brazil, including Gulf of Mexico
- Coastal and outer coral reefs; lagoons, reef faces, slopes
- 1–55 m (3.3–179 ft) ↔ 160 cm (63 in)

Cubera Snapper
Lutjanus cyanopterus
Family Lutjanidae (snappers)

Solitary or in aggregations. Voracious predator that eats fishes and crustaceans; important predator of spiny lobster. Off Belize forms large spawning groups (as many as 10,000 individuals) in offshore habitats. Spawning groups often attract whale sharks, which feed on gametes. Spawning occurs from June to August. Fairly undistinctive species: gray or dark brown overall. Solitary individuals wary and difficult to approach, but individuals in spawning groups often oblivious to divers.

- East Africa and Red Sea, east to Society Islands, north to southern Japan and south to Australia
- Coastal and outer coral and rocky reefs; seagrass meadows, lagoons, reef channels, reef faces, slopes
- 1–150 m (3.3–488 ft) ↔ 50 cm (20 in)

Humpback Snapper
Lutjanus gibbus
Family Lutjanidae (snappers)

Solitary or in schools. Forms stationary groups during day (especially mid-sized individuals), sometimes with other snappers. Groups drift near reef edge. Most hunting done after dark. Feeds on wide range of benthic invertebrates, including cephalopods, crustaceans, echinoderms, serpent stars and fishes. Forms spawning assemblages around full moon.

Gray Snapper

Lutjanus griseus

Family Lutjanidae (snappers)

- ⊕ New England and Bermuda, south to Brazil, including Gulf of Mexico
- ⊙ Coastal and outer coral reefs; lagoons, seagrass, mangroves, estuaries, reef faces, slopes
- ↧ 1–180 m (3.3 to 585 ft)
- ↔ 89 cm (35 in)

Solitary and in aggregations. Young most often in shallow seagrass and mangrove habitats; adults in offshore habitats. Feeds on smaller fishes, crustaceans, snails and cephalopods. Most feeding occurs after dark. Spawns at dusk, usually offshore in larger groups. Female may produce 1.1–5.9 million eggs. Lives for at least 24 years. Gray or reddish brown overall, often with dark line running from lip through eye.

Bluestripe Snapper

Lutjanus kasmira

Family Lutjanidae (snappers)

- ⊕ Red Sea to Marquesas and Tuamotu Islands, north to southern Japan and south to Lord Howe Island; introduced around Hawaiian Islands
- ⊙ Outer coral reefs; lagoons, reef channels, reef faces, slopes
- ↧ 1–265 m (3.3–875 ft)
- ↔ 35 cm (13.8 in)

Juveniles inhabit seagrass meadows or found around patch reefs. Adults congregate near prominent reef features; also shelters in caves. At night adults move onto sandy habitat to feed. Eats crustaceans, cephalopods and small fishes. Courtship begins when male nips and rubs female's body. More than one male may join the pair, with as many as 10 males spiraling up with single females to release gametes.

⊕ Red Sea and East Africa, east to Solomon Islands
☉ Coastal and outer reefs; lagoon patch reefs, reef faces, slopes
↧ 10–90 m (3.3–293 ft)   ↔ 30 cm (12 in)

Bigeye Snapper
Lutjanus lutjanus
Family Lutjanidae (snappers)

During day, adults often in large aggregations that mill around caves or coral promontories until night falls. They then move into adjacent habitats to feed. Indian snapper (*L. madras*) is similar species but lacks prominent yellow line down side and has greater distance between tip of snout and eye.

⊕ Baja and Gulf of California, south to Ecuador and many offshore islands
☉ Coastal and insular rocky reefs; reef faces, slopes
↧ 3–28 m (10–91 ft)   ↔ 30 cm (12 in)

Blue and Gold Snapper
Lutjanus viridis
Family Lutjanidae (snappers)

Occurs in small to large schools; occasionally solitary where not abundant. Diurnal groups drift over boulder-strewn bottoms or along reef face over sand, often mixing with groups of grunts when feeding. Groups apparently disperse at dusk to feed on surrounding reef and sand bottom. Diet consists of crustaceans and small fishes.

Midnight Snapper
Macolor macularis
Family Lutjanidae (snappers)

⊕ Maldives to Fiji, north to Yaeyama Islands and south to New Caledonia
⊙ Coastal and outer coral reefs; bays, reef channels; reef faces, slopes
↕ 3–50 m (10–163 ft)
↔ 60 cm (24 in)

Solitary or in loose groups. Juveniles always on own; adults sometimes form large groups. Nocturnal species that feeds on relatively small prey, namely zooplankton. Long gill-rakers help strain small prey items. Adults have blue spots and lines on head and fins. Similar juveniles of black snapper (*M. niger*) have white-tipped instead of clear tail lobes.

Yellowtail Snapper
Ocyurus chrysurus
Family Lutjanidae (snappers)

⊕ New England and Bermuda, south to Brazil, including Gulf of Mexico
⊙ Coastal and outer coral reefs; lagoons, reef faces, slopes; juveniles in seagrass beds
↕ 1–180 m (3.3–585 ft)
↔ 76 cm (29.2 in)

Found singly or in loose groups. Swims above reef looking for feeding opportunities. Follows substrate-disturbing species (e.g., stingrays, goatfishes). Also feeds frequently after dark. Primary diet fishes, crabs and shrimps. Spawns year-round in many locations; some sites exhibit seasonal peaks. Females produce 100,000–1.5 million eggs per spawn. May be aggressive mimic of yellow goatfish. Can live 14 years or more.

- 🌐 Malaysia to Papua New Guinea, north to Ryukyu Islands and south to Great Barrier Reef
- ⊙ Coastal and outer coral reefs; deep lagoons, reef faces, slopes
- ↧ 2–50 m (7–163 ft)   ↔ 100 cm (39.4 in)

Chinaman Fish
Symphorus nematophorus
Family Lutjanidae (snappers)

Solitary. Adults more often in deep water, juveniles in shallows. Feeds mostly on fishes but also eats crustaceans and mollusks. Forms spawning assemblages. Similar to sailfin snapper (*Symphorichthys spilurus*), which also has blue lines on body, but has large back spot at tail base.

- 🌐 East Africa, east to Line Islands, north to southern Japan and south to Great Barrier Reef
- ⊙ Coastal and outer coral reefs; patch reefs, reef faces, slopes
- ↧ 7–30 m (23–98 ft)   ↔ 40 cm (16 in)

Blue and Yellow Fusilier
Caesio teres
Family Caesionidae (fusiliers)

Occurs in schools. Feeds in water column on zooplankton. Forms spawning groups sometimes numbering more than 1,000 individuals. Group spawns around time of full moon. Similar to yellowback fusilier (*C. xanthonota*) but has yellow from top of head, down back to tail.

Ruddy Fusilier

Pterocaesio pisang

Family Caesionidae (fusiliers)

🌐 East Africa, east to Fiji, north to Ryukyu Islands and south to New Caledonia
☉ Coastal and outer coral reefs; lagoons, reef faces, slopes
↧ 7–30 m (23–98 ft)   ↔ 21 cm (8.3 in)

Schooling fish with as many as 100 in group. Sometimes forms mixed schools with other fusiliers. Found in current-prone habitats, where feeds on zooplankton. Blue-green on back and pinkish on belly, with dark tips on tail; yellow eyes and snout.

Bluestreak Fusilier

Pterocaesio tile

Family Caesionidae (fusiliers)

🌐 East Africa to Marquesas Islands, north to southern Japan and south to New Caledonia
☉ Coastal and outer coral reefs; reef faces, slopes
↧ 1–60 m (3.3–195 ft)   ↔ 25 cm (9.8 in)

Occurs in dense schools that feed high in water column on zooplankton. Prefers current-prone habitats. At night hides in reef crevices and among stony corals. Iridescent blue stripe along side; base color at night mainly brick red.

- Red Sea to Samoa, north to Ryukyu Islands and south to New Caledonia
- Coastal coral reefs; lagoons, estuaries
- 1–12 m (3.3–39 ft)   ↔ 35 cm (14 in)

Oblong Mojarra
Gerres oblongus
Family Gerreidae (mojarras)

Solitary or in loose groups. Feeds by digging polychaete worms and small crustaceans from sand bottom. Also bites off siphon tips of burrowing clams. Juveniles feed on some algae. In some locations forms breeding groups near outer edge of reef.

- Gulf of California, south to Peru, including offshore islands
- Coastal and outer coral reefs; lagoons, channels, reef faces, slopes
- 3–30 m (10–98 ft)   ↔ 51 cm (20 in)

Burrito Grunt
Anisotremus interruptus
Family Haemulidae (grunts)

Solitary and in groups. During day forms loose groups along edges of rocky reefs. Large individuals more often solitary. Does some feeding during day, but most prey intake occurs after dark, when disperses over rocky reef to find food. Annelid worms, mollusks, crustaceans and small fishes eaten.

Black Margate
Anisotremus surinamensis
Family Haemulidae (grunts)

⊕ Florida to Brazil, including Gulf of Mexico
⊙ Coastal and outer coral reefs; lagoon patch reefs, reef faces, slopes
↓ 3–60 m (10–195 ft)   ↔ 76 cm (29.9 in)

Solitary or in small groups. Resides at entrances of caves, under overhangs or among wreckage. Primary food sea urchins, which are crushed with pharyngeal tooth plates; often has purple spots on lips caused by spine penetration. Feeds on crustaceans, mollusks and small benthic fishes to a lesser degree. Most foraging occurs after dark. Occasionally visits wrasse cleaning stations. High arching back and dark patch of scales on side make it easy to identify.

Porkfish
Anisotremus virginicus
Family Haemulidae (grunts)

⊕ Bermuda and Florida, south to Brazil
⊙ Coastal and outer coral reefs; lagoon patch reefs, reef faces, slopes
↓ 3–40 m (10 to 130 ft)   ↔ 41 cm (16.1 in)

Solitary or in groups. Found on shallow walls, under ledges or at cave mouths or under large plating elkhorn coral. Groups disperse at night to feed in adjacent habitats. Adults feed on wide variety of invertebrates, including mollusks, crustaceans, worms and serpent stars. Juveniles regularly clean; adults parasite-pick on rare occasions. Tends to be oblivious of divers.

- South Carolina and Bermuda, south to Brazil
- Coastal and outer coral reefs; lagoon patch reefs, back reefs, reef faces, slopes
- 1–20 m (3.3–65 ft)   ↔ 30 cm (11.8 in)

French Grunt
Haemulon flavolineatum
Family Haemulidae (grunts)

Solitary or in groups. Adult groups mill among elkhorn corals, ship wreckage, sponges or sea fans. Groups can consist of thousands of individuals in areas where species is abundant. Move to feeding area at night and then disperse to hunt worms, chitons, sea cucumbers, cephalopods, crustaceans and echinoderms. Individuals will face off, open jaws wide and push against each other (known as kissing displays).

- New England and Bermuda, south to Brazil, including Gulf of Mexico
- Coastal and outer coral reefs; lagoon patch reefs, reef faces, slopes
- 3–29 m (10–94 ft)   ↔ 45 cm (17.7 in)

White Grunt
Haemulon plumieri
Family Haemulidae (grunts)

Solitary or in shoals. Seagrass beds serve as nursery area for young. Adults groups drift over reef, often in gorgonian fields or under overhangs. Does not move off reef in groups; solitary individuals hunt on reef or nearby habitats. Individuals will engage in kissing displays (see French grunt, above). Forms spawning groups in spring. Easy to approach, especially when in groups. Stripes on head are distinguishing characteristic.

Bluestriped Grunt

Haemulon sciurus
Family Haemulidae (grunts)

- ⊕ South Carolina and Bermuda, south to Brazil, including Gulf of Mexico
- ☉ Coastal and outer coral reefs; lagoon patch reefs, back reefs, reef faces, slopes
- ↧ 1–20 m (3.3–65 ft)
- ↔ 45 cm (17.7 in)

Solitary or in groups. Juveniles more abundant in seagrass beds. Adults hover near reef drop-offs or over patch reefs, often among gorgonians and sponges. Groups migrate to feeding habitats (e.g., seagrass beds, rubble and sand bottoms) after dark, then break up to feed on crustaceans, worms, snails, bivalves and sea urchins. Easy to approach, especially when in groups.

Graybar Grunt

Haemulon sexfasciatum
Family Haemulidae (grunts)

- ⊕ Gulf of California, south to Panama and Galapagos Islands
- ☉ Coastal and insular rocky reefs; rock-strewn bottoms
- ↧ 3–30 m (10–98 ft)
- ↔ 71 cm (28 in)

Solitary and in shoals. Forms "roosting groups" during day but at night disperses to surrounding sand flats and slopes to hunt. Feeds on worms, clams, crustaceans and small fishes, some dug from sand. Also does some feeding during day among rocks.

⊕ East Africa to Samoa, north to Ryukyu Islands and south to Mauritius and New Caledonia
◉ Coastal and outer coral reefs; lagoons, reef channels, reef faces, slopes
↕ 1–30 m (3.3–98 ft)   ↔ 86 cm (33.9 in)

Many-spotted Sweetlips

Plectorhinchus chaetodonoides
Family Haemulidae (grunts)

Solitary or in groups (adults only). Adults hide during day under table corals or ledges or in caves. Frequent visitor to cleaning stations. At night feeds on mollusks, crustaceans and small fishes. Juveniles exhibit unusual swimming behavior, with head down and undulating body; appearance and behavior may mimic swimming flatworm.

⊕ Philippines and Bali to Niue, north to Ryukyu Islands and south to New Caledonia
◉ Coastal and outer reefs; lagoon patch reefs, channels, reef faces, slopes
↕ 2–50 m (7–163 ft)   ↔ 72 cm (28 in)

Diagonal-banded Sweetlips

Plectorhinchus lineatus
Family Haemulidae (grunts)

Adults found singly or in groups. Refuging groups form at bases of bommies, under overhangs or in cave entrances during day. When sun goes down, individuals move onto shallow sand and reef flats to feed. Juveniles occur singly. Diet primarily crustaceans. Forms spawning groups at new moon.

Ribbon Sweetlips

Plectorhinchus polytaenia
Family Haemulidae (grunts)

- Bali to Papua New Guinea, north to Philippines and south to northwestern Australia
- Coastal and outer coral reefs; lagoons, channels, reef faces, slopes
- 3–40 m (10–130 ft)
- 50 cm (19.7 in)

During day adults often take refuge in groups in current-prone areas, hanging under ledges or table corals. At night moves into sandy habitat to forage on bivalves, worms and crustaceans.

Oriental Sweetlips

Plectorhinchus vittatus
Family Haemulidae (grunts)

- East Africa to Samoa, north to Ryukyu Islands and south to Mauritius and New Caledonia
- Coastal and outer coral reefs; lagoons, reef faces, slopes
- 2–25 m (7–81 ft)
- 86 cm (33.9 in)

Solitary or in small groups. Diet consists of variety of invertebrates living in sand flats and on slopes adjacent to reefs. Moves into these areas at night to feed. Similar to diagonal-banded sweetlips (*P. lineatus*) but has black lines down body and yellow on fins and head (black lines diagonal in *P. lineatus*). Juvenile in inset photo.

- 🌐 Florida, south to northern South America
- ⊙ Coastal and outer coral reefs; reef faces, slopes
- ↧ 15–50 m (49–165 ft)
- ↔ 23 cm (9.1 in)

Boga
Inermia vittata
Family Inermiidae (bonnetmouths)

Schooling fish found on clear offshore reefs. Feeds on zooplankton. Sometimes mixes with zooplankton-feeding Creole wrasse. Belongs to bonnetmouth family Inermiidae but sometimes erroneously included in grunt family. Active, nervous fish, often difficult to approach.

- 🌐 Cocos-Keeling Islands, east to Tuamotu Islands, north to southern Japan and south to Lord Howe Island
- ⊙ Coastal and outer coral reefs; seagrass meadows, lagoons, outer reef slopes
- ↧ 2–25 m (7–81 ft)
- ↔ 50 cm (19.7 in)

Yellowtail Emperor
Lethrinus atkinsoni
Family Lethrinidae (emperors)

Solitary or in small groups. Feeds on mollusks, crustaceans and fishes. Shoves snout into soft substrate and sorts out edible infaunal creatures. Uses molar-like teeth to crush hard-shelled prey; spits out sand. May change sex from female to male. Yellow around eye and yellow tail.

Longface Emperor

Lethrinus olivaceus
Family Lethrinidae (emperors)

⊕ East Africa and Red Sea, east to Line Islands, north to southern Japan and south to New Caledonia
⊙ Coastal and outer coral reefs; lagoons, outer reef slopes
↕ 1–185 m (3.3–601 ft)   ↔ 1 m (3.3 ft)

Solitary or in groups (sometimes quite large). Feeds at night on invertebrates that hide in sand. Prefers hard-shelled invertebrates but also eats squid and fishes. Changes sex from female to male. Spawns in groups on reef edge a few days past new moon. Males suffused with crimson during spawning season.

Humpnose Bigeye Bream

Monotaxis grandoculis
Family Lethrinidae (emperors)

⊕ Red Sea to Hawaiian Islands, north to Ryukyu Islands and south to New Caledonia
⊙ Coastal and outer reefs; sandy lagoon flats, outer slopes
↕ 1–100 m (3.3–330 ft)   ↔ 60 cm (24 in)

Young fish solitary; adults on own or form loose groups (up to 50 individuals). Groups often hover near edge of reef, over sand substrate, and disperse after dark to feed. Feeds on mollusks, crustaceans, serpent stars and sea urchins. Forms spawning groups. Juveniles have four white lines on body that can be turned off and on. Juvenile in inset photo.

- Laccadive Islands, east to Fiji, north to southern Japan and south to Lord Howe Island
- Coastal and outer coral reefs; coral patches in lagoons, back reefs, reef faces, slopes
- 1 to 30 m (3.3 to 98 ft)   ↔ 23 cm (9.1 in)

Bridled Monocle Bream
Scolopsis bilineata
Family Nemipteridae (breams)

Juveniles solitary; adults often in pairs. On rare occasions in large aggregations. Juveniles tend to be found in areas with coral cover; adults stray farther over adjacent sand bottoms. Adults often followed by wrasses and other opportunistic followers. Sometimes follows goatfishes. Protogynous hermaphrodite. Mimics poison-fang blennies.

- North Carolina and Bermuda, south to Brazil
- Coastal and outer coral reefs; lagoons, reef faces, slopes
- 1–75 m (3.3–244 ft)   ↔ 56 cm (22 in)

Saucereye Porgy
Calamus calamus
Family Sparidae (sea breams and porgies)

Solitary. Young fish found in seagrass beds; adults more often near coral reefs. Takes mouthfuls of substrate as probes for prey. Main diet bivalves, worms, crabs, brittle stars and sea urchins. Incisor-like teeth in front of jaws to grasp prey; molar-like teeth in sides of jaws to crush them. Very wary and difficult to approach.

Spotted Drum
Equetus punctatus
Family Sciaeniidae (drums)

- Florida and Bermuda, south to Brazil
- Coastal and outer coral reefs; lagoon patch reefs, back reefs, reef faces, slopes
- 5–30 m (15–98 ft)
- 25 cm (9.8 in)

Solitary. Usually found under overhangs or in crevices and caves during day. Moves out from refuges at night to hunt. Main foods crabs, shrimps and small snails. Very long dorsal fin (more so in juvenile); adults have white spots on rear dorsal fin and tail. Similar jackknife fish (*E. lanceolatus*) lacks spots and juvenile has dash on snout, where young *E. punctatus* has spot.

Yellow Goatfish
Mulloidichthys martinicus
Family Mullidae (goatfishes)

- Florida and Bermuda, south to Brazil, including Gulf of Mexico
- Coastal and outer coral reefs; lagoons, reef faces, slopes
- 1–49 m (3.3–159 ft)
- 40 cm (15.7 in)

Young fish found in seagrass meadows; adults take refuge at reef–sand margin of reef face during day. At night moves onto adjacent sand habitats to hunt. Uses sensory chin barbels to locate buried prey, namely crustaceans, worms, bivalves and serpent stars. Occasionally feeds during day and often followed by opportunistic predators (e.g., jacks, wrasses). Two spawning peaks: February to March and September to October.

⊕ Red Sea to Hawaiian, Marquesas and Tuamotu Islands, north to southern Japan and south to Lord Howe Island

⊙ Coastal and outer coral reefs; lagoons, reef flats, reef faces, slopes

↧ 1–113 m (3.3–367 ft)   ↦ 38 cm (15.0 in)

Yellowfin Goatfish
Mulloidichthys vanicolensis
Family Mullidae (goatfishes)

Juveniles solitary or in small groups. Adults in large schools that hang near lagoon patch reefs or under ledges. At night shoals disperse onto surrounding sand habitats to feed. Diet consists of gastropods, brittle stars and echinoids. Similar to yellowstripe goatfish (*M. flavo-lineatus*) but yellowfin has shorter snout and no blue trim along yellow lateral stripe. Yellow stripe of *M. vanicolensis* changes into oblong dusky blotch when it hunts.

⊕ East Africa to Tuamotu and Marquesas Islands, north to southern Japan and south to Lord Howe Island

⊙ Coastal and outer coral reefs; lagoons, reef faces, slopes

↧ 5–100 m (16–325 ft)   ↦ 40 cm (15.7 in)

Dash-dot Goatfish
Parupeneus barberinus
Family Mullidae (goatfishes)

Found singly or in groups (juveniles more often group than adults). Occurs over sand and mud. Feeds mostly on polychaetes and crustaceans. Vigorously displaces substrate using barbels, creating large clouds of sediment. Often followed by wrasses and small jacks. Easy to approach, especially when feeding. Two color morphs: yellow phase has yellow line above black line that extends from eye to base of caudal fin; pale phase lacks yellow coloration.

Spotted Goatfish
Pseudupeneus maculatus
Family Mullidae (goatfishes)

🌐 New Jersey and Bermuda, south to Brazil, including Gulf of Mexico
⊙ Coastal and outer coral reefs; lagoons, reef faces, slopes (on sand and rubble)
↧ 1–35 m (3.3 to 114 ft)   ↔ 30 cm (11.9 in)

Solitary or in small groups. Uses barbels to flip debris and probe sand in attempt to locate prey. Main foods include crabs, shrimps, worms and small fishes. Does most of its hunting during day. Forms mixed aggregations with grunts, wrasses and surgeonfishes. Often accompanied by wrasses as it feeds. At night lies on bottom and color becomes pale. Group or pair spawner.

Golden Sweeper
Parapriacanthus ransonneti
Family Pempheridae (sweepers)

🌐 Seychelles, east to Fiji, north to southern Japan and south to Western Australia and Lord Howe and Norfolk Islands
⊙ Coastal and outer coral reefs; lagoon patch reefs, reef faces, slopes
↧ 3–30 m (10–98 ft)   ↔ 10 cm (3.9 in)

Occurs in schools. Hides under overhangs and caves during day; moves out to feed on zooplankton at night. Yellow and gold on anterior portion of body and head. Posterior part of body is reddish; vertical black line at base of tail. Closely related *P. guentheri* known from Maldives and Red Sea.

- Florida to Brazil
- Coastal and outer coral reefs; lagoon patch reefs, reef faces, slopes
- 3–30 m (10–98 ft)   ↔ 15 cm (5.9 in)

Glassy (Copper) Sweeper

Pempheris schomburgkii
Family Pempheridae (sweepers)

Tends to prefer clear water, often in shipwrecks and among pier pilings. Groups spend day milling in caves or under overhangs. At night moves out to feed on nocturnal zooplankton. Easy fish to approach. Differentiated from sympatric short-fin sweeper (*P. poeyi*) by dark band at base of anal fin (*P. poeyi* has no markings).

- Red Sea to Samoa, north to Philippines; also Mediterranean Sea
- Coastal and outer coral and rocky reefs; lagoon patch reefs, reef faces, slopes
- 2–25 m (7–81 ft)   ↔ 20 cm (7.9 in)

Vanikoro Sweeper

Pempheris vanicolensis
Family Pempheridae (sweepers)

Found in schools. Inhabits caves or large recesses among coral branches. Leaves hiding place at dusk to feed on zooplankton, returning to same diurnal haunt before dawn. Black margin on anal fin, black tip on dorsal fin and black margin on rear edge of caudal fin.

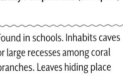

Ray-Finned Fishes

Threadfin Butterflyfish
Chaetodon auriga
Family Chaetodontidae
(butterflyfishes)

🌐 Red Sea to Hawaiian, Marquesas and Ducie Islands, north to southern Japan and south to Lord Howe and Rapa Islands
◉ Coastal and outer coral reefs; also rocky reefs; lagoons, reef flats, reef faces, slopes
↕ 1–61 m (3.3–198 ft)　　　　↔ 23 cm (9.1 in)

Adults occur singly or in pairs (most often) or small groups. Omnivore that feeds on soft corals, stony corals, polychaete worms, anemones and hard corals. Forages among coral rubble, in reef crevices and on sand. Only butterflyfish that will associate with foraging goatfishes. At night returns to traditional shelter site, from which it will chase intruding conspecifics and other fishes (including groupers and damsels).

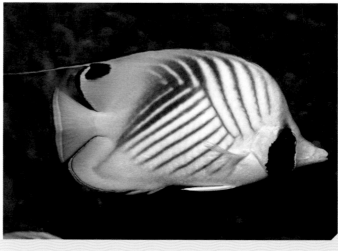

Foureye Butterflyfish
Chaetodon capistratus
Family Chaetodontidae
(butterflyfishes)

🌐 Bermuda south to Venezuela, including Gulf of Mexico
◉ Coastal and outer coral reefs; lagoon patch reefs, back reefs, reef faces, slopes
↕ 1–20 m (3.3–65 ft)　　　　↔ 15 cm (5.9 in)

Found singly or in pairs (rarely forms groups). Found on soft, coral-rich reefs. Feeds heavily on polyps of soft corals, stony corals and zoanthids (eats worms, tiny crustaceans and tunicates to a lesser degree). Pairs forage and take refuge at night in specific home range. Courts and spawns over prominent reef features; spawning takes place just after sunset. Pair sometimes interrupted by bachelor males that attempt to steal paired female; in most cases bachelor is chased away by paired male.

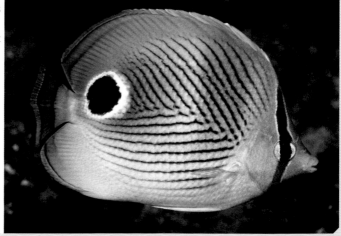

⊕ Southeast Arabian peninsula and Gulf of Oman, north to Pakistan, east to Bali and south to Maldives
⊙ Coastal and outer coral and rocky reefs; lagoons, reef flats, reef faces, slopes
↧ 3–15 m (10–49 ft)   ↔ 16 cm (6.3 in)

White Collar Butterflyfish

Chaetodon collare

Family Chaetodontidae (butterflyfishes)

Forms pairs or groups (up to 20 individuals). Sometimes forms groups with bannerfish. Feeds on coral polyps, fan worms and algae. Known to spawn between November and May in Indian Ocean (may be affected by monsoon season). Young fish lacks red tail. Adults easy to approach and photograph.

⊕ Cocos-Keeling to Hawaiian Islands, north to southern Japan and south to Rapa Islands
⊙ Coastal and outer coral reefs; lagoons, reef flats, reef faces, slopes
↧ 1–30 m (3.3–98 ft)   ↔ 23 cm (9.1 in)

Saddled Butterflyfish

Chaetodon ephippium

Family Chaetodontidae (butterflyfishes)

Adults found singly or in pairs; juveniles solitary. Pairs live in large home range; sometimes separate for a while but exhibit elaborate greeting display when reunite. Feeds on algae and variety of inveretbrates, including stony corals, sponges, tunicates and worms. Has been known to crossbreed with other butterflyfishes.

Blacklip Butterflyfish
Chaetodon kleinii
Family Chaetodontidae
(butterflyfishes)

⊕ East Africa to Hawaii and Samoa, north to southern Japan and south to Lord Howe Island
⊙ Coastal and outer coral reefs; lagoons, reef flats, reef faces, slopes
↧ 4–122 m (13–397 ft)   ↔ 23 cm (9.1 in)

Adults occur singly or in pairs or small groups. Feeds on filamentous algae and macroalgae fronds, soft coral polyps, anemones, hydroids, minute benthic crustaceans and zooplankton. Groups also attack damselfish nests, overwhelming defending damsel. Also swims into water column to eat plankton with other zooplanktivores.

Raccoon Butterflyfish
Chaetodon lunula
Family Chaetodontidae
(butterflyfishes)

⊕ East Africa to Hawaiian Islands, north to southern Japan and south to Lord Howe and Rapa Islands
⊙ Rocky and coral reefs; lagoon patch reefs, reef flats, reef channels, reef faces, slopes
↧ 1–70 m (3.3–228 ft)   ↔ 20 cm (7.9 in)

Young fish solitary; adults found singly or in pairs (usually) or groups. Groups sometimes take refuge under overhangs during day; tends to do most of feeding after dark. At night, hunt for opisthobranch mollusks, sea anemones, tunicates, polychaete worms, peanut worms, small crustaceans and sea urchin tube feet. In some locales does more diurnal hunting, feeding more on corals. Relatively large eyes compared to other butterflyfishes, which may be adaptation to nocturnal lifestyle.

- Indonesia to Hawaiian and Tuamotu Islands, north to southern Japan and south to Lord Howe and Rapa Islands
- Coastal and outer coral reefs; coral-rich areas, lagoons, back reefs, reef flats, slopes
- 3–30 m (10–98 ft) ↔ 12 cm (4.7 in)

Pacific Redfin Butterflyfish

Chaetodon lunulatus

Family Chaetodontidae (butterflyfishes)

Juveniles solitary but may aggregate in coral colonies before dark; adults occur in pairs. Eats only stony coral. Uses lower jaw and comblike teeth to scrap off up to 10 polyps per bite. Home-ranging, but pair members will chase off members of own kind if get too close. Males set up spawning territories one to two hours before sunset and spawn with partner. Similar to Indian Ocean redfin butterflyfish (*C. trifasciatus*), but *C. trifasciatus* has blue on sides and orange bar at base of tail.

- East Africa to Line Islands, north to Ryukyu and Marshall Islands and south to Great Barrier Reef
- Coastal and outer coral reefs; lagoon patch reefs, reef faces, slopes where stony corals abundant
- 2–25 m (7–82 ft) ↔ 18 cm (7.1 in)

Meyer's Butterflyfish

Chaetodon meyeri

Family Chaetodontidae (butterflyfishes)

Juveniles solitary; adults found singly or in pairs. Pair will defend feeding territory from members of own kind and other coral-feeding butterflyfishes. Feeds only on polyps of stony corals, neatly incising flesh without ingesting any of coral's skeleton. One of butterflyfish species that are good indicators of reef health (because so dependent on live stony corals to survive).

Ornate Butterflyfish

Chaetodon ornatissimus
Family Chaetodontidae
(**butterflyfishes**)

⊕ Sri Lanka to Hawaiian, Marquesas and Ducie Islands, north to southern Japan and south to Lord Howe and Rapa Islands
⊙ Coastal and outer coral reefs; lagoons, reef flats, reef faces, slopes
↕ 1–36 m (3.3–117 ft)   ↔ 18 cm (7.1 in)

Adults found singly or in pairs or small groups; juveniles solitary. Pairs often defend feeding territory, which includes rich stony corals. Pair members often separate when feeding. Eats coral polyps, scraping 16–50 polyps off in single bite, using lower jaw and associated tooth pad. Also ingests lots of coral mucus.

Golden Butterflyfish

Chaetodon semilarvatus
Family Chaetodontidae
(**butterflyfishes**)

⊕ Red Sea and Gulf of Aden
⊙ Coastal coral reefs; back reefs, reef faces, slopes
↕ 3–20 m (10–66 ft)   ↔ 23 cm (9.1 in)

Juveniles solitary; adults form pairs or (rarely) groups of dozens of individuals. Often adults hang under table corals (*Acropora* spp.) during day. Grouping may enable them to descend upon territories of aggressive farming damsels that can be overwhelmed by their numbers. One study reports it feeding heavily on macroalgae.

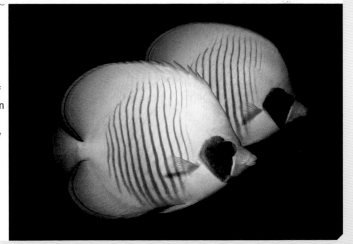

🌐 Bermuda, south to Brazil, including Gulf of Mexico
◉ Coastal and outer coral reefs; lagoon patch reefs, reef faces, slopes
↧ 3–52 m (7–169 ft)   ↔ 16 cm (6.3 in)

Banded Butterflyfish
Chaetodon striatus
Family Chaetodontidae
(butterflyfishes)

Solitary or in pairs. Most abundant among rich stony coral growth. Eats tube-worm feeding tentacles, stony coral polyps and zoanthids. Off Brazil, loose groups feed on zooplankton in water column and adult will sometimes clean parrot-fishes, surgeonfish and grunts. Spawns in pairs. Sister species of *C. striatus* in Eastern Pacific is East Pacific banded butterflyfish (*C. humeralis*), which is similar in appearance but has several bands on tail rather than one, as in *C. striatus*.

🌐 Northwestern Australia and Great Barrier Reef
◉ Coastal coral reefs; sponge reefs; reef faces, slopes (often in sheltered turbid conditions)
↧ 1 to 30 m (3.3 to 98 ft)   ↔ 20 cm (7.9 in)

Margined Coralfish
Chelmon marginalis
Family Chaetodontidae
(butterflyfishes)

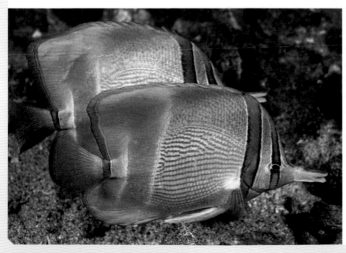

Found singly or in feeding groups. Uses long snout to nip off tube-worm tentacles and ingest crusta-ceans. When quarreling, males ram each other with heads and push each other like bighorn sheep. Very similar to beaked butterflyfish (*C. rostratus*): juveniles almost iden-tical but adult *C. marginalis* lacks black eyespot at base of dorsal fin.

Orange-banded Coralfish

Coradion chrysozonus
Family Chaetodontidae (butterflyfishes)

⊕ Thailand and Malaysia, east to Solomon Islands, north to Ryukyu Islands and south to Western Australia and Great Barrier Reef
⊙ Coastal coral and rocky reefs; lagoons, reef faces, slopes
↕ 3–60 m (3.3–195 ft)   ↔ 14 cm (5.5 in)

Solitary. Feeds on invertebrates living on outer surface of sponges (e.g., small crustaceans) but also eats zooplankton. Similar to highfin coralfish (*C. altivelis*), but *C. chrysozonus* has ocellus on soft portion of dorsal fin, and third body bar is wider and mostly orangish yellow rather than brown.

Big Longnose Butterflyfish

Forcipiger longirostris
Family Chaetodontidae (butterflyfishes)

⊕ East Africa to Hawaiian, Marquesas and Pitcairn Islands, north to Bonin Island and south to New Caledonia and Austral Islands
⊙ Coastal and outer coral reefs; lagoons, reef faces, slopes (coral-rich areas)
↕ 5–208 m (16–676 ft)   ↔ 22 cm (8.7 in)

Occurs singly or in pairs. Long nose is employed to get at prey in reef crevices and among coral branches. Sucks tiny shrimps and crab larvae into pipette-like snout. Unusual all-brown color form is most common around Hawaiian Islands. Similar to longnose butterflyfish (*F. flavissimus*) but has small black spots on throat and longer snout. Two species overlap in range, but where one is common, other is usually scarce.

⊕ East Africa to Society Islands, north to Arabian Gulf and southern Japan and south to Lord Howe Island

⊙ Coastal and outer coral reefs; deep lagoons, reef channels, reef faces, slopes

↧ 2–75 m (7–246 ft) ↔ 25 cm (9.8 in)

Longfin Bannerfish
Heniochus acuminatus
Family Chaetodontidae
(butterflyfishes)

Occurs singly or in pairs or groups (does not form groups as often as closely related schooling bannerfish). Feeds on zooplankton, comb jellies, filamentous algae and sessile invertebrates. Sometimes cleans other fishes of parasites, including mola mola. Very similar schooling bannerfish (*H. diphreutes*) has less pronounced snout, breast is more robust and anal fin is not as rounded.

⊕ East Africa to Tuamotu Islands, north to southern Japan and south to New South Wales, Australia, Norfolk Island and Tonga

⊙ Coastal and outer coral reefs; lagoon patch reefs, reef faces, slopes

↧ 2–20 m (7–66 ft) ↔ 23 cm (9.1 in)

Masked Bannerfish
Heniochus monoceros
Family Chaetodontidae
(butterflyfishes)

Adults occur singly or in pairs; young individuals solitary and shy. Feeds on colonial ascidians and polychaete worms. Mature adults develop hump on forehead and prominent horn in front of each eye, may be used to butt consexual rivals in head-to-head duels. Similar to singular bannerfish (*H. singularis*), but *H. monoceros* has yellow anal fin (black in *H. singularis*).

Barberfish

Johnrandallia nigrirostris
Family Chaetodontidae
(butterflyfishes)

- ⊕ Gulf of California to Panama, including offshore islands
- ☉ Coastal and insular rocky reefs; reef faces, slopes
- ↧ 3–40 m (3.3–130 ft)   ↔ 20 cm (7.9 in)

Solitary or in pairs or shoals. Feeds on algae and benthic invertebrates (snails, crustaceans). Part-time cleaner that removes ectoparasites from other bony fishes as well as scalloped hammerhead sharks. Sets up cleaning stations at specific sites, often cleaning clients in groups. At night, black stripe on back fades and light blotch appears on side.

Longsnout Butterflyfish

Prognathodes aculeatus
Family Chaetodontidae (butterflyfishes)

- ⊕ Florida, south to Venezuela, including Gulf of Mexico
- ☉ Coastal and outer coral reefs; reef faces, slopes
- ↧ 1–140 m (3.3–455 ft)   ↔ 10 cm (3.9 in)

Usually solitary. Most abundant on deep reefs (30 m/98 ft or more). Occurs among soft corals and sponges. Often lives in caves. Feeds on tube worms, spaghetti worms and appendages of sea urchins. Mates meet at spawning site at dusk and release pelagic gametes above substrate after spiraling into water column. Fairly easy species to approach if you move slowly. Replaced by Brazilian longsnout butterflyfish (*P. brasiliensis*) in Brazil.

- ⊕ Eastern Pacific from Santa Catalina Island, California, south to Guadalupe Island, Cabo San Lucas, West San Benito Island and Galapagos Islands
- ◉ Coastal and insular rocky reefs; most often on boulder-strewn bottoms, rock walls, deep slopes
- ↧ 12–150 m (39–488 ft); most often below 100 m (325 ft)   ↔ 16 cm (6.3 in)

Scythe Butterflyfish
Prognathodes falcifer
Family Chaetodontidae (butterflyfishes)

Solitary. Associates with black coral bushes and thought to feed on polyps as well as benthic invertebrates. Also part-time cleaner, engaging in this behavior in caves. Most often seen at safe diving depths off Galapagos. Similar species in Western Atlantic, bank butterflyfish (*P. aya*), lacks scythe-like marking on side.

- ⊕ East Africa, east to Samoa, north to southern Japan and south to New Caledonia
- ◉ Outer coral reefs; pinnacles, reef slopes, drop-offs
- ↧ 3–60 m (10–195 ft)   ↔ 25 cm (9.8 in)

Flagfin Angelfish
Apolemichthys trimaculatus
Family Pomacanthidae (angelfishes)

Solitary or in pairs or, on rare occasions, groups. Adults feed on sponges and tunicates; juveniles graze on algae. Small juveniles have black spot on rear portion of dorsal fin and black band on anal fin. Large adults have filament on dorsal surface of caudal fin. May hybridize with yellowtail angelfish (*A. xanthurus*); resulting progeny are Armitage angelfish (formerly known as *A. armitagei* but now known to be hybrid).

Bicolor Angelfish

Centropyge bicolor
Family Pomacanthidae (angelfishes)

🌐 Malaysia, east to Phoenix Islands, north to southern Japan and south to northwestern Australia and New Caledonia
⊙ Coastal and outer coral reefs; lagoon patch reefs, reef faces, slopes
↧ 2–20 m (7–65 ft)　　　　　　↔ 15 cm (5.9 in)

Haremic. Males defend territory that contains one to seven females. Protogynous hermaphrodite. If male dies, female in harem takes his place within 20 days. Feeds on detritus and microalgae. Spawns at dusk; females move to special spawning site. Large adults have dusky face. Similar to Cocos pygmy angelfish (*C. joculator*) but lacks blue ring around eye.

Lemonpeel Angelfish

Centropyge flavissimus
Family Pomacanthidae (angelfishes)

🌐 Cocos-Keeling Islands, east to Marquesas, north to Ryukyu Islands and south to New Caledonia
⊙ Coastal and outer coral reefs; lagoon patch reefs, back reefs, reef faces, slopes
↧ 1–25 m (3.3–81 ft)　　　　　　↔ 10 cm (3.9 in)

Adults found in pairs or harems (up to three females). Males chirp and grunt to communicate with females. Feeds on algae. In Micronesia often crossbreeds with half-black angelfish (*C. vroliki*). In some areas lemon-peel yellow; in other locations golden orange. Juveniles have blue-bordered eyespot in center of body. Mimicked by juvenile chocolate surgeonfish (*Acanthurus pyroferus*).

⬛ Palau to Hawaiian, Marquesas and Ducie Islands, south to Great Barrier Reef and Pitcairn Islands; most common at Palau, Caroline, Marshall and Society Islands

◉ Coastal and outer coral reefs (more common around oceanic rather than continental reefs); lagoon patch reefs, reef faces, slopes

↧ 2–60 m (7–195 ft) ↔ 10 cm (3.9 in)

Flame Angelfish

Centropyge loriculus
Family Pomacanthidae (angelfishes)

Haremic. Males defend territory that contains one to several females. Protogynous hermaphrodite. Feeds on detritus and microalgae. Tends to be shy and difficult to approach. Pops out from hiding place and then dashes back in if feels threatened. Color can vary from one location to next (e.g., those from Marquesas almost all orange). Males have blue on rear of dorsal and anal fins.

⬛ Northern Queensland to northwestern Australia and Papua New Guinea

◉ Coastal coral reefs; sponge beds, lagoons, reef faces, slopes

↧ 1–30 m (3.3–98 ft) ↔ 25 cm (9.8 inches)

Scribbled Angelfish

Chaetodontoplus duboulayi
Family Pomacanthidae (angelfishes)

Occurs singly or in pairs or small groups. Feeds on sponges and tunicates. When courting, male rapidly swims around female while leaning to side and nuzzles base of her anal fin with snout; pair then ascends into water column to release gametes. Males more brilliant blue, with fine lines on side and white patch over gill cover; females spotted. Male's face becomes pale during courtship.

Black-spot Angelfish
Genicanthus melanospilos
Family Pomacanthidae (angelfishes)

🌐 Malaysia to Fiji, north to Ryukyu Islands and south to Rowley Shoals and New Caledonia
◉ Coastal and outer coral reefs; fore-reef drop-offs
↧ 20–50 m (66–164 ft)　　　　　↔ 18 cm (7.1 in)

Adults form male–female pairs or small groups. In groups, males dominant, chasing off bachelor males; females not aggressive. Feeds on zooplankton high in water column during day. Usually in habitats with rich sponge and coral growth. Males similar to zebra angelfish (*G. caudovittatus*) from Red Sea, but male zebra angel has black on dorsal fin. Male in main photo, female in inset photo.

Queen Angelfish
Holacanthus ciliaris
Family Pomacanthidae (angelfishes)

🌐 Florida and Bermuda, south to Brazil
◉ Coastal and outer coral reefs; found on sponge- and coral-rich reefs; lagoon patch reefs, back reefs, reef faces, slopes
↧ 2–70 m (7–228 ft)　　　　　↔ 45 cm (17.7 in)

Solitary. Found on sponge- and coral-rich reefs. Feeds on many different species of sponge but also eats tunicates, hydroids and bryozoans. Juveniles part-time cleaners. Adults haremic, with large territory of male including two to four mates. Spawns at sunset. Will crossbreed with very similar blue angelfish (*H. bermudensis*); latter most common on shallow continental reefs. Juvenile in inset photo.

- 🌐 Gulf of California to Ecuador and offshore islands (e.g., Cocos, Galapagos)
- ⊙ Coastal and insular rocky reefs; rock-strewn bottoms, rocky walls, slopes
- ↧ 1–80 m (3.3–260 ft)   ↔ 36 cm (14.2 in)

King Angelfish
Holacanthus passer
Family Pomacanthidae (angelfishes)

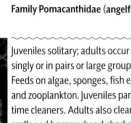

Juveniles solitary; adults occur singly or in pairs or large groups. Feeds on algae, sponges, fish eggs and zooplankton. Juveniles part-time cleaners. Adults also clean scalloped hammerhead sharks and mantas around islands. Forms long-term pair bonds where uncommon; males set up temporary territories and spawn with numerous females where species abundant. Males have yellow pelvic fins, while in females they are white.

- 🌐 Georgia and Bermuda, south to Brazil, including Gulf of Mexico
- ⊙ Coastal and outer coral reefs; lagoon patch reefs, back reefs, reef faces, slopes
- ↧ 3–92 m (10–299 ft)   ↔ 20 cm (7.9 in)

Rock Beauty
Holacanthus tricolor
Family Pomacanthidae (angelfishes)

Solitary. Juveniles found among fire corals or reef crevices; adults prefer caves and crevices. Diet is sponges and algae. Young fish feed on mucus of cryptic fishes (e.g., morays and squirrelfishes). Haremic species, with male territory overlapping feeding territory of two to four females. Shy fish, difficult to approach — patience and stealth required for close observation.

Gray Angelfish
Pomacanthus arcuatus
Family Pomacanthidae (angelfishes)

⊕ New England, south to Brazil, including Gulf of Mexico
⊙ Coastal and outer coral reefs; lagoon patch reefs, back reefs, reef faces, slopes
↧ 1–29 m (3.3–94 ft)   ↔ 50 cm (19.5 in)

Solitary or in pairs or groups. Juveniles found in more shallow habitats, including seagrass beds; adults in coral-rich habitats. Adults feed on variety of sessile invertebrates, including sponges, zoanthids and gorgonians, as well as algae. Juveniles part-time cleaners. Pair-bonding species where scarce, but where common is polygamous (adults form groups consisting of both sexes). Easy fish to approach and photograph.

Emperor Angelfish
Pomacanthus imperator
Family Pomacanthidae (angelfishes)

⊕ East Africa and Red Sea, east to Hawaiian Islands (where it is rare), north to southern Japan and south to New Caledonia and New South Wales, Australia
⊙ Coastal and outer coral reefs; lagoon patch reefs, channels, reef flats, reef faces, slopes
↧ 3–80 m (10–260 ft)   ↔ 38 cm (15.0 in)

Adults usually seen singly, although males have large territory that includes two or more females. Juveniles solitary and may do some part-time cleaning. Spawns at specific site in territory. Feeds on sponges and tunicates. Produces grunting vocalizations during aggression and reproduction. Males have blue in front of eye, gray in females. Juvenile in inset photo.

⊕ Malaysia east to Solomon Islands, north to Ryukyu Islands and south to northwestern Australia

⊙ Coastal and outer coral reefs; lagoon patch reefs, channels, reef faces, slopes

↓ 3–40 m (10–130 ft)   ↔ 25 cm (9.8 in)

Blue-girdled Angelfish
Pomacanthus navarchus
Family Pomacanthidae (angelfishes)

Solitary (may be haremic). Feeds on sponges and tunicates. Juveniles very secretive, inhabiting crevices and caves; may be part-time cleaners. Adults often shy and difficult to approach. Adult very distinctive; juveniles of this and other Indo–Western Pacific *Pomacanthus* species very similar — blue with white and/or light blue lines.

⊕ Florida to Brazil, including Gulf of Mexico

⊙ Coastal and outer coral reefs; lagoons, back reefs, reef faces, slopes

↓ 1–100 m (3.3 to 325 ft)   ↔ 38 cm (14.8 in)

French Angelfish
Pomacanthus paru
Family Pomacanthidae (angelfishes)

Solitary or in pairs. Omnivorous, with algae and sponges comprising most of diet. Juveniles part-time cleaners; often cleaned by shrimps and other parasite-picking species. Pairing where not common, haremic where abundant. Pairs congregate at edge of reef, rising in water column and releasing gametes. Adults bold and easy to approach.

Six-banded Angelfish

Pomacanthus sexstriatus
Family Pomacanthidae (angelfishes)

⊕ Malaysia east to Solomon Islands, north to Ryukyu Islands and south to New Caledonia and Rowley Shoals

⊙ Coastal and outer reefs; lagoons, reef faces, slopes

↕ 2–50 m (7–163 ft)   ↔ 46 cm (18.1 in)

Juveniles solitary, often on siltier reefs or around pier pilings. Adults found singly or in pairs. Lives in large home range. Juveniles of this and other species of Pacific *Pomacanthus* are dark with light blue and white markings (pattern varies among species), which may help young fish settle into adult home ranges or territories without being recognized as future competitor.

Regal Angelfish

Pygoplites diacanthus
Family Pomacanthidae (angelfishes)

⊕ Red Sea, east to Tuamotu Islands, north to Ryukyu Islands in southern Japan and south to New Caledonia and Queensland, Australia

⊙ Coastal and outer coral reefs; clear lagoon pinnacles and patch reefs, channels, reef faces, slopes

↕ 3–80 m (10–260 ft)   ↔ 25 cm (9.8 in)

Juveniles solitary. Adults haremic; male territory contains one to four females. Reclusive, usually seen in caves or under overhangs, sometimes swimming with belly toward cave ceiling. Spawning begins just before sunset at specific spawning sites in territory. Population in Indian Ocean have orange on breast and underside of head; these areas gray in Pacific *P. diacanthus*.

- East Africa and Red Sea, east to French Polynesia, north to southern Japan and south to Australia
- Rocky and coral reefs; lagoons, reef flats, reef faces, slopes
- 1–25 m (3.3–81 ft) ↔ 45 cm (18 in)

Topsail Rudderfish

Kyphosus cinerascens

Family Kyphosidae (sea chubs)

Small to large shoals. Active during day. Browses on algae on hard substrates or on floating algal fragments; also eats zooplankton and sea skaters (*Halobates* spp.), wingless marine insects. At night often seen singly, usually swimming above substrate. Differs from other sea chubs in that rear portion of dorsal fin is distinctly higher (hence its name).

- Canada and Bermuda, south to Brazil, including Gulf of Mexico
- Coral and rocky reefs; lagoons, reef faces
- 1–30 m (3.3–98 ft) ↔ 76 cm (30 in)

Chub

Kyphosus sectatrix

Family Kyphosidae (sea chubs)

Solitary or in shoals. Young often assemble around *Sargassum* algae rafts. Also found in seagrass beds. Adults swim rapidly along reef face. Feeds mainly on algae but also ingests crabs and mollusks. Off Brazil has been observed feeding on fecal material and vomit of spinner dolphins. *K. sectatrix* and *K. incisor* impossible to differentiate without counting fin rays and gill rakers; two species will school together. Shy, but will occasionally swim near a diver.

Bluestriped Chub
Sector ocyurus
Family Kyphosidae (sea chubs)

🌐 Cabo San Lucas, Mexico, south to Peru and offshore islands; also Japan and Hawaiian and Society Islands

☉ Coastal and insular rocky reefs; open ocean; sometimes near reef walls and drop-offs; also around flotsam (e.g., logs)

↧ 1–30 m (3.3–98 ft) ↔ 70 cm (28 in)

Small schools. Feeds on floating algae and zooplankton. More elongate body than most chubs, indicating more pelagic lifestyle.

Stripey
Microcanthus strigatus
Family Kyphosidae (sea chubs)

🌐 Japan, south to Australia and New Caledonia; also Hawaiian Islands

☉ Coastal rock reefs (rarely around coral reefs); estuaries (brackish water), harbors, lagoons, reef faces, slopes

↧ 1–140 m (3.3–455 ft) ↔ 20 cm (7.9 in)

Solitary or in groups. Often aggregates under ledges or in caves. Feeds on algae and crustaceans (has brush-like teeth). May be three distinct species but currently considered all the same.

- ⊕ Rhode Island to Uruguay
- ⊙ Rocky and coral reefs; lagoons, reef faces, mangroves, estuaries, pier pilings
- ↓ 1–20 m (3.3–65 ft)   ↔ 15 cm (5.9 in)

Sergeant Major
Abudefduf saxatilis
**Family Pomacentridae
(damselfishes)**

Diet consists of zoanthids, zooplankton, algae and barnacles. Solitary when feeding on substrate, but when foraging in the water column, forms groups. Males form spawning territories to which they attract multiple female mates. Male breeding color dark blue. Pink eggs laid on rocks (note in photo on left) that male defends and tends. Easy to approach.

- ⊕ East Africa and Red Sea, east to Rapa and Marshall Islands, north to Japan and south to Australia
- ⊙ Coastal and outer coral reefs; lagoon patch reefs, channels, reef faces, slopes
- ↓ 1–15 m (3.3–49 ft)   ↔ 17 cm (6.7 in)

Scissortail Sergeant
Abudefduf sexfasciatus
**Family Pomacentridae
(damselfishes)**

Occurs singly or in groups; forms larger shoals when feeding in water column. Feeds on zooplankton and filamentous algae. Distinguished from others in genus by black borders on tail.

Indo-Pacific Sergeant

Abudefduf vaigiensis
Family Pomacentridae
(damselfishes)

⊕ East Africa and Red Sea, east to Line Islands, north to Japan and south to Australia and New Zealand

⊙ Coastal and outer coral reefs; lagoon patch reefs, back reefs, channels, reef faces, slopes

↕ 1–12 m (3.3–39 ft) ↔ 20 cm (7.9 in)

Forms small to large groups. Feeds on zooplankton and benthic algae (when former less abundant). Males set up spawning territories, dashing into water column to attract mates. Female deposits eggs in male's nest, which he aggressively defends. During spawning, male color intensifies. Eggs hatch in four days.

Golden Damselfish

Amblyglyphidodon aureus
Family Pomacentridae
(damselfishes)

⊕ Similan Islands to Fiji, north to Ryukyu Islands and south to New Caledonia

⊙ Coastal and outer reefs; clear lagoon pinnacles, reef channels, reef walls

↕ 12–45 m (39–146 ft) ↔ 14 cm (5.5 in)

Juveniles form small groups; adult solitary or in pairs. Tends to inhabit areas with sea fans and black and soft corals. Feeds on zooplankton. Male prepares nesting site on gorgonian and sea whip branches; nips off live tissue where female deposits eggs. Male guards eggs until hatch. Easy to approach.

Red Sea, Gulf of Aden and Chagos archipelago

Coastal reefs; lagoons, reef faces, slopes; in sea anemones *Entacmaea quadricolor*, *Heteractis aurora*, *H. crispa*, *H. magnifica* and *Stichodactyla gigantea*

4–25 m (22–81 ft)   14 cm (5.5 in.)

Red Sea Anemonefish
Amphiprion bicinctus
Family Pomacentridae
(damselfishes)

Forms small groups consisting of adult pair and several nonbreeders. Protandric hermaphrodite. Female lays clutch of eggs numbering 600–1,600 at base of anemone; vigorously defends and mouths eggs and fans them with fins. Defends host from butterflyfish that eat anemones. Has declined in parts of Red Sea because of habitat degradation.

Papua New Guinea to Tuamotus, north to Marianas and south to Great Barrier Reef

Coastal and outer coral reefs; lagoons, reef faces, slopes; most often in *Entacmaea quadricolor* and *Stichodactyla mertensii* but also other anemones

1–30 m (3.3–98 ft)   15 cm (5.9 in)

Orangefin Anemonefish
Amphiprion chrysopterus
Family Pomacentridae
(damselfishes)

Social unit is adult pair and one or two juvenile fish. Loosely associates with sea anemones, often moving high in water column. Spends most of day feeding on zooplankton and algae near host. May share anemone with threespot dascyllus (*Dascyllus trimaculatus*). May hybridize with orange skunk anemonefish (*A. sandaracinos*); resulting progeny thought to be whitebonnet anemonefish (*A. leucokranos*), once considered valid species.

Clark's Anemonefish

Amphiprion clarkii
Family Pomacentridae
(damselfishes)

⊕ Arabian Gulf east to Fiji, north to Japan and south to Maldives and Great Barrier Reef
⊙ Rocky and coral reefs; wide range of habitats; in all 10 anemone species known to host anemonefishes
↧ 1–55 m (3.3–179 ft)   ↔ 14 cm (5.5 in)

Usually adult pair with subadults and juveniles or, in smaller anemones, two subadults. Adult pair dominant in group. Individuals immigrate to different groups to try to improve social status. In some areas commonly shares anemone with other anemonefish species (e.g., pink anemonefish) or non-related fishes (e.g., cardinalfishes). Feeds mainly on zooplankton and algae. Spawns year-round in tropics. Life span at least 13 years in the wild.

Red Saddleback Anemonefish

Amphiprion ephippium
Family Pomacentridae (damselfishes)

⊕ Andaman Islands to Java
⊙ Coastal and outer coral reefs; lagoons, reef faces; in *Entacmaea quadricolor* and *Heteractis crispa*
↧ 1–15 m (3.3–49 ft)   ↔ 12 cm (4.7 in)

Social unit typically adult pair and one to three juvenile fish. Strongly attached to anemone host but individuals may move from one social unit to another. Very aggressive; will defend host from predators (e.g., butterflyfishes). Similar species off Western Australia: Australian anemonefish (*A. rubrocinctus*).

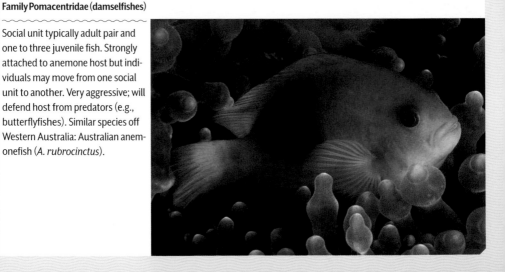

⊕ Gulf of Thailand, east to Palau, north to southern Japan and south to Java
☉ Coastal coral reefs; lagoons, reef faces; in *Entacmaea quadricolor*
↕ 1–12 m (3.3–39 ft) ↔ 14 cm (5.5 in)

Tomato Anemonefish

Amphiprion frenatus
Family Pomacentridae
(damselfishes)

Social unit is adult pair; juveniles and subadults solitary. Feeds on algae, crustaceans and zooplankton. Female much larger than male and tends to be deep red with black on back and top of head; male bright orange overall. Similar to dusky anemonefish (*A. melanopus*) which has black pelvic fins.

⊕ Papua New Guinea and Solomon Islands, south to Great Barrier Reef
☉ Coastal coral reefs; protected lagoons, reef crests, reef faces; in sea anemones *Heteractis magnifica*, *H. crispa*, *Stichodactyla mertensii* and *S. gigantea*
↕ 4–25 m (22–81 ft) ↔ 80 cm (31 in.)

Clown Anemonefish

Amphiprion percula
Family Pomacentridae
(damselfishes)

Found in adult pairs; in larger sea anemones also with juveniles. Some possess very striking color patterns, with lots of black between white body bars (most common in individuals that live in carpet anemones, *Stichodactyla*). Others similar to close relative *A. ocellaris*, false clownfish, but species differ in dorsal spine counts and slightly shorter dorsal spines in *A. percula*; also limited overlap in geographical range (*A. ocellaris* found off Thailand, Micronesia, Indonesia and Japan).

Ray-Finned Fishes

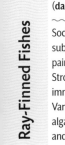

Pink Anemonefish

Amphiprion perideraion
Family Pomacentridae
(damselfishes)

⊕ Cocos-Keeling and Christmas Islands and southeast Thailand, east to Samoa, north to Ryukyu Islands and south to Great Barrier Reef and New Caledonia

⊙ Coastal and outer coral reefs; lagoons, reef faces, slopes; most often in sea anemones *Heteractis magnifica* and *H. crispa*

↧ 3–30 (10–98 ft)   ↔ 11 cm (4.3 inches)

Social groups can be all juveniles, subadults and juveniles or adult pair with subadults and juveniles. Strongly tied to its anemone; rarely immigrates to other social units. Varied diet includes zooplankton, algae, small benthic crustaceans and even tips of anemone tentacles. Spawns on rock or rubble near anemone; clutch normally around 300 eggs. Similar species in Fiji and Samoa: Pacific anemonefish (*A. pacificus*), which is pinkish brown with single white stripe on back.

Blue Chromis

Chromis cyanea
Family Pomacentridae
(damselfishes)

⊕ Florida to Venezuela, including Gulf of Mexico

⊙ Coastal and outer coral reefs; lagoons, reef faces, slopes

↧ 3–55 m (10–179 ft)   ↔ 13 cm (5.1 in)

Occurs singly or in small groups. Found on healthy coral- and sponge-rich reefs with good water movement. Feeds on zooplankton. Young mix with juvenile brown chromis and stay closer to shelter than adults. Color can be bright blue to almost black; darker phase more common when fish is near seafloor (may help it blend better). Spawns throughout year, laying eggs on substrate. Male defends eggs until they hatch (usually in three days). Easy to approach.

- Florida and Bermuda, south to Brazil, including Gulf of Mexico
- Coastal and outer coral reefs; lagoon patch reefs, reef faces, slopes
- 2–40 m (7–130 ft)   ↔ 17 cm (6.7 in)

Brown Chromis
Chromis multilineata
Family Pomacentridae
(damselfishes)

Small to large schools that hover over reef and feed on zooplankton. Tends to stray farther from cover of reef to feed than blue chromis. Often visits goby cleaning stations. Forms spawning assemblages that can include thousands of fish. Males form temporary spawning territories. Females lay eggs, which male guards, lifting hermit crabs and sea urchins from nest with mouth. Easy to approach.

- Red Sea to French Polynesia, north to Ryukyu Islands and south to New Caledonia
- Coastal and outer coral reefs; lagoons, reef flats, reef channels, reef faces, slopes
- 1.5–12 m (5–39 ft)   ↔ 10 cm (3.9 in)

Blue-green Chromis
Chromis viridis
Family Pomacentridae
(damselfishes)

Often in large shoals (numbering in hundreds). Sometimes hovers over staghorn coral, in which it disappears if threatened. Feeds primarily on planktonic crustaceans but will also consume algae. Male sets up temporary spawning territories and attempts to entice females back to territory to lay their eggs. Male fans eggs and chases away intruders. Similar blackaxil chromis (*C. atripectoralis*) has dark spot on pectoral fin axil.

Blue Devil

Chrysiptera cyanea

Family Pomacentridae
(damselfishes)

🌐 Indonesia to Solomon Islands, north to Ryukyu and west Caroline Islands and south to northwestern Australia and Great Barrier Reef

⊙ Coastal and outer reefs; lagoons, reef flats, reef faces

↧ 1–10 m (3.3–33 ft)   ↔ 8 cm (3.1 in)

Found in small to large colonies consisting of males, females and juveniles. Mature males territorial. During spawning season, female visits number of males before spawning with preferred (usually larger) male. Females may line up at nesting sites of such males, waiting to deposit eggs. Feeds mostly on filamentous algae, minute crustaceans and planktonic fish eggs. In some populations male has bright orange tail.

Humbug Dascyllus

Dascyllus aruanus

Family Pomacentridae
(damselfishes)

🌐 East Africa and Red Sea, east to Line, Marquesas and Tuamotu Islands, north to southern Japan and south to Lord Howe and Rapa Islands

⊙ Coastal and outer coral reefs; lagoon patch reefs, reef faces, slopes; in stony corals

↧ 1–12 m (3.3–39 ft)   ↔ 8 cm (3.1 in)

Forms pairs or groups; group size a function of coral colony inhabited. Adult male defends colony; females form groups with pecking order (size determines place on social ladder). Individuals rarely move more than 1 m (3.3 ft) from coral colony. Feeds on zooplankton, fish eggs and algae. Similar to black-tailed dascyllus (*D. melanurus*), which has a black tail (white in *D. aruanus*).

- ⊕ Cocos-Keeling Islands east to Samoa, north to southern Japan and south to Lord Howe Island
- ⊙ Coastal and outer reefs; lagoons, reef flats, reef faces, slopes
- ↧ 1–50 m (3.3–163 ft)　　　　　　　↤ 8 cm (3.1 in)

Reticulated Dascyllus   327

Dascyllus reticulatus
**Family Pomacentridae
(damselfishes)**

Usually forms groups composed of single male, females and juveniles. Male chases other males away from harem. Deposits eggs on rubble or flat rock near base of its coral colony; eggs usually hatch in 2–2.5 days. Associates with branching stony corals. Feeds on zooplankton and algae. Similar to Indian dascyllus (*D. carneus*), but differs in having less black on dorsal fin and no blue highlights on scales.

- ⊕ Red Sea and East Africa to Line and Pitcairn Islands, north to southern Japan and south to Lord Howe Island
- ⊙ Coastal and outer reefs; lagoon patch reefs, back reefs, reef faces, slopes
- ↧ 1–55 m (3.3–179 ft)　　　　　　　↤ 14 cm (5.5 in)

Threespot Dascyllus

Dascyllus trimaculatus
**Family Pomacentridae
(damselfishes)**

Adults found singly or in pairs; juveniles form groups. Latter often live in sea anemones with anemonefishes. Will swim into water column to feed on zooplankton but also eats algae. Male attracts females to nesting site by "signal jumping" (dashes up in water column, then darts back to substrate). Pair scoot along bottom and deposit gametes, which male defends. Similar species, orangefin dascyllus (*Dascyllus auripinnis*), has orange sides and fins. Juvenile in inset photo.

Yellowtail Damselfish

Microspathodon chrysurus

Family Pomacentridae (damselfishes)

⊕ Florida and Bermuda and throughout Caribbean Sea

⊙ Coastal and outer coral reefs; lagoon patch reefs, back reefs, reef faces, slopes

↧ 1–10 m (3.3–33 ft)　　　　↔ 21 cm (8.3 in)

Solitary; territorial. Prefers habitats with strong surge; often associates with fire coral. Feeds on algae along with associated detritus and tiny invertebrates. Infrequently cleans other fishes. Some adults defend spawning territories, while others roam. Spawning occurs between full and new moon and occurs at dawn. Clutch can contain as many as 19,000 eggs, which male aggressively defends. Juveniles dark with blue spots; adults brown with yellow tail. Frenetic but easy to approach. Juvenile in inset photo.

Blackbar Damsel

Plectroglyphidodon dickii

Family Pomacentridae (damselfishes)

⊕ East Africa, east to Line, Marquesas and Tuamotu Islands, north to Japan and south to Lord Howe Island

⊙ Coastal and outer reefs; lagoon patch reefs, reef channels, reef faces

↧ 1–12 m (3.3–39 ft)　　　　↔ 9.5 cm (3.7 in)

Solitary or in small groups, often in habitats with moderate surge. Lives within colonies or thickets of branching corals (e.g., *Acropora*, *Pocillopora*), on which it feeds; eats coral polyps as well as algae, hydroids, sea anemones, copepods and fish eggs. Easily recognized by black bar on posterior portion of body and yellow caudal peduncle and tail (white in juveniles).

- Christmas Island (Indian Ocean) and Bali, Flores and Moluccas (Indonesia), north to Borneo and Palau
- Coastal reefs; patch reefs, rubble flats, slopes
- 2–15 m (7–49 ft)   ↔ 7 cm (2.8 in)

Goldbelly Damsel

Pomacentrus auriventris
Family Pomacentridae
(damselfishes)

Adults form pairs or loose groups. Remains near cover and feeds on passing zooplankton. Male defends nesting site visited by numerous females to lay their eggs. Eggs fanned and defended by male. Similar to neon damsel (*P. coelestis*) but has more yellow on ventrum, sides and dorsal fin.

- Moluccas to Samoa, north to Izu Islands and south to northwestern Australia, New Caledonia and Great Barrier Reef
- Coastal and outer reefs; lagoon patch reefs, reef faces, slopes
- 1–45 m (3.3–146 ft)   ↔ 9 cm (3.5 in)

Princess Damsel

Pomacentrus vaiuli
Family Pomacentridae
(damselfishes)

Occurs singly. Territorial, chasing out conspecifics and other fishes with similar diet. Rarely moves far from seafloor. Feeds on algae, detritus and small invertebrates associated with algal mat. Speckled damselfish (*P. bankanensis*) similar species, differing in having white tail.

Ray-Finned Fishes

Ray-Finned Fishes

Spinecheek Anemonefish

Premnas biaculeatus
Family Pomacentridae (damselfishes)

- ⊕ Indonesia and Philippines to New Guinea, north Great Barrier Reef and Vanuatu
- ☉ Coastal and outer reefs; lagoon patch reefs, reef faces; in sea anemone *Entacmaea quadricolor*
- ↧ 1–16 m (3.3–52 ft)
- ↔ 16 cm (6.3 in)

Usually in pairs with large female and much smaller male (more brightly colored). Most aggressive of all anemonefishes, excluding relatives from preferred anemone hosts. Feeds on algae, small benthic invertebrates and zooplankton. Deposits 150–900 eggs near base of sea anemone; eggs tended by male, who mouths, fans and defends them. In some populations (Sumatra), body bars are gold rather than white.

Yellowtail Tamarin Wrasse

Anampses meleagrides
Family Labridae (wrasses)

- ⊕ Red Sea to Tuamotu Islands, north to southern Japan and south to Lord Howe Island
- ☉ Coastal and outer coral reefs; lagoons, reef faces, slopes
- ↧ 4–60 m (13–195 ft)
- ↔ 22 cm (8.7 in)

Male guards harem of females; group forages and moves about together over expansive home range. During courtship male swims rapidly in wide circles and loops. Also "flutter display," where he hangs in water column and flutters pectoral fins. Feeds on small benthic invertebrates. Similar to white-spotted tamarin wrasse (*A. melanurus*) but has all-yellow tail.

⊕ Red Sea and East Africa to Andaman Sea and Christmas Island
⊙ Coastal and outer reefs; reef faces, slopes
↧ 6–40 m (20–130 ft)　　　　　　↔ 25 cm (9.8 in)

Diana's Hogfish
Bodianus diana
Family Labridae (wrasses)

Solitary or in pairs; juveniles occur singly, often in caves or under overhangs. Part-time cleaners. Adults feed on wide range of invertebrate prey. Juveniles brown with white markings. Very similar redfin hogfish (*B. dictynna*) is Pacific form; differs in having spots on median fins.

⊕ Central Gulf of California to Chile; Cocos, Malpelo, Revillagigedo and Galapagos Islands
⊙ Rocky reefs; often amid large macroalgae stands, mixed areas of rock rubble, sand and large boulders
↧ 4.5–76 m (15–251 ft)　　　　　　↔ 76 cm (29.9 in)

Cortez Hogfish
Bodianus diplotaenia
Family Labridae (wrasses)

Juveniles form small groups that clean other fish; adults solitary or in small aggregations. Feeds on mollusks, crustaceans, urchins and small fishes. Will follow other fishes that disturb substrate (e.g., goatfishes). Males territorial during daytime but in late afternoon large males form temporary spawning territories; single male may spawn with up to 100 females. Juvenile in inset photo.

Ray-Finned Fishes

Spanish Hogfish
Bodianus rufus
Family Labridae (wrasses)

- ⊕ Florida and Bermuda, south to Brazil
- ☉ Coastal and outer coral reefs; lagoons, back reefs, reef faces, slopes
- ↧ 1–60 m (3.3–195 ft)
- ↦ 40 cm (15.7 in)

Solitary. Opportunist, always looking for lunch. Feeds primarily on crabs, serpent stars and sea urchins but also many other invertebrates. Quick to investigate when sees foraging eel or diver moving rubble. Juveniles part-time cleaners, often joining forces with cleaner gobies. Male protects harem of up to 12 females; patrols territory while feeding in his domain. Easy to approach.

Red-breasted Wrasse
Cheilinus fasciatus
Family Labridae (wrasses)

- ⊕ Red Sea to Samoa, north to Ryukyu Islands and south to New Caledonia
- ☉ Coastal and outer reefs; lagoons, reef channels, reef faces, slopes
- ↧ 4–130 m (13–425 ft)
- ↦ 38 cm (15 in)

Solitary. Feeds on mollusks, crustaceans and small fishes. Lifts pieces of rubble in mouth to uncover hidden prey; follows grubbing goatfishes. In afternoon male finds prominent feature in territory, which females visit. Male circles female, then pair swim in parallel, rising in water column to release gametes; male spawns with multiple females. Male has bright orange area behind head.

- Red Sea to Tuamotu Islands, north to Ryukyu Islands and south to New Caledonia
- Coastal and outer reefs; lagoons, reef channels, reef faces, slopes
- 1–60 m (3.3–195 ft) ↔ 2.3 m (7.5 ft)

Humphead Wrasse
Cheilinus undulatus
Family Labridae (wrasses)

Solitary or in loose groups (usually single male and two or more females). Occupies large home range, returning every night to preferred sleeping site. Feeds on bivalves, crustaceans, sea stars (including crown-of-thorns), sea urchins and fishes. Sometimes associated with goatfishes or jacks. Can be common in areas where not heavily fished; rare in most locations.

- Eastern Andaman Sea, east to Palau, north to southern Japan and south to Great Barrier Reef
- Coastal reefs; patch reefs, coral rubble, seagrass beds
- 1–35 m (3.3–116 ft) ↔ 13 cm (5.1 in)

Bluesided Fairy Wrasse
Cirrhilabrus cyanopleura
Family Labridae (wrasses)

Forms small to large loose groups, mainly females and juveniles. Feeds up to several meters over seafloor on zooplankton. Groups sometimes joined by other zooplankton-feeding fishes. Spawns later in afternoon, when male begins dashing about group, displaying to females and chasing other males (color intensifies). Spawns in water column. Some males have yellow patch on side.

Creole Wrasse

Clepticus parrae

Family Labridae (wrasses)

- 🌐 Florida and Bermuda, south to South America
- ☉ Coastal and outer coral reefs; reef faces, slopes
- ↕ 1–40 m (3.3–130 ft)
- ↔ 30 cm (11.8 in)

Young and adults form roving shoals. Groups visit cleaning stations and do headstands and change color as inspected and cleaned. In late afternoon huge shoals migrate to spawning grounds on outer reef, where males fight for females. Produces pelagic eggs. Easy to approach, especially when being cleaned. South of Amazon, replaced by Brazilian creole wrasse (*C. brasiliensis*).

Yellowtail Coris

Coris gaimard

Family Labridae (wrasses)

- 🌐 Christmas Island (Indian Ocean) and Indonesia, east to Hawaiian, Marquesas and Tuamotu Islands, north to southern Japan and south to New Caledonia and Austral Islands
- ☉ Coastal and outer reefs; lagoons, reef flats, reef faces, slopes; usually in areas of mixed coral, rubble and sand or on sand patches
- ↕ 3–50 m (10–165 ft)
- ↔ 38 cm (15.0 in)

Solitary. Feeds during day on bivalves, crabs, hermit crabs and sea urchins. When hunting, throws over rocks with mouth or digs in sand with snout to uncover prey. Buries itself under sand when threatened and at night. Juveniles reddish orange with white spots and white tail; adults have dark body with blue spots and yellow tail. Juvenile coloration shown in inset.

🌐 Red Sea to northwest Hawaiian and Tuamotu islands, north to southern Japan and south to New Caledonia

◉ Coastal and outer reefs; lagoons, reef faces, slopes; most often areas with rich stony coral growth

↧ 1– 42 m (3.3–137 ft)　　　　↤ 35 cm (14 in)

Slingjaw Wrasse

Epibulus insidiator

Family Labridae (wrasses)

Solitary. Juveniles rather secretive; adults parade around reef. Sometimes associates with others fishes, such as yellow goatfish, when hunting or will hide among schools of algae-eating fishes to sneak up on prey. Extensible jaw that can be shot forward to snatch prey from reef crevices. Main prey crustaceans and small fishes. Dwarf slingjaw (*E. brevis*) is similar but males brown with yellow on throat and females yellow or whitish.

🌐 Cocos-Keeling Islands, Christmas Island and Rowley Shoals (eastern Indian Ocean), east to Hawaiian and Pitcairn Islands, north to southern Japan and south to Lord Howe Island, New Caledonia and Rapa Island

◉ Coastal and outer coral and rocky reefs; lagoons, back reefs, reef faces, slopes

↧ 1–30 m (3.3–98 ft)　　　　↤ 28 cm (11 in)

Bird Wrasse

Gomphosus varius

Family Labridae (wrasses)

Solitary species that dashes about reef, occasionally stopping to hunt for prey. Uses long snout to wrest small bivalves, crustaceans and small fishes from reef crevices and from between coral branches. Forms hunting partnerships with goatfishes. Males green with black pectoral fins; females light anteriorly and dark on rear of body and tail. Male in main photo, female in inset photo.

Yellowhead Wrasse

Halichoeres garnoti
Family Labridae (wrasses)

- Florida and Bermuda, south to Brazil, including northern Gulf of Mexico
- Coastal and outer coral reefs; lagoons, back reefs, reef faces, slopes
- 2–80 m (7–260 ft)
- 18 cm (7.1 in)

Solitary. Juveniles often found among soft and stony corals, adults near reef–sand interface. Uses mouth to flip stones and rubble when searching for hiding food. Uses rocks as anvils to break apart hard-bodied prey. Spawning occurs in late morning to early afternoon. Juvenile yellow overall with bright blue line in middle of body; super males have bright yellow head and blue-green on body.

Checkerboard Wrasse

Halichoeres hortulanus
Family Labridae (wrasses)

- Red Sea to Marquesas and Tuamotu Islands, north to southern Japan and south to Great Barrier Reef
- Coastal and outer coral reefs; lagoons, back reefs, reef faces, slopes
- 1–30 m (3.3–98 ft)
- 27 cm (10.6 in)

Solitary. Feeds on snails, crustaceans, worms and small fishes. Often follows goatfishes and other species that disturb seafloor. Will try to outrun a threat instead of bury itself under sand; will take refuge in sand at night. While individuals from Indian Ocean lack second yellow spot under dorsal fin, they are considered same species as that in Pacific.

East Africa to Samoa, east to Line Islands, north to southern Japan and south to southeastern Australia

⊙ Coastal and outer reefs; lagoons, rubble reef flats, reef faces, slopes

↧ 1–30 m (3.3–98 ft)   ↔ 38 cm (15 in)

Pastel Ring Wrasse

Hologymnosus doliatus

Family Labridae (wrasses)

Juveniles solitary or in loose groups; initial-phase individuals form loose groups; males solitary. Feeds on fishes more than most other wrasses — its more elongate body belies its speed — but also eats a variety of invertebrates. Adults often follow foraging octopuses and goatfishes. Juveniles white with red stripes along body; terminal-phase males have light band behind pectoral fins.

Red Sea to Mexico, north to southern Japan and south to Lord Howe Island, including Gulf of California to Panama and Galapagos Islands

⊙ Coastal sand plains adjacent to coral reefs

↧ 2–90 m (7–98 ft)   ↔ 41 cm (16.1 in)

Peacock Razorfish

Iniistius pavo

Family Labridae (wrasses)

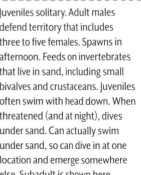

Juveniles solitary. Adult males defend territory that includes three to five females. Spawns in afternoon. Feeds on invertebrates that live in sand, including small bivalves and crustaceans. Juveniles often swim with head down. When threatened (and at night), dives under sand. Can actually swim under sand, so can dive in at one location and emerge somewhere else. Subadult is shown here.

Bluestreak Cleaner Wrasse

Labroides dimidiatus
Family Labridae (wrasses)

- ⊕ Entire Indo-Pacific except Hawaiian Islands (replaced there by *L. phthirophagus*)
- ⊙ Coastal and outer reefs; lagoon patch reefs, back reefs, reef faces, slopes
- ↧ 1–40 m (3.3–132 ft)
- ↔ 11.5 cm (4.5 in)

Social structure varies between populations. Juveniles solitary and territorial. Adults occur in pairs that maintain a territory, usually around some conspicuous reef feature (e.g., promontory). Set up cleaning stations visited by hundreds of fish a day, which wrasses pick parasites from (also eat scales and slime from clients). Spawns throughout day, usually during outgoing tide.

Twinspot Wrasse

Oxycheilinus bimaculatus
Family Labridae (wrasses)

- ⊕ East Africa to Hawaiian Islands, north to southern Japan and south to Vanuatu
- ⊙ Coastal and outer reefs; seagrass meadows, estuaries, harbors, lagoon patch reefs, reef faces, slopes
- ↧ 2–110 m (7–358 ft)
- ↔ 15 cm (5.9 in)

Solitary or in small groups (probably male with females). Males territorial. Will fight by shaking opponent while locking jaws. Feeds on benthic invertebrates. Follows foraging goatfishes. Color variable, but always with yellow patch at base of pectoral fin. Distinguished from close relatives by pointed tail.

- Red Sea to Samoa, north to Ryukyu Islands and south to New Caledonia
- Coastal and outer reefs; lagoon patch reefs, channels, reef faces, slopes
- 1–38 m (3.3–124 ft)   ↔ 35 cm (13.8 in)

Linecheeked Wrasse
Oxycheilinus diagrammus
Family Labridae (wrasses)

Solitary. Feeds on fishes, crustaceans, brittle stars and urchins. Follows goatfishes, triggerfishes and stingrays to pounce on prey items they disturb; changes color (turns light, with line down body) to resemble goatfish it joins with. Also swims alongside larger fishes or in fish shoals to disguise presence and sneak up on wary prey. Color variable. Similar ringtail wrasse (*O. unifasciatus*) has white ring around tail base.

- Red Sea to Panama, north to Ryukyu and Hawaiian Islands and south to Lord Howe and Tuamotu Islands
- Coastal and outer reefs; lagoons, reef flats, channels, reef faces, slopes
- 1–20 m (3.3–66 ft)   ↔ 27 cm (10.6 in)

Rockmover Wrasse
Novaculichthys taeniourus
Family Labridae (wrasses)

Solitary. Juveniles may mimic plant material, swimming in unusual sinusoidal fashion. Will flip rocks and rubble with mouth in attempt to expose hidden prey. Feeds on variety of invertebrates and small fishes. Dives into sand if threatened. Will construct sleeping mounds: rubble that it buries itself under at night. Adults often associated with goatfishes and jacks. When courting, male circles female with fins spread, then rises into water and releases gametes. Juvenile in inset photo.

Ray-Finned Fishes

Filamented Flasher Wrasse

Paracheilinus filamentosus
Family Labridae (wrasses)

⊕ Indonesia, Papua New Guinea, Solomon Islands, Philippines and Belau
⊙ Coastal reefs; among rubble and macroalgae
↧ 3–35 m (10–114 ft)   ↔ 10 cm (3.9 in)

Forms groups made up mainly of females. May mix with other flasher wrasses and related fairy wrasses (*Cirrhilabrus* spp.). Spawns in later afternoon; male dashes about group with fins extended and exhibits amazing colors ("flashing"). Male more colorful, with long dorsal fin filaments. More than one similar species may now be referred to as *P. filamentosus*.

Bluehead Wrasse

Thalassoma bifasciatum
Family Labridae (wrasses)

⊕ Florida and Bermuda, south to South America, including southeastern Gulf of Mexico
⊙ Coastal and outer coral reefs; lagoons, back reefs, reef faces, slopes
↧ 1–40 m (3.3 to 132 ft)   ↔ 18 cm (7.1 in)

Forms loose groups, initial-phase individuals among tentacles of giant sea anemone (*Condylactis gigantea*). Feeds off substrate on small crustaceans, damselfish eggs and zooplankton. Initial-phase individuals (inset photo) part-time cleaners. Spawning usually occurs in middle of day at traditional spawning sites. Pair and group spawning. Initial phase yellow; terminal phase has blue head and green body. Juvenile phase in inset photo.

⊕ East Africa to Line Islands, north to southern Japan and south to the Lord Howe Island

⊙ Coastal and outer reefs; lagoons, reef flats, reef faces, slopes

↨ 1–15 m (3.3–50 ft)   ↔ 20 cm (7.9 in)

Sixbar Wrasse
Thalassoma hardwicke
Family Labridae (wrasses)

Occurs singly or in small groups. Young fish usually found among branching stony corals. Feeds mainly on crustaceans, both benthic and planktonic. Spawns during daytime, all year round in at least some locations. Spawning occurs in or near reef channels.

⊕ Gulf of California to Panama and Galapagos Islands

⊙ Coastal and insular rocky and coral reefs; variety of habitats

↨ 1–64 m (3.3–208 ft)   ↔ 15 cm (5.9 in)

Cortez Rainbow Wrasse
Thalassoma lucasanum
Family Labridae (wrasses)

Found singly or in small groups. Initial-phase fish occasionally form large groups numbering in hundreds when invading damselfish nests to eat eggs. Feeds on benthic invertebrates as well as zooplankton. Spawns daily, late morning and afternoon. Initial-phase fish group-spawn; terminal-phase males form temporary spawning territories and spawn with single individuals.

Moon Wrasse

Thalassoma lunare

Family Labridae (wrasses)

- 🌐 East Africa, east to Line Islands, north to southern Japan and south to Lord Howe Island
- ☉ Coastal and outer reefs; almost all reef zones (even estuaries)
- ↧ 1–20 m (3.3–66 ft)
- ↔ 25 cm (9.8 in)

Solitary; adults may be haremic. Diet varied and includes a number of bottom-dwelling invertebrates and fishes; will also feed on zooplankton. Adults often join zooplankton-feeding fishes when feeding high in water column. Known to invade damselfish nests and feed on their eggs, sometimes in groups. Sometimes cleans other fishes (adults will pick parasites off manta rays). Juveniles sometimes swim among sea anemone tentacles.

Klunzinger's Wrasse

Thalassoma rueppellii

Family Labridae (wrasses)

- 🌐 Red Sea
- ☉ Coastal reefs; lagoons, back reefs, reef flats, reef faces, slopes
- ↧ 1–25 m (3.3–83 ft)
- ↔ 20 cm (7.9 in)

Juveniles solitary; adults often seen on own, but males defend harem of females. Feeds on variety of benthic invertebrates and small fishes. Sometimes swims along with large parrotfishes as they feed, snapping up small prey items chased out by feeding parrots. At night hides in reef crevices.

Florida, south to Venezuela
Lagoons, outer reef slopes
5–15 m (17–49 ft)   ↔ 15 cm (5.9 in)

Rosy Razorfish
Xyrichtys martinicensis
Family Labridae (wrasses)

Lives in colonies of 5–100 individuals, mainly females. Male defends 3–35 females in colony, chasing off rival males. Pairs spawn in late afternoon, releasing gametes about 1 m (3.3 ft) above substrate. When threatened and at night, dives under sand surface. Can swim under the sand, so can re-emerge in different location.

East Africa and Red Sea, east to French Polynesia, north to southern Japan and south to Australia
Coastal and outer reefs; lagoons, reef flats, reef faces, slopes
2–40 m (7–130 ft)   ↔ 1.3 m (4.2 ft)

Bumphead Parrotfish
Bolbometopon muricatum
Family Scaridae (parrotfishes)

Juveniles solitary; adults usually in small shoals (up to 40 individuals). Juveniles usually in shallow inner lagoon; also in seagrass and on reef flats. Moves out to reef channels and outer reef habitats as matures. Feeds on algae and stony corals (important contributor to sand around reef). Aggregates to spawn. Pair spawning occurs in early morning. At night rests in caves or on shallow sand flats. Endangered by overfishing in some areas.

Spotted Parrotfish

Cetoscarus ocellatus

Family Scaridae (parrotfishes)

⊕ East Africa, east to Society and Tuamotu Islands and Micronesia
⊙ Coastal and outer reefs; clear lagoons, reef faces, slopes
↧ 1–30 m (3.3–98 ft)   ↔ 80 cm (32 in)

Juveniles solitary. Terminal-phase males territorial, maintaining a harem. Initial-phase individuals home-ranging, sometimes forming groups when foraging. Eats algae and stony corals. Will group and pair spawn. Juveniles very different in color from adults. Similar *C. bicolor* limited to Red Sea. Terminal phase in top photo. Intermediate phase in middle photo. Juvenile phase in bottom photo.

⊕ East Africa and Red Sea, east to French Polynesia, north to southern Japan and south to Australia

⊙ Coastal and outer coral reefs; lagoon patch reefs, reef faces, slopes

↧ 1–25 m (3.3–81 ft)　　　　　↔ 47 cm (19 in)

Bridled Parrotfish

Scarus frenatus
Family Scaridae (parrotfishes)

Solitary. Haremic; terminal-phase males defend groups of females. One of most aggressive scarids, forming territories from which it excludes members of own kind and other parrotfishes. Initial-phase individuals occasionally form small shoals. Feeds on algae. Terminal phase has light area on tail base with blue crescent on tail; initial phase brown, black and salmon color.

⊕ East Africa and Red Sea, east to Panama and Gulf of California, north to southern Japan and south to Australia

⊙ Coastal and outer rocky and coral reefs; lagoons, back reefs, reef faces, slopes; more often in murky water than other scarids

↧ 2–30 m (7–98 ft)　　　　　↔ 75 cm (30 in)

Blue-barred Parrotfish

Scarus ghobban
Family Scaridae (parrotfishes)

Solitary or in roving groups. Lives in large home range but not thought to be territorial. Feeds on filamentous algae but also ingests some sand and detritus. Sometimes followed by opportunistic wrasses as it forages. Initial phase in inset photo.

Redlip or Ember Parrotfish

Scarus rubroviolaceus
Family Scaridae (parrotfishes)

- ⊕ East Africa and Red Sea, east to Panama, north to southern Japan and south to Australia
- ⊙ Coastal and outer rocky and coral reefs; lagoons, back reefs, reef faces, slopes
- ↓ 1–30 m (3.3–98 ft)
- ↔ 70 cm (28 in)

Solitary, in pairs or in large shoals (initial-phase individuals). Adult male has protruding forehead. Initial phase red and brown; terminal phase shades of green with two bands on lower jaw.

Princess Parrotfish

Scarus taeniopterus
Family Scaridae (parrotfishes)

- ⊕ Florida and Bermuda, south to Brazil
- ⊙ Coastal and outer coral reefs; lagoons, reef faces
- ↓ 2–25 m (7–81 ft)
- ↔ 35 cm (13.8 in)

Usually over coral-rich reefs but also in seagrass beds. Feeds on algae, detritus, seagrasses and sponges. Terminal-phase males territorial, with three to five females. Initial-phase fish often form foraging groups. Usually spawns in pairs. Somewhat wary but can usually be approached if done in non-threatening manner.

⊕ Florida and Bermuda, south to Brazil, including Gulf of Mexico
⊙ Coastal and outer coral reefs; lagoons, back reefs, reef faces, slopes
↨ 3–50 (10 to 163 ft)   ↔ 37 cm (14.6 in)

Stoplight Parrotfish
Sparisoma viride
Family Scaridae (parrotfishes)

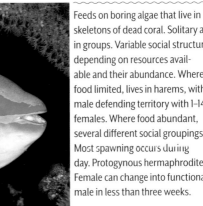

Feeds on boring algae that live in skeletons of dead coral. Solitary and in groups. Variable social structure depending on resources available and their abundance. Where food limited, lives in harems, with male defending territory with 1–14 females. Where food abundant, several different social groupings. Most spawning occurs during day. Protogynous hermaphrodite. Female can change into functional male in less than three weeks.

⊕ Red Sea, east to Fiji, north to Ryukyu Islands and south to Lord Howe Island
⊙ Coastal and outer reefs; lagoons, reef flats, channels, sand and rubble slopes
↨ 2–22 m (7–73 ft)   ↔ 26 cm (10.2 in)

Speckled Sandperch
Parapercis hexophthalma
Family Pinguipedidae (sandperches)

Haremic. Male's territory home to 1–3 females. Females set up own territories in male's larger area. Feeds on small fishes, shrimp, crabs and polychaete worms. Easily approached and even attracted to divers flipping over pieces of rubble — cannot help but come to see what diver may have uncovered.

Blackfin Sandperch
Parapercis snyderi
Family Pinguipedidae (sandperches)

⊕ Andaman Sea and Indonesia, north to southern Japan and south to Great Barrier Reef
☉ Coastal reefs; lagoons, sand and rubble slopes; often silty habitat
↓ 2–45 m (7–146 ft)　　　　　↔ 10 cm (3.9 in)

Haremic, male with harem of 3–10 females. Males have overlapping home ranges. Females change sex. Spawning occurs around sunrise; males spawn with all females in harem every evening. Neighboring males may try to intercept spawning pair and release own sperm. Black patch on front of dorsal fin; black tail margin.

Elegant Sand Diver
Trichonotus elegans
Family Trichonotidae (sand divers)

⊕ Indonesia to Fiji, north to southern Japan and south to Coral Sea
☉ Coastal reefs; sand flats and slopes
↓ 2–40 m (7–130 ft)　　　　　↔ 18 cm (7 in)

Forms loose groups. Haremic: one male with 4–5 females. Feeds on crustaceans drifting near seafloor. Will dive and swim under sand (can disappear in one place and reappear meters away). Buries itself under sand at night. Male has long dorsal filaments. Mates in early evening; eggs deposited on seafloor, then fertilized eggs picked up by female, which incubates them in gill chamber.

- Red Sea, east to Samoa
- Coastal sand and mud flats and slopes, often adjacent to coral reefs
- 5–150 m (16–487 ft)   ↔ 45 cm (18 in)

Whitemargin Stargazer

Uranoscopus sulphureus
Family Uranoscopidae (stargazers)

Solitary. Spends almost all life under sand. Usually only top of head seen by divers during night dives. Uses lure: long filaments on lower jaw that are thrown into water column to attract fish prey. Cirri on jaws keep sand from falling into mouth. Venomous spine on "shoulder" can cause painful wound.

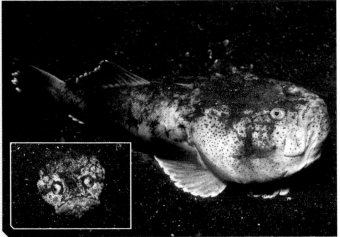

- Southern Japan to Great Barrier Reef
- Coastal reefs; lagoon patch reefs, reef faces, slopes
- 2–20 m (7–66 ft)   ↔ 5 cm (2 in)

Striped Triplefin

Helcogramma striatum
Family Tripterygiidae (triplefin blennies)

Occurs singly or in loose groups. Often rests on stony corals or sponges or among tunicates. Feeds on zooplankton. Most common and attractive of triplefins in Indo-Pacific. The fish in this family get their name from the dorsal fin, which is split into three distinct sections. Most of the 200-odd species in the family occur in the intertidal zone. There are 38 species in the genus.

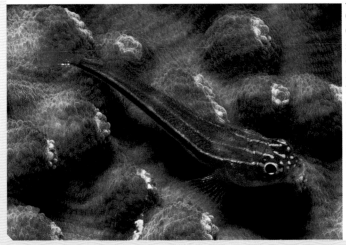

Diamond Blenny

Malacoctenus boehlkei

Family Labrisomidae (blennies)

- 🌐 Bahamas, south to Bonaire
- ⊙ Coastal and outer reefs; lagoon patch reefs, back reefs, reef faces, slopes
- ↧ 5–70 m (16 to 228 ft) ↤ 6.4 cm (2.5 in)

Solitary. Lives under base of giant sea anemone (*Condylactis gigantea*); can contact tentacles without harm to itself. Dashes from one coral crevice to another or perches on top of coral surveying surroundings. During spawning season, male's head becomes bright yellow. Spawning occurs during day. Eggs deposited in crevice, guarded and cared for by male.

Mexican Barnacle Blenny

Acanthemblemaria macrospilus

Family Chaenopsidae (tube blennies)

- 🌐 Southern Baja California, south to Acapulco, Mexico, and Revillagigedo Islands
- ⊙ Coastal and insular rocky reefs; rock walls and boulders
- ↧ 1–15 m (3.3–49 ft) ↤ 5 cm (2 in)

Solitary. Inhabits empty barnacle shells and mollusk tubes, often in high-surge areas. Spends most of time hiding but occasionally dashes out from cover to capture passing zooplankton or pick off benthic invertebrate nearby. Eggs laid in shelter site, guarded by male until they hatch.

⊕ Bahamas to Tobago
⊙ Coastal coral reefs; reef flats and faces
↕ 2–8 m (7–26 ft)   ↔ 5.1 cm (2.0 in)

Secretary Blenny
Acanthemblemaria maria
Family Chaenopsidae (tube blennies)

Solitary. Lives in limestone areas exposed to surge, in empty holes of tube worms. Dashes out from hole to snag passing zooplankton. Swims back into hole when approached but usually sticks out head to inspect patient intruder. Several similar species: *A. maria* has alternating brown and pale bars and white streak below eye, while similar spinyhead blenny (*A. spinosa*) dark brown overall with white head.

⊕ Florida to Venezuela
⊙ Coastal coral reefs; lagoons, back reefs
↕ 5–20 m (16–65 ft)   ↔ 8.5 cm (3.3 in)

Yellowface Pikeblenny
Chaenopsis limbaughi
Family Chaenopsidae (tube blennies)

Solitary. Usually lives among sand and rubble. Territorial, defending preferred shelter site and adjacent feeding area. Larger individuals usurp homes from smaller specimens, often leading to dynamic battles in which combatants raise fins and open mouth wide to intimidate each other. If smaller fish does not back down, combatants push jaws together and attempt to overpower opponent. Female less colorful than male (male shown here).

Sailfin Blenny

Emblemaria pandionis

Family Chaenopsidae (blennies)

⊕ Florida and Bahamas to northern South America, including northern Gulf of Mexico
⊙ Coastal rocky and coral reefs; lagoon patch reefs, reef faces
↧ 1–12 m (3.3–39 ft)   ↔ 5 cm (2 in)

Forms colonial groups, most often in holes in coral fragments. Feeds on zooplankton. Breeding male guards hole, in which one or more females deposit eggs. Male has much higher dorsal fin than female, which it raises and lowers when displaying to neighbors ("flagging"), and large pectoral fins. Color of male very dark during spawning period.

Arrow Blenny

Lucayablennius zingaro

Family Chaenopsidae (blennies)

⊕ Bahamas and Caribbean Sea
⊙ Coastal and outer coral reefs
↧ 13–106 m (42–345 ft)   ↔ 3.8 cm (1.5 in)

Solitary. Most abundant at greater depths (21 m/70 ft or more). Hovers just off substrate, moving in erratic fashion with tail curled around toward head. When sees a tiny fish or crustacean, launches itself forward by suddenly straightening body. Takes refuge and female deposits eggs in holes in reef. Male guards eggs.

⊕ East Africa to Society Islands, north to Ryukyu Islands and south to New Caledonia
⊙ Coastal reefs; lagoon patch reefs, reef flats, reef faces
↕ 1–6 m (3.3–20 ft)   ↔ 13.5 cm (5.3 in)

Red-spotted Blenny
Blenniella chrysospilos
Family Blenniidae (blennies)

Solitary or in groups. Eats algae, detritus and associated micro-invertebrates. Found in habitat influenced by high wave energy in intertidal zone. Regularly flips (or "skips") from one tide pool to next, often leaving water for short periods. During breeding season male maintains territory that harbors nesting site (usually a crevice). Larger males spawn with more females than smaller ones. Guards demersal eggs. Adults eaten by various piscivorous fishes (e.g., morays, groupers) and sea snakes.

⊕ Helen Atoll, Halmahera, Admiralty Islands, New Britain, Milne Bay, Papua New Guinea and Solomon Islands
⊙ Outer reefs; reef faces, slopes
↕ 1–25 m (3.3–81 ft)   ↔ 5 cm (2 in)

Clown Blenny
Ecsenius axelrodi
Family Blenniidae (blennies)

Solitary. Perches on coral promontories, diving for shelter when threatened. Feeds by rasping unicellular algae from hard substrates. Lays demersal eggs in a nest; eggs attached to sides or roof of shelter hole by tiny threads. Male does not tend eggs until ready to hatch, then vigorously fans them with fins. Two distinct color phases: banded and striped.

Bicolor Blenny

Ecsenius bicolor
Family Blenniidae (blennies)

⊕ Maldives to Phoenix Islands, north to Ryukyu Islands and south to Great Barrier Reef
⊙ Coastal and outer reefs; lagoon patch reefs, reef faces, slopes
↕ 1–25 m (3.3–81 ft)   ↔ 11 cm (4.3 in)

Solitary. Grazes on microalgae, although ingests stony coral polyps on occasion. Seeks shelter in reef crevices and empty serpulid worm tubes. Lays eggs in hiding place. When stressed, exhibits white or bluish white spots and lines. Four distinct color phases: uniform brown color; bicolored; striped with yellow tail; striped without yellow tail.

Leopard Blenny

Exallias brevis
Family Blenniidae (blennies)

⊕ East Africa and Red Sea, east to Hawaii, north to southern Japan and south to Australia
⊙ Outer reefs with rich stony coral growth; lagoon patch reefs, reef faces, slopes
↕ 2–20 m (7–65 ft)   ↔ 14.5 cm (5.7 in)

Solitary. Male territorial. Feeds mainly on stony coral polyps but spreads out feeding activity so rarely kills coral colonies. Male removes all polyps from portion of colony to serve as egg deposition site. Female moves from one territory to another, depositing eggs in nests of up to 10 different males. Male defends nest until eggs hatch but may occasionally eat eggs. Male red in color.

⊕ Florida and Gulf of Mexico, south to Brazil
⊙ Coastal rocky reefs; pier pilings, oil platforms, buoys, rocky reef faces
↕ 1–3 m (3.3–10 ft)   ↔ 5.8 cm (2.3 in)

Tesselated Blenny
Hypsoblennius invemar
Family Blenniidae (blennies)

Solitary. Resides in empty barnacles (*Megabalanus antillensis*), which defends from other blennies. Feeds on algae and passing zooplankton. Lays adhesive eggs in hideout. This gorgeous blenny not encountered much in Caribbean. When located, usually just peeks out from barnacle home, although will occasionally dart out to capture zooplankton. Bright orange spots on head make it easily recognizable.

⊕ Indonesia east to Samoa, north to Ryukyu Islands and south to Great Barrier Reef and New Caledonia
⊙ Coastal and outer coral reefs; lagoons, reef faces, slopes
↕ 1–30 m (3.3–98 ft)   ↔ 11 cm (4.3 in)

Yellowtail Fangblenny
Meiacanthus atrodorsalis
Family Blenniidae (blennies)

Occurs singly or in pairs; rarely forms small groups. Hovers in water column, dashes forward (swimming in eel-like fashion), then stops abruptly and resumes hovering. Found in open because of venomous fangs used to bite predators in mouth if ingested. Feeds on tiny crustaceans and zooplankton. In Fiji replaced by canary fangblenny (*M. oualanensis*), which is all yellow.

Redlip Blenny

Ophioblennius atlanticus
Family Blenniidae (blennies)

🌐 Bermuda and North Carolina, south to Trinidad Island; also rarely in northern Gulf of Mexico
☉ Coastal and outer reefs; lagoon patch reefs, reef faces, slopes
↧ 1–18 m (3.3–59 ft)   ↔ 19 cm (7.5 in)

Solitary; territorial. Bulk of diet organic detritus but also algal material, including diatoms and different types of blue-green algae. Most spawning in first three hours of daylight during week of full moon. Spawns year-round, with female laying up to 4,000 eggs per month. Male spawns with more than one female. Larger males with larger nests have greater reproductive success. Does not change sex.

Mexican Fanged Blenny

Ophioblennius steindachneri
Family Blenniidae (blennies)

🌐 Northern Gulf of California to Peru, including Galapagos Islands
☉ Coastal and insular rocky reefs; surge zones, drop-off ledges
↧ 1–18 m (3.3–56 ft)   ↔ 18 cm (7.1 in)

Solitary. Territorial, usually with two or three preferred shelter sites in territory. Defends area vigorously from own kind and other intruders. Uses expandable jaws to rasp algae and detritus from rocks, incidentally ingesting some small invertebrates. Female deposits white egg mass in rocky crevice, which male fertilizes and then defends.

🌐 East Africa to Papua New Guinea, north to southern Japan and south to New Caledonia
⊙ Coastal reefs; estuaries, bays, reef faces
↧ 1–10 m (3.3–33 ft)   ↔ 11 cm (4.3 in)

Shorthead Fangblenny

Petroscirtes breviceps
Family Blenniidae (blennies)

Occurs singly or in pairs. Sometimes rests among macroalgae. Feeds on small crustaceans and algae. Mimics striped fangblenny (*Meiacanthus grammistes*), which has venomous fangs. Lays adhesive eggs in shells and benthic debris (e.g., pop cans, bottles).

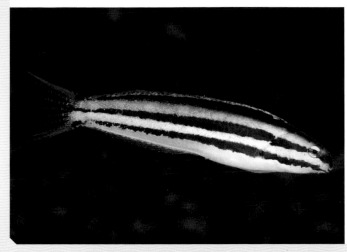

🌐 East Africa, east to French Polynesia, north to southern Japan and south to Great Barrier Reef
⊙ Coastal reefs; lagoon patch reefs, reef faces, slopes
↧ 4–40 m (13–130 ft)   ↔ 12 cm (4.7 in)

Bluestriped Fangblenny

Plagiotremus rhinorhynchus
Family Blenniidae (blennies)

Solitary. Swims in water column. Aggressive mimic; different color forms may mimic different species. One looks similar to bluestreak cleaner wrasse, while orange color phase resembles lyretail anthias (this color phase often swims among these fishes). Feeds by biting mucus and scales off other fishes; also eats benthic invertebrates. Usually takes refuge in empty serpulid worm tubes.

Red Clingfish
Acyrtus rubiginosus
Family Gobiesocidae (clingfishes)

⊕ Bahamas, south to Lesser Antilles and Honduras
⊙ Coastal and outer reefs; reef crests and faces (usually in areas exposed to surge)
↧ 1–30 m (3.3–98 ft)   ↔ 3.5 cm (1.4 in)

Solitary. Small, flat, highly cryptic fish that takes refuge among spines of sea urchin *Echinometra lucunter*, on gorgonians or in reef crevices. Modified pelvic fins help it adhere to substrate. Feeds on benthic crustaceans and zooplankton. Deposits demersal eggs in reef crevices. Small-headed clingfish (*Apletodon dentatus*) also found with sea urchins (different species of echinoderms) during part of life cycle.

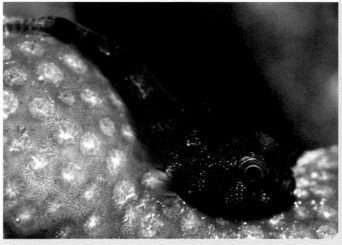

Urchin Clingfish
Diademichthys lineatus
Family Gobiesocidae (clingfishes)

⊕ Arabian Sea, east to Indonesia, north to southern Japan and south to Australia
⊙ Coastal and outer coral reefs; reef faces, slopes; *Diadema* sea urchins
↧ 3–20 m (10–65 ft)   ↔ 5 cm (2 in)

Solitary or in pairs. Associates with long-spined sea urchins. Young fish feed mainly on urchin pedicellariae and sphaeridia (appendages urchins use for movement and feeding). Larger *D. lineatus* also ingest small bivalves, copepods and invertebrate eggs. Swims with snakelike undulations. Unlike many clingfish, which are cryptic, swims in open.

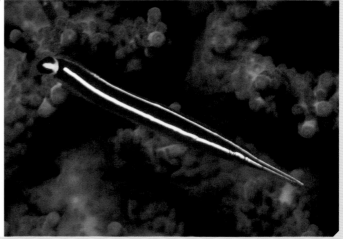

⊕ Ryukyu Islands, south to Great Barrier Reef; Christmas Island (Indian Ocean)
⊙ Coastal and outer coral reefs; reef faces; always among arms of crinoids
↧ 8–20 m (26–65 ft)　　　　　　　↔ 5 cm (2 in)

Crinoid Clingfish

Discotrema crinophila
Family Gobiesocidae (clingfishes)

Solitary or in pairs. Apparently feeds on other animals that live among crinoid arms (e.g., crustaceans, worms). Cryptic; often seen only if you look carefully into the crinoid — usually hangs out on oral disc. Similar to *D. monogrammum*, which is also found in crinoids, but latter species lacks stripe down back.

⊕ Indonesia
⊙ Coastal sand and mud flats and slopes, often adjacent to coral reefs
↧ 5–40 m (17–132 ft)　　　　　　↔ 15 cm (5.9 in)

Orange and Black Dragonet

Dactylopus kuiteri
Family Callionymidae (dragonets)

Solitary. Hops along seafloor or propels itself forward with pectoral and caudal fins. When threatened, throws up long dorsal spines and exhibits eyespot at base of fin, which may frighten some predators. Picks small invertebrates off substrate. Partially buries itself under sand during night. Juvenile white over much of body; adults are mottled. Similar to fingered dragonet (*D. dactylopus*), which has more filamentous first dorsal spines.

Mandarinfish
Synchiropus splendidus
Family Callionymidae (dragonets)

- 🌐 Java, east to Micronesia, north to Ryukyu Islands and south to Great Barrier Reef
- ☉ Coastal reefs; protected areas, including lagoons with rubble, rubbish and waterlogged leaf litter
- ↧ 1–18 m (5–59 ft)
- ↔ 6 cm (2.4 in)

Haremic; male defends group of females. Males fight viciously, often biting one another or jaw-locking; larger males dominate and spawn with more females. Lives deep among rubble or debris, where feeds and socially interacts. Later in afternoon and on overcast days becomes bolder, emerging from rubble to feed. Courtship begins at dusk. Pelagic eggs.

Giant Shrimpgoby
Amblyeleotris fontanesii
Family Gobiidae (gobies)

- 🌐 Sumatra, east to west Indonesia and Palau and north to southwest Japan
- ☉ Coastal reefs; sand or mud flats and slopes
- ↧ 5–30 m (16–98 ft)
- ↔ 25 cm (9.8 in)

Solitary. Occupies burrow of large reddish brown snapping shrimp; shrimp remains in contact with goby when working outside burrow. More often on silty bottoms than many other members of genus. "Mother of all shrimpgobies" — much larger than most other species. Small orange spots on head and five brown bands on body.

🌐 Great Barrier Reef to Samoa, north to Japan
◉ Coastal reefs; back reefs, reef faces (on sand patches among coral), slopes
↧ 4–34 m (13–111 ft)   ↔ 9 cm (3.5 in)

Spotted Shrimpgoby
Amblyeleotris guttata
Family Gobiidae (gobies)

Solitary. Vigorously defends burrow from conspecific intrusion. During breeding season, females and males occupy same burrow; eggs laid in burrow chamber. Lives with snapping shrimp. Rarely moves far from burrow entrance. Feeds on zooplankton and food exposed by digging activity of shrimp. Orange spots on head and body.

🌐 Indonesia to Australia, north to Philippines and Micronesia
◉ Coastal reefs; usually sand patches on reef faces and slopes
↧ 10–48 m (33–156 ft)   ↔ 9 cm (3.5 in)

Randall's Shrimpgoby
Amblyeleotris randalli
Family Gobiidae (gobies)

Solitary. Often found under ledges or on cave floors. Spectacular dorsal fin with eyespot that is raised and lowered when swims out of burrow. Will spend more time hovering over burrow entrance than others in genus. Lives with snapping shrimp. Feeds on zooplankton and small invertebrates that live in sand. Eaten by sea snakes and sandperches.

Wire Coral Goby

Bryaninops yongei
Family Gobiidae (gobies)

⊕ Red Sea to Hawaiian, Rapa and Marquesas Islands, north to southern Japan and south to Great Barrier Reef

⊙ Coastal and outer coral reefs; reef faces, reef walls, slopes; associates with wire coral (*Cirripathes anguina*)

↕ 3–45 m (10–146 ft)   ↔ 3.5 cm (1.4 in)

Young live on smaller sea whips; large *C. anguina* occupied by monogamous adult pairs. Larger whips may harbor adult pair and one or more juveniles. Capable of bidirectional sex change. During spawning, male removes polyps from host and female deposits eggs on exposed skeleton. Transparent, with diffused bars on upper part of body that help it blend with host.

Peppermint Goby

Coryphopterus lipernes
Family Gobiidae (gobies)

⊕ Florida to Central America

⊙ Coastal and outer coral reefs; patch reefs, reef faces, slopes

↕ 1–13 m (3.3–42 ft)   ↔ 3 cm (1.2 in)

Solitary or in small groups (2–5 individuals). Found over stony coral colonies, resting on coral and dashing up to capture passing zooplankton. Changes sex from female to male. Masked goby (*C. personatus*) is similar species with series of small white blotches on side; lacks blue on face as in *C. lipernes*.

⊕ Andaman Sea to southeast Caroline Islands, north to southern Japan and south to Great Barrier Reef

☉ Coastal reefs; sand and mud flats and slopes

↧ 1–15 m (3.3–49 ft)   ↔ 7 cm (2.8 in)

Banded Shrimpgoby
Cryptocentrus cinctus
Family Gobiidae (gobies)

Solitary or in loose groups. Forms pairs during reproductive season. Lives with snapping shrimp. Does not move far from shelter, feeding on passing zooplankton and small benthic invertebrates. Lays eggs in burrow. Several different color forms: most yellow with blue spots, but also lighter phase with brown banding; another is dark brown overall. Similar to barred shrimp-goby (*C. fasciatus*), which does not have markings on dorsal fins.

⊕ Bahamas, Grand Cayman, Lesser Antilles, Belize and Honduras

☉ Coastal and outer reefs; isolated patch reefs, reef faces, slopes

↧ 8–30 m (26–98 ft)   ↔ 2.5 cm (1.0 in)

Orangesided Goby
Elacatinus dilepis
Family Gobiidae (gobies)

Solitary or in pairs or small groups. Sits on live corals, sponges or limestone substrate. Beautiful little goby, rarely seen. Little known about its biology. Not a cleaning species. Color very distinctive. Once placed in genus *Gobiosoma*; now 20 species recognized in *Elacatinus* in tropical Western Atlantic.

Sharknose Goby

Elacatinus evelynae
Family Gobiidae (gobies)

- Bahamas, south to north coast of South America
- Coastal and outer coral reefs; lagoon patch reefs, back reefs, reef faces, slopes
- 1–45 m (3.3–146 ft)
- 4 cm (1.6 in)

Cleaner species; removes juvenile isopods and dead tissue. Cleans wide range of clients, servicing as many as 100 individual fish in an hour. Monogamous pair maintains cleaning station; will stay at same site for years. Deposits eggs in crevices. Several different color forms (yellow, blue or white striped); all have V mark on snout.

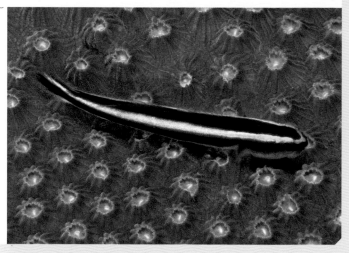

Goldspot Goby

Gnatholepis thompsoni
Family Gobiidae (gobies)

- Florida and Bahamas, south to northern South America
- Coastal and outer coral reefs; lagoons, reef faces, slopes
- 5–50 m (16–163 ft)
- 8.2 cm (3.2 in)

Solitary or in loose groups. Found on sand and rubble bottoms near reef edge. Ducks into rubble interstices or crevices. Takes mouthfuls of sediment and sorts out algae, detritus and tiny crustaceans (does ingest some sand with food items). Distinguished from other sand-dwelling gobies by black line under eye and gold spot above pectoral fin. Easy to approach.

- ⊕ Cocos-Keeling Islands, east to Great Barrier Reef and north to southern Japan
- ☉ Coastal and outer reefs; lagoon patch reefs, reef flats, reef faces
- ↧ 2–15 m (7–49 ft)　　　　　↔ 3.5 cm (1.4 in)

Yellow Coral Goby
Gobiodon okinawae
Family Gobiidae (gobies)

Forms groups. Always found in association with branching stony corals, often living deep in colony, but also hovers just over colony. Feeds on tiny crustaceans, protozoa, coral mucus and tissue. Produces toxic skin mucus similar to that produced by soapfishes (Grammistini), thought to have anti-predation function. Genus contains more than 20 species; *G. okinawae* is only yellow species.

- ⊕ Philippines, south to Great Barrier Reef and east to Marshall Islands
- ☉ Coastal reefs; sand patches on reef faces or slopes, at base of patch reefs
- ↧ 3–30 m (10–98 ft)　　　　　↔ 7 cm (2.8 in)

Rainford's Goby
Koumansetta rainfordi
Family Gobiidae (gobies)

Solitary; rarely forms small groups. Hovers over substrate, occasionally dropping down to take mouthful of filamentous algae or detritus. Filters non-edible materials through gills and swallows tiny invertebrates. Similar to Hector's goby (*K. hectori*), which is dark brown with yellow lines.

Soft Coral Ghost Goby

Pleurosicya boldinghi
Family Gobiidae (gobies)

🌐 East Africa to Papua New Guinea, north to southern Japan and south to Australia
◉ Coastal and outer reefs; reef faces, slopes
↧ 15–45 m (49–146 ft)   ↔ 3.5 cm (1.4 in)

Solitary or in pairs. Found on soft corals, especially those in genus *Dendronephthya*. Feeds on plankton, including what gets trapped on coral host. Light in color, sometimes with hint of hue of host. Lays eggs on seafloor.

Common Ghost Goby

Pleurosicya mossambica
Family Gobiidae (gobies)

🌐 East Africa and Red Sea, east to French Polynesia, north to southern Japan and south to Australia
◉ Coastal and outer reefs; lagoon patch reefs, reef faces, slopes
↧ 2–30 m (7–98 ft)   ↔ 3.5 cm (1.4 in)

Solitary. Found on wide variety of hosts, including sponges, tunicates, soft corals, tridacnid clams, macroalgae and seagrass. Feeds on tiny benthic and planktonic crustaceans. Color highly variable, in part dependent on host color. Lays benthic eggs on host.

- ⊕ Indonesia, east to Palau, north to Philippines and south to Great Barrier Reef
- ☉ Coastal sand and mud flats, slopes
- ↧ 2–30 m (7–98 ft) ↔ 7 cm (2.8 in)

Twinspot Goby
Signigobius biocellatus
Family Gobiidae (gobies)

Adults form monogamous pairs that share burrow. Deposits eggs in burrow, then male sealed in burrow to tend eggs for a while. He emerges and pair close up opening and construct new home near nursery burrow. Eventually parents open nursery burrow and single juvenile fish emerges. Takes mouthfuls of sand and filters out edible invertebrates. Spends most daylight hours feeding. Hovers over bottom. When agitated, swims forward and backward with all fins erected.

- ⊕ Indonesia to Fiji, north to Japan and south to Great Barrier Reef
- ☉ Coastal sand slopes
- ↧ 15–25 m (49–81 ft) ↔ 5 cm (2 in)

Yellownose Shrimpgoby
Stonogobiops xanthorhinica
Family Gobiidae (gobies)

Solitary or in pairs; sometimes in colonies. Unlike most shrimpgobies, hovers over seafloor snapping up zooplankton. Usually lives with red and white–banded snapping shrimp (*Alpheus randalli*). Sometimes lives near similar blackray shrimpgoby (*S. nematodes*), which has long black dorsal filament; in areas where one is less common, may form heterospecific pair.

Orange-dashed Goby

Valenciennea puellaris
Family Gobiidae (gobies)

⊕ Red Sea to Samoa, north to southern Japan and south to southern Great Barrier Reef
⊙ Coastal and outer reefs; lagoons, reef faces, slopes
⬇ 2–20 m (7–65 ft)   ↔ 17 cm (6.7 in)

Solitary or in pairs. Lives in burrow dug by using large mouth. Takes substrate in mouth and filters out worms and tiny crustaceans. Forms long-term pair bond. Females prefer to pair up with larger males. Lays eggs in burrow, in which male is sealed — he fans and mouths eggs. After they hatch, male opens burrow and wafts larvae into water column with pectoral fins.

Decorated Dartfish

Nemateleotris decora
Family Ptereleotridae (dartfishes)

⊕ Mauritius and the Maldives to Samoa, north to Ryukyu Islands and south to New Caledonia
⊙ Coastal and outer coral reefs; reef faces, slopes
⬇ 18–70 m (60–231 ft)   ↔ 9 cm (3.5 inches)

Occurs singly or in pairs. Most often over sand, rubble and hard coral substrate at base of reef. Hovers over burrow entrance, into which disappears if threatened. Faces into current and picks off passing zooplankton. Related fire dartfish (*N. magnifica*) usually found at more shallow depths, although the two sometimes occur together.

- East Africa, east to Hawaiian Islands, north to Ryukyu Islands and south to New Caledonia
- Coastal and outer coral reefs; over sand patches on reef faces and slopes
- 6–61 m (20–201 ft)   ↔ 8 cm (3 in)

Fire Dartfish
Nemateleotris magnifica
Family Ptereleotridae (dartfishes)

Forms pairs or groups (latter more common for adolescent individuals). Lives in burrow that it hovers over and disappears into if threatened and at night. Feeds on zooplankton. Raises and lowers long dorsal fin; may use it to communicate with other pair member. Sometimes parasitized by copepod parasite that attaches to head or fin.

- Philippines to Line Islands, north to southern Japan and south to New South Wales, Australia
- Coastal sand and rubble slopes
- 3–50 m (7–165 ft)   ↔ 12 cm (4.7 inches)

Threadfin Dartfish
Ptereleotris hanae
Family Ptereleotridae (dartfishes)

Juveniles often form groups; where common, adults sometimes form colonies. Hovers over burrow, into which it darts if threatened. Same burrow may be home to shrimp-goby and snapping shrimp. When male displays to female or rival males, fully extends pelvic fins and erects all median fins.

Ray-Finned Fishes

Atlantic Spadefish
Chaetodipterus faber
Family Ephippidae (spadefishes)

⊕ Massachusetts and Bermuda, south to Brazil, including Gulf of Mexico
⊙ Coastal and outer coral and rocky reefs; lagoons, reef faces, slopes
↓ 3–35 m (10–114 ft)   ↔ 91 cm (35.8 in)

Solitary or in small to large groups (in the hundreds). Juveniles found in mangroves, blending with mangrove pods and dead leaves; adults in open water over hard sandy bottoms, wrecks and oil platforms. Feeds on sponges, hydroids, soft corals, zoanthids, worms, crustaceans, echinoderms, tunicates and plant material. Most feeding done during midday.

Pinnate Batfish
Platax pinnatus
Family Ephippidae (spadefishes)

⊕ Indonesia, east to Solomon Islands, north to southern Japan and south to New Caledonia
⊙ Coastal and outer reefs; lagoons, back reefs, reef faces, slopes
↓ 2–25 m (7–81 ft)   ↔ 37 cm (15 in)

Occurs singly; adults sometimes form small groups. Young fish thought to mimic noxious flatworm in color and swimming behavior. Feeds on wide range of benthic invertebrates and algae; in some areas (Great Barrier Reef) important for control of reef-smothering macroalgae. Adults very different in color from juveniles. Unlike in close kin, snout more protruding in adult fish.

- Red Sea and East Africa, east to Micronesia, north to southern Japan and south to New Zealand
- Coastal and outer reefs; lagoons, back reefs, reef faces, slopes; mangrove and seagrass habitats
- 3–15 m (10–49 ft)   ↔ 41 cm (16 in)

Longfin Batfish
Platax teira
Family Ephippidae (spadefishes)

Usually forms small groups. Often hangs around pier pilings. Feeds on variety of sessile invertebrates. Juveniles look like drifting leaves or algae. Differs from relatives in having rounded forehead (as adult), very long pelvic fins and black patch at pelvic fin base.

- Arabian Gulf to Vanuatu, north to Hainan and Philippines and south to northern Queensland
- Coastal reefs; bays, estuaries, mangroves, lagoons, reef faces (often in turbid water)
- 1–15 m (3.3–49 ft)   ↔ 53 cm (21 in)

Java Rabbitfish
Siganus javus
Family Siganidae (rabbitfishes)

Juveniles and adolescent individuals form small groups; larger fish form pairs. Feeds on algae attached to substrate, as well as plant fragments dislodged from bottom by wave action. Wavy gray lines on body and dark blotch on tail distinguish it from close relatives. Like other rabbitfishes, has venomous dorsal spines.

Masked Rabbitfish

Siganus puellus
Family Siganidae (rabbitfishes)

Cocos-Keeling Islands and south China Sea to Gilbert Islands, north to Ryukyu Islands and south to southern Great Barrier Reef and New Caledonia

Coastal and outer coral reefs; lagoon patch reefs, reef faces, slopes

1–30 m (3.3–98 ft)   38 cm (15 in)

Juveniles found in shallows among staghorn coral or form loose feeding aggregations with other herbivores. Forms pairs as matures and moves into more exposed habitats. Juveniles feed on algae; subadults and adults eat algae, sponges and colonial tunicates. Wavy blue lines, vertical on fore body, horizontal on rear portion.

Foxface Rabbitfish

Siganus vulpinus
Family Siganidae (rabbitfishes)

Sumatra to Gilbert Islands, north to Philippines and south to Great Barrier Reef and New Caledonia

Coastal and outer coral reefs; lagoons, back reefs, crests, reef faces, slopes (often in areas with rich coral growth)

2–30 m (7–98 ft)   24 cm (9.4 inches)

Juveniles solitary; adults form tight long-term pair bonds (similar to butterflyfishes). Young fish often hide among branching corals. Grazes on algae growing on dead coral bases. Often joins feeding assemblages made up of parrotfishes, surgeonfishes and other rabbitfishes. Onespot rabbitfish (*S. unimaculatus*) likely a color variant of this species.

- East Africa (not Red Sea), east to Mexico, north to southern Japan and south to Great Barrier Reef
- Coastal and outer coral and rocky reefs; lagoons, back reefs, reef faces, slopes
- 1–180 m (3.3–585 ft)   16 cm (6.3 in)

Moorish Idol
Zanclus cornutus
Family Zanclidae (Moorish idol)

Solitary or in groups; sometimes forms large spawning groups. Planktonic phase 6–8 weeks; settles out on reef at 8 cm (3 in) in length. Long pelagic phase responsible for wide geographical range. Primary food algae and sponges. Uses long snout to get at sponges in reef interstices. Long dorsal filament helps direct turbulence away from body.

- Massachusetts and Bermuda to northwestern Gulf of Mexico and south to Brazil
- Coastal and outer coral and rocky reefs; lagoons, back reefs, reef faces, slopes
- 2–25 m (7–83 ft)   35 cm (14 in)

Ocean Surgeonfish
Acanthurus bahianus
Family Acanthuridae (surgeonfishes)

Solitary or in loose groups. Ingests large quantities of inorganic matter, including sand, pebbles and small shells. Also feeds on small fragments of various algae and seagrasses. Joins foraging groups of parrotfishes or blue tangs and invades more productive territories tended by damselfishes. Color variable, ranging from grayish blue to dark brown, but always white band around base of lunate tail.

Blue Tang

Acanthurus coeruleus

Family Acanthuridae (surgeonfishes)

⊕ New York and Bermuda, south to Brazil, including Gulf of Mexico
⊙ Coastal and outer coral and rocky reefs; lagoons, back reefs, reef faces, slopes
↧ 2–40 m (7–130 ft)   ↔ 39 cm (15.4 in)

Solitary (juveniles territorial); also in small to large shoals. Feeds on algae and seagrass. In some areas sets up cleaning stations that green sea turtles visit to have shells, head and flippers groomed of algae, parasites and necrotic skin. Where not common, spawns in pairs. Where abundant, group-spawns (some groups have thousands of individuals). Juveniles yellow overall with blue ring around eye.

Powderblue Surgeonfish

Acanthurus leucosternon

Family Acanthuridae (surgeonfishes)

⊕ East Africa to Bali (Indonesia)
⊙ Coastal and outer reefs; lagoons, reef flats, reef faces, slopes
↧ 1–25 m (3.3–81 ft)   ↔ 38 cm (15 in)

Highly territorial species. Feeding area defended by male–female pair; exclude members of own kind as well as other herbivores from area. Will abandon territory on occasion to form feeding shoals. Young found at greater depths than adults, in habitats with rich stony coral growth. Feeds on smaller forms of filamentous algae.

⊕ East Africa to Polynesia, north to southern Japan and south to New Caledonia
⊙ Outer reefs; turbulent reef flats, crests, reef faces
↕ 1–6 m (3.3–20 ft)   ↔ 38 cm (15 in)

Lined Surgeonfish
Acanthurus lineatus
Family Acanthuridae (surgeonfishes)

Solitary. Feeds on larger filamentous algae and fleshy macroalgae. Very territorial, attacking conspecifics as well as other algae-eating fishes. Borders of territories often contiguous with those of conspecific neighbors; forms monospecific colonies just below reef crest. Has larger caudal peduncle spine then almost all other surgeonfishes — and apparently a fervent desire to use it!

⊕ East Africa and Red Sea, east to French Polynesia, north to southern Japan and south to Great Barrier Reef
⊙ Coastal and outer reefs; lagoons, reef faces, slopes (often in turbid water)
↕ 5–25 m (16–81 ft)   ↔ 50 cm (20 in)

Yellowmask Surgeonfish
Acanthurus mata
Family Acanthuridae (surgeonfishes)

Solitary or in small groups. Sometimes hangs underneath schooling zooplankton feeders, ingesting their feces. Primary food zooplankton. Has yellow mask running through eye and gray pectoral fins; similar yellowfin surgeonfish (*A. xanthopterus*) has yellow pectoral fins.

Ray-Finned Fishes

Whitecheek Surgeonfish

Acanthurus nigricans
Family Acanthuridae (surgeonfishes)

🌐 Christmas Island and Indonesia, east to Hawaii, north to southern Japan and south to Great Barrier Reef
⊙ Coastal and outer reefs; lagoons, back reefs, reef faces, slopes
↧ 1–40 m (3.3–130 ft)   ↦ 21 cm (8.3 in)

Solitary or forms large feeding groups that invade territories of damselfish and other surgeonfishes. Algae eater. Similar to powder brown surgeonfish (*A. japonicus*) but differs in having small patch of white under eye. *A. japonicus* has white bar that extends from bottom of eye to edge of mouth.

Sohal Surgeonfish

Acanthurus sohal
Family Acanthuridae (surgeonfishes)

🌐 Red Sea and Arabian Gulf
⊙ Coastal reefs; reef flats, reef faces; prefers turbulent areas
↧ 1–10 m (3.3–33 ft)   ↦ 41 cm (16 in)

Solitary, highly territorial species; will defend "garden" from other herbivores (parrotfishes, other surgeonfishes, rabbitfishes). Dashes about territory (usually at boundary), occasionally stopping to graze on filamentous algae and macroalgae. Has large venomous spine in front of caudal fin.

🌐 East Africa to Panama, north to southern Japan and south to eastern coast of Australia
⊙ Coastal and outer reefs; lagoons, reef flats, reef faces, slopes
↧ 1–5 m (3.3–16 ft)   ↔ 26 cm (10.2 in)

Convict Surgeonfish
Acanthurus triostegus
Family Acanthuridae (surgeonfishes)

Solitary and in groups. Grazes on algae off hard substrates. Dominated by other, more aggressive surgeonfishes, so forms large feeding shoals (can number more than 100 individuals) to overwhelm defenses of territorial acanthurids and damselfishes. Solitary, territory-holding *A. triostegus* limited to reef habitats less attractive to more dominant surgeonfishes.

🌐 East Africa and Red Sea, east to Hawaiian Islands, north to southern Japan and south to New South Wales
⊙ Coastal and outer reefs; lagoons, patch reefs, reef faces, slopes
↧ 2–122 m (7–397 ft)   ↔ 60 cm (24 in)

Spotted Unicornfish
Naso brevirostris
Family Acanthuridae (surgeonfishes)

Solitary or in loose shoals. Macroalgae a favorite food, but as grows and "horn" gets longer, feeds more on zooplankton; also eats feces of other fishes. All in genus have special scales (similar to shark scales) that serve to reduce turbulence along body so can move through water with greater ease and speed. Horn on head grows longer as fish grows. Hides in reef at night.

Elegant Unicornfish

Naso elegans
Family Acanthuridae (surgeonfishes)

⊕ Red Sea, east to Bali (Indonesia)
⊙ Coastal and outer reefs; lagoons, reef flats, reef faces, slopes
↧ 1–20 m (3.3–65 ft)   ↔ 45 cm (17.7 in)

Solitary or in groups (sometimes large). Feeds on macroalgae. Will try to outrun predators rather than seeking shelter in reef; however, slumbers in reef crevices at night. Male has long streamers on tail. Similar to orangespine unicornfish (*N. lituratus*) but has yellow along dorsal fin; both species found around Bali.

Bignose Unicornfish

Naso vlamingii
Family Acanthuridae (surgeonfishes)

⊕ East Africa, east to Galapagos Islands, north to southern Japan and south to Great Barrier Reef
⊙ Outer reefs; lagoons, reef faces, slopes or drop-offs
↧ 4–50 m (13–163 ft)   ↔ 55 cm (22 in)

Most often forms groups. Feeds in current-prone habitats on zooplankton; also on feces of predatory fishes (barracudas, jacks). Both males and females develop long streamers on tail. Changes color when being cleaned to make parasites more conspicuous to cleaner-fish.

🌐 East Africa, east to Samoa, north to southern Japan and south to New South Wales
⊙ Outer reefs; channels, reef faces, slopes
↧ 2–40 m (7–130 ft) ↔ 31 cm (12 in)

Palette Surgeonfish
Paracanthurus hepatus
Family Acanthuridae (surgeonfishes)

Solitary or in groups; young often in shoals that shelter in branching coral colonies. Usually lives in current-prone habitat. Swims over reef, feeding on zooplankton carried in current; also eats some algae. During spawning period, forms groups consisting of one male and 2–7 females. Pair spawn in water column, at which time male's color fades.

🌐 Costa Rica south to Ecuador (including offshore islands) — not found in Gulf of California
⊙ Coastal rocky reefs; rocky reef faces, slopes
↧ 1–25 m (3.3–81 ft) ↔ 60 cm (24 in)

Razor Sawtail
Prionurus laticlavius
Family Acanthuridae (surgeonfishes)

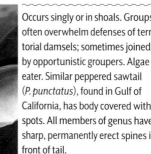

Occurs singly or in shoals. Groups often overwhelm defenses of territorial damsels; sometimes joined by opportunistic groupers. Algae eater. Similar peppered sawtail (*P. punctatus*), found in Gulf of California, has body covered with spots. All members of genus have sharp, permanently erect spines in front of tail.

Pacific Sailfin Tang
Zebrasoma veliferum
Family Acanthuridae (surgeonfishes)

⊕ East Africa and Red Sea, east to Indonesia
☉ Coastal and outer reefs; lagoons, reef flats, reef faces, slopes
↧ 1–30 m (3.3 to 98 ft)   ↔ 30 cm (12 in)

Juveniles solitary; adults found in pairs. Sometimes forms large shoals of 5–100 fish that raid damselfish territories. When threatened, young fish erects fins to increase apparent size. In at least some locations, during spawning season, mature male forms small spawning territory to which attracts females. Feeds on algae.

Great Barracuda
Sphyraena barracuda
Family Sphyraenidae (barracudas)

⊕ Circumtropical
☉ Coastal and outer coral reefs; lagoons, back reefs, slopes
↧ 1–100 m (3.3–325 ft)   ↔ 1.5 m (4.9 ft)

Adults usually solitary but sometimes aggregate. Juveniles found in mangroves, seagrass and even brackish water; adults more often on deep reef, sometimes even in open ocean. Apex predator that feeds on wide variety of fishes. Feeds during day, depending mainly on sight to locate food. Very quick, dashing after prey that gets too close — said to swim at speed of at least 58 kph (36 mph). Danger to man exaggerated; attacks very rare.

🌐 Peru and Ecuador; also Cocos and Galapagos Islands
◉ Coastal and insular reefs; reef faces, slopes
↕ 1–24 m (3.3–78 ft)　　　　　　　↔ 91 cm (36 in)

Pelican Barracuda
Sphyraena idiastes
Family Sphyraenidae (barracudas)

Forms schools (3–20 individuals) segregated by size. Schools of larger fish tend to inhabit deeper water; smaller individuals more coastal. Fish-eater, sometimes slicing larger prey into bite-sized morsels. Silvery gray with white on belly. Shy fish, difficult for divers to approach; not dangerous. Young fish often have yellow line running from tip of jaw to middle of body, as well as spots.

🌐 Bermuda and Florida, south to Uruguay
◉ Coastal rocky and coral reefs; seagrass meadows (juveniles), lagoons, reef faces, slopes; often over muddy substrate
↕ 1–65 m (3.3–211 ft)　　　　　　　↔ 46 cm (18 in)

Southern Sennet
Sphyraena picudilla
Family Sphyraenidae (barracudas)

Forms schools (sometimes large groups). Feeds on fishes and squid. Dusky blue on back, shading to silvery white on sides and belly; two faint yellow stripes on body. Guaguanche (*S. guachancho*) is another, smaller species in Western Atlantic; it has one distinct yellow stripe down middle of body.

Chevron or Blackfin Barracuda

Sphyraena qenie
Family Sphyraenidae (barracudas)

🌐 East Africa and Red Sea, east to Panama
⊙ Coastal and outer reefs; seagrass meadows, lagoons, reef faces, slopes
↧ 5–50 m (16–163 ft)　　　　　↔ 1.7 m (5.6 ft)

Young solitary or in groups; form refuge shoals during day. At night individuals disperse to feed on fishes. Shoals may occur in same location for many days or months. Similar to pickhandle barracuda (*S. jello*), which has yellow tail and wavy bars on body, while chevron has black tail and chevron-shaped markings.

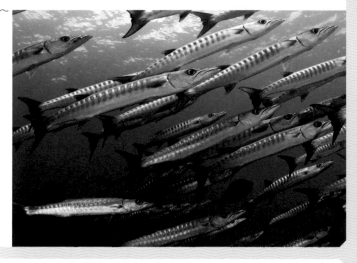

Dogtooth Tuna

Gymnosarda unicolor
Family Scombridae (mackerels and tuna)

🌐 East Africa and Red Sea, east to French Polynesia, north to southern Japan and south to Australia
⊙ Offshore reefs; deep lagoons, channels, reef faces, slopes; open ocean
↧ 2–100 m (7–325 ft)　　　　　↔ 1.8 cm (6 ft)

Solitary predator. Feeds on small shoaling fishes (including fusiliers and fairy wrasses) and squid (to a lesser degree). Also known to attack groups of spawning surgeonfishes and wrasses. This is only tuna regularly seen near coral reefs.

- ⊕ Southern California, south to Chile; also offshore islands, including Galapagos
- ⊙ Offshore reefs; reef faces, walls; open ocean
- ↧ 1–12 m (3.3–39 ft) ↔ 1 m (39 in)

Pacific Sierra
Scomberomorus sierra
**Family Scombridae
(mackerels and tuna)**

Solitary or in schools; sometimes forms large groups. Built for speed, uses hunting prowess to subdue small schooling fishes such as anchovies and herrings. In Mexico spawns near coast July–September; in Costa Rica spawning occurs August–November. Silver with many orange oval marks on body. Sometimes approaches divers but often difficult to get near. Important game and food fish.

- ⊕ East Africa, east to Fiji, north to Ryukyu Islands and south to Great Barrier Reef
- ⊙ Coastal sand flats and slopes adjacent to reefs
- ↧ 1–30 m (3.3–98 ft) ↔ 15 cm (5.9 in)

Angler Flatfish
Asterorhombus fijiensis
Family Bothidae (lefteye flounders)

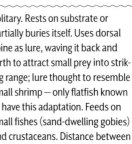

Solitary. Rests on substrate or partially buries itself. Uses dorsal spine as lure, waving it back and forth to attract small prey into striking range; lure thought to resemble small shrimp — only flatfish known to have this adaptation. Feeds on small fishes (sand-dwelling gobies) and crustaceans. Distance between eyes wider in males than females.

Peacock Flounder
Bothus lunatus
Family Bothidae (lefteye flounders)

🌐 Florida and Bermuda, south to Brazil
⊙ Coastal sand flats and slopes near reefs
↧ 2–100 m (7–325 ft)   ↔ 46 cm (18.1 in)

Solitary. Feeds on schooling fishes as well as larger reef fishes, mantis shrimps and octopuses. When first hatches, eyes positioned above mouth; as it grows, eyes migrate to left side of body. Color can change suddenly to enhance camouflage or communicate mood. Large territorial male guards harem of females; courts and spawns just before sunset. Expels pelagic eggs above bottom.

Flowery Flounder
Bothus mancus
Family Bothidae (lefteye flounders)

🌐 East Africa and Red Sea, east to Mexico and offshore islands (Revillagigedo, Clipperton and Cocos Islands), north to Japan and south to Australia
⊙ Coastal sand and rocky flats and slopes
↧ 2–150 m (7–488 ft)   ↔ 42 cm (17 in)

Solitary. Hunts mainly during day but also does some feeding at night. Eats squid, crustaceans and fishes. Found on sand and rock substrate, often in full view. Pectoral fins of male more elongate and held vertically when displaying or courting females. Gray with blue spots and circular markings.

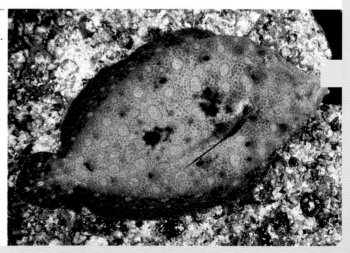

- ⊕ East Africa and Red Sea, east to Society Islands, north to southern Japan and south to Lord Howe Island
- ☉ Coastal sand or mud flats and slopes
- ↧ 3–250 m (10–813 ft)   ↤ 39 cm (15.3 in)

Leopard Flounder
Bothus pantherinus
Family Bothidae (lefteye flounders)

Solitary. Buries itself under sand to avoid detection. Feeds on crustaceans and fishes. Eyes very close together (distance about equal to eye diameter).

- ⊕ Gulf of Thailand to Taiwan, south to Great Barrier Reef and New Caledonia
- ☉ Coastal bays and estuaries; sand and mud flats and slopes
- ↧ 5–70 m (10–130 ft)   ↤ 22 cm (8.7 in)

Cockatoo Flounder
Samaris cristatus
Family Samaridae (crested flounders)

Solitary. Seen on seafloor or moving over bottom during day. Feeds on benthic fishes and crustaceans. Has long white dorsal fin rays held under body when fish is resting. When threatened, unfurls dorsal rays and throws them forward in an amazing display, apparently to scare off would-be predators or increase apparent size so predators will not try to swallow it.

Peacock Sole

Pardachirus pavoninus
Family Soleidae (true soles)

⊕ Maldives to Samoa, north to southern Japan and south to New South Wales and Tonga
⊙ Coastal sand flats and slopes
↧ 3–40 m (10–130 ft)
↔ 22 cm (8.7 in)

Solitary. Buries itself completely or partially under substrate to avoid detection by predators. Feeds on worms, crustaceans and small fish. Exudes toxic body slime from glands at base of anal and dorsal fins that deter many piscivores from eating it. Bright yellow spots and light ocelli on body.

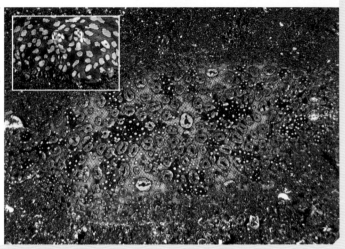

Banded Sole

Soleichthys heterorhinos
Family Soleidae (true soles)

⊕ East Africa and Red Sea, east to Samoa and north to southern Japan
⊙ Coastal sand flats and slopes
↧ 2–20 m (7–65 ft)
↔ 15 cm (5.9 in)

Solitary. Buries itself under sand, with only snorkel-like nostril protruding from substrate. While can be seen moving about on soft and hard substrate during day, is more active after dark. Probably feeds on small crustaceans, worms and tiny benthic fishes (e.g., gobies). Typically "crawls" over seafloor but can also swim in open water with undulating motion.

🌐 East Africa and Red Sea, east to Hawaii, north to Japan and south to Australia

☉ Coastal and outer reefs; lagoons, back reefs, reef flats, reef faces, slopes

↧ 2–50 m (7–163 ft)   ↔ 30 cm (12 in)

Orange-lined Triggerfish

Balistapus undulatus

Family Balistidae (triggerfishes)

Solitary. Omnivore, feeding on coral-line algae, sponges, hydroids, stony corals, clams, worms, crustaceans, urchins, brittle stars, tunicates and fishes. Lays eggs in nest excavated among sand and rubble. Eggs stick to substrate; guarded by both parents. Sexually dichromatic: female has orange stripes between eyes and mouth, lacking in male.

🌐 Massachusetts to Brazil, including Gulf of Mexico

☉ Coastal and outer coral and rocky reefs; lagoons, back reefs, reef faces, slopes

↧ 2–275 m (7–894 ft)   ↔ 60 cm (23.4 in)

Queen Triggerfish

Balistes vetula

Family Balistidae (triggerfishes)

Solitary. Eclectic diet, including all kinds of invertebrates (conchs, slipper lobsters, crabs, serpent stars, urchins). Blows stream of water from mouth to knock over urchins, then bites through vulnerable oral surface. Opportunistic wrasses often hang around as it eats urchins, to feed on scraps. Often easy to approach and curious.

Clown Triggerfish

Balistoides conspicillum

Family Balistidae (triggerfishes)

- ⊕ East Africa to Samoa, north to southern Japan and south to Lord Howe Island
- ⊙ Outer reefs, reef faces, slopes
- ↓ 5–75 m (16–244 ft)
- ↔ 50 cm (20 in)

Solitary. Juveniles most common on steep drop-offs deeper than 20 m (66 ft), where they live under ledges and in caves. Feeds on variety of invertebrates, including bivalves, crustaceans, sea urchins and crinoids. Shoots jets of water from mouth into sand to uncover prey items, which attracts wrasses. Lays eggs in nest in sand.

Titan Triggerfish

Balistoides viridescens

Family Balistidae (triggerfishes)

- ⊕ Red Sea to Tuamotu Islands, north to southern Japan and south to New South Wales and New Caledonia
- ⊙ Coastal and outer reefs; lagoons, back reefs, reef faces, slopes
- ↓ 1–50 m (3.3–163 ft)
- ↔ 75 cm (30 in)

Solitary and haremic. Feeds on wide range of invertebrates and fishes; will even eat crown-of-thorns sea stars. Breaks up coral with jaws and turns over rubble to get at hidden prey. Male has large territory containing territories of 2–4 females. Female lays eggs in nest in sand and defends and fans them. At this time females can be very aggressive; have even been known to injure divers. Eggs hatch in a day.

⊕ East Africa to Hawaiian and Galapagos Islands, north to southern Japan and south to Great Barrier Reef

⊙ Coastal and outer reefs; reef faces, slopes

↧ 1–60 m (3.3–195 ft)   ↔ 30 cm (12 in)

Pinktail Triggerfish

Melichthys vidua

Family Balistidae (triggerfishes)

Occurs singly or in pairs or small groups. Most often in current-prone habitats. Feeds on zooplankton and fish feces (sometimes hangs under groups of predatory fishes to eat their fecal material). Also hangs around groups of spawning fishes, feeding on eggs as released. Lays eggs in nest in sand; cared for by parents.

⊕ East Africa and Red Sea, east to French Polynesia, north to southern Japan and south to Great Barrier Reef

⊙ Coastal and outer reefs; reef faces, slopes

↧ 5–40 m (16–130 ft)   ↔ 50 cm (20 in)

Redtooth Triggerfish

Odonus niger

Family Balistidae (triggerfishes)

Juveniles solitary; adults form loose groups. Typically in current-swept areas. Feeds on passing zooplankton; occasionally nibbles on encrusting invertebrates such as sponges. When threatened, dashes head-first into a crevice. Forms communal spawning groups; females establish nesting sites visited by males. Both sexes defend eggs from wrasses and other egg predators.

Red Sea Picasso Triggerfish

Rhinecanthus assasi
Family Balistidae (triggerfishes)

⊕ Red Sea and Arabian Gulf
⊙ Coastal reefs; lagoons, back reefs, reef flats, reef faces, slopes
↕ 2–15 m (7–49 ft)   ↔ 30 cm (12 in)

Solitary. Feeds on algae and wide variety of benthic invertebrates. Blows water jet from mouth at sand to uncovered buried prey. Male digs nest in sand; female deposits eggs and male guards them until they hatch. Larvae enter plankton. Easy to approach underwater. Similar to Picasso triggerfish (*R. aculeatus*), found from east Africa to Hawaiian Islands but not in Red Sea.

Scythe Triggerfish

Sufflamen bursa
Family Balistidae (triggerfishes)

⊕ East Africa east to Hawaiian Islands, north to southern Japan and south to Great Barrier Reef
⊙ Outer reefs; lagoons, back reefs, reef faces, slopes
↕ 3–90 m (10–293 ft)   ↔ 24 cm (9.4 in)

Solitary. Feeds on detritus, algae, bivalves, snails, worms, crabs, sea urchins and tunicates. Lighter belly; scythe marking (brown or yellow) behind pectoral fin. Related flagtail triggerfish (*S. chrysopterus*) has yellow bar behind eye, blue on chin and chest and white-margined tail.

⊕ Micronesia to offshore islands of eastern Pacific and north to Japan
⊙ Outer coral and rocky reefs; reef faces, slopes
↕ 10–100 m (33–325 ft)   ↔ 22 cm (8.7 in)

Crosshatch Triggerfish
Xanthichthys mento
Family Balistidae (triggerfishes)

Forms loose groups in which females outnumber males. Most often in current-prone areas, where feeds on zooplankton high in water column. Sexes different in color: male has bright red tail; that of females is yellow (also other color differences). Most spawning occurs in summer months. Egg scatterer; does not form nests like some other triggers.

⊕ North Carolina and Bermuda, south to Brazil
⊙ Outer reefs; reef faces, walls, slopes
↕ 1–80 m (3.3–260 ft)   ↔ 25 cm (9.8 in)

Sargassum Triggerfish
Xanthichthys ringens
Family Balistidae (triggerfishes)

Solitary or in small groups. Juveniles associate with flotsam (*Sargassum* algae rafts) near ocean surface; adults usually below 30 m (98 ft). Adults also prefer current-prone habitat, where they swim into water column to feed. Diet mainly zooplankton but also eats some benthic invertebrates (e.g., crabs, sea urchins).

Ray-Finned Fishes

Scrawled Filefish

Aluterus scriptus
Family Monacanthidae (filefishes)

⊕ Circumtropical
☉ Coastal and outer coral and rocky reefs; lagoons, reef faces, slopes
↧ 3–120 m (10–390 ft)   ↔ 1.1 m (3.6 ft)

Solitary or in groups. Lives on coral reefs among gorgonians, around pier pilings and even high in water column. Groups of young hang out under flotsam (e.g., plant material, trash, *Sargassum* algae). Feeds on algae, seagrasses, hydrozoans, gorgonians, zoanthids and tunicates. Spawns in pairs; egg-scatterer. Sometimes spawns over coral colonies, adopting head-down posture and releasing gametes over coral branches.

Whitespotted Filefish

Cantherhines macrocerus
Family Monacanthidae (filefishes)

⊕ Florida and Bermuda, south to Brazil
☉ Coastal and outer coral reefs; lagoons, back reefs, reef faces, slopes
↧ 2–40 m (7–130 ft)   ↔ 46 cm (18 in)

Occurs singly or in pairs. Feeds on sponges and gorgonians; also consumes some algae. Two color forms: one mainly plain orange and gray, other with white spots on head and body. Male has larger spines at tail base than female. Usually approachable and sometimes curious.

- Malaysian peninsula, east to Great Barrier Reef and north to southern Japan
- Coastal reefs; lagoons, reef faces, slopes
- 2–25 m (7–82 ft)   ↔ 31 cm (12.2 in)

Leafy Filefish
Chaetodermis penicilligerus
Family Monacanthidae (filefishes)

Solitary. Has leaflike appendages on head and body that help it blend with seagrass and algae it often associates with. Feeds on benthic invertebrates. Sometimes afflicted by copepod parasites. Easy for divers to approach if move slowly.

- North Carolina and Bermuda, south to Antilles
- Coastal and outer coral reefs; lagoons, back reefs, reef faces, slopes
- 2–50 m (7–163 ft)   ↔ 10 cm (3.9 in)

Slender Filefish
Monacanthus tuckeri
Family Monacanthidae (filefishes)

Solitary. Lives among gorgonian/soft coral branches, adopting vertical posture to enhance camouflage. At night positions body along main branch of coral home. Feeds on zooplankton swept past in ocean currents. Long planktonic larval stage (around 42 days); relatively large 3.2 cm (1.3 in) when settles out of plankton.

Longnose Filefish

Oxymonacanthus longirostris
Family Monacanthidae (filefishes)

- ⊕ East Africa, east to Samoa, north to southern Japan and south to Australia
- ⊙ Coastal and outer reefs; lagoons, back reefs, reef faces, slopes
- ↧ 1–35 m (3.3–114 ft)
- ↔ 9 cm (3.5 in)

Juveniles solitary or in small groups; adults form pairs. Forms long-term pair bonds; both individuals share and defend feeding territory, center of which is preferred food, *Acropora* (staghorn) coral. Specializes in removing polyps from coral skeleton. Spawns daily, laying eggs on algae. Because of specialized diet, coral bleaching events have heavy impact.

Mimic Filefish

Paraluteres prionurus
Family Monacanthidae (filefishes)

- ⊕ East Africa, east to Great Barrier Reef and New Caledonia and north to southern Japan
- ⊙ Outer reefs; reef faces, slopes
- ↧ 6–25 m (20–81 ft)
- ↔ 10 cm (3.5 in)

Solitary or in small groups (rarely). Feeds on benthic invertebrates. Perfect replica of toxic saddled toby (*Canthigaster valentini*), so swims in open boldly, as most predators do not eat fish it mimics; differs from toby in characteristic first dorsal fin with file-like spine. Andaman mimic filefish (*P. arquat*) mimics Slarnder's toby (*Canthigaster petersii*).

⊕ New Jersey and Bermuda, south to Brazil
◉ Coastal and outer coral reefs; lagoons, back reefs, reef faces, slopes
↧ 3–80 m (10 to 260 ft)   ↦ 50 cm (19.7 in)

Honeycomb Cowfish
Acanthostracion polygonius
Family Ostraciidae (trunkfishes)

Lives among gorgonians or seagrass. Sponges, soft corals, tunicates and shrimp preferred food. Male occurs singly and defends small group of females. Boxfishes do not change sex. Produces pelagic eggs released during ascent into water column. Wary; will swim off when approached too closely.

⊕ Massachusetts and Bermuda, south to Brazil, including Gulf of Mexico
◉ Coastal and outer coral reefs; lagoons, back reefs, reef faces, slopes
↧ 2–50 m (7–163 ft)   ↦ 47 cm (18.5 in)

Smooth Trunkfish
Lactophrys triqueter
Family Ostraciidae (trunkfishes)

Solitary or in loose groups. Main food tunicates and sponges; also mollusks, crustaceans and worms. Exposes buried invertebrates by blowing jets of water out of mouth toward sand bottom ("hydraulic jetting"). Male forms temporary mating territory visited by females. Exudes toxic slime but still eaten by sharks.

Longhorn Cowfish
Lactoria cornuta
Family Ostraciidae (trunkfishes)

🌐 East Africa and Red Sea, east to French Polynesia, north to southern Japan and south to Australia

◉ Coastal and outer reefs; seagrass beds, sand and mud flats and slopes

↧ 1–50 m (3.3–163 ft)   ↔ 46 cm (18 in)

Solitary; possibly haremic. Feeds on polychaete worms, small bivalves and other invertebrates in sand. Uses jets of water to uncover buried prey, which attracts attention of opportunists such as wrasses. Adult has much longer tail than juvenile.

Thornback Cowfish
Lactoria fornasini
Family Ostraciidae (trunkfishes)

🌐 East Africa, east to Hawaiian Islands, north to Japan and south to Australia

◉ Rocky and coral coastal and outer reefs; lagoons, reef faces, slopes

↧ 2–80 m (7–260 ft)   ↔ 15 cm (5.9 in)

Juveniles solitary; adults haremic. Territory of male contains home ranges of 3–4 females. Feeds on tunicates and sponges off hard substrate, as well as polychaete worms from sand. Blows jets of water at sand to expose buried prey. When defending territory or during courtship, color intensifies. Spawns at sunset; spawning event synchronized by high-pitched hum produced by male.

⊕ East Africa and Red Sea, east to French Polynesia, north to Japan and south to New Zealand
⊙ Coastal and outer reefs; lagoons, back reefs, reef faces, slopes
↕ 1–35 m (3.3–114 ft)　　　　　↔ 45 cm (18 in)

Yellow Boxfish

Ostracion cubicus
Family Ostraciidae (trunkfishes)

Juveniles solitary; adults haremic. Male defends area containing 3–4 females. Feeds on sponges, tunicates, mollusks, worms and algae. Spawns in late afternoon, rising high in water column to release gametes. Juveniles bright yellow with black spots; large adults grayish purple with yellow tail base and bump on snout. Juvenile in main photo, adult in inset photo.

⊕ East Africa, east to Baja, north to southern Japan and south to Great Barrier Reef
⊙ Coastal and outer coral and rocky reefs; lagoons, back reefs, reef faces, slopes
↕ 2–30 m (7–98 ft)　　　　　↔ 18 cm (7.1 in)

Spotted Boxfish

Ostracion meleagris
Family Ostraciidae (trunkfishes)

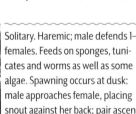

Solitary. Haremic; male defends 1–3 females. Feeds on sponges, tunicates and worms as well as some algae. Spawning occurs at dusk: male approaches female, placing snout against her back; pair ascend 1–2 m (3.3–7 ft) above substrate to release pelagic gametes. Produces highly toxic slime to dissuade predators. Male shown here.

Papuan Toby
Canthigaster papua
Family Tetraodontidae (pufferfishes)

- Indonesia and Philippines to Great Barrier Reef and New Caledonia
- Coastal and outer reefs; lagoons, back reefs, reef faces, slopes
- 2–35 m (7–114 ft)
- 10 cm (3.9 in)

Solitary or in pairs (probably haremic). Most often on coral-rich reefs. Feeds on benthic invertebrates, including corals, crustaceans and echinoderms. Lays eggs on substrate. Similar to Indian toby (*C. solandri*), which has large blue to white spots on body and yellowish orange tail (*C. papua* also has orange under snout).

Sharpnose Puffer
Canthigaster rostrata
Family Tetraodontidae (pufferfishes)

- Florida and Bermuda, south to Venezuela
- Coastal and outer coral reefs; lagoons, back reefs, reef faces, slopes
- 1–40 m (3.3–130 ft)
- 12 cm (4.7 in)

Solitary or in pairs. Eats sponges, crustaceans, worms, snails, sponges, tiny clams, seagrasses and coralline algae. Haremic; male defends territory that contains 1–6 females. Smaller bachelor males attempt to spawn with harem members. Spawns in morning; eggs laid on algae, with no parental care.

- 🌐 Red Sea to Tuamotu Islands, north to southern Japan and south to Lord Howe Island
- ⊙ Coastal and outer reefs; lagoons, back reefs, reef flats, reef faces, slopes
- ↧ 1–55 m (3.3–182 ft)
- ↔ 10 cm (3.9 in)

Saddled Toby

Canthigaster valentini

Family Tetraodontidae (pufferfishes)

Male-dominated harems, with 1–7 female territories within male's larger territory. Some bachelor, non-territorial males move into male's territory if he disappears. Feeds on algae and wide range of invertebrates, including tunicates, corals, crustaceans, polychaete worms, echinoderms and sponges. Spawns at dusk; lays eggs on substrate. Like parents, eggs and larvae are toxic.

- 🌐 East Africa and Red Sea, east to Panama, north to Japan and south to Australia
- ⊙ Coastal and outer coral and rocky reefs; lagoons, back reefs, reef faces, slopes
- ↧ 1–50 m (3.3–163 ft)
- ↔ 50 cm (19.6 in)

Hispid Puffer

Arothron hispidus

Family Tetraodontidae (pufferfishes)

Solitary. Highly varied diet includes sea squirts, sea urchins, serpent stars and sea stars (including crown-of-thorns), as well as other invertebrates and algae. Gray to brown body with white spots and white rings around pectoral fins. Similar to reticulate puffer (*A. reticulatus*), which has white bands from head to belly.

399

Ray-Finned Fishes

Map Puffer

Arothron mappa
Family Tetraodontidae (pufferfishes)

- ⊕ East Africa to Samoa, north to Japan and south to New Caledonia
- ⊙ Coastal and outer coral reefs; lagoons, back reefs, reef faces, slopes
- ↓ 4–30 m (13–98 ft)
- ↔ 60 cm (23.4 in)

Solitary. Juveniles often sit among sponges on invertebrate-encrusted pier pilings; adults found on shipwrecks, in caves and under table corals. Feeds heavily on sponges, biting off large chunks with beaklike jaws; also eats coralline, bubble and calcareous green algae, sea squirts, snails and crabs. Skin and internal organs highly toxic.

Guineafowl Puffer

Arothron meleagris
Family Tetraodontidae (pufferfishes)

- ⊕ East Africa to Panama, north to southern Japan and Hawaiian Islands and south to Lord Howe, Rapa and Easter Islands
- ⊙ Coastal and outer coral and rocky reefs; lagoons, back reefs, reef faces, slopes
- ↓ 1–14 m (3.3–46 ft)
- ↔ 50 cm (19.6 in)

Solitary. Main food is tips of branching and encrusting hard corals; also eats soft corals, calcareous algae, detritus, sponges, tunicates, bryozoans, crustaceans and bivalves. Brown to purplish black, with white spots; also all-gold color phase. Fed on by sharks, especially Galapagos and tiger sharks.

⊕ East Africa, east to Line Islands, north to southern Japan and south to New Caledonia
⊙ Coastal and outer reefs; lagoons, reef faces, slopes
↓ 3–25 m (10–81 ft)   ↔ 33 cm (13 in)

Blackspotted Puffer
Arothron nigropunctatus
Family Tetraodontidae (pufferfishes)

Found singly or in pairs. Prefers coral-rich areas, often near caves or crevices during day. Rests among coral or sponges at night. Feeds mainly on hard corals — preferring to nip tips off branching species — and sea anemones; also eats algae, bivalves, amphipods, crabs and sea cucumbers. Color variable: brown to blue-gray, with black spots on body; some individuals yellow on belly and sides, rarely completely gold.

⊕ Maine, south to Brazil; rare or absent in Caribbean Sea
⊙ Coastal reefs; seagrass beds, bays, lagoons
↓ 1–20 m (3.3–65 ft)   ↔ 25 cm (9.8 in)

Striped Burrfish
Chilomycterus schoepfi
Family Diodontidae (porcupinefishes)

Solitary. Feeds mainly on snails and hermit crabs, which it crushes with fused teeth and powerful jaws. Has spines on head and body like porcupinefish (*Diodon* spp.) but cannot inflate; spines always erect (in *Diodon* spp. spines lie flat on body until fish inflates). Much of locomotion generated by jetting water out of gill slits. Dark brown stripes differentiate it from other burrfish in region.

Balloonfish

Diodon holocanthus
Family Diodontidae
(porcupinefishes)

- Circumtropical
- Coastal and outer reefs; lagoons, back reefs, reef faces, slopes
- 1–100 m (3.3–330 ft)
- 29 cm (11 in)

Solitary. Juveniles often sit among sponges on invertebrate-encrusted pier pilings; adults found on shipwrecks, in caves and under table corals. Feeds heavily on sponges, biting off large chunks with beaklike jaws; also eats coralline, bubble and calcareous green algae, sea squirts, snails and crabs. Skin and internal organs highly toxic.

Porcupinefish

Diodon hystrix
Family Diodontidae
(porcupinefishes)

- Circumtropical
- Coastal and outer rocky and coral reefs; lagoons, reef faces, slopes
- 2–50 m (7–163 ft)
- 91 cm (3 ft)

Solitary. Regularly seen hovering over reef or taking refuge in caves or under overhangs during day. Juveniles pelagic until about 20 cm (7.9 in). Actively hunts for sea urchins, snails and hermit crabs after dark. Spots on fins, unlike ballonfish (*D. holocanthus*). Even though spiny and can inflate, regularly eaten by tiger sharks.

A rainbow of colors in the eye of a parrotfish (*Scarus* sp.). Belize.

Chapter 4

Elasmobranchs

Sharks and Rays

Sharks and rays are some of the best known — and most maligned — of all sea creatures. Much of their notoriety is due to the bad press they receive when an occasional aggressive encounter occurs between a shark and our species. Sharks have been known to bite and, occasionally, kill people. While these incidents occur infrequently, considering the number of people who enter the ocean every day, they give rise to sensational and frightening stories that stir up dread in the psyches of those who do not really know what sharks are all about.

The shark's flattened relatives, the stingrays, also have a bad rep with some members of the public. They have a dagger-like spine on their tail that they use for defense, typically against the large sharks that eat them. But if a bather should accidentally tread on a stingray, it may employ this caudal weaponry, which can result in a painful wound on the foot or leg. In a handful of unusual instances, larger stingrays have inflicted lethal puncture wounds to a vital organ — case in point: the death of Steve Irwin. Even though sharks and rays do occasionally harm *Homo sapiens*, the danger they pose to our species has been greatly exaggerated. They are vital members of tropical ecosystems, and they are also some of the most majestic and spectacular animals to observe in their natural habitat.

There are 440 species of sharks and around 500 species of rays currently recognized. They belong to the class Chondrichthyes, which includes all fishes that have a cartilaginous skeleton and jaws. The class includes two subclasses: the Holocephalii (known as chimeras) and the Elasmobranchii (sharks and rays). Many classification schemes divide elasmobranchs into two superorders: the Squalomorphii (sharks) and the Rajomorphii (stingrays, electric

A huge manta ray (*Manta birostris*), with a wing span of more than 4 m (13.2 ft), glides through the blue. Unique combinations of white shoulder markings and spot patterns on the underside help scientists identify individual animals. Baja, Mexico.

This "over-under" view shows lemon (*Negaprion brevirostris*) and tiger (*Galeocerdo cuvier*) sharks and brave scuba divers on a shallow sandbank in the northern Bahamas.

rays, skates, sawfishes and guitarfishes). The Squalomorphii are sometimes referred to as *selachians*, while the term *batoids* is sometimes used for the Rajomorphii. Squalomorphs have multiple gill openings and rows of constantly regenerating teeth. The males also have unique reproductive organs, called claspers, that are modifications of the pelvic fins. During mating, the male elasmobranch rotates a clasper forward, inserts one (in rare cases, both) into the cloaca of the female and inseminates her.

Sharks vary in form, ranging from almost eel-like (frill sharks, *Chlamydoselachus* spp.) to torpedo-shaped (mako sharks, *Isurus* spp.). When most sharks swim, they undulate the body, using the longer upper tail lobe to propel themselves forward (the tail, with its long upper lobe and short lower lobe, is referred to as a heterocercal caudal fin). The fast-swimming fusiform species, such as mackerel sharks, are more stiff-bodied; they are pushed forward by a tail with lobes of equal size (known as a homoceral caudal fin). Epaulette sharks (*Hemiscyllium* spp.) rely on a different means of locomotion altogether. They use their muscular pectoral and pelvic fins to walk over the seafloor, moving more like a salamander than a typical shark. Most rays employ their pectoral fins for propulsion as well. They either undulate the disc margin (stingrays and stingarees) or swim through the water by flapping their large, winglike pectoral fins (mantas, bat rays, eagle rays). Some rays have a well-developed caudal fin (guitarfishes, torpedo rays) and swim in a more typically sharklike fashion.

Not only do fins serve to propel sharks, their pectoral fins provide lift to prevent an active shark from plunging downward as its swims. In the thresher sharks (*Alopias* spp.) and the tasselled wobbegong (*Eucrossorhinus dasypogon*), the tail is used to help capture prey. The former use their tail to herd and strike small schooling fishes, while the tasselled wobbegong uses its tail as a lure to attract fish prey into striking range — it curls the tail over its head and waggles it so it looks like a swimming fish. In many elasmobranchs, fins are also used as a holdfast during mating: male sharks and rays of many species will bite the pectoral fin of the female, grasping it while they copulate.

Top
A popular conception of the great white shark (*Carcharodon carcharias*) — primal fear! South Africa.

Bottom
Beware the tail spine of the long-tailed stingray (*Dasyatis thetidis*). New Zealand.

A male banded guitarfish (*Zapteryx exasperata*). Note the two claspers, the fingerlike projections alongside the body protruding from the back of the disc. In male elasmobranchs the claspers are modified pelvic fins that function as a penis. Baja, Mexico.

Sharks and rays have interesting digestive tracts; they include a specialized intestine with a structure known as a spiral valve. This helps increase the absorptive surface area, which means they need less intestine than a similar-sized animal. Elasmobranchs also have skin that is very different from that of bony fishes. They have placoid scales, or dermal denticles, that make them feel rough, especially if rubbed from tail to head. These toothlike scales not only protect them from abrasion and injury but also make them more hydro-dynamically efficient, by reducing turbulence as the shark moves through the water. The more sedentary elasmobranchs (some rays and skates) have fewer placoid scales (some are naked); they may have enlarged denticles that serve to maintain contact between male and female during mating. In some sharks the skin of the female is thicker than that of the male, in order to protect it from the "love bites" that occur during courtship and mating.

Sharks and rays are found in a variety of aquatic ecosystems. While most are marine animals, some spend their entire lives in fresh water (freshwater stingrays, family Potamotrygonidae) and others live in both fresh and seawater — for example, the bull shark (*Carcharhinus leucas*). While many sharks and rays live in relatively shallow coastal habitats, there are fairly large mesopelagic and bathypelagic elasmobranch communities. Elasmobranchs that live in deeper water include frilled sharks (family Chlamydoselachidae), cow sharks (Hexanchidae), goblin sharks (Mitsukurinidae), certain dogfishes (*Etmopterus* spp.) and catsharks (*Apristurus* spp.), as well as a number of skates (Rajidae). Some deepwater dogfishes have light-producing organs, known as photophores, that help them find one another and possibly attract prey.

Though often considered to be primitive, small-brained creatures, elasmobranchs are far from this popular misconception. They have relatively large brains for their body size and engage in some very complex behaviors. They certainly have very refined sensory systems that can detect minute olfactory and weak electrical cues to help them find their prey. The "five-o'clock shadow" you see on the snouts of elasmobranchs is actually electro-receptors known

The spotted ratfish (*Hydrolagus colliei*), a temperate species, is a chimera, an example of the subclass Holocephalii of the class Chondrichthyes. British Columbia, Canada.

Indonesian speckled epaulette sharks (*Hemiscyllium freycineti*), heads downward, mating. The male holds on to the female by biting her pectoral fin. Then, while they are wrapped around each other, the male will insert a clasper into her cloaca. Papua New Guinea.

People spend thousands of dollars to dive with great white sharks (*Carcharodon carcharias*) from the safety of cages. Guadalupe Island, Baja, Mexico.

as ampullae of Lorenzini. These help locate prey and may also help some species find a mate (male stingrays may use them to find mates buried in the sand). They have an adequate visual system that is particularly effective in low-light conditions, and they can "hear" a struggling fish hundreds of meters away, although the auditory abilities of elasmobranchs vary widely between species.

All sharks and rays are carnivorous. Some species exhibit very generalized diets, while others are highly specialized eaters. Even the more opportunistic species usually exhibit some prey preferences. For example, the adult tiger shark (*Galeocerdo cuvier*), which is often considered the most undiscriminating of all selachians, prefers sea turtles, sea snakes and seabirds. Species with more specialized tastes include the Atlantic weasel shark (*Paragaleus pectoralis*), which feeds on squid; the crested Port Jackson shark (*Heterodontus galeatus*), which feeds heavily on sea urchins; the great hammerhead (*Sphyrna mokarran*), a stingray and cownose ray specialist; and the cownose ray (*Rhinoptera bonasus*), which feeds almost exclusively on bivalve mollusks. Some of the largest of all the elasmobranchs feed on plankton, including the whale shark (*Rhincodon typus*), basking shark (*Cetorhinus maximus*), megamouth shark (*Megachasma pelagios*) and manta and devil rays (family Myliobatidae).

Elasmobranchs have three different reproductive modes. The most primitive species lay a leathery egg case (this is known as oviparity). The case may have

long tendrils at each corner or filamentous threads on its surface that
help it attach to the seafloor. Bullhead sharks, bamboo sharks, epaulette sharks, catsharks and skates
exhibit oviparity. There are also
elasmobranchs in which the egg is
fertilized and then encapsulated
in a shell. The young shark develops inside the casing, nourished
by an attached yolk sac, until the
egg hatches within the utcrus and
the young shark is expelled from
the female as a near replica of the
adult (ovoviviparity). Most sharks
and rays exhibit this reproductive mode, including angel sharks,
nurse sharks, whale sharks, mack-

Shark fins drying on the deck of a small boat. After the fins are sliced off the still-living animals, they are dumped back into the ocean. Without fins, unable to hunt and swim, they starve or bleed to death on the bottom. Shark-fin soup is popular in Asia, and worldwide shark populations are quickly being depleted. Many species are now endangered. Thailand.

erel sharks, torpedo rays, stingrays, eagle rays and manta rays. Finally there
are species in which no shell is involved; instead the young shark has a placen-
tal attachment to the mother's uterine wall, much like that seen in mammals.
After the "pup" is fully developed, parturition occurs (viviparity). This mode
is seen only in certain requiem sharks and hammerheads.

Many dive spots in the tropics now offer shark diving or ray feeding. This is
both a good and a bad thing. Baiting sharks helps to get them close enough to
observe and photograph, but it results in unnatural behavior. It is also true that
divers have been bitten during shark feeds, in at least a few cases with fatal results.
In the case of ray feeding, some studies suggest that the stingrays that frequent
tourist-provisioned food sites (such as Stingray City in the Cayman Islands) tend
to be less healthy — with lower body weight; more wounds and scars from aggressive interactions with conspecifics, predation attempts by sharks and collisions
with boat propellers; and more ectoparasites — than those that utilize natural
food sources. The upside is that people who would not normally interact with a
ray or a shark may gain a greater appreciation for them if they have a close encounter, which hopefully will lead to an interest in protecting them and their habitat.

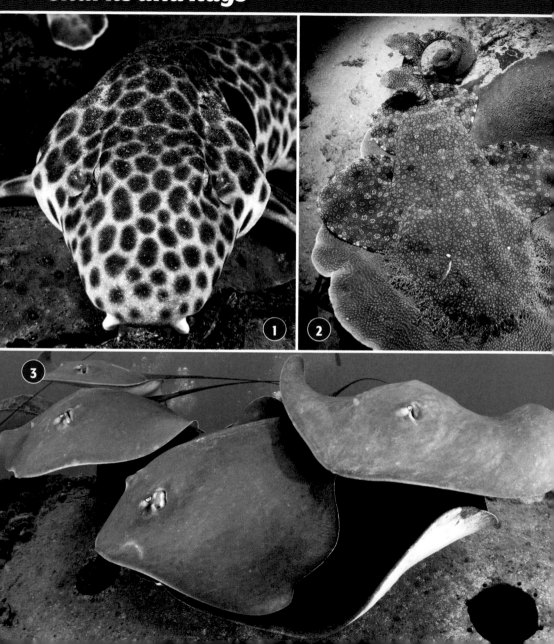

1 A Milne Bay epaulette shark (*Hemiscyllium michaeli*) "walks" along the bottom on its fins. Papua New Guinea.

2 A tasselled wobbegong shark (*Eucrossorhinus dasypogon*) rests on top of coral. Sometimes it curls its tail forward over its head, wiggles it to attract fish and then lunges upward to eat dinner. Indonesia.

3 A female marbled stingray (*Taeniura meyeni*) below smaller pink whiprays (*Himantura fai*), swimming together above the wreck of the SS *Yongala*. Australia.

4 The torpedo-shaped great white shark (*Carcharodon carcharias*). Guadalupe Island, Baja, Mexico.

5 Bull sharks (*Carcharhinus leucas*) gathering in the shallows. This species is responsible for many of the shark attacks on (and deaths of) humans, in part because it ventures into fresh water, moving up rivers, where many people would not expect to find them. Bahamas.

1 Tiger shark (*Galeocerdo cuvier*). The little dots on its snout are electro-receptor sensory pores called the ampullae of Lorenzini. Bahamas.

2 Great hammerhead shark (*Sphyrna mokarran*). The unmistakable, bizarrely alien head of the hammerhead has a battery of special sensory cells on its underside that spread over a large area to help it to detect its prey — stingrays and cownose rays. Bahamas.

3 Whale sharks (*Rhincodon typus*) gulp-feeding on plankton. Baja, Mexico.

4 The zebra shark (*Stegostoma fasciatum*) is oviparous, which means that its young are not born "live" but instead from leathery egg cases deposited on the bottom. Australia.

5 The sand tiger shark (*Carcharias taurus*), here surrounded by baitfish, is an example of an ovoviviparous species (this is also called aplacental viviparity). North Carolina, USA.

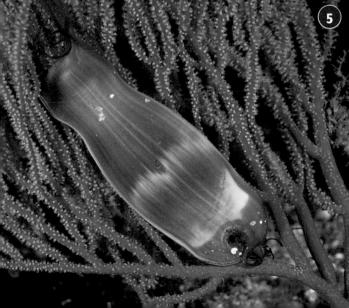

1 Gray reef sharks (*Carcharhinus amblyrhynchos*). Australia.

2 A slow, cautious approach allows a diver to move near a spotted wobbegong shark (*Orectolobus maculatus*) resting on the sandy bottom. Australia.

3 Tasselled wobbegong shark (*Eucrossorhinus dasypogon*), close-up of eye. Indonesia.

4 Pelagic thresher shark (*Alopias pelagicus*), visiting a cleaning station at dawn to be serviced by cleaner fish such as the wrasse to the right. Philippines.

5 Egg case of a swell shark (*Cephaloscyllium ventriosum*), a temperate species, attached to a gorgonian. California.

Bluntnose Sixgill Shark

Hexanchus griseus

Family Hexanchidae (cow sharks)

⊕ Wide-ranging in tropical and temperate seas

⊙ Deepwater species sometimes found on rocky reefs; outer continental shelves and slopes.

↧ 18–1,875 m (59–6,094 ft); exhibits tropical submergence (found at greater depths in tropical areas)

↔ 4.8 m (16 ft)

Solitary. Main food fishes and sharks; less often crustaceans, rays, seals, carrion (e.g., sunken whale carcasses) Spends day near seafloor. Makes vertical migrations: moves into lesser depths when sun goes down, then back to deep as sun rises. Found in deeper waters in autumn and winter. Ovoviviparous; litter size 22–108. Observed by divers near Vancouver Island, Canada. Not aggressive toward divers.

Galápagos Horn Shark

Heterodontus quoyi

Family Heterodontidae (bullhead sharks)

⊕ Galápagos Islands and other islands off Peru

⊙ Rocky reefs around islands

↧ 16–30 m (52–98 ft)

↔ 57 cm (22 in)

Solitary. Rests in crevices and caves during day. Active at night, feeding on sea urchins and other hard-shelled invertebrates. Supraorbital ridges low, with light bands in between; first dorsal origin behind pectoral fin base; spots over half of eye length. Eaten by sharks.

⊕ Tropical Australia, Papua New Guinea and Indonesia
☉ Coral reefs; lagoon patch reefs, back reefs, reef flats, reef faces, slopes
↧ 1–40 m (3.3–130 ft)   ↤ 1.3 m (4.2 ft)

Tasselled Wobbegong Shark
Eucrossorhinus dasypogon
Family Orectolobidae (carpet sharks)

Solitary. Rests under table corals, in lettuce corals, among ship wreckage or in caves during day, with tail curled up. Ambush predator; eats bony fishes and cephalopods. Schools of sweepers and/or cardinalfishes swim above it in caves. Will wag tail over head, mimicking swimming behavior of fish to lure prey into striking range. "Coughing" behavior may be threat display. Placid.

⊕ Temperate Australia, from southern Queensland to Western Australia
☉ Coastal and insular rocky reefs
↧ 1–30 m (3.3–98 ft)   ↤ 2.9 m (9.5 ft)

Hale's Wobbegong Shark
Orectolobus halei
Family Orectolobidae (carpet sharks)

Solitary or in aggregations. Inactive during day; may move about and hunt at night. Stays on same reef for long periods (some for two years or more). Feeds mainly on bony fishes, cephalopods and elasmobranchs, including smaller wobbegongs. Gestation 10–11 months; parturition September–October; litter size 30–45. Young very cryptic; hide in reef cracks and crevices. Will bite if provoked. Similar ornate wobbegong (*O. ornatus*), much smaller in size.

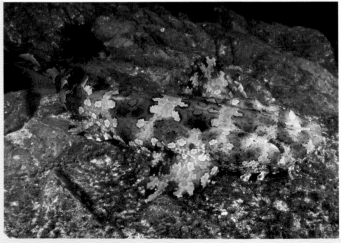

Elasmobranchs

Milne Bay Shark

Hemiscyllium michaeli
Family Hemiscylliidae
(epaulette sharks)

- 🌐 Milne Bay, Papua New Guinea
- ⊙ Coral reefs; lagoons, reef faces
- ↧ 3–15 m (10–49 ft)
- ↔ 72 cm (28 in)

Solitary. Hides in reef crevices during day. At night emerges to hunt benthic invertebrates and sleeping fishes. Walks on paired fins; rarely swims in typical sharklike fashion. Seven other epaulette shark species, but no other found in Milne Bay. Similar Indonesian speckled epaulette shark (*H. freycineti*) found on the West Papuan reefs (shown on page 413).

Zebra Shark

Stegostoma varium
Family Stegostomatidae
(zebra sharks)

- 🌐 East Africa and Red Sea, east to Samoa, north to Japan and south to Australia
- ⊙ Coral and rocky reefs; lagoons, reef channels, reef faces, slopes
- ↧ 1–70 m (3.3–228 ft)
- ↔ 3.5 m (11.5 ft)

Solitary or in groups. Rests on seafloor during day. Feeds on snails, clams, mussels, crabs and bony fishes. Forms breeding aggregations. Males bite females during courtship; at times bite female's tail, causing her to stop struggling. Males bite each other when asserting dominance. Up to seven eggs laid at a time, at six- to eight-day intervals; incubation about 160 days.

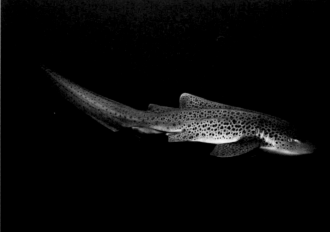

- Society Islands, east to South Africa, north to Red Sea and south to Australia
- Coral and rocky reefs; lagoons, reef flats, channels, reef faces, slopes
- 1–70 m (3.3–228 ft)   ↔ 3.2 m (10.5 ft)

Tawny Nurse Shark
Nebrius ferrugineus
Family Ginglymostomatidae
(nurse sharks)

Solitary; occasionally in groups. Larger individuals move over reef or rest in caves during day. Hunts after dark, feeding on octopuses, squid, crabs, lobsters, sea urchins and bony fishes. Grubs in cervices, under coral heads and among rubble searching for food. Often present at shark feeds in Indo Pacific. Placid, but will bite if provoked.

- Western Atlantic, from Rhode Island to Brazil; Eastern Atlantic from Senegal to Gabon; Eastern Pacific from southern Baja California to Peru
- Coral and rocky reefs; lagoons, mangroves, reef flats, reef faces, slopes
- 1–50 m (3.3–163 ft)   ↔ 4.3 m (14 ft)

Atlantic Nurse Shark
Ginglymostoma cirratum
Family Ginglymostomatidae
(nurse sharks)

Solitary, often keeping head under overhang or entire body in cave during day. Feeds on crustaceans, cephalopods, sea urchins and bony fishes. Uses suction to slurp prey from crevices. Habituates to being fed; will stay in area and "greet" divers if fed often. Forms breeding assemblages in shallow water in spring; parturition occurs 3–4.5 months later; 5–28 young in litter. If provoked will bite and hold on with tenacity of a pit bull.

Elasmobranchs

Whale Shark

Rhincodon typus
Family Rhincodontidae
(whale sharks)

⊕ Worldwide; tropical to warm temperate oceans (latitudes 30°N and 35°S)
⊙ Coral and rocky reefs; open ocean
↓ 1–980 m (3.3–3,185 ft)   ↔ 14 m (46 ft); possibly up to 18 m (60 ft)

Solitary or in loose aggregations (sometimes up to 100 individuals). Feeds on fish eggs, squid, planktonic crustaceans, sardines, anchovies and mackerel. Segregates by size and sex. Temporal abundance often related to prey availability. In Caribbean, locally abundant during mass spawning of snappers and groupers. Long-range migrations — related to plankton blooms and spawning events — of hundreds or even thousands of miles. Ovoviviparous; up to 300 young in litter. Docile.

Sand Tiger Shark

Carcharias taurus
Family Odontaspididae
(sand tiger sharks)

⊕ Western and Eastern Atlantic Oceans; western Indian Ocean; Western Pacific Ocean
⊙ Rocky reefs, shipwrecks
↓ 1–200 m (3.3–650 ft)   ↔ 3.2 m (10.5 ft)

Singly or in aggregations. Found in gutters, caves and around shipwrecks. Slowly swims or even hovers in water column. Ingests air at water's surface and uses stomach as buoyancy compensator. Feeds on bony fishes, sharks and rays. Some migrate to warmer waters in fall and winter and cooler climates in spring and summer. Male bites female during courtship and copulation. Ovoviviparous and embryophagous — developing young engage in intra-uterine cannibalism; two in litter (one per uterus).

- Warm temperate and tropical Indo-Pacific Ocean; South Africa and Red Sea, east to Gulf of California and Galápagos Islands
- Coral and rocky reefs; off reef slopes and seamounts; open ocean
- 1–150 m (3.3–488 ft)   ↔ 3.3 m (10.8 ft)

Pelagic Thresher Shark

Alopias pelagicus
Family Alopiidae (thresher sharks)

Solitary. Feeds mainly on schooling bony fishes and pelagic squid. Uses tail to herd and stun fish before eating. Body temperature higher than surrounding water. Leaps out of water. Two pups per litter; eat eggs that enter uterus during development (oophagy). Visits wrasse cleaning stations on seamounts to be groomed (often at dawn). Seen by divers in Red Sea, Philippines, Indonesia and Gulf of California.

- Worldwide; temperate and some tropical seas
- Coastal and insular rocky reefs
- 1–1,280 m (3.3–4,160 ft), mostly at temperatures of 12°–24°C (54°–75°F)
- ↔ 6.5 m (21.5 ft)

Great White Shark

Carcharodon carcharias
Family Lamnidae (mackerel sharks)

Solitary; occasionally in pairs or aggregations when major food source present. Forms dominance hierarchies based on size — smaller individuals avoid larger conspecifics. Young sharks prey more on bony fishes and elasmobranchs. Adults feed more on pinnipeds and cetaceans (live and dead). Uses stealth to sneak up on seals, then bites and lets them "bleed out" before eating them. Litter size 7–9. One of the few sharks known to "spy-hop." Potentially dangerous; worthy of great respect.

Shortfin Mako Shark

Isurus oxyrinchus
Family Lamnidae (mackerel sharks)

- ⊕ Circumtropical; tropical and temperate seas
- ⊙ Rocky and coral reefs; mostly open ocean
- ↓ 1–400 m (3.3–1,300 ft)
- ↔ 3.9 m (12.9 ft)

Solitary. Feeds on sharks, rays and bony fishes (including billfishes). Large adults eat occasional marine mammals. Gestation 12–18 months; litter size 4–16. Juveniles prefer mixed warmer layers of water above thermocline, spending most time near surface. Large adults may hang out below thermocline and make excursions into deep water. Warm-blooded, with rete mirabile (network of blood vessels) to increase body temperature (same as for white shark). Usually shy if bait not present. Potentially dangerous.

Coral Cat Shark

Atelomycterus marmoratus
Family Scyliorhinidae (cat sharks)

- ⊕ Arabian Sea, east to Papua New Guinea and north to Philippines
- ⊙ Coastal coral reefs; lagoons, reef faces
- ↓ 1–15 m (3.3–49 ft)
- ↔ 70 cm (28 in)

Coral-reef species with elongate body that allows movement in reef crevices and among branching corals. During day hides in crevices or under benthic debris; at night emerges to hunt invertebrates and sleeping fishes. Lays eggs in cases with tendrils at each corner; juveniles hatch in 4–6 months. A number of similar species, some awaiting description.

⊕ Western and Eastern Atlantic Ocean
⊙ Coral and rocky reefs; sand flats, mangroves, lagoons, reef faces, slopes
↧ 1–92 m (3.3–299 ft)   ↔ 3.4 m (11.2 ft)

Lemon Shark
Negaprion brevirostris
Family Carcharhinidae
(requiem sharks)

Solitary, but will aggregate in preferred habitats. Covers a home range of 18–93 sq km (7–36 sq mi). Feeds throughout day and night, although most active during twilight. Primary food of juveniles bony fishes and shrimps; adults eat fishes and elasmobranchs. Litter size 4–17. Usually indifferent, but can be aggressive in baited situations. Possible agonistic display consists of figure-eight swimming and jaw gaping.

⊕ East Africa and Red Sea, east to Panama, north to southern Japan and south to Australia
⊙ Coral and rocky reefs; lagoons, reef flats, reef faces, slopes
↧ 1–40 m (3.3–130 ft)   ↔ 2.1 m (6.9 ft)

Whitetip Reef Shark
Triaenodon obesus
Family Carcharhinidae
(requiem sharks)

Solitary or in aggregations. Rests in caves, under ledges or in reef gutters during day. Hunts at night, ferreting about reef and plunging head into cracks and crevices, searching for sleeping fishes, crabs, lobsters and octopuses. Often returns to same daytime resting place after night foraging. Cleaned by wrasses and gobies. Gestation 13 months; litter size 1–5. Indifferent toward or shy of divers.

Silvertip Shark

Carcharhinus albimarginatus
Family Carcharhinidae
(requiem sharks)

- ⊕ East Africa to Panama, north to Japan and south to Australia
- ☉ Coral and rocky reefs; reef faces, slopes, offshore banks
- ↧ 1–800 m (3.3–2,600 ft)
- ↔ 3 m (9.9 ft)

Occurs singly or in loose groups. Feeds on pelagic and benthic bony fishes, sharks and rays. Gestation 11 months; young born in summer; litter size 1–11. Sometimes visits wrasse cleaning stations. Curious about divers; occasionally aggressive in baited situations.

Gray Reef Shark

Carcharhinus amblyrhynchos
Family Carcharhinidae
(requiem sharks)

- ⊕ East Africa, east to Hawaiian Islands, north to southern Japan and south to Lord Howe Island
- ☉ Coral reefs; around low coral islands and atolls; all reef habitats
- ↧ 1–274 m (3.3–891 ft)
- ↔ 2.6 m (8.4 ft)

Solitary or in diurnal loose groups (often near reef drop-offs) or polarized schools (usually close to seafloor). Group members disperse to hunt after dark. Diet mainly bony fishes. Gestation 9–12 months; litter size 1–6. Potentially dangerous; has been implicated in more bites on divers than any other shark. Classic agonistic display includes pectoral fin lowering, back arching and nose raising with exaggerated swimming.

- ⊕ Circumtropical
- ⊙ Open ocean; sometimes off reef faces
- ↧ 1–500 m (3.3–1,650 ft)   ↔ 3.3 m (10.9 ft)

Silky Shark
Carcharhinus falciformis
**Family Carcharhinidae
(requiem sharks)**

Singly or in loose groups (juveniles aggregate more often). Associates with schooling fishes (mackerel, tuna, jacks, scad) and squid. Will feed with bottlenose dolphins on schooling fishes — both predators cause them to form tight groups, then dash into school and capture fish. Litter size 2–15. Lifespan up to 22 years or more. Usually indifferent toward or curious about divers.

- ⊕ Cosmopolitan in tropical and warm temperate seas
- ⊙ Oceanic islands; coral and rocky reefs
- ↧ 1–180 m (3.3–585 ft)   ↔ 3 m (9.9 ft)

Galápagos Shark
Carcharhinus galapagensis
**Family Carcharhinidae
(requiem sharks)**

Singly or in loose groups. Juveniles often in shallower habitats; adults more common on drop-offs and steep reef slopes. Feeds on reef fishes (moray eels, parrotfishes, surgeonfishes, squirrelfishes), cephalopods and crustaceans; off Galápagos Islands preys on sea lions. Litter size 6–16. Curious toward divers. Threat display consists of head-swinging and exaggerated swimming motions.

Bull Shark
Carcharhinus leucas
Family Carcharhinidae
(requiem sharks)

⊕ Circumglobal
⊙ Tropical and subtropical seas; most abundant near continental coastlines; swims up rivers and even enters some lakes
↧ 1–150 m (3.3–488 ft)   ↔ 3.4 m (11.2 ft)

Solitary, but may aggregate around food sources. Segregates by sex. Juveniles found in estuarine habitats. Feeds on variety of food items: bony fishes, sea turtles, marine mammals, crabs, squid and carrion. Adults prefer other sharks and rays as food. Gestation 10–11 months; 1–13 pups per litter. Divers should respect this shark, but usually not aggressive without bait present. Implicated in attacks on bathers.

Blacktip Shark
Carcharhinus limbatus
Family Carcharhinidae
(requiem sharks)

⊕ Circumglobal
⊙ Tropical and subtropical seas; turbid inshore waters (lagoons, mangrove swamps, estuaries), sand flats, reef channels, reef faces, slopes, seamounts
↧ 1–64 m (3.3–208 ft)   ↔ 2.6 m (8.6 ft)

Segregates by sex; females more prevalent in shallow water. Juveniles and adolescents often form mixed schools with similar-sized shark species. Feeds on benthic and schooling fishes. Hunts more during day than at night. Large groups feed on schools of mullet, with sharks leaping from the water during foraging melee. Gestation 11–12 months; litter size 1–10. Mostly shy, circling at a distance, or leaves area altogether. Some become bold and aggressive.

⊕ Circumglobal
⊙ Open ocean; sometimes approaches coastlines near high islands
↧ 1–240 m (3.3–780 ft)   ↔ 3.5 m (11.6 ft)

Oceanic Whitetip Shark
Carcharhinus longimanus
Family Carcharhinidae
(requiem sharks)

Singly or in loose groups. Forms large aggregations around food sources (e.g., whale carcasses). Associates with pilot whales. Chases and challenges silky sharks, even when latter larger. Feeds on squid, bony fishes and pelagic stingrays. Gestation 12 months; litter size 1–15. Bold, known to persistently circle divers (sometimes for hours) and make occasional close passes. Several cases of unprovoked attacks on divers.

⊕ Red Sea, east to Society Islands, north to Japan and south to Australia
⊙ Coral reefs; lagoons, channels, reef faces, slopes
↧ 1–75 m (3.3–244 ft)   ↔ 1.8 m (5.9 ft)

Blacktip Reef Shark
Carcharhinus melanopterus
Family Carcharhinidae
(requiem sharks)

Solitary, but aggregates in reef channels at low tide, moving onto reef flats at flood tide. Limited home range, about 2.5 sq km (about 1 sq mi). Feeds mostly on reef fishes but also cephalopods and crustaceans; chases down surgeonfishes and stingrays and attacks groups of spawning surgeonfishes. Juveniles preyed upon by other sharks and large groupers. Gestation 8–9 months; litter size 3–4. Bites waders on calf but rarely bothers divers.

Caribbean Reef Shark
Carcharhinus perezi
Family Carcharhinidae
(requiem sharks)

⊕ Florida to Brazil
⊙ Coral reefs; lagoons, reef faces, slopes
↕ 1–350 m (3.3–1,137 ft)
↔ 3 m (9.9 ft)

Solitary or in loose groups. Stays in same general area for long periods. Juveniles occupy deep lagoons; adults move into shallower water at night and spend days in cooler deep waters. Diet consists of bony fishes. Will lie on bottoms of caves and under ledges in apparent torpor, as if sleeping. Litter size 4–6. Common at shark feeds. Responsible for a number of attacks on divers, almost always in baited situations.

Tiger Shark
Galeocerdo cuvier
Family Carcharhinidae
(requiem sharks)

⊕ Circumglobal
⊙ Subtropical and tropical reefs; most reef habitats; also open ocean
↕ 1–371 m (3.3–1,206 ft)
↔ 5.5 m (18.2 ft)

Solitary, but may aggregate around large food source. Adopts nonchalant, relaxed pace but moves quickly when necessary. Adults occupy deeper water during day, move onto shallow reefs at night and sometimes on overcast days, when light levels low. Juveniles and adolescents regular inhabitants of shallow water during day. Varied diet: bony fishes, sharks, rays, sea turtles, sea snakes, sea birds and marine mammals. Gestation 12–16 months; litter size 10–82. Lifespan 45–50 years.

⊕ Circumglobal

⊙ Tropical to temperate seas; usually open ocean; some near offshore islands

↧ 1–220 m (3.3–715 ft)   ↔ 3.8 m (12.5 ft)

Blue Shark

Prionace glauca

Family Carcharhinidae (requiem sharks)

Solitary or in aggregations near food sources. Feeds heavily on krill, squid and schooling bony fishes (anchovies, herring, sardines). In Pacific moves northward in summer and southward in winter. In Atlantic rides Gulf Stream across Atlantic, catches other currents down European and African coasts, then hitches ride on Atlantic North Equatorial Current back to Caribbean. Segregates by size and sex. Gestation 9–12 months; litter size 4–135. Usually indifferent toward or shy of divers. More aggressive when baits present.

⊕ Circumglobal; warm temperate and tropical seas

⊙ Open ocean; around seamounts, lagoons, reef faces, slopes

↧ 1–275 m (3.3–894 ft)   ↔ 4.2 m (13.9 ft)

Scalloped Hammerhead Shark

Sphyrna lewini

Family Sphyrnidae (hammerheads)

Young individuals aggregate in lagoons; adults form daytime refuging groups (50–225 individuals), often around seamounts. At night moves into mesopelagic zone to feed on squid and schooling fishes. Large adults eat other sharks. During day, much social interaction between group members, including unusual behavior patterns: corkscrew swims, head-shaking and hitting (butting against another with head). Cleaned by reef fishes (king angels, cleaner wrasses) in some areas. Sometimes shy.

Great Hammerhead Shark

Sphyrna mokarran

Family Sphyrnidae (hammerheads)

- ⊕ Circumtropical
- ☉ Coral and rocky reefs; lagoons, reef faces, slopes; open ocean
- ↧ 1–300 m (3.3–975 ft) ↔ 6 m (19.8 ft)

Solitary. Avoided by other sharks, possibly because of proclivity toward eating elasmobranchs. Feeds on stingrays (a favorite of adults), bony fishes (including tarpon), squid and crustaceans. Uses hammer to pin stingrays to seafloor and bite off their pectoral fins. Gestation 11 months; litter size 3–42. Usually not aggressive, but may make close passes to investigate.

Giant Guitarfish

Rhynchobatus djeddensis

Family Rhynchobatidae (guitarfishes)

- ⊕ South Africa to Red Sea; Japan to New South Wales, Australia
- ☉ Coral and rocky reefs; intertidal areas, lagoons, reef faces, slopes
- ↧ 1–50 m (3.3–163 ft) ↔ 3.1 m (10.2 ft)

Solitary or in aggregations. Often swims onto tidal flats to feed at flood tide. Eats clams, crustaceans and benthic fishes, which it digs out of sand. Birthing occurs in summer, often in shallows, including estuarine habitats; litter size around 10. Often shy and difficult to approach.

- ⊕ North Carolina to northern Argentina, including Gulf of Mexico
- ☉ Sandy shorelines, sometimes near coral reefs
- ↧ 1–40 m (3.3–130 ft)　　　　↔ 45 cm (17.7 in)

Lesser Electric Ray
Narcine brasiliensis
Family Narcinidae (numbfishes)

Solitary or in loose groups. Main diet worms and occasionally benthic fishes and crustaceans. Uncovers infaunal prey by undulating posterior disc margin. Nocturnal, burying itself under sand during day. Moves from shallow inshore waters to deeper areas in winter. Off Florida, females move into surf zone to give birth in late summer; litter size 2–17. Has electric organs; can emit shock of up to 37 volts. Harmless to divers.

- ⊕ Western and Eastern Atlantic Ocean
- ☉ Bays, tidal flats, estuaries (including brackish conditions)
- ↧ 1–40 m (3.3–130 ft)　　　　↔ disc width 1.2 m (3.9 ft)

Smooth Butterfly Ray
Gymnura micrura
Family Gymnuridae (butterfly rays)

Kitelike shape with short tail. Active, swimming just above bottom. Uses swim/glide locomotion, beating pectoral fins to gain momentum, then gliding for a distance before beating fins again. Rests on substrate or buries itself under sand or mud. Fish-eater, but also grubs for bivalves and crustaceans. Nursery areas usually turbid coastal waters; litter size 2–10.

Southern Stingray

Dasyatis americana
Family Dasyatidae
(whiptail stingrays)

- ⊕ New Jersey to Brazil
- ☉ Lagoons, seagrass beds, reef faces, slopes
- ↧ 1–53 m (3.3–172 ft)
- ↔ disc width 1.5 m (5 ft)

Occurs singly or in pairs or aggregations. Inactive during day, often buried in sand. Feeds at night. Swims over or rests near cleaning stations to be cleaned by bluehead wrasse and Spanish hogfish. Mating consists of following by male, biting of pectoral fin and copulation (male swings under female and inserts single clasper). Males and females promiscuous; litter size 2–10. Will allow divers to hand-feed (e.g., at Stingray City); known to bite divers in this context but does minimal damage.

Diamond Stingray

Dasyatis brevis
Family Dasyatidae
(whiptail stingrays)

- ⊕ Eastern Pacific Ocean
- ☉ Bays, seagrass meadows, kelp beds, near rocky reefs
- ↧ 1–70 m (3.3–228 ft)
- ↔ disc width 1.2 m (3.9 ft)

Solitary or in small groups. Rests on substrate or buries itself just underneath. Eats mollusks, worms and crustaceans. Probes sand with snout and undulates front portion of disc to excavate prey. Fed on by orcas and large sharks. Easy to approach. Similar sympatric species, longtail stingray (*Dasyatis longus*), has longer tail (twice the length of disc).

⊕ Society Islands, Thailand and India
◉ Lagoons, reef faces, slopes
↧ 1–20 m (3.3–65 ft) ↔ disc width 1 m (3.3 ft)

Pink Whipray
Himantura fai
Family Dasyatidae
(**whiptail stingrays**)

Solitary but can be quite social (often 2–8 individuals bury selves together). Rests on or buried under substrate. Preys on crustaceans, doing much of feeding at night. Shows strong site fidelity, living in same general area for long periods. Larger females most dominant in groups. Fed in some Polynesian lagoons for tourists.

⊕ East Africa and Red Sea, east to French Polynesia, north to Philippines and south to Australia
◉ lagoons, tidal flats, sand patches on reef faces
↧ 1–20 m (3.3–65 ft) ↔ disc width 90 cm (35.4 in)

Bluespotted Ribbontail Ray
Taeniura lymma
Family Dasyatidae (whiptail stingrays)

Solitary and in aggregations (during mating period). Feeds during day and at night. Digs feeding pits in sand when mining for mollusks, crustaceans and benthic fishes. Moves into tidal zone at flood tide to feed. Seeks refuge under table corals and in staghorn coral beds and shipwreck debris. Often visits cleaning stations to be cleaned by wrasses. Can be shy and difficult to approach underwater.

Marbled Stingray

Taeniura meyeni

**Family Dasyatidae
(whiptail stingrays)**

⊕ East Africa and Red Sea, east to Panama, north to southern Japan and south to Australia
⊙ Rocky and coral reefs; estuaries, lagoons, reef faces, slopes
↧ 2–500 m (7–1,625 ft)   ↔ disc width 1.6 m (5.3 ft)

Solitary or in aggregations. Lies on sand, rock and coral bottoms. Feeds on bivalves, crabs, shrimps and benthic fishes. Jacks and cobia commonly swim just above or below as ray moves over bottom, possibly using it as blind to approach prey. Fed for divers in Maldive Islands. The amount of black marbling on this ray varies from one individual to another.

Reticulated Round Stingray

Urobatis concentricus

Family Urotrygonidae (round stingrays)

⊕ Sea of Cortez, Panama and Galápagos Islands
⊙ Rocky reefs and bays (on sand and rocky substrate)
↧ 1–65 m (3.3–211 ft)   ↔ 60 cm (23.6 in)

Usually solitary; may form groups during breeding season. Feeds on small crabs and worms. Male grasps female by pectoral fin and flips underneath so pair is belly to belly during copulation; inserts one clasper. Unreceptive female may stab male with tail spine. Preyed on by sharks.

⊕ North Carolina, Gulf of Mexico and throughout Caribbean to Trinidad
⊙ Coral reefs, harbors, bays, lagoons
↧ 1–25 m (3.3–81 ft)   ↦ 67 cm (26 in)

Yellow Stingray
Urobatis jamaicensis
Family Urotrygonidae
(round stingrays)

Solitary. Excavates holes in sand by undulating anterior disc margin to expose buried prey. Eats shrimps, small fishes, clams and worms. When mating, more than one male may attempt to copulate with same female. Litter size 2–4. Numbers have dropped significantly in past decade.

⊕ Circumglobal
⊙ Coral and rocky reefs; lagoons, channels, reef flats, reef faces, slopes; open ocean
↧ 1–80 m (3.3–260 ft)   ↦ disc width 3.5 (11.5 ft)

Spotted Eagle Ray
Aetobatus narinari
Family Myliobatidae
(eagle and manta rays)

Solitary or in pairs or large schools (200+ individuals). Probes sand with snout to locate bivalves, gastropods and hermit crabs. Groups move from reef channels and reef faces onto reef flats and lagoons during flood tide to feed and avoid predators. Prey for several large sharks. Only left ovary and uteri functional; gestation 12 months; litter size 1–2. Shy and difficult to approach. DNA study suggests two different species, one in Western and Central Pacific and one in Eastern Pacific and Atlantic Oceans.

Manta Ray

Manta birostris

Family Myliobatidae
(eagle and manta rays)

- ⊕ Circumglobal
- ⊙ Coral and rocky reefs; lagoons, reef faces, slopes; also open ocean
- ↧ 1–120 m (3.3–390 ft)   ↔ disc width 6.7 m (21.9 ft)

Solitary or in groups (up to 50 individuals). Feeds on planktonic crustaceans and small schooling bony fishes. Females outnumber males in most populations. Females breed every other year. Gestation 1 year, with some populations giving birth in summer; 1–2 pups per litter. Aggregates around cleaning stations. Fed on by large sharks and orcas. Smaller *Manta alfredi* (found mainly in Indo-Pacific) has more spots on belly, light mouth and no tail spine.

Spine-tail Devil Ray

Mobula japanica

Family Myliobatidae
(eagle and manta rays)

- ⊕ Indo-Pacific Ocean
- ⊙ Coral and rocky reefs; lagoons, reef faces, slopes; open ocean
- ↧ 1–20 m (3.3–65 ft)   ↔ disc width 3.1 m (10.1 ft)

Schooling species; segregates by size. Groups may number in hundreds. Will leap out of water, somersaulting before falling back into sea. Uses Gulf of California as feeding and mating grounds. Filter-feeder that specializes in krill. Hosts remoras and followed by pilotfishes and jacks. Has tail spine, long tail with white along sides, dark blue to black on back, and white-tipped dorsal fin. Mouth is under head in *Mobula* species (subterminal) and at end of head in *Manta* species (terminal).

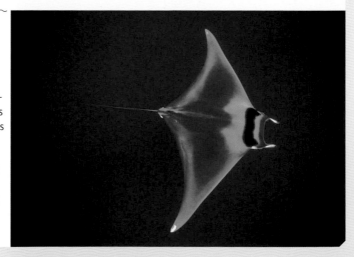

⊕ Circumtropical
⊙ Open blue water, usually at or near surface
↓ 1–30 m (3.3–98 ft)   ↔ 3 m (9.8 ft)

Sicklefin Devil Ray

Mobula tarapacana
Family Myliobatidae
(eagle and manta rays)

Solitary or in small groups (up to 10 individuals). Sometimes swims in circular formation. Feeds on krill, other larger zooplankton and small fishes (jacks, pufferfishes); fish-eating habits of this species rare for devil rays. Often parasitized by isopods and copepods, which are fed on by hitchhiking remoras. Has counter-current heat exchangers in pectoral fins and brain to keep body and head warmer. Tail spine; tail short, with strongly falcate fins.

Elasmobranchs

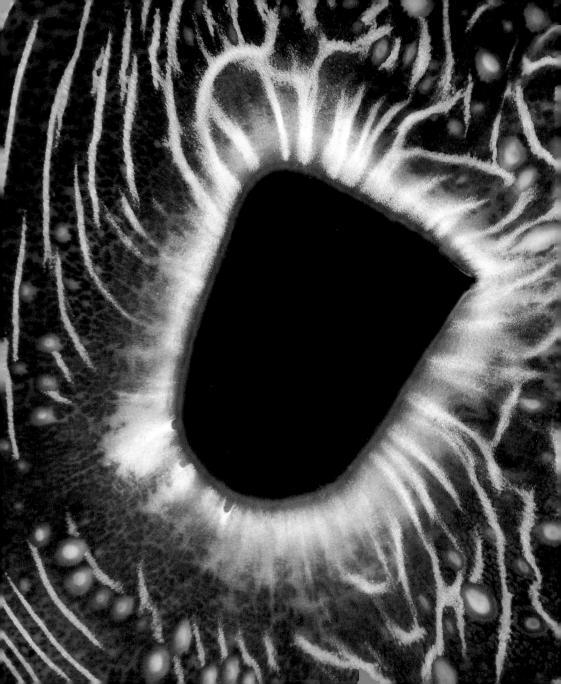

While they are not a true biological group, the term *invertebrate* is used generically to refer to any animal that lacks a backbone. This is a very large collection, containing about 97 percent of all known animal species! Coral reefs are home to more invertebrates than any other marine ecosystem. Though we do not yet know exactly how many invertebrate species live on coral reefs, the number is likely to be at least in the hundreds of thousands, perhaps even millions. To give you some idea how well represented invertebrate life is on coral reefs, a recent study conducted in New Caledonia collected 2,738 species of mollusks alone.

Invertebrates include the "backbone" of the tropical reef, the stony corals, as well as their "softer" relatives the soft corals, sea anemones, sea jellies and comb jellies. Within the stony coral labyrinth, and in the adjacent sand/rubble plains and flats, live many spineless critters, including numerous species of worms, sea slugs, snails, clams, octopuses, shrimps, crabs, sea stars and sea cucumbers. The tunicates, though often included in the invertebrates, actually belong to the kingdom Chordata (vertebrates).

Sponges

Sponges may be one of the most underappreciated groups of invertebrates. The phylum Porifera is huge, containing more than 5,000 species placed in four classes. Many sponges are found on coral reefs; in fact, several groups contribute to reef construction. In certain tropical Western Atlantic and Caribbean coral-reef habitats, they exceed corals in number of species, biomass and the area of substrate covered. For example, on one reef in Belize, scientists counted 300 species of sponge and only 47 stony corals. Many sponges, especially in deep reef habitats, have yet to be described.

Rich sponge growth (various species) on the reef edge at 18 m (60 ft) deep. Belize.

Previous Page
The psychedelic cosmos of a giant clam siphon and mantle, Australia.

Sponges are the simplest or most "primitive" of the multicellular animals. They lack true tissues as well as actual organs (and no, they don't wear pants). Instead they are made up of cells supported by several different skeletal elements — spongin (collagen fibers), calcareous spicules and/or siliceous spicules — all wrapped in a tough skin. Another significant sponge feature is incurrent pores that permeate the skin, leading to the interior cavity, called the atrium. Sponges also have a larger opening, the osculum, which leads from the atrium to the surrounding aqueous environment. Water moves through the sponge, entering the incurrent pores and exiting the osculae. These animals are sessile (incapable of locomotion) and have no nervous system. Sponges exhibit the full gamut of architectural forms, however, from simple encrusting types to elaborate tubular designs.

Sponges feed by filtering water through their incurrent pores and body chamber(s) and out through the osculae. Current is produced within the sponge's body by the beating of hairlike flagella found on specialized cells. They can filter an incredible amount of water each day — one study documented a leuconoid sponge just 1 cm (0.5 in) high that pumped 22.5 L (6 gal) of water through its body per day. Cells within the body cavity ingest microscopic food particles, many too small to be seen by a standard microscope. Larger food items include bacteria and dinoflagellates. Waste produced by the sponge is simply carried away by the water filtering through the animal.

Most sponges possess both male and female sex organs. Sperm is released into the water column and enters the bodies of other sponges, fertilizing the eggs. Developing larvae drift as plankton until they reach the settling stage, when they attach themselves to appropriate substrate.

Although the sponges that most divers notice are brightly colored, the majority of species are quite drab. Those more chromatically blessed may exhibit vivid colors because of toxins they contain, or to protect themselves from ultraviolet rays. A number of tropical species that grow in exposed areas are toxic; they can cause paralysis or death if ingested in large quantities. Along the east coast of Mexico, 75 percent of sponges may be toxic.

In spite of toxic, spicule-packed tissues and a consistency much like fiberglass, some highly specialized fishes include sponges in their diets, and some feed almost exclusively on them. In one study, about 10 percent of the reef fish species surveyed fed frequently on sponges (e.g., angelfishes, boxfishes). These fishes apparently

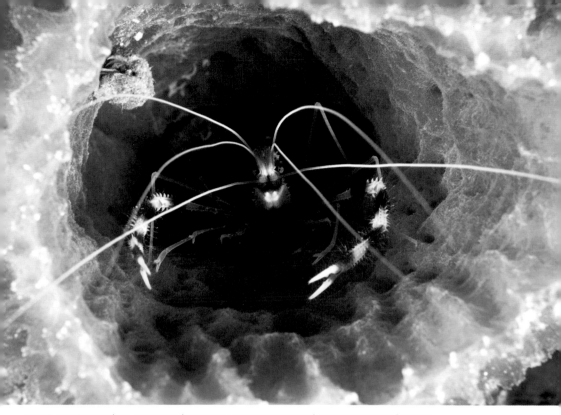

A banded coral shrimp (*Stenopus hispidus*) shelters in an azure vase sponge (*Callyspongia plicifera*) waiting for fish to come by, so it can clean them of parasites. Belize.

feed on toxic sponges in quantities small enough not to affect them deleteriously, or perhaps they are immune to the poisonous substances. Other marine animals that feed on sponges include many sea slugs and hawksbill sea turtles.

An important function of sponges is to provide sanctuary for other reef animals, from tiny bacteria to conspicuous fishes. Some sponges contain blue-green algae (cyanobacteria). The relationship may be mutualistic in nature, with the algae producing nutrients for the sponge while the sponge provides a growing substrate. A single sponge may also serve as home for hundreds of larger organisms, such as mollusks, crabs, shrimps, sea stars, serpent stars and fishes. A small number of reef fishes, including several gobies and a cardinal-fish, are obligatory sponge-dwellers (that is, they are always found in sponges).

Sponges

1 A brown volcano sponge (*Ectyoplasia ferox*) spawning, releasing gametes in sticky strands. Dominica.

2 The giant barrel sponge (*Xestospongia muta*) can grow to 2 m (6.5 ft) tall. Dominica.

3 Tube sponge (*Callyspongia* sp.). Indonesia.

4 This sponge, *Chalinula nematifera*, was formerly known as *Nara nematifera* and *Haliclona nematifera*. Indonesia.

5 This elephant ear sponge (*Ianthella basta*) is 1 m (3.3 ft) across. Solomon Islands.

6 Orange elephant ear sponge (*Agelas clathrodes*). This large specimen is up to 3 m (10 ft) wide and grows 25 m (80 ft) deep along a wall. Bonaire.

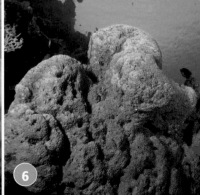

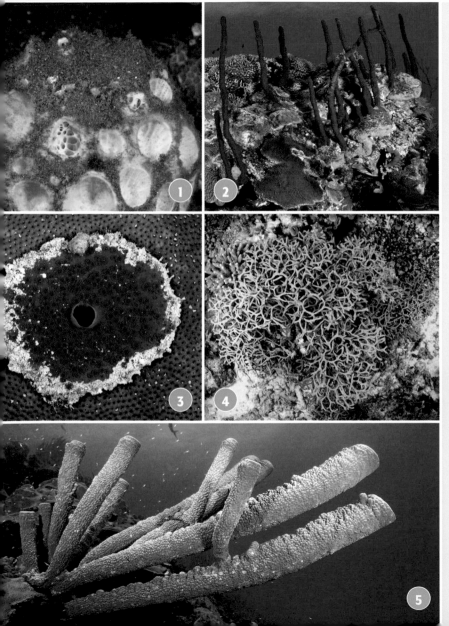

1 Golf ball sponge (*Cinachyra* sp.). Indonesia.

2 Erect rope sponges (*Amphimedon compressa*). Belize.

3 A red boring sponge (*Cliona delitrix*) bores into a coral head. Belize.

4 This handsome sponge is possibly a *Cribrochalina* sp. Indonesia.

5 Stovepipe sponge (*Aplysina archeri*). Bonaire.

Sea Anemones

Sea anemones (phylum Cnidaria, order Actinaria) share the class Anthozoa with approximately 6,000 other invertebrate species. Some other groups in this class include stony and soft corals, black corals, tube anemones, zoanthids and corallimorpharians (mushroom anemones). Sea anemones are solitary polyps with a columnar body and an oral disc equipped with hollow tentacles. Food is ingested and waste expelled through a slit-shaped mouth in the disc's center. Anemones range from 1.5 cm (0.6 in) to more than 1 m (3.3 ft) in diameter. The sea anemone's base either adheres to hard substrate or digs into the sand or mud. All sea anemones occur in marine habitats, and they are especially abundant in shallow tropical seas.

The main defense mechanism of sea anemones is stinging cells, or nematocysts, in their tentacles. In some species the stinging cells are strong enough to incapacitate a medium-sized fish, while in others only slight irritation will occur. Nematocysts of the "hell's fire" anemones (family Actinodendronidae) are very potent — they can ruin a careless diver's day! (At least some of these odd anemones appear to mimic algae and soft corals.) Sea anemones also use their nematocysts offensively to capture prey, which usually consist of zooplankton. Some larger anemone species with more powerful stings even feed on small fishes or crustaceans.

Venom-laced micro-harpoons in its nematocysts are not the sea anemone's only form of defense. Species that dwell in soft substrates withdraw under the sand or mud when assaulted, while some reef-dwelling forms pull into holes or crevices. In the Indian and Pacific Oceans the anemone's best defense against predators is the anemonefishes that use their tentacles as a refuge. When such fish are removed from anemones, they are quickly set upon and eaten by hungry butterflyfishes. Other anemone predators include spadefishes, grunts, boxfishes, pufferfishes and triggerfishes.

Sea anemones have unicellular algae, known as zooxanthellae, in their tissues. Through photosynthesis, the zooxanthellae deliver nutrients to the host anemone. Sea anemones can also absorb some organic nutrients directly from seawater; one benefit of hosting anemonefishes is that the ammonia and feces they expel provide a nutrient source for the anemone. And anemonefishes and

Close-up of the stinging tentacles of a bulb tentacle sea anemone (*Entacmaea quadricolor*). Indonesia.

A Clark's anemonefish (*Amphiprion clarkii*) hiding in a bulb tentacle sea anemone (*Entacmaea quadricolor*). An example of mutualism — a classic symbiotic relationship in which both parties benefit. Anemonefish are also called clownfish. Indonesia.

zooxanthellae are not the only marine organisms that use anemones for shelter. Many shrimps, crabs and other species of fish make their homes among the anemone's stinging tentacles. Some appear to develop an immunity to its toxins, while others do not trigger firing of the anemone's microscopic arsenal. Other fishes found around anemones (certain cardinalfishes and wrasses) nimbly maneuver between the tentacles, avoiding contact. Certain sea anemones attach themselves to other animals, living on the shells of large hermit crabs or attaching to jellyfish or comb jellies. The "pom pom" crab (*Lybia* spp.) will pick up two small anemones, one in each claw, and use them to sting predators that get too close.

Top
Fiery blooms of zoanthids (*Parazoanthus* sp.). Australia.

Bottom
A boxer or "pom pom" crab (*Lybia tessellata*) protects itself by carrying stinging sea anemones. Indonesia.

Sea Anemones

1 A leathery sea anemone (*Heteractis crispa*), with its long tentacles often tipped in purple, is host to a Clark's anemonefish. Philippines.

2 An orange ball corallimorph (*Pseudo-corynactis caribbeorum*), its tentacles extended to feed at night. Dominica.

3 Magnificent sea anemone (*Heteractis magnifica*) with false clown anemonefish (*Amphiprion ocellaris*). Indonesia.

4 Haddon's sea anemone (*Stichodactyla haddoni*) is host to saddleback anemonefish (*Amphiprion polymnus*). Indonesia.

5 Zoantharians (*Protopalythoa* sp.) form a colony of anemone-like animals. Each "umbrella" is 1 cm (0.4 in) in diameter. Indonesia.

1 The gorgonian wrapper sea anemone (*Nemanthus annamensis*) attaches to gorgonians and black corals. Galápagos Islands.

2 A tube-dwelling sand anemone of the family Cerianthidae. This sea anemone is common in shallow, sandy areas. Galápagos Islands.

Coral (*Acropora* sp.) spawning at night, releasing eggs. Fiji.

Stony Corals

The stony corals (phylum Cnidaria, order Scleractinia) — also called scleractinians or hard corals — are major components of a coral reef. Over thousands of years the calcareous skeletons of these tiny animals accumulate and are cemented together by algae, sponges and other corals. This process has led to the formation of some of nature's most awe-inspiring structures. Most coral species that are important reef-builders are in a group known as hermatypic corals. These have single-celled symbiotic algae (zooxanthellae) living in their tissues that, via photosynthesis, convert sunlight into nourishment for their hosts. Ahermatypic corals lack these algae, so they capture their food with stinging polyps or absorb nutrients from the surrounding seawater (to varying degrees, hermatypic species feed this way as well). Not being dependent on the sun, ahermatypic species can grow in dark caves and under overhangs.

Corals most often grow in colonies; an isolated coral colony is known as a coral head. Colonies exhibit many different growth forms. In some cases they grow to maximize the amount of colony surface (the number of polyps) exposed to the sun's energy. In other cases their structure is determined by additional, abiotic factors such as wave action. Common growth forms include columnar, which creates columns; massive, where the colony is similar in all directions; encrusting, where it grows over the substrate; branching; foliaceous, or leaflike; and laminar, or platelike. To properly identify corals to the species level, taxonomists rely heavily on detailed examination of a specimen's corallites — the calcereous skeletons that surround individual polyps. It can be quite a challenge for non-experts to accurately identify many of the hundreds of varieties of corals found on the reef.

A coral's skin produces large amounts of mucus, which protects it from certain predators and also from drying out if exposed to air during low tide. This mucus is a vital source of food for certain fishes, which either nip it off the coral (certain butterflyfishes) or ingest pieces that the coral sloughs off (some damsels). But even though scleractinians may seem to be adequately defended, some reef fishes eat the polyps themselves. The most important corallivores are butterflyfishes. Many feed on corals by picking or scraping the polyps from the skeleton; certain filefishes and wrasses feed similarly. Triggerfishes and pufferfishes don't bother about neatly excising the polyps — they just bite off entire tips of coral branches.

Stony corals reproduce both sexually and asexually. When it comes to sexual reproduction, most scleractinians are broadcast spawners, with fertilization occurring after individual polyps release eggs and/or sperm into the water column. Many engage in mass spawning, with numerous species releasing gam-etes synchronously during a single evening each year. During these events, so many sex cells are released that egg predators are overwhelmed, resulting in "gamete slicks" on the water's surface. After the eggs are fertilized, the young coral develop in the plankton. Eventually the planula larvae settle out onto suitable substrate, where they grow and reproduce themselves (asexually) to form a colony. Stony corals can also reproduce asexually by fragmentation. In certain species (e.g., some *Acropora*), when a piece breaks off, it may fall to the seafloor, reattach and grow into a large colony.

Lace coral (*Stylaster* sp.), a delicate, finely branched hydrocoral found in caves. This is an ahermatypic coral, which does not contain symbiotic zooxanthellae algae. Papua New Guinea.

Stony Corals

1 Cabbage coral (*Turbinaria* cf. *reniformis*). Australia.

2 Lobed coral (*Porites lobata*) dominates this shallow reef. Hawaii.

3 Table coral (*Acropora indonesia*), 2.5 m (8.2 ft) across, on a shallow reef top. Indonesia.

4 Boulder brain coral (*Colpophyllia natans*) with bluestriped grunts (*Haemulon sciurus*) around the top. Florida.

5 Cactus coral (*Pavona cactus*), with its distinctive shape, is usually found in protected areas. Indonesia.

6 Finger coral (*Porites attenuata*). Indonesia.

Stony Corals

1 Mountainous star coral (*Montastraea faveolata*) forms giant mushroom-like mounds on a reef slope 18 m (59 ft) deep. Bonaire.

2 Star column coral (*Pavona clavus*). Fiji.

3 Mushroom coral (*Fungia fungites*). Fiji.

4 Elkhorn coral (*Acropora palmata*), once common in the Florida Keys and the Caribbean, now rare. Belize.

5 Staghorn coral (*Acropora cervicornis*). Belize.

6 Table corals (*Acropora hyacinthus*). Indonesia.

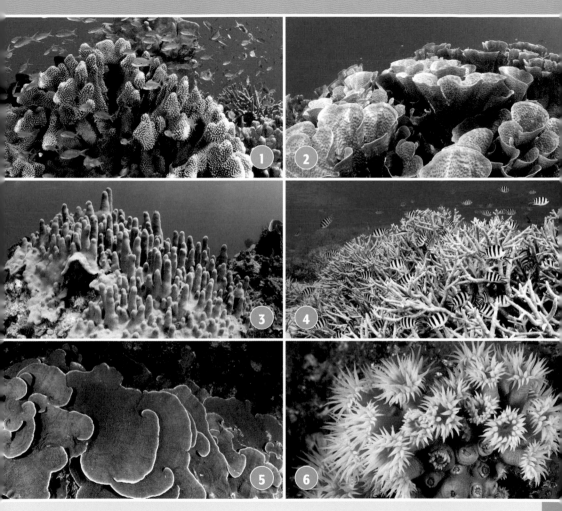

1 Cauliflower coral (*Pocillopora eydouxi*) with a cloud of scalefin anthias (*Pseudanthias squammipinnis*). Fiji.

2 Whorls of chalice coral (*Echinopora lamellosa*). This healthy colony is in shallow water bordering mangrove habitat. Indonesia.

3 Pillar coral (*Dendrogyra cylindrus*). Dominica.

4 A dense, healthy thicket of branching staghorn coral (*Acropora formosa*) in shallow water shelters scissortail sergeants (*Abudefduf sexfasciatus*). Australia.

5 A large colony of tiered corals, sometimes called serpent coral (*Pachyseris speciosa*), in the family Agariciidae. Australia.

6 Cup corals (*Tubastraea faulkneri*) at night. Some of the polyps have their feeding tentacles extended. Australia.

Soft Corals

The phylum Cnidaria, subclass Octocorallia — soft corals — includes some of the most spectacular sessile invertebrates on the coral reef. For example, the colors and forms of the Indo-Pacific soft coral genera *Dendronephthya* and *Scleronephthya* are unrivaled. Likewise, large stands of pastel-colored sea fans create dramatic seascapes on coral reefs in the tropical Atlantic. These animals are found on coral reefs around the world and are usually the first corals to colonize deep reefs and those damaged by hurricanes. This is an extremely varied group that includes the lesser-known blue corals, sea pens, stoloniferans (e.g., pipe organ coral) and sea whips, as well as the gorgonians and more common soft corals.

The actual number of octocoral species is somewhat of a mystery, as the taxonomic state of this group seems to be in disarray. In many cases, microscopic examination of their sclerites — mineralized internal structures that provide rigidity and aid in defense — is necessary to identify a soft coral to the species level. Most soft corals have an internal skeleton, made up of a flexible horny material or calcareous sclerites, and polyps with eight pinnate (featherlike) tentacles (stony coral polyps usually have tentacles in multiples of six). Not all the soft corals are actually soft. Some, such as the blue corals and pipe organ corals, have a calcium carbonate skeleton. Other members of the group have an axial skeleton — for example, sea pens. Soft corals also display a variety of different growth forms, including bushy, branching, encrusting, lobate, pinnate, umbellate and more. As with stony corals, the form of many soft corals is a function of their environmental conditions.

Some octocorals harbor zooxanthellae in their tissues that provide them with an important source of energy. These species are most common on shallow tropical reefs, where the sun's intensity is greatest. Others rely totally on ingesting food to meet their nutritional needs. Such species are sometimes found in less well-illuminated habitats, such as under overhangs and in caves.

Soft corals are a rich source of carbohydrates, proteins and especially lipids, but they are unpalatable to most generalized carnivores because of their toxic metabolites, repugnant smells, spiny spicules and sclerites. However, certain specialized reef fishes feed on them, including members of the butterflyfish family. Select invertebrates such as the egg cowrie (*Ovula ovum*) and the solar-powered nudibranch

---

Two kinds of soft corals, tan leather corals (*Sinularia flexibilis*) above bright *Dendronephthya* soft corals. Fiji.

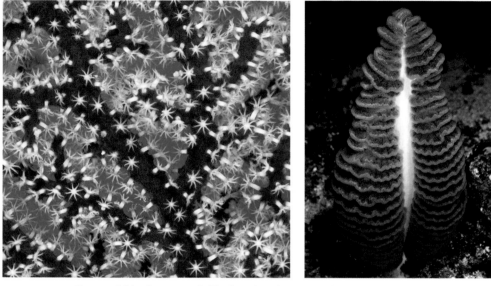

Close-up of eight-pinnate-tentacled feeding polyps of gorgonian sea fan (*Siphonogorgia* sp.). Australia.

Pteroeides species. Indonesia.

(*Phyllodesmium longicirrum*) have also evolved to prey on leather corals (*Sarcophyton* spp.). Soft corals produce chemicals — terpenoids, sarcophines and diterpenes — to deter competitors for space from growing near them; this is called allelopathy.

Soft corals reproduce both asexually and sexually. Some species engage in mass spawning events similar to those seen in their stony coral relatives. Some utilize internal fertilization and brood their young; the fertilized eggs of these species are brooded in pouches on the polyp's surface (e.g., *Briareum* spp.) or in the dermis (e.g., *Xenia* spp.). Other soft corals are broadcast spawners; that is, they release eggs and sperm into the water column, where fertilization occurs. Most soft corals are gonochoristic (with separate males and females) but there are some that are hermaphrodites.

Top
Close-up of a soft coral (*Dendronephthya* sp.) showing its red polyps and white spicules in the trunk. Spicules and sclerites are mineralized components that provide structural support and also help deter predators. Indonesia.

Bottom
A scuba diver peers over sea fans, including *Annella mollis* (the yellow one). Australia.

Soft Corals

1 Knotted sea fans (*Melithaea* sp.). Fiji.

2 Stinging hydroid (*Aglaophenia cupressina*). Don't touch this one — its feathery branches deliver a painful sting! Hydroids are not true "soft corals." They are in the phylum Cnidaria with soft corals and stony corals, but under the class Hydrozoa, order Hydroidea.

3 Mushroom leather coral (*Sarcophyton* sp.). Indonesia.

4 Common sea fans (*Gorgonia ventalina*). Florida.

5 Sea plumes (*Pseudopterogorgia* sp.) 1.5 m (5 ft) tall. Bonaire.

6 Soft corals (*Chironephthya* sp.) hang like a rainbow curtain at 30 m (98 ft) deep along a steep wall. Fiji.

1   Tree fern coral (*Clavularia* sp.) is also called palm coral. This octocoral's polyps are nearly 2 cm (0.8 in) in diameter. Papua New Guinea.

2   Deepwater sea fan (*Iciligorgia schrammi*). Belize.

3   Tree soft corals (*Dendronephthya* sp.). Maldives.

4   Sea whip corals (*Ellisella* sp.). Fiji.

5   Leather coral (*Sinularia flexibilis*) at a dive site called Kansas, Fiji.

6   Spiral wire coral (*Cirripathes* sp.) extends from a reef wall at a depth of 30 m (100 ft). Fiji.

Sea Jellies

The sea jellies (phylum Cnidaria, subclass Medusozoa), which are often called jellyfishes, are very simple creatures made mainly of water — about 95% H_2O, to be exact. They are divided into four clades, or groups: Scyphozoa ("true jellies"), with approximately 200 species; Staurozoa, about 50 species; Cubozoa, with about 20 species; and Hydrozoa, which has about 1,000 to 1,500 species. While beautiful and elegant when drifting through the ocean, these animals turn into gelatinous blobs when removed from the water. That's because jellies have no supportive internal or exoskeleton. Instead they comprise three principal cell layers: the epidermis (outer layer), gastrodermis (inner layer) and mesoglea (middle layer). The mesoglea gives them their jellylike quality and is responsible for buoyancy and helping maintain shape underwater.

While other cnidarians such as corals and anemones have a medusa phase in their life cycle, they actually spend most of their time as polyps. The opposite is true in the majority of sea jellies. The jelly medusa typically consists of a large bell — it can be 2 cm (0.8 in) to 2 m (6.6 ft) in diameter — that is often scalloped along the edges. Some sea-jelly groups have tentacles that extend from the bell's edge. These tentacles are often armed with nematocysts (stinging cells) used for defensive purposes and to immobilize their prey. The potency of the venom associated with the stinging cells varies considerably. Some species have a virulent toxin that can cause welts on human skin or, even worse, interfere with the central nervous system. Dozens of people have died from the extraordinarily potent venom of the sea wasp, or box jelly (*Chironex fleckeri*), a member of the Cubozoa group.

When a tentacle contacts prey (usually plankton, crustaceans or small fishes), it immobilizes or ensnares its quarry. The food is then passed to the mouth. Not all jellies are active predators, however. Some are suspension feeders that collect plankton in mucus on the underside of the bell, known as the subumbrella. And upsidedown jellies (*Cassiopea* spp.) harbor zooxanthellae algae that deliver nutrients to their host.

The gonads of sea jellies are located in the gastrodermis. Most are dioecious — that is, either male or female. When they reach maturity, eggs or sperm are released into the gastrovascular cavity and expelled from the mouth.

Some marine animals associate with jellies. Crabs and juvenile jacks and

Red bell jellyfish (*Crambione mastigophora*), a rhizostome jelly. Australia.

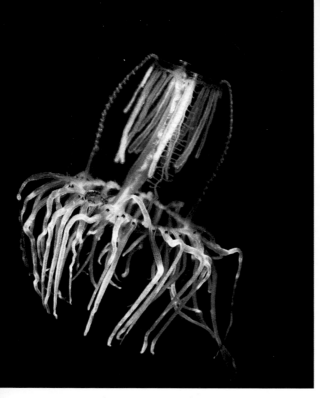

Red-eye jellyfish (*Polyorchis penicillatus*), a temperate-water species about 3 cm (1.2 in) long. Note the red ocelli, or "eyespots" — which are very primitive light-sensitive "eyes" — and the gonads inside the bell. Eastern North Pacific Ocean from Alaska to Baja, Mexico.

Man-of-war fish (*Nomeus gronovii*) live among the stinging tentacles of a Portuguese man-of-war (*Physalia physalis*) siphonophore. Dominica.

butterfish utilize them as cover because shelter is hard to find in open water. The man-of-war fish (*Nomeus gronovii*) lives among the stinging tentacles of the Portuguese man-of-war (*Physalia physalis*), a jellyfish-like siphonophore in the class Hydrozoa. These clever fish feed on the tentacles and gonads of the host while at the same time receiving protection from many pelagic predators.

Jellies are eaten by a number of different fish species, including spadefishes and certain angelfishes and filefishes, as well as sea turtles and some sea birds. Humans also include sea jellies on their bill of fare. They have been an important food source in China since 300 CE, and approximately 425,000 tonnes are harvested annually worldwide.

Occasionally sea-jelly numbers explode exponentially. Such "blooms" can be

A bloom of moon jellies (*Aurelia* sp.), a non-stinging type of jelly. Australia.

problematic, both for swimmers at popular beaches and also for industry. Huge jelly swarms that burst fishing nets and kill valuable farmed fish have been front-page news recently. Immense numbers of jellies can reduce wild fish stocks, as the gelatinous horde devours piscine larvae nonstop. In fact there is concern that jellies may overtake fish numbers in certain ecosystems. Though jelly blooms can be natural phenomena, evidence suggests that these outbreaks are occurring more frequently because of human activities. Reasons for these population increases include overfishing, which removes jelly predators and their food competitors; pollutants that stimulate rapid growth of the plankton food sources preferred by jellies; hypoxic sea conditions, which are tolerated by jellies but unsuitable for fishes; and translocation of jellies in the ballast water of ships. A warming ocean caused by climate change may also favor jellies. While they may look fragile, these animals can survive and even thrive in suboptimal conditions.

Sea Jellies

1 The moon jellyfish (*Aurelia aurita*) is a commonly sighted species around the globe. Mexico.

2 Papuan jellyfish (*Mastigias papua*). Indonesia.

3 Box jelly (*Chironex fleckeri*), also called a "sea wasp." Thailand.

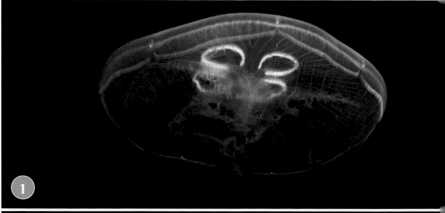

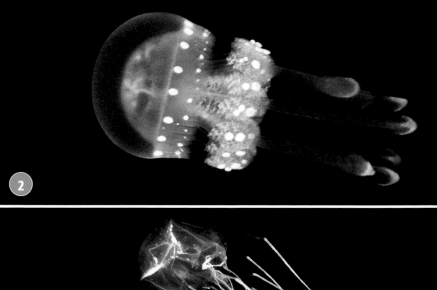

4 Found in all tropical and subtropical oceans of the world, the Portuguese man-of-war (*Physalia physalis*), also known as the bluebottle, is a jellyfish-like marine invertebrate of the family Physaliidae. It is a siphonophore. Belize.

5 Upsidedown jellyfish (*Cassiopea* sp.) near seagrass. This jelly rests on the bottom, upside down on top of its bell, with the oral arms pointing upward. Bahamas.

Comb Jellies

For a long time the ctenophores, or comb jellies, were placed in the phylum Cnidaria. But now biologists recognize the 150-odd species in their own unique phylum, Ctenophora. These invertebrates are globelike and gelatinous, with eight bands of cilia arranged in vertical comblike rows, known as ctenes, along the body. The cilia beat synchronously to move the ctenophore slowly through the water. Light reflects off the ctenes, creating a kaleidoscope of color. They range in size from several millimeters to 1.5 meters (5 feet).

While divers may find ctenophores mesmerizing, their role as important oceanic predators has often been overlooked. Most feed on small zooplankton (including other ctenophores), but some include sea jellies, krill and small fishes in their diets. Certain species eat ten times their weight in food per day. Some comb jellies extrude long, branched, sticky threads that ensnare small planktonic prey. The ctenophore then "reels in" these threads and pulls them across the mouth to ingest the meal. Others use elaborate oral lobes to capture food items. While none produces its own nematocysts, some feed on sea jellies and then use the prey's stinging cells for their own defense.

Pelagic ctenophores reproduce sexually, with most species possessing the sex organs of both genders. While most are ocean rovers, some ctenophores (*Coeloplana* spp.) live a benthic lifestyle, usually associating with plants or other animals. Benthic ctenophores are often mistaken for sea slugs or acoel flatworms. They have a pelagic larval stage, during which time they possess cilia; these are lost once they settle out of the plankton. Upon finding a suitable organism on which to live, they develop a color pattern similar to that of the host. These animals may reproduce asexually.

Top
This comb jelly (*Beroe forskalii*) grows to 15 cm (6 in) long. Its eight rows of cilia beat together to provide locomotion and glow with rainbow colors when light strikes them. Widespread in temperate and tropical seas worldwide.

Bottom
Platyctene ctenophores (*Coeloplana astericola*) are strange bottom-dwelling comb jellies that superficially resemble flatworms. Here they are living on a sea star (*Echinaster luzonicus*). Philippines.

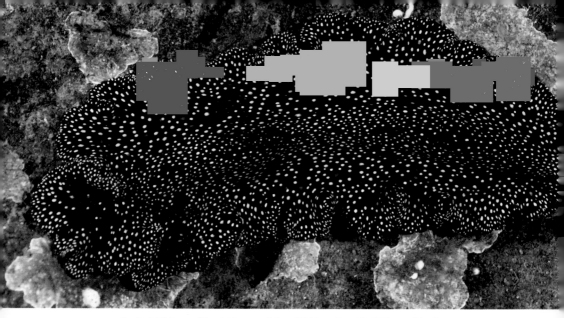

A colorful flatworm (*Pseudobiceros* sp.), 5 cm (2 in) long, from the Galápagos Islands.

Polyclad Flatworms and Acoels

Flatworms (phylum Platyhelminthes) are very primitive creatures without a body cavity, respiratory organs or a vascular system. Most of the 10,000-plus flatworm species are parasitic, including the tapeworms (class Cestoda) and flukes (Trematoda); there are fewer free-living species. The polyclad flatworms (class "Turbellaria," order Polycladida) are a more conspicuous group that most divers see: many sport dazzling colors and some reside on coral reefs. They are similar in overall appearance to sea slugs but lack the prominent gills seen in most nudibranchs.

Biologists suggest that at least some polyclads exhibit aposematic (warning) coloration because they taste bad and/or are toxic. Several species of fishes (e.g., pinnate batfish, sole in the genus *Soleichthys*) may be Batesian mimics of certain flatworms, meaning that they resemble them in color and, in some cases, the way they swim. Predators that learn to avoid eating these particular flatworms may also be reluctant to slurp up the flatworm mimics.

Polyclad flatworms move with the help of tiny cilia on the body's ventral surface that beat like oars to propel the worm forward over an excreted mucus layer; some also swim by undulating their body margins. They have a simple brain and photoreceptive cells that can detect changes in light levels. Most polyclads are predatory, feeding on sessile invertebrates, including sponges, bryozoans and tunicates. A structure called the pharynx plicatus and secretions of digestive fluids are used to break down and ingest prey.

Polyclads rely primarily on chemoreception to find food and mates. Chemosensory cells are particularly abundant on the undersurface of the pseudotentacles folds of the anterior margin of the flatworm's "head." The majority of polyclads are simultaneous hermaphrodites, with both male and female functional reproductive organs. One flatworm inseminates another by piercing its mate's body with its penial stylet, injecting sperm into the tissue (this is known as hypodermal insemination). The sperm then migrate through the body to be stored in the seminal receptacle. After fertilization the eggs pass through a shell gland that coats them with yolk and shell material. Finally, an egg mass is deposited on the substrate.

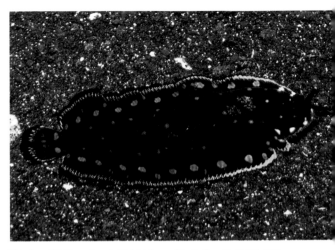

This 5 cm (2 in) juvenile sole (*Soleichthys* sp.) looks like a toxic flatworm. This type of mimicry gives the flatfish some protection from would-be predators. Indonesia.

Acoels have long been included in the phylum Platyhelminthes, along with many other organisms wrongly classified with the "true" flatworms. (The acoels have yet to be given a proper phylum, so they are simply recognized as acoelomorphs.) Divers typically see acoels — although in most cases they may not recognize that they are seeing them! — living on large-polyped stony corals such as bubble coral. They look like little brown freckles. Acoels are very primitive animals with a simple cell membrane, a bundle of nerve cells that functions as an archaic brain, eyespots (simple light detectors), a mouth, a statocyst (balancing organ) and cilia all over the body that propel them. Their diet includes algae, cyanobacteria and microcrustaceans. Some also have symbiotic algae (either zooxanthellae or zoochlorellae) living in their tissues that provide them with food. They can reproduce rapidly by "budding" (asexual reproduction) but also engage in sexual reproduction.

Flatworms

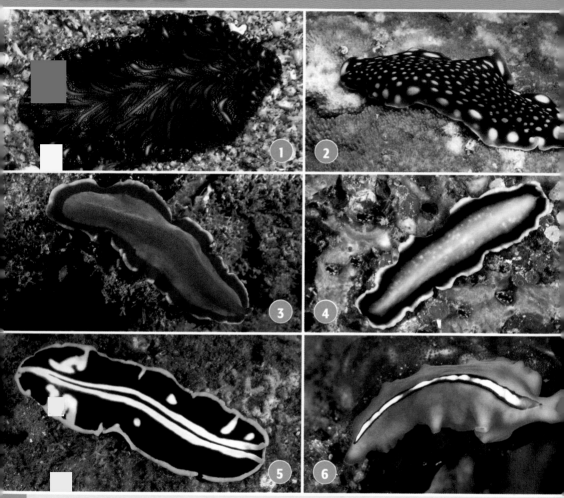

1. The Persian carpet flatworm (*Pseudobiceros bedfordi*) grows to 10 cm (4 in). Indonesia.

2. Linda's flatworm (*Pseudoceros lindae*), 4 cm (1.6 in) long. Australia.

3. The fuchsia flatworm (*Pseudoceros ferrugineus*) feeds on colonial tunicates. Australia.

4. Broadstriped flatworm (*Pseudoceros paralaticlavus*). Indonesia.

5. Tiger flatworm (*Pseudoceros dimidiatus*). Indonesia.

6. Racing stripe flatworm (*Pseudoceros bifurcus*). Philippines.

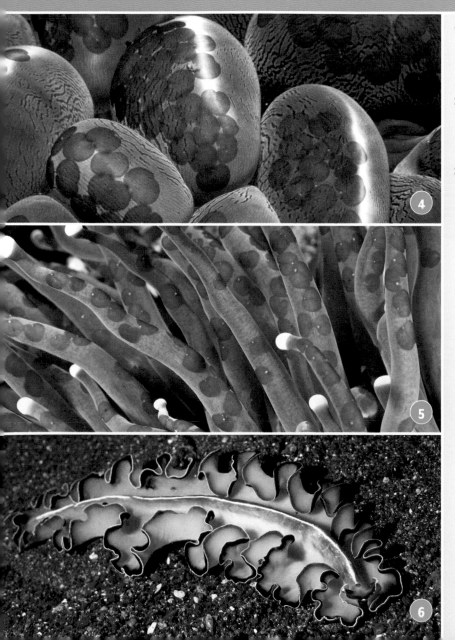

Polychaete Worms

Although there are many types of worms in coral-reef environments, those most often encountered by divers belong to the class Polychaeta, part of the phylum Annelida. There are more than 8,000 described species. Most practice a cryptic way of life, hiding in reef crevices, under rubble or in sand or mud. The "typical" polychaete has a long, segmented body with paddle-like appendages called parapodia on each segment, and a "head" complete with eyes, antennae and a ventrally placed mouth that can have sizeable jaws and/or teeth.

Polychaete worms can be divided into two groups based on lifestyle. The first consists of free-living species, called errant polychaetes. These move about on the bottom, digging burrows in the soft substrate or lurking among coral rubble or within coral interstices. Most are very secretive and more active at night, in part because they are prey items for many reef fishes. Some errant polychaetes live commensally in the burrows of other worms or crustaceans or live on hermit crabs, corals, sea stars, urchins or sea cucumbers.

Many species scavenge but some are voracious predators. For example, the leviathan of the group, the Bobbit worm (*Eunice aphroditois*), has relatively large, bony jaws it uses to grab passing fishes. After snatching its prey it jerks it beneath the sand surface and consumes it. This worm can reach a length of at least 3 meters (10 feet)! The well-known fire worm, *Hermodice carunculata*, feeds on stony corals and gorgonians and also scavenges on carrion. Some errant polychaetes have sharp bristles (setae) that cause burning and irritation if they penetrate the skin.

The second group in the class are known as sedentary polychaetes. These are more diminutive in size and construct permanent refuge chambers on or in the substrate. Christmas tree worms (serpulids) and fan worms (sabellids) project a spiral crown from their tubes to filter-feed. This feeding apparatus is made up of featherlike structures called radioles; when the worm is threatened, the radioles are rolled up and rapidly pulled into the tube.

The tube of sabellid worms is composed of sand grains and mucus. In serpulids, the tube is calcareous and has an operculum that plugs the tube's end when the worm withdraws. Not only do these hard tubes provide shelter for the worm, empty serpulid tubes serve as a home for different fishes, including the tube blennies.

A magnificent feather duster (*Sabellastarte magnifica*), a large segmented worm. This polychaete retracts its feathery crown into its tube when disturbed. Dominica.

Polychaete Worms

1 Social feather duster worms (*Bispira brunnea*). Dominica.

2 Bearded fireworm (*Hermodice carunculata*). Dominica.

3 Colonial serpulid worms (*Filogranella elatensis*) have fine white calcareous tubes from which reddish tentacles emerge. Indonesia.

4 A Christmas tree worm (*Spirobranchus* sp). Indonesia.

5 The Bobbit worm (*Eunice aphroditois*), a predatory polychaete worm that grows to 3 m (10 ft) long, is seen here with its head protruding from its burrow in the sand. Papua New Guinea.

Marine Snails

Within the phylum Mollusca, the gastropods form the largest group, with about 55,000 species. In older classification schemes (and in this book, for convenience's sake) snails were placed in the subclass Prosobranchia, but modern research has since blown the old scheme to bits (it has been shown to be polyphyletic) and now this group is under revision. This expansive group includes all the well-known shelled gastropods, including the conchs, cones, cowries, murexes, volutes and whelks. They vary in size from tiny to quite large. The "mother of all snails" is *Syrinx aruanus*, whose shell can measure 91 cm (36 in).

Snails have a head (unlike the bivalves) and a shell into which they withdraw for protection, and they exhibit torsion (twisting) of the body—if one were to look down on a shell-less animal, one would see that most of the body behind the head is twisted 180 degrees counterclockwise. Snails use their muscular foot to pull themselves along the substrate. Most also have an operculum attached to the foot, which acts as a hatch to plug the shell opening when head and foot are retracted inside. Many have sensory tentacles on the head, and eyes at the base of the tentacles. These eyes are not good for much except noting shadows and finding dark places to hide. When it comes to finding food, most snails rely on olfactory cues. Snails also have a proboscis (a trunk-like structure) equipped with a radula, the equivalent of a tongue with teeth.

Many snails are algae eaters that docilely browse on microalgae on the substrate. Others are rapacious carnivores, drilling through the shells of their relatives to ingest the tasty innards. And then there's *Hydroginella caledonica*, which behaves like a vampire bat, parasitizing sleeping fishes. It inserts its proboscis into the fish's tissue and sucks out the body fluids.

Few animals are safe from wily snails. Almost all of the animal phyla represented on tropical reefs are fed on by one or more snail species; this includes sponges, stony and soft corals, polychaete worms, peanut worms, other snails, bivalves, crustaceans, serpent stars, sea stars and fishes. Snails may be highly specialized feeders or exhibit dietary breadth. The golden wentletrap (*Epitonium billeeanum*) preys entirely on orange cup coral (*Tubastrea* spp.). Certain drupe snails are voracious stony-coral predators whose numbers occasionally explode, dramatically affecting coral colonies. Many of the spindle (*Phenacovolva* spp.) and egg cowries (*Primovula* and *Prosimnia* spp.) feed on gorgonians, which they often perfectly mimic, right down to "pseudo polyps" on the mantle. The egg cowrie (*Ovula ovum*) devours soft corals. Whelks and murexes use brute force to get to the internal organs of bivalves, pulling the shells apart with their foot. Even the poisonous-spine-clad crown-of-thorns is consumed by the Triton's trumpet (*Charonia tritonis*), a huge "über snail" that dines on other sea stars and sea cucumbers as well.

Cone snails (genus *Conus*) feed on more mobile prey, including polychaete worms, other gastropods and even small fish. These snails have a modified radular tooth similar to a barbed hypodermic needle. When a cone locates prey, it propels this harpoon-like tooth from the proboscis into its quarry and injects venom to paralyze its victim. Some of the *Conus* species produce a venom that can be lethal to humans, although reported deaths are rare. The most venomous species is the geographic cone (*Conus geographus*) from the Central Indo-Pacific. There may be more than 50,000 different conotoxins (neurotoxic peptides) present in the venom of living *Conus* species.

Unlike their relatives the sea slugs, most prosobranchs exhibit separate sexes. In many species (e.g., cowries) fertilization is internal and the female lays parchment-like egg capsules or a gelatinous material that contains the developing embryos. In certain cowrie species the female will cover the developing eggs with her foot until they hatch and release veliger larvae that usually feed on phytoplankton. The veliger propels itself with winglike structures known as velum.

A Triton's trumpet (*Charonia tritonis*) eating a sea star. Indonesia.

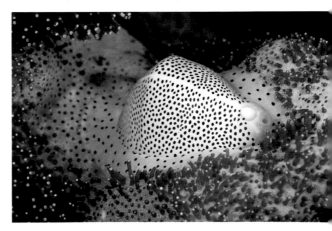

A toenail egg cowrie (*Calpurnus verrucosus*), 3 cm (1.2 in) long, feeds on a soft coral's polyps. Philippines.

Marine Snails

1 Tiger egg cowrie (*Cuspivolva tigris*) on a gorgonian sea fan. The 1 cm (0.4 in) snails feed on these *Euplexaura* sp. octocorals. Thailand.

2 Articulate harp snail (*Harpa articularis*), whose shell grows to 11 cm (4.3 in). The yellow spots on the large mantle's skirt help to distinguish this species from other, similar ones. Papua New Guinea.

3 The highly venomous textile cone snail (*Conus textile*). Papua New Guinea.

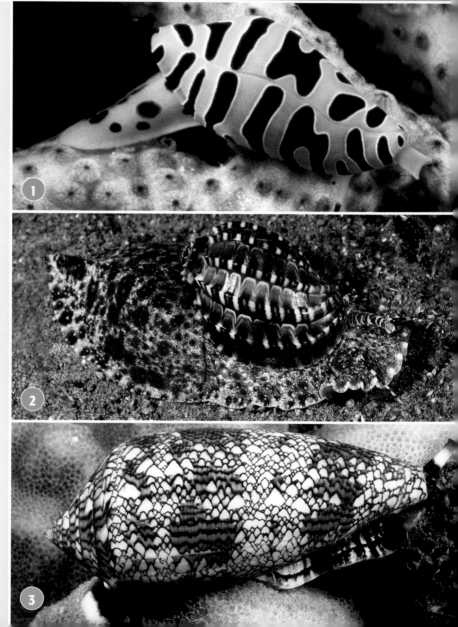

4 Auger snail (*Terebra affinis*). Indonesia.

5 Golden wentletrap (*Epitonium billeeanum*) snails laying eggs on cup corals. The snails get their orange pigmentation from eating cup coral polyps. Their eggs resemble polyps, which helps protect them from predation. Baja, Mexico.

6 Murex snails (*Murex* sp.) are highly prized in the shell trade. Indonesia.

Marine Snails

1 The tiger cowrie (*Cypraea tigris*) is a large, common marine snail that grows to 15 cm (6 in). Hawaii.

2 Moon snail (*Naticarius alapapilionis*). Indonesia. Australia.

3 An adult common egg cowrie (*Ovula ovum*). This large snail grows to 10 cm (4 in) and feeds on soft corals — note the gray branching animal in the background. Thailand.

4 Aubergine cowrie (*Erosaria albuginosa*), which grows to 2.5 cm (1 in). Costa Rica.

5 Clear sundial snail (*Architectonica perspectiva*). Papua New Guinea.

6 Gray bonnet helmet snail (*Phalium glaucum*). Indonesia.

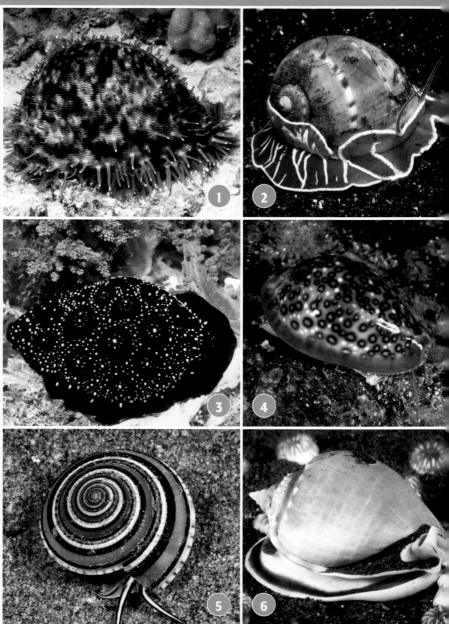

1 Flamingo tongue snail (*Cyphoma gibbosum*) on a sea fan. Belize.

2 Panama horse conch (*Pleuroploca princeps*). This large snail grows up to 40 cm (15.7 in) or more! Galápagos.

3 A lettered cone snail (*Conus litteratus*) sticking its proboscis beneath the sand. Indonesia.

4 A juvenile queen conch (*Lobatus gigas*) in mangrove habitat. This snail was previously known as *Strombus gigas*. Bahamas.

5 Bubble conch snail (*Strombus bulla*). Notice the eyes and tentacles of this 6 cm (2.4 in) snail. Indonesia.

6 Ridged egg cowrie (*Diminovula culmen*), 1 cm (0.4 in) long. Feeds on soft coral's polyps. Indonesia.

Sea Slugs

Sea slugs are in a subclass of the phylum Mollusca, Opisthobranchia, which has more than 3,000 species. They are divided into five groups: the cephalaspidea (headshield slugs), sacoglossa (sapsucking slugs), anaspidea (sea hares), notaspidea (sidegill slugs) and nudibranchia (nudibranchs). These animals have no shell, or if present it is greatly reduced in size. They have advanced gills for respiration and are simultaneous hermaphrodites, with both male and female functional sex organs. Oral tentacles help locate food and rhinophores on top of the head sense chemicals in the water.

Sea slugs exhibit a variety of feeding strategies. Most feed on sessile invertebrates such as sponges, hydroids and bryozoans. Some specialized opisthobranchs — for example, *Roboastra* species — eat other sea slugs, while another genus, *Chelidonura*, make their living hunting acoel flatworms. Still other species feed on corals. For example, members of the genus *Phyllodesmium* eat soft corals, not only acquiring nutrients by consuming the coral's flesh but also exploiting the unicellular algae (zooxanthellae) that live within the tissues of their prey. The *Phyllodesmium* species transport the coral's zooxanthellae into their cerata (elongate structures on the back) and other parts of their bodies via digestive glands. The algae cells then photosynthesize, providing the slug with needed nutrients. Because of this unusual mutualistic behavior, these slugs are nicknamed "solar-powered nudibranchs." Not all sea slugs are carnivorous, however; a number of species graze on algae and cyanobacteria (blue-green algae).

Sea slugs also exhibit interesting ways to avoid being eaten. Many are extremely well-camouflaged and blend in with their food sources, while others burrow under the sand (e.g., *Euselenops luniceps*) or are more active at night. There are sea slugs with more elaborate defensive strategies too, such as employing the stinging cells found in their prey for their own defense. For example, many aeolid nudibranchs eat hydroid cnidarians. As they feed on them, some of the hydroid's stinging cells are not discharged but instead are transported through the slug's digestive system to accumulate in organs known as cnidosacs. These organs are usually located in the cerata — spiky projections on the back of aeolid nudibranchs that are connected to the digestive tract. If the sea slug is harassed by a potential predator, the recycled stinging cells can be employed against the enemy.

In other aeolids, the cerata are thrown off when the slug is harried by a predator — this is known as autotomy. The amputated cerata produce copious amounts

Two Chamberlain's nembrotha nudibranchs (*Nembrotha chamberlaini*), which are simultaneous hermaphrodites, illustrating mating behavior. Philippines.

of slime and wiggle about, which is thought to distract the would-be predator and allow the sea slug to get away. Instead of using autotomy, sea hares excrete a cloud of purple ink to distract an attacker. Numerous slugs dissuade predators by accumulating or producing foul-tasting or toxic secretions. In some cases these chemicals are extracted from their food (such as algae, sponges or soft corals), while in other species acidic secretions are produced and exuded from specialized glands in the skin.

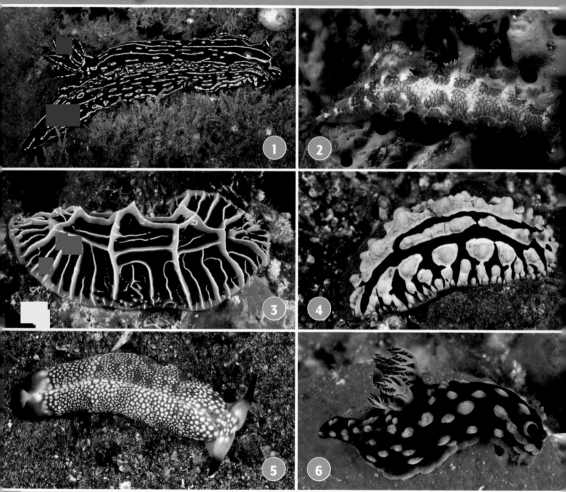

1. A Florida regal sea goddess nudibranch (*Hypselodoris edenticulata* — possibly a synonym of *H. picta*). Order Nudibranchia, family Chromodoridae. Florida.

2. A dendronotid nudibranch (*Marionia* sp.), 10 cm (4 in) long. Family Tritoniidae. Indonesia.

3. *Reticulidia halgerda* nudibranch. Order Nudibranchia, suborder Doridina, family Phyllidiidae. Fiji.

4. Swollen phyllidia nudibranch (*Phyllidia varicosa*). Order Nudibranchia, suborder Doridina, family Phyllidiidae. Papua New Guinea.

5. A *Plakobranchus* sea slug, probably *P. ocellatus*. This is a member of the sapsucking slugs group of opisthobranchs (order Sacoglossa, family Plakobranchidae). Papua New Guinea.

6. Crested nembrotha nudibranch (*Nembrotha cristata*). Order Nudibranchia, suborder Doridina, family Polyceridae. Indonesia.

1 Ocellated nudibranch (*Phyllidia ocellata*). Order Nudibranchia, suborder Doridina, family Phyllidiidae. Indonesia.

2 Showy headshield slug (*Philinopsis speciosa*). This highly variable aglajid opisthobranch is closely related to nudibranchs and other sea slugs. Order Cephalaspidea, family Aglajidae. *P. cyanea* is a synonym for this species.

3 Geometric nudibranch (*Chromodoris geometrica*). Order Nudibranchia, suborder Doridina, family Chromodoridae. Indonesia.

4 This nudibranch sea slug (*Armina* sp.) feeds on sea pens. Order Nudibranchia, suborder Arminina, family Arminidae. Indonesia.

5 *Ceratosoma magnificum*, a nudibranch sea slug. Order Nudibranchia, suborder Doridina, family Chromodoridae. Indonesia.

6 Kubaryana's nembrotha nudibranch (*Nembrotha kubaryana*). Order Nudibranchia, suborder Doridina, family Polyceridae. Indonesia.

Sea Slugs

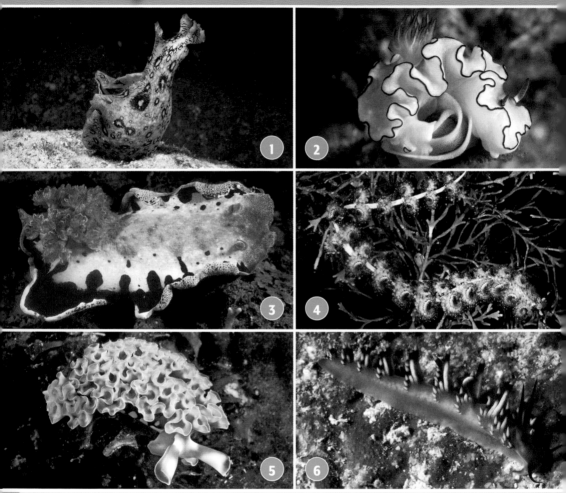

1 Spotted sea hare (*Aplysia dactylomela*). This herbivorous sea slug grows to 20 cm (8 in) and can discharge a cloud of purple ink for defense. Order Anaspidea, family Aplysiidae. Dominica.

2 A dark-margined glossodoris (*Glossodoris atromarginata*) laying eggs. The coiled ribbon contains thousands of eggs.

3 The huge Spanish dancer nudibranch (*Hexabranchus sanguineus*) can grow to 60 cm (23.6 in) in size! Indonesia.

4 A dragon nudibranch (*Pteraeolidia ianthina*), which can grow to 10 cm (4 in) long, is here seen crawling on *Halimeda* algae. Order Nudibranchia, suborder Aeolidina, family Glaucidae. Indonesia.

5 The lettuce sea slug (*Tridachia crispata*) grows to 5 cm (2 in) long. Order Sacoglossa, family Elysiidae. Bonaire.

6 This nudibranch sea slug, *Cuthona sibogae*, is 3 cm (1.2 in) long. Order Nudibranchia, suborder Aeolidina, family Tergipedidae. Fiji.

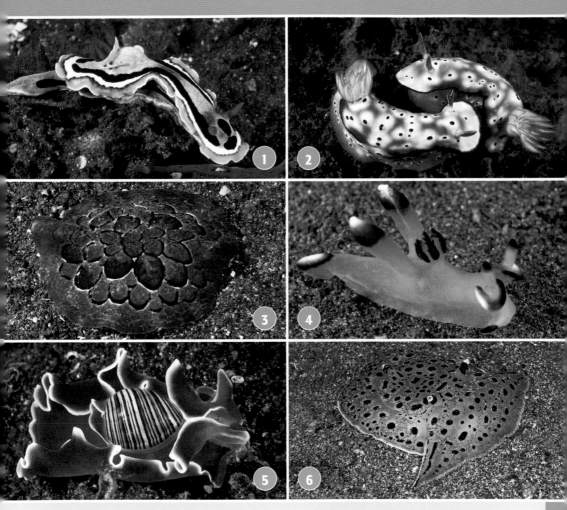

1　This 3 cm (1.2 in) long nudibranch (*Chromodoris annae*), like most sea slugs, is brightly colored. This feature helps protect them from predators by advertising their bad taste. Papua New Guinea.

2　Two nudibranch sea slugs (*Risbecia tryoni*) preparing to mate. Papua New Guinea.

3　This pleurobranch (*Pleurobranchus forskalii*) is nocturnally active. Order Notaspidea, family Pleurobranchidae. Indonesia.

4　Pacific thecacera nudibranch (*Thecacera pacifica*). Order Nudibranchia, suborder Doridina, family Polyceridae. Indonesia.

5　Brown-line paper bubble shell (*Hydatina physis*). This 4 cm (1.6 in) colorful headshield slug is found circum-tropically in the Indo–Western Pacific and Atlantic Oceans. Order Cephalaspidea, family Hydatinidae.

6　The moon-headed sidegill slug (*Euselenops luniceps*) grows to 7 cm (2.8 in). Indonesia.

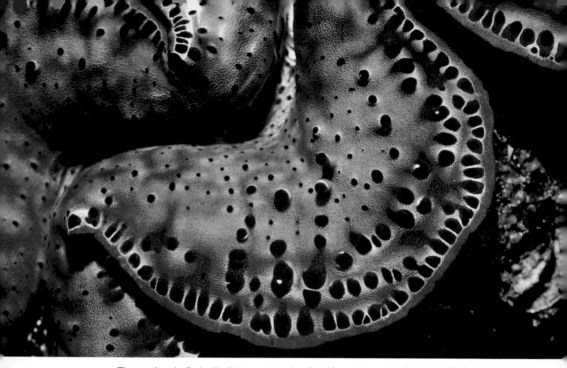

The mantle — the fleshy "lips" between the valves (shells) — of a giant clam (*Tridacna* sp.), showing its psychedelic colors. Tonga.

Bivalves

Oysters, mussels and clams are members of the invertebrate order Bivalvia in the phylum Mollusca. As the name suggests, bivalves possess a shell comprising two parts, called valves. These are hinged by ligaments and completely enclose the animal's body; the shell is pulled closed by adductor muscles. Bivalves have a muscular foot that is used in burrowing, but they lack the radula present in many other mollusks. They have highly developed gills that play an important role in feeding and respiration. Many bivalves exhibit separate sexes, although there are some hermaphrodites in the group. Fertilization is external and the larvae are planktonic.

Some bivalves burrow into soft bottom materials while others attach to hard structures with byssal threads or by cementing one of their valves to the substrate. Certain members of this group are capable of drilling into solid structures such as coral, rock and wood; they do this by slowly rocking from side to side and opening and closing the valves. A few bivalves are parasitic. The sea star scallop (*Thyca crystallina*) is parasitic on sea stars, using its proboscis to suck fluid and tissue from its host. Other bivalves, such as the scallops, do not attach to the substrate and evade predators by swimming. They do this by rapidly slapping their valves closed, which causes them to move by jet propulsion.

The majority of bivalves are found on soft sea bottoms but a number do occur on coral reefs. The most conspicuous coral-reef bivalves are the tridacnids, or giant clams. These clams have colorful siphonal mantles — lip-like structures that can be extended from between the valves or completely

This giant clam (*Tridacna gigas*) is 1 m (3.3 ft) wide. Australia.

withdrawn into the shell. The tissue of the clam's mantle contains iridophores, which are responsible for the amazing iridescent colors they exhibit. These structures and the color they produce protect the clam from harmful ultraviolet radiation.

Tridacnids also have primitive eyes. In fact, large clams can have several thousand of these photoreceptors. While their simple lenses cannot transmit detailed images, they do possess differential color sensitivity, and some respond to ultraviolet light. If there is a sudden change in the light level (say a fish swims overhead), the clam will rapidly retract into its shell, slapping the valves together to protect its soft tissues from attack.

The tridacnid clams host symbiotic algae. As with corals, the relationship is mutualistic. The clam provides a growing substrate and some nourishment for the plant cells, while the algae produce sugars and oxygen used by the clam. This extra source of nourishment has enabled some of these bivalves to reach massive proportions. The largest of the bunch, *Tridacna gigas*, reaches a length of more than 1.2 m (47 in). A large tridacnid clam can be decades or even centuries old.

Bivalves

1 The burrowing giant clam (*Tridacna crocea*) is the smallest "giant clam" at up to 15 cm (6 in) wide. Its shell is recessed deeply into the cracks of the reef. Kiribati.

2 Rough fileclam (*Lima scabra*). Dominica.

3 The fluted giant clam (*Tridacna squamosa*) grows to 40 cm (15.7 in). The prominent leaflike flutes on the surface of its shell help to identify this species. Indonesia.

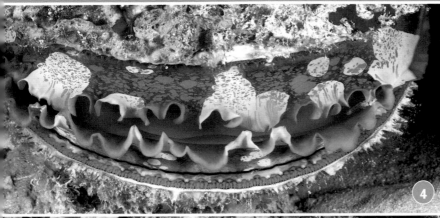

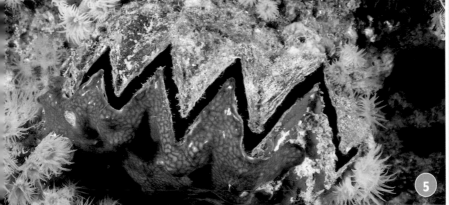

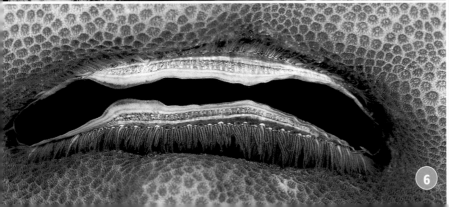

4 Variable thorny oyster (*Spondylus varians*). Australia.

5 The shell of this honeycomb oyster (*Hyotissa hyotis*), 15 cm (6 in) across, is encrusted with sponges. Australia.

6 The brightly colored mantle of the iridescent scallop (*Pedum spondyloideum*) helps identify this small mollusk, which lives in the crevices of living coral colonies. Indonesia.

Cephalopods

The order Cephalopoda of the phylum Mollusca includes approximately 650 species of nautiluses, cuttlefishes, squids and octopuses. Many are very mobile and spend less time on the seafloor than other mollusks. This group contains the largest of all invertebrates: the giant squid (*Architeuthis dux*). This monster reaches a maximum length of at least 16 meters (52 feet) and a body circumference of 4 meters (13 feet).

The Latin name *cephalopod* means "head-footed," and most members of this group are simply that — one big head and many long "feet." Squids and cuttlefishes have an internal shell but the octopuses do not. This internal shell is important for buoyancy, as it contains fluid and gas that can be regulated to make the animal more or less buoyant. Nautiluses are the only cephalopods that have well-developed external shells. Squid and cuttlefish have fins on their bodies, while the octopuses lack them; the fins can be used for stabilization, steering and propulsion. When they need to move quickly, these animals use jet propulsion, rapidly expelling water from a funnel in the mantle cavity, which propels the cephalopod in the opposite direction. Squids are able to attain impressive speeds using this jet propulsion. Some will actually jump out of the water and have been known to land on ship decks 4 meters (13 feet) above the water's surface.

A cephalopod's head is surrounded by large, prehensile tentacles, or "arms," which often bear suckers. Octopuses have eight arms, while the cuttlefishes have eight arms plus two feeding tentacles. The arms are used for locomotion — in those species that spend considerable time on the seafloor, such as the octopuses — and also in prey capture. In some species the arms serve a reproductive role as well. For example, male octopuses have a modified third arm that is used to pass sperm packets into the female's oviduct. They do this by sticking the end of the arm through the female's gill opening and into her reproductive organ.

The cephalopods have highly developed sensory organs. The eyes of squids, cuttlefishes and octopuses are very similar to those of vertebrates, while nautilus eyes are simpler, functioning like a pinhole camera. Cephalopod tentacles are rich in chemoreceptor and tactile cells, especially in octopuses, that enable the animal to use its arms to discriminate between different textures and chemical cues. Cephalopods are also notable for their ability to learn, problem-solve and

The pharaoh cuttlefish (*Sepia pharaonis*) grows to a body length of 25 cm (10 in). Thailand.

The Caribbean reef octopus (*Octopus briareus*) hunts at night, "parachute" or "tent feeding." It traps prey — here, a crab — under the webbing between its tentacles. Dominica.

memorize, which some people feel makes them the most "intelligent" inverte-brates in the sea.

Cephalopods are voracious carnivores that feed on a wide range of active inver-tebrates as well as fishes. The nautiluses are thought to scavenge and catch bottom-dwelling crustaceans. Cephalopods have a horny beak that they use for biting and ripping up prey. Some octopuses also produce toxic saliva, which is most highly developed in the deadly blue-ringed octopuses (*Hapalochlaena* spp.) — a bite from one of these beautiful creatures can kill a grown man, and the bites of other octo-pus species can cause joint pain, similar to arthritis, for months or even years. The enzyme-rich saliva of the octopuses helps to digest their prey's flesh before and as it is consumed. A radula (a rasp-like structure) is used to pull bits of food into the "mouth." The Caribbean reef octopus (*Octopus briareus*) hunts at night, its flex-ible tentacles probing beneath rocks and in coral crevices. When it locates suitable prey such as a crab, its arms spread wide and the webbing between them expands to form a tent, effectively trapping dinner underneath.

Cephalopods are fed upon by many marine organisms, including sharks, rays, bony fishes, whales and seals. They are well known for their ability to expel clouds of ink when attacked, which may distract the would-be predator. The ink may also affect a predator's sense of smell and taste. Another defense is the ability to change color in an instant. Some even modify their skin texture, developing dermal flaps that help mask their outline against the seafloor. Not only does this help them avoid detection by predators, it can also serve to camouflage their presence from prey. One of the most interesting color transformations exhibited by cephalopods is the "passing cloud display,"

A brilliant squid from the family Loliginidae. Australia.

in which waves of shimmering color pass along the body. In cuttlefishes the wave originates at the head and passes down the body until it reaches the tips of the arms, while in octopuses it moves in the opposite direction. Cuttlefish often exhibit this behavior when they are stalking their prey. They may do this to confuse or distract their quarry or to blend in with the "glitter lines" of sunlight that dance over the shallow ocean bottom.

Cephalopods' extraordinary chromatic repertoire is possible thanks to layers of special cells just under their skin. Light-reflecting iridophores contribute the metallic blues, greens and golds, while leucophores are responsible for white spots. Chromatophores, which contain elastic sacs of different-hued pigments, help with both color and pattern. Controlled by muscles and under the direction of nerves in the brain, the chromatophores open and close with lightning speed. Working together with impressive orchestration, these cells deliver the seemingly magical control of color for which these quick-change artists are famous.

Cephalopods

1 A day octopus (*Octopus cyanea*) acting as if it's part of the coral reef. Kiribati.

2 The chambered nautilus (*Nautilus pompilius*) is a "living fossil" — an ancestor of modern cephalopods such as octopus and squid. Indonesia.

3 Common octopus (*Octopus vulgaris*). Dominica.

4 The tiny bobtail squid (*Euprymna berryi*), 3 cm (1.2 in) long, creeps along the sandy bottom and buries itself for protection. Philippines.

5 Wunderpus (*Wunderpus photogenicus*). Indonesia.

6 The greater blue-ringed octopus (*Hapalochlaena lunulata*) grows to 7 cm (2.8 in) and is very poisonous. Indonesia.

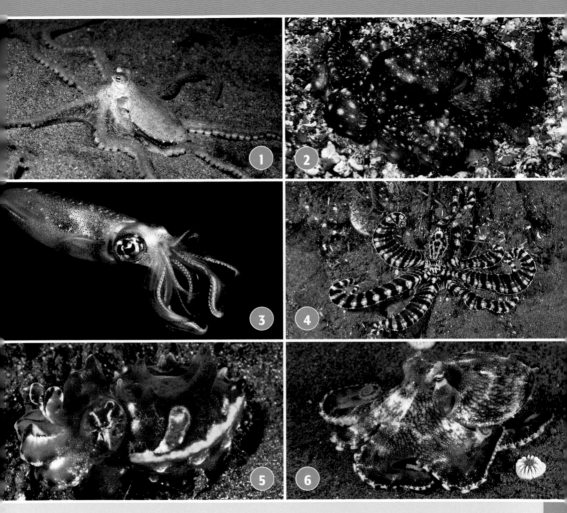

1 The Atlantic longarm octopus (*Macrotritopus defilippi*) is also known as the Lilliput longarm octopus (*O. defilippi*). Dominica.

2 Starry night octopus (*Callistoctopus luteus*). Indonesia.

3 Bigfin reef squid (*Sepioteuthis lessoniana*). Indonesia.

4 Mimic octopus (*Thaumoctopus mimicus*). Papua New Guinea.

5 The flamboyant cuttlefish (*Metasepia pfefferi*) grows to 8 cm (3 in). Indonesia.

6 The veined octopus (*Amphioctopus marginatus*) is also known as the coconut octopus (previously *Octopus marginatus*). Indonesia.

Crustaceans

Crustaceans — members of the phylum Arthropoda, subphylum Crustacea — come in many odd forms, exhibit beautiful chromatic attire, and engage in interesting behaviors. There are more than 38,000 species in the subphylum Crustacea, including the mantis shrimps, shrimps, lobsters and crabs. Most live in marine environments, with many of these occurring on coral reefs. Reef-dwelling crustaceans vary in size from tiny amphipods to massive, formidably armed and armored crabs. A lot of crustaceans — the ostracods, copepods and isopods — are small, inconspicuous members of the coral-reef community.

General crustacean anatomy consists of a segmented body, with head, thorax, abdomen and tail. The head has two pairs of antennae, one pair of mandibles for manipulating food, and two pairs of accessory feeding appendages. The trunk (which is divided into thorax and abdomen) is covered by a carapace that encloses the body and provides armored protection. The trunk usually has ten jointed limbs, eight for locomotion plus two pincer-like claws. Under the abdomen, pleopods (swimmerets) are used for swimming and brooding eggs and during copulation. External feathery gills facilitate gas exchange. In lobsters and shrimps the segmented tail is used to swim backwards.

Crustaceans have an exoskeleton composed of chitin. In order to grow, they must periodically shed their exoskeleton, a process known as molting. Before the old skeleton is shed, a new one is laid down beneath it. The old one splits open and the animal works its way out of the old "shell." At least some crustaceans (certain crabs) eat the old exoskeleton. It takes time for the new skeleton to harden, so just after molting a crustacean is very vulnerable and often hides. This whole process is controlled by hormones.

Most crustaceans crawl, but some swim (at least for short distances), especially when they need to beat a hasty retreat. Some also burrow under sand or mud. Many crustaceans are planktonic throughout their lives while others have a planktonic phase in their life cycle. Others are parasitic (certain copepods and isopods). The barnacles are sessile filter-feeders that attach themselves to hard surfaces (including whales and turtle shells). The majority of crustaceans are nocturnal, spending their days in reef crevices, between coral branches or under the sand. The feeding modes of these invertebrates are also highly varied. Many

A peacock mantis shrimp (*Odontodactylus scyllarus*) brooding eggs. Note its compound eyes. Indonesia.

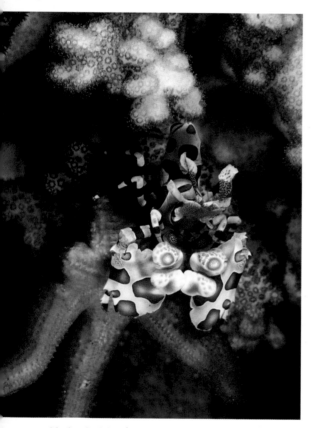

A harlequin shrimp (*Hymenocera elegans*) eating a sea star. This 3 cm (1.2 in) shrimp, a voracious predator, has already cut off two of the sea star's arms and devoured them. Papua New Guinea.

are carnivorous, capturing other marine animals, which they hold and tear apart. Others are scavengers that feed on carrion. Fewer species feed on plankton or are suspension-feeders that eat detritus. Some of the shrimps are cleaners that remove larval crustacean parasites from fishes. Crustaceans are an important food source for a wide variety of fishes.

The general sensory organs of crustaceans are their eyes; statocysts, which detect changes in water pressure or currents; tactile receptors; and chemoreceptors. Most crustaceans have compound eyes, which may be on some form of movable stalk. Their visual acuity tends to be poor — they have problems distinguishing shapes — but at least some possess color vision. They have a wide field of view, especially those species with eyes on stalks.

Most crustaceans are either male or female and do not change sex. When crustaceans copulate, the male holds the female, often using specialized appendages. Males may have a penis or a special appendage for transmitting the sperm. The eggs are usually brooded, often being held with specialized appendages or stored in a brood chamber until they hatch. Many shrimps and lobsters carry their egg mass under the abdomen; the sponge-like egg mass of most crabs is also tightly held under the shortened abdomen. Upon hatching, the larvae enter the plankton for varying lengths of time.

Sea cucumber crab (*Lissocarcinus orbicularis*) 1 cm (0.4 in) in size, lives in commensal symbiotic relationship on a sea cucumber. Indonesia.

Crustaceans

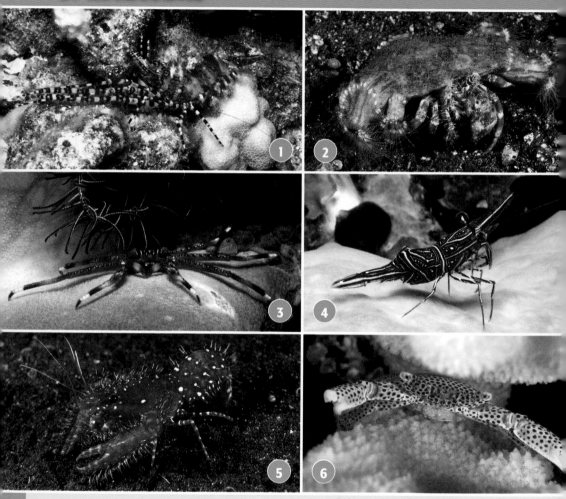

1 Marbled shrimp (*Saron* sp.). This male has long claw arms used for mate-guarding and breeding. Hawaii.

2 Anemone hermit crab (*Dardanus pedunculatus*). The anemones on its shell help protect the crab and the anemones benefit by being taken out to meals, an example of mutualist symbiosis. Papua New Guinea.

3 The flat rock crab (*Percnon planissimum*) moves quickly across the coral, into and out of crevices on the shallow reef. Indonesia.

4 Hingebeak shrimp (*Rhynchocinetes durbanensis*). Indonesia.

5 The red reef lobster (*Enoplometopus occidentalis*) is small — to 10 cm (4 in) — and reclusive. Indonesia.

6 Rust-spotted guard crab (*Trapezia rufopunctata*) carrying eggs. This 2.5 cm (1 in) wide commensal crab lives in *Pocillopora* branching coral. Australia.

1 Spotted spiny lobster (*Panulirus guttatus*). Dominica.

2 Banded coral shrimp (*Stenopus hispidus*), a cleaner shrimp. Dominica.

3 The channel clinging crab (*Mithrax spinosissimus*) is the largest crab on Caribbean reefs, up to 46 cm (18 in) across. Dominica.

4 Sculptured slipper lobster (*Parribacus antarcticus*). Dominica.

5 White-banded cleaner shrimp (*Lysmata amboinensis*). Indonesia.

6 The splendid red spooner crab (*Etisus splendidus*) grows to 15 cm (6 in) wide. Thailand.

Crustaceans

1 Yellowline arrow crab (*Stenorhynchus seticornis*). Dominica.

2 This crinoid squat lobster (*Allogalathea babai*), 2 cm (0.8 in) long, lives exclusively on feather stars (crinoids), an example of commensal symbiosis. Thailand.

3 Peacock mantis shrimp (*Odontodactylus scyllarus*), 15 cm (6 in) long. Indonesia.

4 Adult painted spiny lobster (*Panulirus versicolor*). This lobster grows to 40 cm (15.7 in) and is widespread in the tropical Indo-Pacific Ocean. Indonesia.

5 The porcelain crab (*Neopetrolisthes maculatus*) lives in a commensal symbiotic relationship with sea anemones. Papua New Guinea.

6 Black coral shrimp (*Pontonides ankeri*), 1 cm (0.8 in) long and well camouflaged among the tentacles of whip corals. Indonesia.

1   Blunt decorator crab (*Camposcia retusa*), covered in sponges. Indonesia.

2   Orangutan crab (*Oncinopus* sp.). Fine hairs, often red or brown, give this long-limbed crab its name. Indonesia.

3   Bumblebee shrimp (*Gnathophyllum americanum*), a 1 cm (0.4 in) symbiont that lives on sea cucumbers. Dominica.

4   Emperor shrimp (*Periclimenes imperator*), a 2 cm (0.8 in) commensal shrimp that lives on sea cucumbers in a symbiotic relationship. Papua New Guinea.

5   Blue swimmer crab (*Portunus pelagicus*) eating a sea urchin. Japan.

6   This 2 cm (0.8 in) shrimp (*Laomenes* sp.) is well camouflaged. It lives among the arms of a feather star (crinoid) in a commensal symbiotic relationship. Indonesia.

Crustaceans

1 Golden mantis shrimp (*Lysios-quilloides mapia*) in its burrow. This spearing mantid species grows to 15 cm (6 in) long. Indonesia.

2 Coral hermit crab (*Paguritta harmsi*). This very small (1 cm/0.4 in) crab lives in worm-tube holes in the coral and uses its feathered antennae to snare passing bits of plankton. Solomon Islands.

3 This sea spider is a marine arthropod in class Pycnogonida. Indonesia.

4 Coleman's shrimp (*Periclimenes colemani*). Papua New Guinea.

5 Conical spider crab (*Xenocarcinus conicus*). Indonesia.

6 This lesser sponge crab (*Dromia erythropus*) is carrying a sponge on its back to help it hide from predators. Dominica.

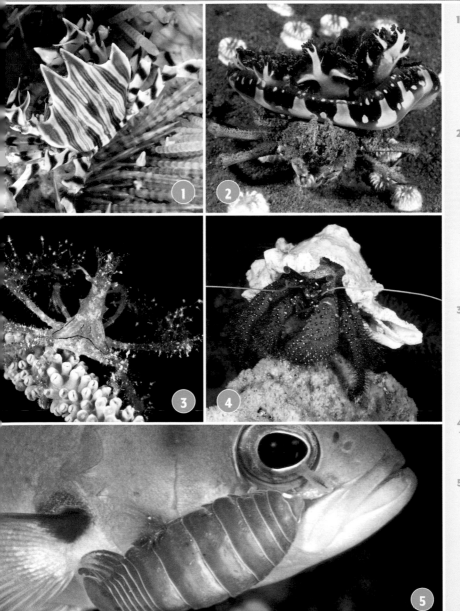

1 Zebra crab (*Zebrida adamsii*). This 1 cm (0.4 in) commensal crab lives among the spines of fire urchins. Indonesia.

2 Decorator crab (*Ethusa* sp.) carrying an upsidedown jellyfish (*Cassiopeia andromeda*) for protection. Stinging cells on the jellyfish help deter fishes and octopuses from eating the crab. Indonesia.

3 A neck crab (*Podochela* sp.), a decorator crab species, clings to a gorgonian soft coral. Note the hydroids attached to its legs. Belize.

4 White-spotted hermit crab (*Dardanus megistos*). Australia.

5 An isopod (*Anilocra laticaudata*) on a creole-fish (*Paranthias furcifer*). The isopod, a crustacean, is a parasite on this fish and often on soldierfish. Bonaire.

Echinoderms:
Sea Stars, Sea Urchins and Sea Cucumbers

More than 6,500 species of sea stars, serpent stars, feather stars, sea cucumbers and urchins represent the phylum Echinodermata. All are marine and almost all spend the majority of their life cycle on the seafloor (there are a few pelagic sea cucumbers). Echinoderms exhibit pentamerous radial symmetry, which simply means they consist of five equal sections arranged around a central axis. These animals lack a head, a brain and a heart. A defining characteristic is their water-vascular system — a network of canals running through the body and appendanges, ending in tube feet. This system is employed in food collection and handling, gas exchange, sensory reception and locomotion.

Echinoderm translates as "spiny skin," but it is actually the internal skeleton, just beneath the skin, that supports the spines. The skeleton and skin give structural support and provide protection from predators. The skin of certain asteroid sea stars is not only tough but also adorned with knobs or thorns. Sea urchins take this one step further: their round bodies are often covered with long, needlelike spines. Some species have venomous spines or pedicellariae — long tubes with tiny pincers at the ends — that inject venom. Urchins also employ their pedicellariae to secure bits of debris, including plant material, rubble and manmade products, which they use to camouflage themselves. Sea cucumbers are protected by their thick, slimy skin, which makes ingestion difficult for most predators.

Feather stars and serpent stars regularly employ a clever defense mechanism called autotomy, which is self-amputation of the appendages. When attacked, these echinoderms can voluntarily release their arm(s), thereby gaining a chance to crawl away from the predator. The morphology of a serpent star, or brittle star, and its readiness to autotomize its limbs apparently determines how palatable it is. Those species that have more robust arms, sharp arm spines and chemical defenses such as acid mucus are less desirable to potential predators.

Sea cucumbers may sacrifice internal body parts to escape potential predators. Some species have unique defense organs known as Cuvierian tubules. These are sticky white threads that are shot from the anus at an attacker to distract or even entangle it. After these structures are expelled, the tubules become detached

The peppermint sea star (*Fromia monilis*) grows to 10 cm (4 in). A number of similar species are found throughout the tropical Indo-Pacific region.

The tube feet of a crown-of-thorns sea star (*Acanthaster planci*). Indonesia.

from the body and are later regenerated. Regeneration of organs and limbs is key to survival for many echinoderms. Some sea stars (e.g., *Linckia* spp.) are able to grow an entirely new body from just a fragment of a severed arm. A diver who finds a bizarrely shaped sea star with tiny arms sprouting from one larger arm has just found a "comet." Given time, it will be crawling around the reef as good as new, looking and functioning just like its symmetrical five-armed brethren.

Echinoderms acquire nutrients in a variety of different ways. Many of the sea urchins are herbivores. Sea stars, which are commonly referred to as "starfish," are highly predaceous, feeding on snails, bivalves, crustaceans, worms and other echinoderms. The dreaded crown-of-thorns feeds on live stony corals. While most serpent stars feed on a variety of smaller invertebrates or are suspension-feeders, one species eats fish. The feather stars, also called crinoids, are plankton-feeders, while many of the sea cucumbers are deposit-feeders, mopping up detritus with their feeding tentacles. Some sea cucumbers feed on plankton and suspended debris.

Reef-dwelling echinoderms are popular hosts for commensal invertebrates and fishes. For example, sea urchin spines often serve as a refuge for certain juvenile groupers and snappers, cardinalfishes and clingfishes. Pearlfishes live inside the body cavities of sea cucumbers, entering through the anus and feeding on the organs. There is a comb jelly that lives on sea stars, and a number of smaller crustaceans reside on many echinoderm species.

In the majority of the echinoderms, the sexes are separate — that is, they are not hermaphrodites. During spawning, gametes are released into the water column, where they mix and fertilization occurs. There is a planktonic larval stage.

Crinoids (family Comasteridae), also known as feather stars, on a healthy coral reef. Indonesia.

Cushion sea stars (*Oreaster reticulatus*) on a shallow sand plain inside the coral reef. Cozumel.

Echinoderms

1 Crown-of-thorns sea star (*Acanthaster planci*). Baja, Mexico.

2 Flower sea urchin (*Toxopneustes roseus*). The large, trumpet-shaped pedicellariae are venomous. The shell debris attached may possibly help protect from UV radiation. Baja, Mexico.

3 Longspine sea urchin (*Diadema* sp.). Its spines can inflict a painful wound. Indonesia.

4 Slate pencil sea urchin (*Heterocentrotus mammillatus*). Hawaii.

5 Watson's sea star (*Gomophia watsoni*). Australia.

6 The red cushion sea star (*Oreaster reticulatus*) inhabits shallow seagrass beds and sand flats 1.5–10.7 m (5–35 ft) deep. Dominica.

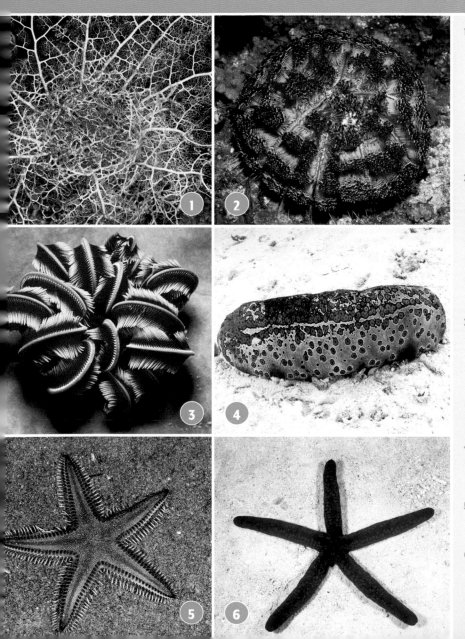

1   A giant basket star (*Astrophyton muricatum*) with its spidery web of finely branched arms unfurled at night to ensnare small fish and plankton. Dominica.

2   The fire sea urchin (*Asthenosoma varium*) is both large — to 20 cm (8 in) in diameter — and dangerous. Its venomous spines can inflict a painful wound. Indonesia.

3   A robust crinoid (possibly *Himerometra robustipinna*) with its arms curled up during the day. It is also called a feather star. Indonesia.

4   Leopard sea cucumber (*Bohadschia argus*). Australia.

5   Sand sea star (*Astropecten polyacanthus*). Indonesia.

6   Blue sea star (*Linckia laevigata*). Australia.

Echinoderms

1 Splendid jewel box sea urchin (*Mespilia* cf. *globulus*), also called globe urchin. Thailand.

2 Double-spined sea urchin (*Echinothrix calamaris*). Its anal sac with spots helps to identify this common urchin. Thailand.

3 Synaptid sea cucumber, from the family Synaptidae. Indonesia.

4 The granular sea star (*Choriaster granulatus*) grows to 25 cm (9.8 in). Philippines.

5 Golden crinoids (*Davidaster rubiginosa*). The darker one with yellow tips (behind and to left) is a different color morph of the same species. Dominica.

6 Legless feather star (*Comanthus alternans*). Indonesia.

1 The chocolate chip sea star (*Protoreaster nodosus*) grows to 30 cm (11.8 in) in diameter. Papua New Guinea.

2 The Galápagos sand dollar (*Encope galapagensis*), buried under sand by day, crawls about in the open at night. Galápagos Islands.

3 A dark red-spined brittle star (*Ophiothrix purpurea*), commonly seen on gorgonians, soft corals and sponges. Indonesia.

4 Pineapple sea cucumber (*Thelenota ananas*). Australia.

5 Bennett's feather stars (*Oxyco-manthus bennetti*), also called crinoids. Indonesia.

6 Sponge brittle star (*Ophiothrix suensonii*) on lavender rope sponge (*Niphates erecta*). Belize.

Tunicates

While often confused with sponges, tunicates are important members of coral-reef communities. There are 2,000 benthic tunicates (also known as sea squirts) in the subphylum Urochordata, class Ascidiacea. They are named for the "tunic" that surrounds the body and serves as a skeletal structure, enabling the animal to maintain its shape. The tunic's rubbery or leathery material contains a cellulose fiber known as tunicin. Tunicates have a non-living covering but grow without having to molt. Some species have blue-green algae (genus *Prochloron*) living in the tunic that, via photosynthesis, provide nutrients.

Tunicates' bright colors apparently serve to warn of their toxic qualities. These toxins include heavy metals (e.g., vanadium, iron) and sulfuric acid that is deposited in and eventually expelled from the tunic. These substances make tunicates undesirable to dine on, at least for most reef organisms. In addition, tunicates with these chemicals in their tunics are rarely overgrown by algae or invertebrates. However, even though they possess an impressive defensive arsenal, specialized gastropods (certain volutes and cowries), sea slugs, polyclad flatworms, angelfishes, batfishes and trunkfishes eat tunicates. Sea slugs in the genus *Nembrotha* even use the ingested chemicals for their own defense.

A solitary tunicate body is typically cylindrical, with two holes — the incurrent and excurrent siphons. Right inside the incurrent siphon is an expanded area known as the branchial basket that comes complete with gill slits. Tiny food particles (e.g., bacteria) collect on mucus produced by a structure called the endostyle. Ciliary action of the gill slits eventually moves the mucus, along with the food particles, into the esophagus and stomach. The food is then processed and waste is ejected from the anus, which is located near the excurrent siphon.

The vast majority of tunicates grow on hard substrates and many species are colonial. They are simultaneous hermaphrodites that expel gametes into the water column when spawning. The larval form is almost tadpole-like and has a "notochord," or primitive backbone. It swims about until it finds an appropriate substrate for settlement. It then adheres to that spot with the help of adhesive papilla and undergoes a very rapid and spectacular metamorphosis — in as little as 20 seconds it absorbs the tail section and notochord into the main body. The tunic then begins to grow, and within hours it has securely fastened the "little squirt" to the substrate.

A tunicate, *Polycarpa aurata*, that exemplifies the bright warning coloration, siphons and rubbery tunic texture of this group of animals. Indonesia.

Tunicates

1 Tunicates
   (*Didemnum*
   spp.) on
   a sponge.
   Malaysia.

2 Salp (*Thetys
   vagina*).
   This jellylike
   creature
   is actually
   a pelagic
   tunicate,
   widespread
   in both the
   temperate and
   tropical Pacific
   and Atlantic
   Oceans.

3 Tunicates
   (*Atriolum
   robustum*).
   Indonesia.

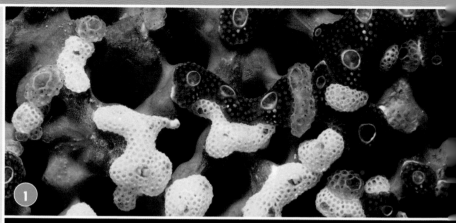

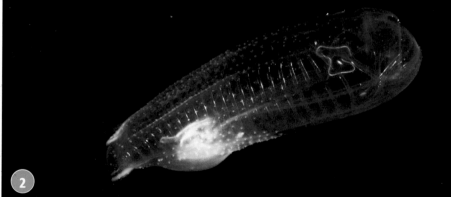

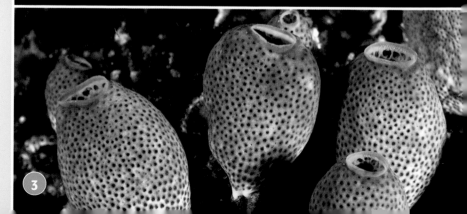

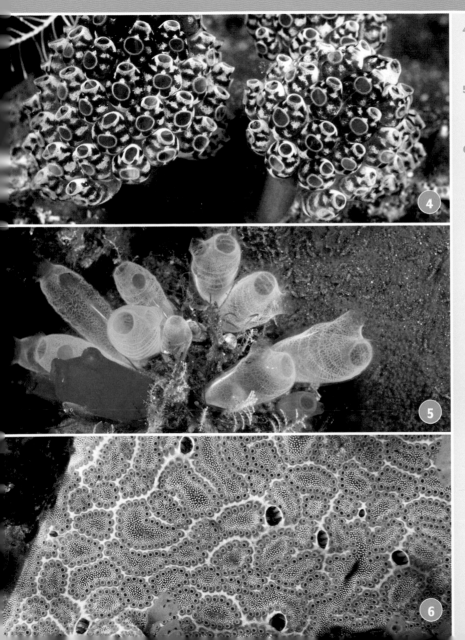

4 Stalked
  tunicates
  (*Oxycorynia
  fascicularis*).
  Indonesia.

5 Tunicates
  (*Rhopalaea*
  sp.), also called
  ascidians.
  Indonesia.

6 A colonial
  tunicate
  (*Botryllus* sp.).
  Indonesia.

Chapter 6

Marine Reptiles

Relatively few reptiles are adapted to living in marine environments. They include sea turtles, sea snakes, a couple of crocodilians and one species of lizard. All of these animals must occasionally swim to the surface to breathe air, but they also exhibit amazing breath-holding abilities. For example, sea snakes can hold their breath for more than 3.5 hours, while one loggerhead sea turtle reportedly stayed underwater for 10 hours. That said, most marine reptiles typically come up for air much more frequently than that, usually every 4 to 6 minutes. Sea turtles engage in an explosive exhale-inhale behavior that quickly purges their lungs of old, oxygen-impoverished air and then fills them with fresh air. Sea snakes supplement normal pulmonary respiration by "breathing" through the skin, taking up oxygen from the water and excreting carbon dioxide. Marine reptiles will also slow their metabolic rate, such as when resting on the seafloor, to reduce oxygen demands. The sea turtles, some sea snakes and crocodiles are bound to the terrestrial environment, where they lay their eggs. The sea snakes in the subfamily Hydrophiinae, however, are ovoviviparous, giving birth to live young at sea.

One marine reptile is well known for the danger it poses to humankind. Saltwater crocodiles reach at least 6 meters (19.8 feet) in length and are extremely opportunistic, preying on a wide range of animal prey, including large mammals. Thus humans would be considered suitable prey. Even so, attacks by "salties" are uncommon, with on average two fatalities annually in Australia. More attacks may occur in more remote places such as Borneo, Sumatra and Myanmar (Burma).

Sea Snakes

The sea snakes comprise the family Elapidae. This group is divided into two subfamilies: the Hydrophiinae (referred to as "true" sea snakes), with 58 species, and the Laticaudinae (sea kraits), with 5 species. Sea kraits spend more

Saltwater crocodile (*Crocodylus porosus*). Australia.

time on land than their Hydrophiinae cousins. In fact, one of the most frequently encountered sea snakes, the yellow-lipped sea krait (*Laticauda colubrina*), splits its time equally between water and land. Sea kraits leave the water to lay their eggs, mate, slough their skin, bask and digest their food. In contrast to sea kraits, members of the subfamily Hydrophiinae spend most, if not all, of their time at sea. They slough their skin at sea, and those that live around reefs will rub their head and body against the coral to get rid of fouling organisms such as bryozoans and barnacles. As mentioned above, these sea snakes also give birth in the water to live young.

Adaptations to an aquatic lifestyle include nostrils with valves that close when the snake is submerged, scales along the lip that help seal the mouth and a salt gland under the tongue that excretes sodium from the body that was ingested with the snake's prey. Large lungs function not only in respiration but also as buoyancy control. They also have a cardiac shunt (it is more pronounced in deep-diving sea snakes) that, along with their ability to release nitrogen from the blood through the skin, helps prevent sea snakes from getting the bends. A paddle-like tail facilitates movement through the water that is at least three times faster than onshore. In fact, some of the Hydrophiinae sea snakes are so specialized to aquatic life that they have trouble moving on land. Sea snakes range in length from 12 centimeters (5 inches) to 2 meters (6.5 feet).

Most sea snakes prey on bony fish: the members of at least 56 different fish families are on the menu. A number of marine serpents found around coral reefs target moray, conger and snake eels, while the beaked sea snake (*Enhydrina schistosa*) is a catfish-eater. One of the most unusual feeding modes involves egg eating (oophagy); the turtle-headed sea snake (*Emydocephalus annulatus*) moves slowly over the bottom, stopping occasionally to ingest the eggs of damselfishes and blennies. But not all sea snakes are such dietary specialists. The olive sea snake (*Aipysurus laevis*) feeds on 19 different fish species, fish eggs, shrimps, crabs and file shells.

Though equipped with a deadly chemical arsenal, sea snakes are an important food for sharks, especially tiger sharks. They are also eaten by larger

A yellow-lipped sea krait (*Laticauda colubrina*) swimming up a coral slope on its way to the surface to breathe. It is also called the banded sea krait or colubrine sea snake. Indonesia.

morays and groupers, some larger crabs, crocodiles, sea eagles and marine mammals. At least one sea snake has been shown to dupe would-be predators by having a tail that looks like its head. The color of the tail and head of the yellow-lipped sea krait are nearly identical, and it twists its tail in a way that makes it look like the head end as the snake probes reef crevices looking for food. This adaptation may deflect attacks by predators away from the more vulnerable head end, increasing the animal's chances of survival. Other causes of sea snake mortality include storms, currents, sun exposure, dehydration, fire, disease and malnutrition. The maximum age for at least one species (the olive sea snake) is 15 years. However, the mortality in the first year of life for some species has been estimated to be between 40 and 90 percent.

Sea snakes are dangerous because of their highly toxic venom, which is composed of a cocktail of neurotoxins, myotoxins, nephrotoxins and nontoxic substances. The primary effects of the venom are paralysis and respiratory failure. Fortunately, sea snakes rarely bite people. In fact they are quite tolerant of human handling (although we don't recommend you test their patience!), and when they do bite, they tend not to inject much venom.

Sea Turtles

Sea turtles have been around for a long time. They date back 130 million years in the fossil record, when they shared the seas with such marine leviathans as *Plesiosaurus* and *Ichthyosaurus*. After so many years of being part of marine ecosystems, the number of sea turtles is generally on the decline because of overharvesting and destruction of their nesting and foraging habitats. Not only are adults targeted for their meat, the eggs are also excavated for food. Some are also at risk of being taken as bycatch. For example, loggerhead (*Caretta caretta*) and leatherback turtles (*Dermochelys coriacea*) are incidentally captured by pelagic long lines and high-seas drift nets. Thousands of sea turtles die in this manner every year. Sea turtles are also prone to ingesting non-degradable marine debris such as plastic bags, bottles, rope, monofilament line and tar balls, which can lead to health issues and death. As a result of these varying pressures, almost all the sea turtle species are considered threatened or endangered.

Currently, seven sea turtle species are recognized, in six different genera. While they are wonderfully adapted to life in the ocean, they are cumbersome

Hawksbill sea turtle (*Eretmochelys imbricata*). Dominica.

on land. Rather than the typical turtle front legs, they have large flippers that they flap like wings to propel themselves through the water; the back legs are also modified. Because of these modifications they have lost the ability to retract their head and forelimbs inside the shell, but their large size and armored head compensate for this loss. Sea turtles have a gland under each eye that removes salt from the body — it is responsible for the tears seen as the female lays her eggs. Instead of teeth they have a beak. It is used to scrape sessile invertebrates (e.g., sponges, soft corals, sea anemones) and algae from the substrate, to browse on seagrass or to grasp and crush crabs, bivalves and sea urchins. One species, the leatherback, has stiff spines in its mouth that point backwards toward the throat, facilitating the capture and swallowing of the gelatinous sea jellies that it eats. The maximum carapace length is 55 centimeters (22 inches) for the smallest species, the Kemp's ridley sea turtle (*Lepidochelys kempii*), and 1.8 meters (6 feet) for the largest species, the leatherback.

Sea turtles begin their lives in a nest under the sand. The pregnant female returns to the beach where she was hatched (known as the natal beach) to dig a pit with her flippers, into which she deposits her eggs. This may be a solitary affair or, in the case of both ridley sea turtle species, females may come ashore en masse in arribadas. During these mass nesting events, hundreds and sometimes thousands of females will occupy a nesting beach. The eggs are sometimes dug up and eaten by ghost crabs, large lizards (e.g., monitor lizards), vultures, armadillos, canine species, feral pigs, mongooses and raccoons (a major egg-eater in North America). After an incubation period of around 45 to 70 days (it depends on the sand temperature), the eggs hatch and young turtles erupt from their sandy incubator. Hatchlings usually emerge at night, and typically all at once, in order to increase the likelihood that at least some will be able to run the gauntlet of waiting predators. In the sea as well, the young turtles are not without their enemies. They are eaten by sharks, groupers, snappers, jacks, mahi-mahi and tuna. Even the largest adult turtles can be prey for tiger sharks, which specialize in feeding on marine reptiles. Orcas also eat adult turtles, including giant leatherbacks.

Mating usually occurs just prior to egg-laying. During courtship, the male will rapidly approach the female and bite and nuzzle her carapace. He will then mount her, using enlarged claws on his fore flippers and the tail to grip the edge of her shell. Copulation can be a lengthy affair, lasting as long as 12 hours in some species. Attendant males (as many as a dozen have been reported) will associate with a mating pair and may attempt to interfere by biting and mounting the copulating turtles. A female may mate with more than one male and her clutch may include eggs fertilized by more than one suitor.

Sea turtles visit cleaning stations to be serviced by cleaner fish, including wrasses, parrotfishes, angelfishes, damselfishes, hogfish and a variety of surgeonfishes. These fishes browse on hitchhiking invertebrates (such as barnacles), algae and dead and diseased tissue from the turtle's skin and shell. Sea turtles will also "self-clean," rubbing their carapace, flippers or head against submerged objects to remove barnacles and algae.

A loggerhead sea turtle (*Caretta caretta*) escaping from a fishing net equipped with a TED (turtle excluder device). Thousands of endangered sea turtles are killed each year by entanglement in fishing gear. Only recently have certain fishermen in a few countries started using nets like this. Photo courtesy of NOAA.

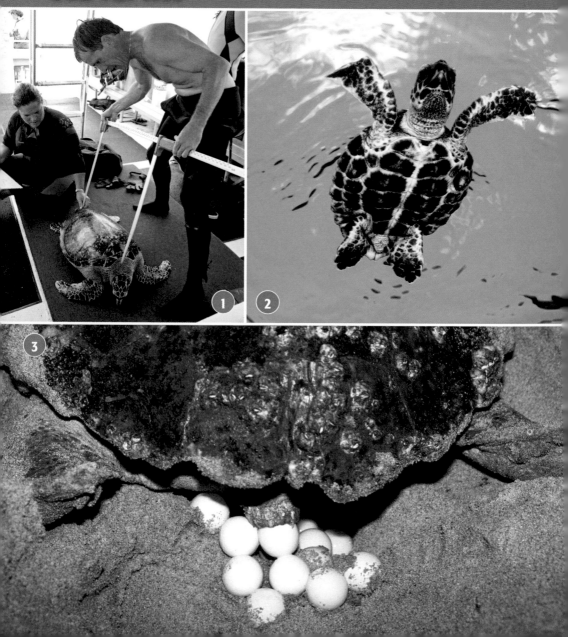

1 Sea turtle biologist Larry Wood uses calipers to measure the length of a hawksbill sea turtle (*Eretmochelys imbricata*). Florida.

2 A hawksbill sea turtle (*Eretmochelys imbricata*) 8 cm (3 in) hatchling soars through innerspace, just under the ocean surface in the Gulf Stream off Florida.

3 This loggerhead sea turtle (*Caretta caretta*) will deposit approximately 100 eggs into its nest on the beach at night. Florida.

4 A loggerhead sea turtle (*Caretta caretta*) nest on the beach has been marked by scientists. Florida.

5 Loggerhead sea turtle hatchlings (*Caretta caretta*) scamper from their nest to the surfline and into the big ocean. Florida.

Marine Iguana

Only one lizard spends considerable time in the marine environment — the marine iguana (*Amblyrhynchus cristatus*). This animal has been an inhabitant of the Galápagos Islands for more than 10 million years. While there is only one species, six subspecies are found on different islands throughout the archipelago. Both sexes tend to be charcoal gray to black during the non-breeding season, an adaptation to help warm them between forays into the cold sea. Males on some islands, such as Fernandina, are brightly colored red and teal during the breeding season. Male *A. cristatus* attain a length up to 1.7 meters (5.6 feet), while females are usually 0.6 to 1 meter (2 to 3.3 feet). The lizard is a good swimmer, aided by a laterally flattened tail.

Marine iguanas feed on macroalgae. While they are indeed amphibious, they spend only about 5 percent of their time in the water. Juveniles and sub-adults tend to be less aquatic; they do most of their feeding in the intertidal zone, often returning to the same foraging site day after day. Juveniles tend to stay in the upper intertidal zone because it is warmer and they have less wave action to contend with: smaller lizards have a more difficult time hanging on to the rocks when a wave comes in. Larger lizards feed sub-tidally. They swim out from shore, dive down — usually no deeper than 10 meters (33 feet) — and browse on algae growing on stones and boulders on the seafloor. Because it is cold-blooded, the marine iguana cannot spend too much time in the cool waters around the Galápagos. They remain underwater for up to 30 minutes, after which they crawl out onto the rocks to bask and increase their body temperature. They attempt to maintain their body temperature at 35° to 37°C (95° to 99°F) during the day.

Breeding occurs once a year and is synchronous. The mating system of marine iguanas consists of males gathering together and forming temporary breeding territories, known as leks. Fights break out between the males as they attempt to occupy territories in the middle of the lek — those in the central territories tend to have greater reproductive success than those on the margins. The male engages in head-bobbing displays to attract females, and when one enters his territory, he will mount and inseminate her. Females usually mate only once per season. After mating, females exhibit aggression toward members of their own sex when defending their own nests and attempting to steal nest sites from consexuals.

About four months after egg-laying, young iguanas begin to emerge from their nest sites. While the newly hatched lizards eat some algae, for the first couple of months of their life their primary diet consists of the feces of adults. They eat feces to populate their alimentary tracts with microbes that help break down the cellulose in the plants that adults eat.

Visitors to the Galápagos Islands are easily able to observe and photograph this remarkable reptile, the only marine lizard. Adult marine iguanas are usually very easy to approach. However, the Galápagos Islands are often greatly affected by El Niño warming events. During certain cycles, the algae on which these lizards feed become scarce. During such years population numbers have declined severely, with recorded mortality rates from starvation of 70 to 80 percent. Nevertheless, populations throughout the region are protected and in fairly good condition.

A marine iguana (*Amblyrhynchus cristatus*) underwater, feeding on *Ulva* green algae. This is the world's only lizard that feeds in the ocean. Galápagos Islands.

Marine iguanas (*Amblyrhynchus cristatus*) clustered together to conserve heat on a cool morning. Galápagos Islands.

Olive Sea Snake

Aipysurus laevis
Family Elapidae

- 🌐 West Papua, Papua New Guinea, Australia, Coral Sea and New Caledonia
- ⊙ Coral and rocky reefs; lagoons, reef flats, reef crests, reef faces, slopes
- ↧ 1–68 m (3.3–221 ft)
- ↔ 2 m (7 ft); females longer and heavier than males

Solitary, but aggregates during breeding season. Home range about 1,800 sq m (19,375 sq ft), along reef edge. Generalist diet: numerous fish species, fish eggs, crustaceans. Hunts in reef crevices and on sand; active both day and night. Young born at sea, 2–6 per litter. May live to 15 years. Many caught and killed in trawl nets.

Yellow-lipped Sea Krait

Laticauda colubrina
Family Elapidae

- 🌐 Andaman and Nicobar Islands, east to Samoa, north to Japan and south to New Zealand
- ⊙ Tropical; semiaquatic; coral reefs
- ↧ 1–10 m (3.3–33 ft)
- ↔ 1.5 m (4.9 ft); 2 kg (4.4 lb); females larger than males

Solitary; forms courting groups in breeding period. Juveniles rarely out of or far from water. Eel-eaters: female eats more conger eels (single prey item per foraging bout); male feeds on smaller moray eels (often multiple prey per bout). Returns to land to digest prey, shed and reproduce. Most courtship and mating takes place in morning; one to several males follow female, then lie along female and twitch, sometimes for days (males not aggressive to one another). Lays eggs, 4–20 per clutch. Requires fresh water to drink.

Marine Reptiles

- ⊕ Temperate to tropical seas
- ⊙ Coastal habitats; open ocean
- ↔ 1 m (3.3 ft.); 159 kg (350 lb)

Loggerhead Sea Turtle

Caretta caretta
Family Cheloniidae

Solitary. Newly hatched juveniles feed on insects and invertebrates associated with floating debris. Adults feed on clams, crustaceans, sponges and corals. Eaten by large sharks (notably tiger sharks). Migrates to tropical areas to feed; migrations can be more than 1,500 km (1,000 mi). Mates with many partners; copulation can last several hours. Newly hatched turtles found along drift lines in open ocean among debris and floating algae (e.g., *Sargassum*).

- ⊕ Circumtropical
- ⊙ Sand flats and slopes with seagrass; visits coral and rocky reefs
- ↔ 1.5 m (4.9 ft); 395 kg (869 lb)

Green Sea Turtle

Chelonia mydas
Family Cheloniidae

Solitary; in groups during breeding/nesting period. Juveniles and adolescences eat sea jellies and man-of-wars. Adults eat seagrass, preferring young grass as more nutrient-rich. Feeds during day; returns to nocturnal shelter site in late afternoon. Reaches maturity in 15–35 years (slow growth due to diet). Nests in tropics; one important area Tortuguero, off Costa Rica. Female returns to same nesting area, male to same location to mate. Some travel long distances in open ocean from feeding to nesting sites — up to 2,250 km (1,400 mi.).

Hawksbill Sea Turtle
Eretmochelys imbricata
Family Cheloniidae

⊕ Tropical seas
⊙ Rocky and coral reefs, bays, estuaries
↔ 1 m (3.3 ft); 127 kg (279 lb)

Solitary. Invertebrate-eater with preference for sponges. When feeding, will dive for around 20 minutes, usually to depths of 10 m (33 ft) or less. When resting at night, may dive for up to 47 minutes; may return to same resting site every night. Often climbs higher up beach than other turtles because of smaller size, even navigating over plant material and rocks. Often nests on offshore islands; does not nest in groups. Average egg clutch around 180. Highly sought after for shell. Endangered.

Leatherback Sea Turtle
Dermochelys coriacea
Family Dermochelyidae

⊕ Circumglobal; cold temperate to tropical seas
⊙ Coastal habitats (rarely around reefs); open ocean
↔ 3 m (10 ft); 916 kg (2,015 lb)

Solitary. Feeds on sea jellies. Makes deep feeding dives of more than 1,000 m (3,250 ft). Dive duration averages 9 minutes, but 3.5 hours possible. Strong swimmer. Long migrations: up to 5,000 km (3,000 mi) from feeding grounds in cold water to nesting areas in tropics and subtropics (e.g., Gabon in western Africa, Indonesia, Central America). Found at temperatures of 6°C (42°F); body temperature can be 18°C (10°F) higher than ambient water. Basks at surface when in cool water. Endangered.

Chapter 7

Marine Mammals

Cetaceans: Whales and Dolphins

The cetaceans — members of the order Cetacea — are some of the most charismatic, awe-inspiring creatures on the planet. You have only to watch people's reactions to a dolphin riding a boat's bow wave to know that these animals have a special place in the hearts of humankind. Young and old, male and female, seafarer and landlubber alike will smile, squeal and ooh and aah as these animals frolic in the water. Why this attraction? It is partly due to the notion that cetaceans are not only intelligent but also "friends" of the human species. There are numerous stories about dolphins acting altruistically to save drowning children or scaring off marauding sharks threatening a hapless swimmer. Of course, many of these stories are based more on anthropomorphizing and sensationalism than fact, but such tales have certainly helped cement the idea that cetaceans are our benefactors, not enemies. Even the killer whale (*Orcinus orca*), the most predatory and potentially dangerous whale species, will share the water with and tolerate the presence of our species, even though it could easily make a meal of us. (The few reported attacks on people by *O. orca* usually involve a captive whale biting its trainer.)

Unfortunately, the "friendship" between humans and cetaceans has often been one-sided. For many years cetaceans were hunted and harvested without restriction. They were killed for their meat and for valuable byproducts such as whale oil, baleen and ambergris. Dolphins were (and still are) taken as bycatch in huge fishing nets or shot because they were viewed as competing for the same food resources. Thankfully, most countries now protect at least some cetaceans from harvest. A moratorium on commercial whaling was instigated in 1982 by the International Whaling Commission; this has helped whale populations increase in recent decades. But today many remain below pre-whaling

Bottlenose dolphins (*Tursiops truncatus*). Honduras.

A playful young male sperm whale (*Physeter macrocephalus*) opening its mouth. Look closely to see where its teeth will eventually break through the gums on the lower jaw. Dominica.

numbers, and some species are still endangered or on the verge of extinction. The most threatened of all is the Yangtze River dolphin (*Lipotes vexillifer*). Its population is considered no longer viable and it may soon be extinct (the last known sighting of an individual was in 2004).

There are currently 81 recognized species of cetaceans. However, new species are still being described, and as molecular studies progress, the number will likely increase. These mammals come in a variety of shapes and sizes; some smaller dolphins reach a maximum length of 1.2 meters (4 feet), while the blue whale is the largest animal ever known, reaching around 33 meters (108 feet). The order Cetacea can be broken up into two major groups: the baleen whales, or mysticetes (four families with 11 species), and the toothed whales and dolphins, or odontocetes (eight families with 70 species). As their group name indicates, rather than teeth, baleen whales possess baleen plates that hang from their upper jaw. Toothed whales and dolphins do have teeth, although in a handful of species they never emerge through the gums. In the mysticetes the baleen acts as a filter to strain small fish (such as herring) and zooplankton (such as copepods and krill) from the seawater, while the dentition of the odontocetes is employed to feed on larger prey items such as crustaceans, squid and fishes. A few in this group (most notably the killer whale) also hunt pinnipeds, in addition to other cetaceans.

The cetaceans make their homes in various ecosystems and habitats. While most are marine animals, some cetaceans live in freshwater rivers (Amazon, Ganges, Indus and Yangtze). Certain species, such as the blue whales, are true open-ocean rovers that rarely approach a coastline, while others spend much of their time near shore. But many inshore species also regularly ply the oceanic environs when moving from mating areas to more productive feeding grounds. Many baleen whales engage in extensive migrations, living closer to the poles in the summer months, where they glut themselves on food, building up blubber reserves in preparation for the long journey to wintertime breeding grounds nearer the equator, where their food is scarce. Some scientists hypothesize that baleen whales give birth in tropical areas to avoid having their offspring attacked by killer whales, which are less common in tropical climes.

Like terrestrial mammals, whales have hair. This consists of bristles on the face, usually found only on young individuals. Rather than nostrils, they have a blowhole on top of the head. Toothed whales have a single blowhole while baleen whales have two, positioned side by side. Cetaceans also have large, complex brains — the sperm whale (*Physeter macrocephalus*) has the largest brain known. Sexual dimorphism occurs in some whales: female baleen whales tend to be larger than males, while in the toothed whales the opposite is true.

Cetacean social organization varies greatly between species and can be significantly different between populations of the same species (these disparities are usually a function of resource availability and predation risk). Baleen whales tend to be less social than toothed whales. Species such as humpbacks and bowhead whales may form long-term feeding pairs. Other species such as minke and fin whales may aggregate in large numbers around a food source, but they are usually not as communal, nor do they engage in complex social behavior like the odontocetes.

Toothed whales tend to live in highly structured social groups. Social units may consist of smaller groups, as for the northern bottlenose whale (*Hyperoodon ampullatus*) — usually three or four individuals — to huge herds, as is often the case with dusky dolphins (*Lagenorhynchus obscurus*), which can form groups numbering

Humpback whales (*Megaptera novaeangliae*): tail flukes of mother, with her newborn calf in background. Tonga.

more than 1,000 individuals. Many inshore dolphin species exhibit a "fission/ fusion" grouping pattern. This is where groups are continually changing in composition: a pod may split into sub-pods, individuals from one pod may join another, or two pods may merge completely. In certain dolphin populations, adult males form tight bonds and may work together to defend a solitary female. In other odontocetes, groups consist of females of multiple generations — up to four generations in certain killer whale communities. In these matrilineal groups, females may cooperate to protect each other's offspring. For example, when nursing mother sperm whales dive deep to catch squid, they will leave their young ones, which are unable to dive as deep as their mothers, in the care of "babysitter" female pod members.

Most cetaceans give birth to a single calf. The duration of neonatal care is relatively short in baleen whales (weaning occurs in less than a year) and longer in odontocetes. In the latter group, this indicates that the mother (and the community) has lots to teach the young whale before it leaves maternal care. For example, young bottlenose dolphins (Tursiops truncatus) are usually dependent on their mothers for several years, and in some cases they may nurse for up to nine years. In the sperm whale, male offspring may nurse for several years or even as long as 13 years. During this time the young whale learns how to hunt and interact with other members of its community, and at least in some species, it learns the vocal repertoire of the population. In some cases (e.g., certain killer whale populations), both male and female young may stay with their maternal "sub-pod," which regularly joins larger pods made up of different family units. In other species, such as the sperm whale, only the female family members remain together. Young males move poleward to feeding grounds where they will grow larger, preparing to challenge dominant males for breeding access to females when they return to the tropics.

When it comes to feeding strategies, whales and dolphins exhibit considerable flexibility. They also show variability within and between populations of the same species. Some cetaceans, such as bottlenose dolphins, feed during both day and night. Others, including dusky dolphins, are nocturnal, diving down to the deep scattering layer to catch squid and fishes that move up to those depths at night. Cetaceans employ fascinating tactics to capture their prey. Humpback whales emit bubbles as they spiral in the water column, creating a bubble cylinder around their prey; at the same time they emit a trumpeting feeding sound. They swim up through the middle of the bubble net and gulp up the prey items that have been trapped within. The bubbles, along with the associated vocalizations, create a "wall of sound" that enhances the net's effectiveness. Dolphins and Bryde's whales are also known to create bubble nets.

Whales and dolphins use their tails to herd or stun their prey, by slapping their flukes on the sea surface; this is known as kick-feeding or lobtailing. Toothed whales have been observed to toss their prey into the air to stun them; for example, killer whales will use their tails to hurl seals into the air. Some even go so far as to pursue their prey out of

Humpback whales (*Megaptera novaeangliae*), mother and calf. The calf was born a month ago here, in the shallow, calm, warm waters of the Silver Bank. Dominican Republic.

the water. The most spectacular case of this hunting tactic involves killer whales in Patagonia purposefully beaching themselves to ambush sea lions. Dolphins too practice amphibious assaults, chasing schooling fishes up onto shore, then wiggling back into the water after consuming the stranded prey. Parents who have mastered these advanced predation strategies pass down the skills to their offspring through social learning.

Other interesting cetacean behaviors include spyhopping, in which the animal pushes its head out of the water (by beating with its tail flukes) to see what is going on above the surface. Killer whales often use this strategy when feeding on animals that live along the shoreline. Breaching is another spectacular cetacean behavior. This is defined as the animal's going airborne, with at least 40 percent of its body leaving the water. The real purpose of breaching is not fully known, but it may help in prey capture or communication, and/or it may simply be a form of play.

The biggest enemy of cetaceans is humans. But dolphins and smaller whales (or the young of larger species) are also eaten by sharks, especially the white shark. The greatest nonhuman threat to cetaceans, however, is killer whales.

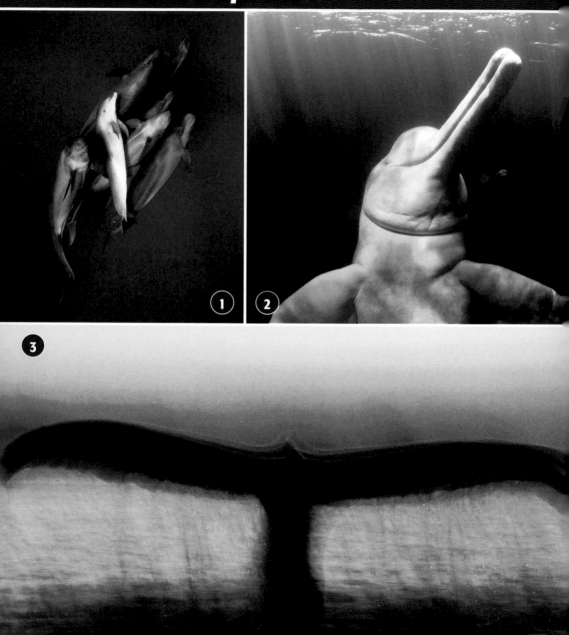

1 False killer whales (*Pseudorca crassidens*) and bottlenose dolphin (*Tursiops truncatus*). Dominica.

2 Amazon river dolphin (*Inia geoffrensis*), also called boto or pink river dolphin. Some are pink, others are bluish gray or off-white. Rio Negro, Brazil, South America.

3 Humpback whale (*Megaptera novaeangliae*) tail flukes at sunset (motion-blurred for effect). Hawaii.

4 Orca (*Orcinus orca*) breaching. It is also known as the killer whale. Worldwide, polar to tropical seas.

5 Sperm whales (*Physeter macrocephalus*) interacting with each other. Dominica.

Pinnipeds: Seals and Sea Lions

While not well represented in tropical oceans, pinnipeds do occur in subtrop-ical and warm temperate seas (many more species are found nearer the poles). One of the most endangered of all the pinnipeds, the Hawaiian monk seal (*Monachus schauinslandi*), is found in the tropics, with just over 1,000 individuals occurring around the Hawaiian Islands. The Mediterranean monk seal (*M. monachus*) is the second-rarest of the seals; just over 450 are thought to live in the Eastern Atlantic and the Mediterranean Sea. The Caribbean monk seal (*M. tropicalis*) is already extinct.

Pinnipeds have a number of adaptations that allow them to live a subaquatic lifestyle. This includes nostrils that close up to prevent water from entering the lungs, and the ability to see above and below the water, using a membrane that covers the eye to see well underwater. Fur and blubber help keep them warm in colder water. Pinnipeds have impressive breath-holding capabili-ties: some species can remain underwater for nearly two hours. When they make deep dives in pursuit of food, their heart rate slows to about one-tenth of normal and the circulatory system diverts blood to sense organs and the ner-vous system. Even though they are pretty "fleet of flipper" in the water, these animals are preyed upon by some sharks (e.g., white sharks) and cetaceans (e.g., killer whales). Breeding and giving birth keep all the pinnipeds tied to solid ground or pack ice.

There are three families in this group: Odobenidae (walruses), Otariidae (eared seals) and Phocidae (earless seals). The earless seals are the most aquatic of the bunch, being better adapted to diving deep and swimming long dis-tances. In fact, many phocids spend most of their time at sea, where they build up fat reserves for the breeding season. After giving birth, they often do not feed very much, relying on stored nutrients to get them through until lactation ends. Earless seals swim by undulating the entire body and are propelled by their well-developed rear flippers. They are very ungainly on land, where they move by pulling themselves along on their front flippers and by pushing off the ground with their abdominal muscles. Most phocids occur in cooler climates (polar to cool temperate latitudes), except for the aforementioned monk seals.

Eared seals, which include sea lions and fur seals, spend more time at the ocean—land interface. They are better able to get around on land, walking on all four rear and front limbs. When swimming, they propel themselves

Juvenile California sea lions (*Zalophus californianus*) interacting with one another. Baja, Mexico.

primarily with their large front flippers. While earless seals are sometimes gregarious (especially when they haul out to give birth to their young), otariids tend to be more social, often living in large colonies. Fur seals (genus *Arctocephalus*) get their common name from their coat, which consists of dense underfur mixed with guard hairs. The largest species in this family is the Steller sea lion (*Eumetopias jubatus*), which can reach a length of 3.25 meters (10.7 feet) and a weight of 1,120 kilograms (2,500 pounds).

Sirenians: Manatees and Dugongs

The unusual creatures of the order Sirenia have been the focal point of legend and lore for centuries. It is hard to believe that, in the distant past, sailors are said to have mistaken them for mermaids. That is what too much time at sea can do to you! Dugongs and manatees, also known as sea cows, are fully aquatic mammals that lack rear limbs — the only thing they have in common with mermaids.

There are two families in the group, the Trichechidae (manatees) and the Dugongidae (dugongs). Though several other sirenian families are now extinct, three species of manatee and one dugong survive today. The easiest way to tell the two families apart is by the tail. Manatees have a paddle-shaped tail, while that of the dugong is fluked like a dolphin's. While they may appear rather ungainly, if speed is required, manatees have been clocked swimming at 30 kilometers (13 miles) an hour for short distances.

Members of both groups are herbivorous, feeding mainly on seagrass. As old teeth become worn down and fall out, new ones grow in at the rear of the jaws to replace them. Another adaptation to a seagrass diet is the alimentary tract. Very long intestines help break down the plant material on which they browse. Because they feed on seagrass, all sirenians are tied to shallow coastal habitats. While primarily herbivores, however, dugongs in some locations will eat polychaete worms and other benthic invertebrates.

Sirenians often frequent protected areas such as mangrove channels, bays and springs. Both species have relatively few enemies, with sharks being the biggest threat, along with saltwater crocodiles and killer whales. Disease seems to be one of the main causes of mortality. Aboriginal peoples also kill these animals for meat in some regions.

The Florida manatee (*Trichechus manatus latirostris*), a subspecies of the West Indian manatee, is the sirenian most often encountered by divers. From November to March, hundreds of these animals congregate in warm, spring-fed rivers in Citrus County, Florida. Dugongs are most often seen in the Red Sea, the Persian Gulf and Western and Northern Australia. With an estimated population of around 10,000, Shark Bay is one of the best places to see them in Australia.

Florida manatees (*Trichechus manatus latirostris*) surfacing to breathe in a shallow river near a warm spring. Florida.

Dwarf Minke Whale

Balaenoptera acutorostrata

Family Balaenopteridae (rorquals)

⊕ Eastern coast of South America to Australia, north to Vanuatu and south to ice edge of subantarctic

⊙ Coastal and open ocean, sometimes around islands

↔ 7.8 m (25 ft)

Feeds on krill and lanternfish. Spends summer months in subantarctic feeding; in winter months moves toward equator to give birth. Single calf born every year; weaned in 5–6 months. Lifespan 50 years. Proficient at breaching, with whole body sometimes leaving water. Small size means more threatened by orcas and possibly larger sharks (whites, tigers). Best place to see is Australia's Great Barrier Reef between March and October.

Bryde's Whale

Balaenoptera brydei

Family Balaenopteridae (rorquals)

⊕ Worldwide

⊙ Subtropics and tropics

↔ Females 15.5 m (50 ft); males 14 m (46 ft)

Solitary or in pairs; rarely, loose aggregations of up to 20. Feeds primarily on small schooling fish such as sardines. Not shy — approaches whale-watching boats. Breaches and surfaces at irregular intervals. Can stay underwater for at least 20 minutes. Dives to 300 m (975 ft). Moan-like vocalizations. About 100,000 individuals worldwide. Omura's whale (*Balaenoptera omurai*), a "pygmy" form, described in 2003; maximum length about 12 m (39 ft).

- ⊕ Worldwide
- ⊙ Polar to tropical seas
- ↔ 33 m (108 ft) in Antarctic; smaller elsewhere

Blue Whale

Balaenoptera musculus
Family Balaenopteridae (rorquals)

Solitary. Krill-feeder; copepods and schooling fishes insignificant part of diet. Moves poleward in spring, toward subtropics in fall. More oceanic than most other baleen whales. Body long and slender, with small dorsal fin; gray with mottling. Gestation 10–12 months; calves nursed for 6–7 months. Reaches sexual maturity at 5–15 years. Worldwide population estimated at 10,000–25,000 individuals. Ice entrapment may be biggest cause of natural mortality. On rare occasions, preyed on by orca.

- ⊕ Worldwide
- ⊙ Open ocean; mainly temperate and polar seas but also in tropics; occasionally close to coast
- ↔ 26 m (85 ft) in southern hemisphere; 22 m (72 ft) in northern hemisphere

Fin Whale

Balaenoptera physalus
Family Balaenopteridae (rorquals)

Social, usually in groups of 2–7 individuals; aggregations of 30 near food sources. Often associates with other cetaceans (humpbacks, minke whales and Atlantic white-sided dolphins). Primarily krill-eater but also feeds on small schooling fishes. Joined by seabirds when feeding near surface. In winter migrates from cool to warmer water, where female gives birth to single calf; gestation 11–12 months. Sexual maturity reached at 6–12 years. Lifespan 80–90 years. Preyed on by orca; young may be attacked by white sharks.

Marine Mammals

Humpback Whale

Megaptera novaeangliae

Family Balaenopteridae (rorquals)

- ⊕ Worldwide
- ⊙ Coastal; open ocean during migration
- ↔ 18 m (59 ft)

Feeds on krill and small schooling fishes, consuming up to 1,360 kg (2,992 lb) a day. Frequently breaches and slaps water with flippers. Spends summer near poles and winter in tropics (e.g., Alaska and Hawaii). One of longest migrations of any mammal — 8,300 km (5,160 mi). Males promiscuous, competing for females with agonistic behaviors (chasing, tail and body thrashing). Best singer of whales; males may sing for hours and can be heard by conspecifics up to 30 km (19 mi) away. Estimated worldwide numbers 60,000–80,000.

Sperm Whale

Physeter macrocephalus

Family Physeteridae

- ⊕ Worldwide, latitude 60°N to 60°S
- ⊙ Polar to tropical oceans; open ocean
- ↔ Males 18 m (59 ft); females 11 m (36 ft)

Main food is large mesopelagic squid (including giant squid) but also eats sharks, skates and other fishes. Dives average 35 minutes but can last more than an hour. Foraging dives can be as deep as 2,000 m (6,600 ft). Calves once every 5 years. Weaning in 3 years or more. Matrilineal social unit, with females of same family sticking together: on average, 12 females and their young. Young males often group together until old enough to breed. Older males solitary, moving toward equator to mate.

- ⊕ Atlantic, Indian and Pacific Oceans
- ☉ Warm temperate, subtropical and tropical seas; shallow coastal habitats
- → 2.6 m (8.5 ft)

Long-beaked Common Dolphin

Delphinus capensis
Family Delphinidae (oceanic dolphins)

Small social units of 10–30 animals, which get together and form larger groups (usually 100–500, sometimes 1,000 or more). Breaches, porpoises and bow-rides. Primary diet is small schooling fishes (anchovies, hakes, pilchards and sardines), squid and krill. Dives to at least 280 m (910 ft) and can hold breath up to 8 minutes. Gestation 10–11 months; birthing interval 1–3 years. Lifespan 40 years.

- ⊕ Worldwide, latitude 60°N to 60°S
- ☉ Temperate, subtropical and tropical seas; usually open ocean; sometimes coastal water in northern Europe
- → 4 m (13 ft)

Risso's Dolphin

Grampus griseus
Family Delphinidae (oceanic dolphins)

Groups of usually 5–50; also found singly and in groups of thousands. May associate with bottlenose and Pacific white-sided dolphins and northern right whale dolphins, as well as gray whales. Feeds mainly at night on krill, cephalopods and schooling fishes (anchovies). Dives to at least 300 m (975 ft). Sometimes parasitized by cookiecutter sharks and lampreys. Lifespan 35 years. Big head and narrow tail stock; tall falcate dorsal fin. Adults pale gray to nearly white.

Short-finned Pilot Whale

Globicephala macrorhynchus
Family Delphinidae (oceanic dolphins)

- ⊕ Circumglobal
- ⊙ Tropical and temperate seas; usually offshore but sometimes near shore
- ↔ Males 7.3 m (24 ft); females 5.5 m (18 ft)

Groups of one male with up to eight females; these pods often join larger groups, which can number up to 50 animals. Groups spread out up to 1 km (0.6 mi) when hunting. Matrilineal social structure; females remain with family pod for life. Gestation 15 months; weans usually in 2 years. Lifespan 45 years for males, 60 years for females. Primary food squid, but also schooling fishes and pelagic octopuses; most hunting done in mesopelagic zone at depths of 305 m (991 ft). Bulbous head with no beak; dorsal fin far forward on body.

Pacific Whitesided Dolphin

Lagenorhynchus obliquidens
Family Delphinidae (oceanic dolphins)

- ⊕ Temperate and occasionally subtropical North Pacific, latitude 38°N to 47°N
- ⊙ Open ocean
- ↔ Males 2.5 m (8.1 ft); females 2.3 m (7.5 ft)

Social unit usually 10–100 but can number into thousands. Associates with northern right whale dolphins (*Lissodelphis borealis*) and Risso's dolphins. Does spectacular aerial acrobatics and likes bow-riding. Feeds on squid and small schooling fish (capelin, sardines, herring). Hunts cooperatively, herding schooling fishes. Dive time 6 minutes. Gestation 12 months; calves born in summer every other year. Lifespan around 40 years. Robust, with short beak and large falcate dorsal fin; sides and belly white, back and flukes black.

- ⊕ Worldwide
- ☉ Temperate and tropical seas, usually open ocean
- ↦ Males 6 m (20 ft); females 5 m (16 ft)

False Killer Whale

Pseudorca crassidens
Family Delphinidae
(oceanic dolphins)

Groups of 10–20; often join to form schools of 40–100 individuals. Groups spread out when hunting to increase chances of locating prey. Sometimes followed by oceanic whitetip sharks. Feeds on fishes and squid and small dolphins (on rare occasions). Feeds both day and night. Gestation 14–16 months; weans at 1.5–2 years. Female reproduces once every seven years. Lifespan 60 years. Slender, with cone-shaped head and no beak; pectoral fins have distinct bulge on front edge.

- ⊕ Worldwide
- ☉ Polar to tropical seas, usually coastal
- ↦ Males 10 m (33 ft); females 8.5 m (28 ft)

Killer Whale or Orca

Orcinus orca
Family Delphinidae
(oceanic dolphins)

Most wide-ranging of all cetaceans. Communal, forming groups of 2–15 individuals. Vocalizes to communicate and identify prey. Three distinct forms in North Pacific: residents, transients and offshores. Transient whales feed on marine mammals; residents prey on fish (primarily salmon); offshore orcas may specialize in shark-eating. Males live up to 60 years, females to 90. Molecular studies suggest at least three possible distinct orca species, including dwarf form in Antarctic.

Pantropical Spotted Dolphin

Stenella attenuata

Family Delphinidae (oceanic dolphins)

⊕ Worldwide
⊙ Tropical and subtropical oceans; usually open ocean
↔ 2.5 m (8 ft)

Forms group of 300–1,000 individuals or more. Mixes with spinner dolphins. Feeds on mesopelagic squid and fishes. Some movement, from more inshore in fall to offshore in spring. Gestation 11 months; weans at 1–2 years. Reproduces year-round; gives birth every 2.5–4 years (dependent on population). Longevity 46 years. Species most affected by tuna purse-seining. Long snout with white tip; no marks at birth but develops spots with age; dark area from head to tail flukes.

Atlantic Spotted Dolphin

Stenella frontalis

Family Delphinidae (oceanic dolphins)

⊕ Atlantic Ocean
⊙ Warm temperate to tropical seas; coastal and continental shelf; sometimes in open ocean
↔ 2.3 m (7.5 ft)

Forms groups of 5–15 but also up to 200 individuals. Sometimes associates with bottlenose dolphins. Frequently breaches, leaps and bow-rides. Feeds on small fishes, cephalopods and bottom-dwelling invertebrates. Flushes out buried prey by probing substrate with snout. Engages in shallow dives of usually less than 10 m (30 ft) but can reach depths of 60 m (195 ft). Holds breath up to 10 minutes. Gives birth every 1–5 years; weans in 1–5 years. Robust, with falcate dorsal fin midway along back; becomes darker and spotted with age.

- ⊕ Worldwide, latitude 35°N to 35°S
- ☉ Tropical and subtropical seas; shallow water to open ocean habitat
- ↔ 2 m (7 ft)

Long-snouted Spinner Dolphin

Stenella longirostris
Family Delphinidae (oceanic dolphins)

Forms large groups in open ocean, with pods of 35–100. Uses shallow bays as resting sites during day. Feeds at night on schooling fishes (lanternfish especially important), squid and sergestid shrimps, which make vertical migrations after dark. One subspecies feeds near coral reefs during day. Often associates with pantropical spotted dolphins and yellowfin tuna (*Thunnus albacares*). Gestation about 11 months; calving interval just over 2 years.

- ⊕ Worldwide, latitude 60°N to 45°S
- ☉ Temperate to tropical seas; coastal habitats and open ocean
- ↔ 3.8 m (12.5 ft)

Bottlenose Dolphin

Tursiops truncatus
Family Delphinidae (oceanic dolphins)

Social units of usually 2–15 individuals; may join together to form groups numbering several hundred. May associate with other cetaceans (e.g., pilot whales, other dolphins). Diet varies but includes schooling fishes, squid and benthic invertebrates. Uses echolocation to find and capture prey. Calves every 3–6 years; gestation 12 months; weans in 18–20 months. Lifespan 45 years for males, 50 for females. Inshore populations often smaller and lighter in color than those from offshore habitats.

California Sea Lion

Zalophus californianus

Family Otariidae (eared seals)

⊕ Gulf of Alaska, south to Mexico
⊙ Coastal rocky reefs
↔ Males 2.4 m (7.9 ft), 360 kg (792 lb); females smaller

Occurs singly or in groups. Feeds on fishes and squid. Average dive 3 minutes, longest around 10; dives as deep as 274 m (891 ft). Assembles, breeds and births on sandy beaches. Female gives birth to single pup after gestation of 11 months. Breeding and pupping takes place May–July. Males defend territory for 45 days, mating with many females. Pups wean in 12–36 weeks. Eaten by white sharks and orca. Lifespan up to 25 years for females.

Dugong

Dugong dugon

Family Dugongidae

⊕ East Africa and Red Sea, east to Vanuatu, north to Japan and south to Australia
⊙ Coastal and insular waters; bays, mangrove channels, seagrass meadows
↕ 1–39 m (3.3–127 ft)
↔ 4 m (13 ft), average 400 kg (880 lb); maximum reported weight 1,016 kg (2,240 lbs)

Forms groups of 2–200. Feeds on seagrass, using muscular lip to dig grasses out of substrate. Males exhibit aggression toward each other (tail-thrashing, lunging) when competing for females. Calves in shallows, on sandbars and in estuaries. Nurses for about 1.5 years. Calf and mother remain together for about 6 years. Can live more than 70 years. Some local populations threatened. Fluked, dolphin-like tail.

⊕ North Carolina south to Florida (where most occur) and west to Louisiana
⊙ Shallow fresh, brackish and sea water; coastal seagrass meadows, rivers, springs
↔ 4 m (13 ft), average 590 kg (1,300 lb); maximum reported weight 1,400 kg (3,000 lbs)

Florida Manatee
Trichechus manatus latirostris
Family Trichechidae

Solitary or in aggregations. Feeds on seagrass, algae and even some terrestrial plant material. Spends 6–8 hours a day feeding. Rests on surface or bottom for 2–12 hours a day. Can hold breath for up to 20 minutes. Males pursue females in heat; female mates with one or more males. One calf (occasionally twins) produced every 2–5 years; gestation 12 months. Calves remain with mother for more than two years. Good sense of hearing; uses vocalizations to maintain contact. Population size approximately 5,000. Rounded, paddle-shaped tail.

Chapter 8

The Open Ocean

A vast blue emptiness — that's how the open ocean may first appear when you don mask and snorkel and leap off a boat far from shore. But look closely and be patient. In addition to the tiny building blocks of the entire marine ecosystem, larger, more charismatic sea creatures await beneath the waves.

These waters teem with microscopic plants (phytoplankton) and animals (zooplankton). Plankton form the food pyramid's base and ensure that life flourishes in this and other marine habitats. Even so, species richness in the open ocean (also referred to as the pelagic zone) is lower than on coral reefs, with only about 10 percent of all known species occurring in this biome. Some of the larger predatory fishes that characterize the open ocean include a variety of sharks, such as whale sharks (*Rhincodon typus*), white sharks (*Carcharodon carcharias*), makos (*Isurus* spp.), threshers (*Alopias* spp.), blue sharks (*Prionace glauca*), oceanic whitetips (*Carcharhinus longimanus*), silky sharks (*C. falciformis*) and hammerheads (*Sphryna* spp.). The pelagic stingray (*Pteroplatytrygon violacea*) is another unique cartilaginous oceanic fish that lives high in the water column, unlike other stingrays, which spend most of their time in repose on the seafloor. Not surprisingly, the pelagic stingray is well adapted to life in open water. It has a large liver that makes it more positively buoyant and it swims by flapping its pectoral fins (like a manta or eagle ray) rather than undulating its disc margin like the bottom-dwelling stingrays.

Fascinating bony fishes also call the open ocean home, including the lancetfishes (*Alepisaurus* spp.), flying fishes (family Exocoetidae), rainbow runners (*Elagatis bipinnulata*), pilotfish (*Naucrates ductor*), banded rudderfish (*Seriola zonata*), pomfrets (family Bramidae), oceanic triggerfish (*Canthidermis maculata*), oilfish (*Ruvettus pretiosus*), ocean sunfish (*Mola mola*) and game fish such as tuna (*Thunnus* spp.), wahoo (*Acanthocybium solandri*) and marlin and sailfish (family Istiophoridae). While they favor the open ocean, some of these fish (both the bony and the cartilaginous) occasionally visit coral reefs to find food or to be cleaned of parasites.

Pelagic fish must expend their calories efficiently. Food sources are few and far between in the open ocean, and long foraging and spawning migrations are often required. Tuna (*Thunnus* spp.) are the epitome of hydrodynamic efficiency. They move through the water constantly at a relatively high rate of speed. They have no

An Atlantic sailfish (*Istiophorus albicans*) feeding on sardines. Some consider this the same species as the Indo-Pacific sailfish (*I. platypterus*). Mexico.

swim bladder, meaning that they would sink if they stopped swimming. A tuna's fusiform (torpedo-like) body shape, smooth skin and finlets on the back and underside all help reduce calorie-costing drag. The lunate (half-moon) shape of the tail produces maximum thrust and less turbulence along the fins' edges. While the fish is swimming, only its tail and caudal peduncle move back and forth.

Tuna also have a highly advanced circulatory system that includes counter-current heat exchangers — rete mirable — that reduce heat loss from the blood. This keeps their body temperature above ambient. So yes, they are functionally "warm-blooded," an impressive trait shared with mackerel sharks (family Lamnidae, including the white, mako and porbeagle sharks) and threshers (family Alopiidae). Because tuna have a higher metabolic rate than other fishes, they also have a larger gill-surface area (seven to nine times that of a trout) and maintain a higher blood pressure and a greater concentration of hemoglobin. These physiological adaptations allow transfer of more oxygen to the muscles, better fueling this extraordinary fish's internal engine.

Most tuna live in schools, with some species forming groups that can number up to 5,000 individual fish. Schooling helps to further improve hydrodynamic efficiency. Groups of tuna also hunt cooperatively, overwhelming and confusing schooling prey fishes. Their migrations are epic — the larger tuna species travel thousands of miles from feeding to spawning grounds.

An oceanic whitetip shark (*Carcharhinus longimanus*), the quintessential open-ocean predator. Hawaii.

The oceanic whitetip shark employs different strategies to survive in the open ocean. Its very large pectoral fins provide extra lift, so it need not swim as rapidly as some other sharks to avoid sinking. Unlike the tuna, the whitetip sculls lazily through the water, throwing its long heterocercal tail (long top lobe, short bottom lobe) and much of its body from side to side as it swims. It boldly investigates any potential meal and is highly opportunistic, often feeding on dead or wounded animals near the ocean's surface. It also uses stealth and cunning to capture faster prey species, including lancetfishes, mahi mahi, oarfishes, barracudas, marlin and even tuna. Some scientists believe that the bright white patches on the oceanic whitetip's fins may resemble a school of fish from a distance. This pseudo-school could serve to lure hungry piscivores closer; before they can realize their mistake, the formidable whitetip subdues them with a quick burst of speed.

Many open-ocean fishes are vertical migrators. Bigeye tuna (*Thunnus obesus*) swim within 100 meters (330 feet) of the surface during the day but dive to 500 meters (1,650 feet) at night to feed along the sound-scattering layer. This is a concentrated layer of plankton and other marine organisms, so named because it reflects and scatters sonar sound waves. White sharks also make deep dives, swimming along the thermocline as they stay alert for tasty waterlogged whale carcasses that have got "hung up" on cooler, heavier water masses. Meanwhile, the bigeye thresher shark (*Alopias superciliosus*) moves from the cool water below the thermocline during daytime to warmer, shallower water at night. (Countercurrent heat exchangers keep the brain and eyes warm, which could allow these organs to function more effectively at depth.) The infamous cookie-cutter shark (*Isistius brasiliensis*) is also a vertical migrator, at night moving from its deepwater diurnal haunts — below 1,000 meters (3,300 feet) — all the way up to the surface. Averaging only 45 centimeters (18 inches) long, it fearlessly ambushes much larger predatory fishes, seals and cetaceans, from which it bites neat plugs of flesh with bandsaw-like teeth.

The big blue is also home to a variety of marine mammals. Baleen whales such as the blue whale (*Balaenoptera musculus*), fin whale (*B. physalus*) and humpback whale (*Megaptera novaeangliae*) move majestically through this biome. Sperm whales (*Physeter macrocephalus*), the largest of all carnivores, cross ocean basins effortlessly and plumb deep ocean trenches hunting giant tentacled prey. Elusive and poorly understood, the beaked whales (family Ziphiidae) are also signature oceanic species that are very rarely encountered within sight of land. A number of dolphin species, including the rough-toothed (*Steno bredanensis*), Fraser's (*Lagenodelphis hosei*) and pantropical spotted dolphins (*Stenella attenuata*), can also be found far offshore in tropical waters beyond the continental shelf.

Sometimes these intriguing fishes and cetaceans make forays to the seaward edge of reefs along coasts or islands or near seamounts. Certain dive sites are renowned for sightings of big pelagic fishes adjacent to reef habitats. For example, divers are drawn to islands in the Eastern Pacific — such as the Galápagos, Socorro and Cocos Islands — to observe open-ocean sharks, cetaceans and occasionally even striped marlin (*Tetrapturus audax*) and sailfish

By-the-wind sailors (*Velella velalla*) cluster together in the thousand. These jellyfish, anthomedusans in the family Valellidae, float on the surface miles offshore. They drift by "sailing" with the wind, their tentacles dangling beneath them. California.

(*Istiophorus platypterus*). Pelagic predators may also visit reef slopes to take advantage of the cleaning services of reef fishes. Pelagic thresher sharks (*Alopias pelagicus*) frequent seamounts in the Philippines to have parasites removed by wrasses, and ocean sunfish visit reef slopes 40 meters (132 feet) deep near Bali, Indonesia, to be cleaned by schooling bannerfish (*Heniochus diphreutes*) and adult emperor angelfish (*Pomacanthus imperator*).

Fishes have long been known to aggregate near flotsam in the open ocean, whether it's a floating palm leaf, logs or even trash. Manmade "fish-attracting devices" (FADs) are installed by fishermen and scientists specifically to attract marine life. Potential prey fishes use the floating objects as a refuge, while predators regularly inspect them for hidden quarry.

Countering all the life we've discovered above, sections of the open ocean are indeed biotically impoverished. Barren areas cover approximately 20 percent of the world's oceans and occur mostly on either side of the equator, in subtropical gyres. Unfortunately, NOAA scientists believe these "ocean deserts" are increasing in size, possibly because of climate change. The primary reason for the lack of life in these areas is that there are fewer primary producers — the all-important phytoplankton — and where there are few producers, there are even fewer consumers.

Sargassum Frogfish

Histrio histrio

Family Antennariidae (frogfishes)

⊕ Circumglobal; tropical and subtropical seas (not reported from Eastern Pacific)
⊙ Open ocean in *Sargassum* algae rafts
↧ Usually near surface; post-larval individuals as deep as 600 m (1,950 ft)
↔ 19 cm (7.5 in)

Solitary. Extremely opportunistic, ingesting any fishes, worms or crustaceans that can be swallowed whole. Also extremely cannibalistic. Adult male and female come together to produce egg raft, which is pelagic and contains thousands of eggs. May spawn every 3–40 days. Adults fed on by dolphinfish and sharks. Inflates with water or air when threatened.

Smallhead Flying Fish

Cheilopogon pinnatibarbatus californicus

Family Exocoetidae (flying fish)

⊕ Oregon to Baja, Gulf of California and Revillagigedo Islands
⊙ Open ocean and coastal habitats
↧ 1–10 m (3.3–33 ft)   ↔ 48 cm (19 in)

Large pectoral and pelvic fins enable fish to leap and glide for hundreds of meters just above water's surface. Can change direction and altitude while gliding (flying fish species with large pectoral fins only, known as "two-wing gliders," travel short distances in straight line). Feeds on zooplankton. Eggs have filaments that stick to floating debris and algae. Important food for dolphinfish, tunas, billfishes, cetaceans and seabirds.

⊕ Peru, Chile and off Galápagos Islands
☉ Open ocean and coastal habitats
↧ 1–200 m (3.3–650 ft)   ↤ 40 cm (16 in)

Pacific Sardine

Sardinops sagax

Family Clupeidae (herring, sardines, shad and relatives)

Forms large schools. Feeds mainly on zooplankton but also some phytoplankton. Spawns twice a year: July–September and February–March. Some migrate into cooler areas during summer and back toward equator in fall. Food for many pelagic predators, including sharks, tuna, seabirds and marine mammals. May live up to 25 years. Similar forms (lineages) from South Africa, east to California and Canadian coast, north to Japan and south to New Zealand.

⊕ Circumglobal; tropical seas
☉ Coastal habitats (as adults); juveniles up to 25 cm (9.8 in) pelagic; rarely if ever around coral reefs
↧ 1–100 m (3.3–325 ft)   ↤ 1.5 m (4.9 ft)

African Pompano

Alectis ciliaris

Family Carangidae (trevallies or jacks)

Solitary. Feeds on variety of crustaceans, cephalopods and small fishes, in open water and off bottom. Juveniles have long filamentous dorsal and anal rays that may mimic medusae of a sea jelly (some of which have a venomous sting). Preyed upon by sharks, mackerel and tunas.

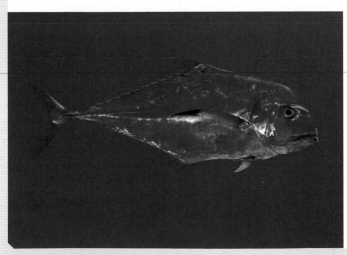

Almaco Jack

Seriola rivoliana
Family Carangidae
(trevallies or jacks)

⊕ Circumglobal; tropical and subtropical seas
⊙ Open ocean, outer reef slopes, bank reefs, seamounts
↓ 5–160 m (16–520 ft)   ↔ 1.6 m (5.2 ft)

Solitary or in small to moderate-sized schools. Juveniles hang near flotsam, including Sargassum rafts. Feeds mainly on fishes (schooling species primarily), but also squid and crustaceans (shrimp, crabs). Groups engage in coordinated attacks on grouping prey, sometimes together with other predatory fishes. Occasionally chafes against sharks, maybe to remove parasites or possibly a case of mobbing, in which fish attempt to irritate and drive off a potential predator. Spawns offshore, producing pelagic eggs.

Dolphinfish

Coryphaena hippurus
Family Coryphaenidae
(dolphinfishes)

⊕ Circumglobal; tropical and subtropical seas
⊙ Open ocean
↓ 1–85 m (3.3–276 ft)   ↔ 2.1 m (6.9 ft); male larger than female

Solitary or in groups. Varied diet includes pelagic fishes, benthic fishes and juveniles of large pelagic species such as tuna, billfishes and jacks; also mysid shrimp and squid. Male has squared-off forehead. Females and small males spend time near floating objects; males live in open water, traveling between female groups. Fast-growing: sexually mature in less than a year; most live less than two years. Fed on by sharks, tuna, marlin, swordfish and marine mammals. Also called mahi mahi and dorado.

- Circumglobal; tropical to warm temperate seas
- Open ocean, occasionally near reef drop-offs
- 1–253 m (3.3–822 ft); usually less than 20 m (65 ft)
- 2.5 m (8.2 ft)

Wahoo

Acanthocybium solandri

Family Scombridae
(mackerels and tuna)

Usually solitary; sometimes in loose groups. Highly mobile pelagic predator. Chases down variety of fish prey; occasionally eats squid. Can reach speeds of 78 kph (48 mph). Seasonal migrations may be longer than 1,000 km (621 mi). Spawning season during summer months in Gulf of Mexico. Spawns every 5–6 days during this period; large female produces up to 1.67 million eggs per spawning event. Fast-growing; most live less than two years, although can live as long as nine years. Adults preyed upon by mako sharks and marlin.

- East Africa and Red Sea, east to Fiji, north to Japan and south to Australia
- Open ocean; sometimes large lagoons, reef faces, slopes
- 10–70 m (33–228 ft)
- 2.4 m (7.9 ft)

Narrow-barred Spanish Mackerel

Scomberomorus commerson
Family Scombridae (mackerels & tuna)

Usually in small schools. Fish-eater (mainly schooling species such as anchovies and jacks) but will also eat squid and shrimp. Feeds both day and night. Some populations migratory, others are not. Spawns October–December off Great Barrier Reef; in other areas, spawning season is longer. Spawns in late afternoon; females spawn every 2–6 days. Flesh can be toxic.

Yellowfin Tuna

Thunnus albacares
Family Scombridae
(mackerels and tuna)

- ⊕ Circumglobal; tropical and subtropical seas
- ⊙ Open ocean; sometimes near coasts
- ↧ 1–100 m (3.3–330 ft); usually above thermocline but sometimes below it
- ↔ 2.8 m (9.2 ft)

School-forming; groups with similar-sized species (e.g., skipjack and bigeye tuna). Associates with dolphins. Often near floating debris and around FADs (may use them to navigate). Feeds on fishes (including flying fish), cephalopods and crustaceans. Reproduces year-round but peaks in summer or when food (e.g., anchovies) abundant. Most spawning at night. Preyed upon by sharks, including cookie-cutter shark, which leaves tell-tale gouges in flesh. Differs from closely related species by having yellow finlets on back.

Atlantic Sailfish

Istiophorus albicans
Family Istiophoridae (billfishes)

- ⊕ Tropical and temperate Atlantic, including Mediterranean
- ⊙ Open ocean; also nearshore
- ↧ Usually above thermocline but occasionally at greater depths
- ↔ 3.15 m (10.3 ft)

Solitary or in groups of 3–30; groups form around clumped prey. Young may form dense schools. Adult's main food pelagic bony fishes, but also eats squid and benthic fishes. Stuns schooling fishes with bill. Migratory: moves into cooler waters during summer months, then back toward equator with cooler conditions and strong winds. During spawning period, one or more males follow female. Spawns near water's surface; eggs pelagic. Very similar to Indo-Pacific sailfish (*I. platypterus*).

⊕ East Africa and Red Sea; west coast of North and South America, north to Japan and south to New Zealand and Cape of Good Hope

⊙ Pelagic; warm temperate, subtropical and tropical seas

↧ 1–290 m (3.3–943 ft)   ↔ 4.2 m (13.7 ft)

Striped Marlin
Tetrapturus audax
Family Istiophoridae (billfishes)

Usually solitary but in small groups during spawning season. May also aggregate around clumped prey. Diet mainly bony fishes but also some squid. Sometimes swims slowly at surface with upper lobe of tail breaking water. Usually swims above thermocline. Some populations exhibit certain degree of site fidelity; others migrate and may travel more than 2,000 km (1,242 mi). Young marlin eaten by many piscivorous fishes, including tuna and dolphinfish. Adults have few enemies, with the exception of large sharks (makos) and killer whales.

⊕ Circumtropical

⊙ Coastal and outer reefs; mainly open ocean; sometimes near reef faces, slopes

↧ 1–480 m (3.3–1,560 ft)   ↔ 3 m (10 ft)

Ocean Sunfish
Mola mola
Family Molidae (ocean sunfishes)

Solitary. Feeds mostly on large zooplankton. During day found near surface, where it often "basks," lying on side. At night dives down to near thermocline to hunt prey. Uses dorsal and anal fins like wings to swim. Most fecund of all vertebrates: female lays as many as 300 million eggs at a time! Often shy of divers but can be approached when being cleaned by bannerfishes and wrasses. Sometimes eaten by killer whales and sharks. Bycatch of drift gill nets.

Chapter 9

Conservation of Tropical Marine Ecosystems

Those who have dived for any length of time are likely to have witnessed changes in the condition of various marine ecosystems. Ocean habitats are intricately linked with those on shore, meaning that the environmental "sins" committed on land typically have an impact on the world's seas. We once believed the oceans' vast size could buffer the pollutants spewed from factories, cruise ships and coastal cities. We also thought that fish stocks would provide an endless supply of protein for the planet's populations. Only in recent decades have we come to the realization that marine ecosystems are fragile and that ocean residents cannot continue to take the many pressures we have placed upon them.

Consider the world's coral reefs. Some of the changes seen over the years are the result of natural succession and processes. For example, a coral community may change composition because a certain coral species overgrows a less vigorous relative. Likewise, a fish species may become more or less abundant with natural fluctuations in larval settlement. Cyclones and hurricanes can cause extensive damage to coral reefs, as did the recent tsunami in Indonesia, Thailand and Sri Lanka. Natural events affect reefs in both small and large ways, but many of the changes we see in the complexion of modern coral-reef communities have been brought about by human influences. In fact, it is estimated that 57 percent of coral reefs around the world are threatened by human activity. In Southeast Asia, 82 percent of the reefs are thought to be at high to very high risk. Caribbean reefs are also in trouble, with 61 percent considered to be at high to very high risk.

Coral reefs are not the only marine ecosystems negatively affected by anthropogenic (human) causes. Kelp forests on rocky reefs in temperate waters have degraded in recent decades because of warmer water temperatures, from disturbances to once-balanced relationships between kelp herbivores and their predators, and from land-borne pollutants. Oceanic habitats are threatened by huge debris fields that include tons of plastic. The "Great Pacific Garbage Patch" is such an area — currents of the North Pacific Gyre have trapped chemical sludge and plastic materials in a pelagic raft of debris. The plastic breaks down into particulates that are suspended in the

---

This coral reef was destroyed by a cyclone. North-eastern Australia.

sea's surface layer; they are ingested by zooplankton and small bait fishes and work their way through the food chain, doing damage all along the way. Large oceanic fishes, especially sharks, are threatened by fishing practices that lay waste to pelagic predator communities. According to the International Union for Conservation of Nature, about one-third of all oceanic shark and ray species are endangered.

In this section we will examine some of the major threats to tropical marine ecosystems and conclude with suggestions to help the oceans that we love.

Land-Based Pollution

On a local level, much of humans' impact on reefs is related to coastal development. For example, studies found a 40 to 60 percent reduction in coral diversity on Indonesian reefs subjected to land-based pollution such as sewage, sedimentation and industrial waste. Whether it's a village or a tourist resort, the resulting pollutants increase nutrient levels on adjacent coral reefs, leading to more vigorous macroalgae growth. While the symbiotic algae inside the coral's tissues are reef benefactors, external macroalgae are usually enemies to stony corals. They compete with them for space and will overgrow scleractinian colonies, shading them from life-giving sunlight. Algae can suppress zooxanthellae photosynthesis, cause hypoxia in areas where the coral and algae are in contact, and may even spread disease to neighboring corals. Coastal agricultural activities can exacerbate reef degradation. For example, runoff from fertilizer used at date palm plantations has stimulated growth of macroalgae on coral reefs off Papua New Guinea. The algae (*Padina* sp.) have overgrown and choked out staghorn coral like virulent weeds in a backyard garden.

Development also contributes to sediment pollution. Terrestrial sediments dislodged by dredging, coastal construction, mining, logging and farming wash into coastal waters and smother corals. Most of the reef-building stony corals cannot shed these sediments. Rampant coastal development is also harmful to adjacent seagrass beds and mangrove forests that are important to the health of reef communities.

Overexploitation

Small-scale artisanal fisheries have been important to coastal and insular human populations for millennia. In most cases these fishers did not have the equipment to do extensive damage to local fish communities, and it was to their

Coral overgrown with algae, likely because of increased nutrient levels from pollution and/or warmer water temperatures. Hawaii.

benefit not to cause irreparable harm to the coral reefs that supported them. Now many reefs sustain pressure not only from indigenous fisherman but also from large vessels operated by companies from faraway lands that exploit areas with little regard for the long-term health of the habitat or marine fauna. Such newcomers could be trap-netters that move into an area or a primitive "mother ship" with an associated flotilla of canoes that overexploit the marine resources on one reef before moving off to another to continue their carnage.

A shocking case of overexploitation is the global shark fishery. In the past, sharks were hunted for their livers and for their flesh. More recently sharks have been targeted for their fins, used as an ingredient in sharkfin soup, which is popular in certain Asian countries. This delicacy commands high prices, and as a result the shark-finning industry has burgeoned. Its methods are cruel beyond measure: The shark's fins are hacked off while it's still alive, then the mutilated fish is dumped overboard. It sinks to the bottom — unable to swim and thus unable to feed — where it starves and/or suffocates, eventually to be consumed by scavengers. An estimated 26 to 73 million sharks are being finned yearly.

A high-tech modern-day commercial tuna-fishing boat using a huge seine net. Baja, Mexico.

In some areas where sharks were once abundant, they are now scarce or even absent altogether. It has been estimated that the populations of certain larger shark species — bull, dusky, oceanic whitetip, tiger, and smooth and scalloped hammerhead sharks — have plummeted by 95 percent since 1970. The reduction of shark populations has had a top-down effect on the rest of the food chain. For example, mollusk numbers in US coastal waters have declined significantly because there are fewer large sharks. The reason? Large sharks eat cownose rays (*Rhinoptera bonasus*), and these rays love to eat shellfish. With fewer sharks, there are more rays around (an estimated tenfold increase) to consume scallops and clams.

On many reefs, divers rarely see large groupers, snappers or humphead wrasses anymore. These species are being captured for the live reef-fish food trade. Big predatory fishes that form spawning groups — often in predictable places at specific times — are easily targeted by fishermen. Two or three years of intensive fishing can result in elimination of large numbers of broodstock, which has an enormous impact on the overall abundance of these species.

Fish populations in the open ocean are also at risk. The threat comes from fisheries that employ immense factory ships. Giant purse-seiners target the food supply of predators (e.g., sardines, anchovies, herring) as well as the predators themselves (e.g., tuna), while long-lining vessels target billfishes, tuna and sharks. The bycatch includes dolphins, sea turtles, and seabirds, although many countries are making efforts to reduce the number of sea mammals killed by tuna fishermen. No longer are the fleets restricted in how far they can fish from their home base. Because the catch can now be processed, frozen and stored on these vessels, they can travel greater distances. Some scientists estimate that the biomass of large predatory fishes has dropped by 90 percent since industrialized fishing began.

Destructive Fishing Methods

Blast (bomb) fishing likely damages more coral reefs than any other fishing method. It has been reported in at least 40 countries and is most widespread in Southeast Asia. Fishermen use inexpensive homemade bombs that are dropped into the water among schooling fishes. The explosion damages the fishes' swim bladders; divers then enter the water and collect the stunned or dead fish. The blast not only incapacitates the focal fishes but also eradicates non-targeted juveniles and invertebrates. On shallow reefs, the explosions cause incredible damage to the reef structure, blowing portions of the reef into rubble. Coral spat (larvae) are unable to settle on the unstable rubble.

Cyanide fishing also has a negative impact on coral reefs. Cyanide was originally employed to capture fishes for the aquarium trade, but in the 1970s its use broadened to include stunning larger predators (namely groupers and humphead wrasses) and rock lobsters for food. The live reef-fish food trade has become a large industry in the tropical Indo-Pacific: more than 30,000 metric tons of live reef fish are imported annually to a variety of Asian markets.

Cyanide is relatively cheap and easy to use. Crushed sodium cyanide tablets are placed in a squirt bottle along with seawater, then the solution is squirted into coral crevices or over coral colonies. Doped fish shoot or float out from their hiding places and are netted by the collector. Collectors will also break up corals to gain access to stunned fishes hiding within. Perhaps as many as 75 percent of the fish die within hours of being collected with cyanide, and even more die later. Far worse is the extensive "collateral environmental damage." The poisonous cyanide cloud can kill live corals and other sessile invertebrates. Cyanide also impedes zooxanthellae photosynthesis, causing the coral to expel these symbiotic algae, which can result in coral tissue detachment and increased microbial

A fish trap used by native Dominica islanders. This very indiscriminate method of fishing kills many reef species that are not good food fish. Those deemed not tasty are simply thrown away.

infections. Speaking of a nearly dead reef on which cyanide fishers were methodically working, biologist Mark Erdman states, "It appears the sad fate of these reefs that they may be cyanided until they are reduced to barren carbonate skeletons."

Coral Collection and Mining

Coral is collected for a number of different purposes. One of the most destructive practices is coral mining. In the Maldives large areas of reef are commonly removed for construction projects. The calcium carbonate (i.e., limestone) is used to make cement and building materials and for roads.

Live corals are harvested and bleached for souvenirs and curios. Fortunately this practice is not as widespread as it once was, because of increased public awareness. While it used to be common to use coral skeletons as decorations in marine aquariums, most aquarists now use faux corals or maintain "living-reef" aquariums. These are composed of "live" rock — typically large chunks collected from major rubble tracts — and live coral colonies. More than 400,000 pieces are brought in annually by the largest importer (the United States) alone. Aquarists have made great advances in propagating live stony and soft corals, and in the future, mariculture may provide most of the coral colonies available in the aquarium trade.

Echinoderm Issues

The disappearance and the overabundance of certain echinoderms has also affected coral reefs. In the 1980s and '90s there were mass die-offs of *Diadema* sea urchins in the tropical Atlantic. Sea urchins keep algae crops on coral reefs in check. If their numbers dwindle, algae flourish, and where macroalgae grow, stony corals do not thrive. In Jamaica, after a mass mortality event of sea urchins, macroalgae coverage increased to 95 percent and coral cover was reduced as much as 60 percent.

The crown-of-thorns sea star (*Acanthaster planci*) is another echinoderm that has had an impact on coral reefs. Unlike the sea urchin, whose presence helps keep reefs healthy, when there is a radical increase in *A. planci* numbers, coral reefs suffer. Growing to around a meter (3.3 feet) in diameter, these large sea stars are predators of stony corals. On most reefs they are uncommon and have little influence on stony coral communities, but certain areas — for example, the Great Barrier Reef — have experienced population booms that have resulted in significant

Longspine sea urchins (*Diadema* sp.) are important herbivores on the reef. They graze on algae, helping to prevent the algae from exploding and smothering stony corals. Their long spines can inflict a painful wound. Philippines.

reduction in coral cover. The crown-of-thorns has large spines on its body that exude a toxin, so it has few predators. These sea stars are eaten by triton snails, the humphead wrasse, a few larger triggerfishes and pufferfishes. Overexploitation has reduced the numbers of these first two species in many places.

The Big Problems

There are also overarching global problems relating to climate change that may possibly cause the demise of modern coral reefs.

In recent times, as in the past, ocean temperatures have risen. As mentioned in the preface, corals and their associated zooxanthellae algae are sensitive to thermal shock. If the water gets too warm, corals evacuate their life-giving algae. Coral bleaching has been occurring with more regularity in the past couple of decades. There have been massive bleaching events in places such as the Maldives, the Great Barrier Reef and Micronesia. If water temperatures do not remain high for too long, the corals can be re-inoculated with their algae symbionts and begin to grow again; or, if all their tissue is not destroyed, they can regrow on dead portions of the colony. But if the thermal stress continues, the stony corals die and macroalgae move in. Macroalgae make it difficult for stony coral larvae to settle out onto the substrate and for coral communities to regenerate, especially in areas where herbivores have been overfished.

Generally speaking, coral bleaching occurs when the water temperature exceeds summer maximums by 1° to 2°C (1.8° to 3.6°F) for several weeks or more. That being said, temperature tolerance in stony corals varies between species and from one location to another. There is also a correlation between the coral's growth type and its resistance to heat stress; finely branching species tend to be more susceptible to water warming than massive, boulder-type growth forms.

Along with the stress caused by warmer water comes increased frequency of major disease outbreaks. Some of these include black band disease (thought to be related to cyanobacteria), white syndrome diseases (including white band, white pox and white plague, all thought to be bacterial in nature), skeletal-eroding band disease (caused by a ciliated protozoan). On healthy reefs these diseases are usually not a threat to coral communities, but in areas exposed to high water temperatures and pollutants, pathogens can destroy the already reeling invertebrates.

As if thermal stress and disease were not enough, ocean acidification may be even more dangerous to reefs and ocean biodiversity as a whole. Scientists have estimated that over the past 250 years there has been a 30 percent increase in the acidity of the oceans, and they speculate that the worst is yet to come. The phenomenon of higher acidity (lower pH) is thought to be occurring because of an increase in carbon dioxide in the earth's atmosphere. If carbon dioxide emissions are not reduced, geologists and climatologists hypothesize that ocean acidity will increase another 50 percent by 2100, resulting in near total demise of coral reefs in the middle of this century.

Why does this change in ocean chemistry cause problems for coral reefs? It affects the coral's ability to create its calcium carbonate skeleton. If the pH drops too much, corals cannot lay down their calcareous skeletons or the skeletons will become fragile and nonfunctional. Rising ocean acidity will not only affect stony corals, it will also be lethal to coralline algae, shelled mollusks, crustaceans and echinoderms, as well as a host of other, smaller plants and animals that are important in the ocean's food chain.

Coral bleaching. The hard coral (*Pocillopora* sp.) on the left is white because it has lost its symbiotic zooxanthellae algae. Warmer water temperatures caused by climate change can stress corals. If sea temperatures don't return to normal soon, the coral will die. Kiribati.

Diseased brain coral (probably *Colpophyllia natans*). The white (left) half of the coral is afflicted with white plague disease, caused by a bacterial pathogen. Belize.

A diver soars over sea fans, sponges and soft corals on a vibrant shallow reef. Belize is a popular Caribbean scuba destination, and the government's protection plan is working.

Some Success Stories

Okay, enough gloom and doom. Thankfully there are some success stories in marine conservation. One involves the goliath grouper (*Epinephelus itajara*), one of the largest bony fishes found in the tropics. This beast, which can grow to 364 kilograms (800 pounds), was fished to near extinction. A moratorium was placed on catching this fish in Florida in 1990 and in the Gulf of Mexico in 1992. Since then it has made a comeback on the reefs of southern Florida. And there are many benefits to the return of the goliath grouper. It is, for example, one of a few species that will eat invasive lionfishes. Goliath groupers are also good for tourism. Resident groupers draw scuba enthusiasts, who always get a buzz when they encounter these inquisitive gentle giants.

The story of the giant clam (family Tridacnidae) has both bad and good elements. Heavily exploited for food for many years, their numbers decreased precipitously, with some species disappearing altogether from certain areas. But mariculture has brought many tridacnids back from the brink, as well as providing a living for many island peoples. In the Western Pacific, giant clams are being raised for food and for the aquarium trade, taking the pressure off wild populations.

Some conservation success stories involve ecotourism. Though an increase in tourism can lead to problems for reefs such as waste and sedimentation, it can also help to save them. Governments are more likely to protect coral reefs when they contribute to the economy of a region. For example, in Belize it is estimated that coral reefs contribute 12 to 15 percent of the country's GDP. Most of this money comes from the many scuba divers who visit every year to explore the beautiful healthy marine habitats. As a result, the government of Belize is doing more to protect its coral reefs.

In some cases it is not government but local dive operators who are protecting their waters. For example, at certain resorts in the Philippines the employees police the surrounding reefs and deter blast fishing. Resorts that depend on ecotourism are careful about anchor placement or use permanent mooring buoys to minimize coral damage. Because much of the local population relies on the resorts for jobs and ecotourism dollars, they are quick to protect their valuable reef resources.

Making a Difference

As ambassadors for coral reefs and the world's oceans, it is up to us to be proactive, not just reactive. Help sustain healthy oceans and the diversity of life that inhabits them. Here are some things you can do.

Make Smart Seafood Choices

Support sources of sustainable seafood. Learn more about the best seafood choices, good alternatives and species to avoid: www.montereybayaquarium.org and www.fishchoice.com.

Don't eat shark. Just say no and discourage barbarous shark-finning practices by decreasing the demand.

While raising marine animals for food may seem like a good idea, there are drawbacks to some forms of mariculture. The construction of facilities for raising shrimp in coastal ponds has led to destruction of mangrove habitat in Thailand, India, Costa Rica and Ecuador. Salmon densely packed into floating pens have a greater incidence of disease and parasites. And these problems don't limit themselves to captive salmon populations but spread to adjacent wild stocks too.

These high concentrations of fish also produce a tremendous amount of untreated waste, as well as byproducts of the pharmaceuticals used to treat the fish. In addition, huge quantities of wild forage fish (e.g., sardines and herring) are removed from the sea just to feed farm-raised fish (e.g., salmon and tuna). Most conservationists would tell you to avoid captive-raised salmon for these reasons.

Support Protected Areas
A marine protected area (MPA) is a section of coastline or reef where fishing and other activities that can damage the habitat are managed, while in a fish replenishment area (FRA) no fishing is allowed at all. In both cases the goal is to maintain biodiversity. In the MPA or FRA, resident adult fishes (broodstock) can supply vast tracts of unmanaged coastline with their pelagic progeny, ensuring preservation of fish populations on reefs in and around the protected areas. In marine reserves, the density of fishes targeted by fisheries can be more than twice as high.

Choose Captive-Raised Fishes for Aquariums
Marine aquarists should always purchase captive-raised marine animals such as seahorses. They should also support groups that promote net-caught fishing — in other words, no cyanide.

Think Twice about Souvenirs
Don't buy coral-reef souvenirs, tortoiseshell sunglasses, cowrie necklaces, dried sea stars and other such trinkets as souvenirs.

Lose the Plastic
Reduce the amount of plastics that end up in our oceans, where they do untold amounts of damage.

Never Release Marine Plants or Animals into the Wild
Adding any organism to an area where it does not naturally occur can have dire ecological consequences. It may, for example, cause the demise of another species with similar resource requirements. A captive fish released into the wild can also expose wild populations to pathogens and parasites not found in the area, which could lead to catastrophic disease epidemics. One ecological disaster that may have resulted from aquarium releases is the lionfish invasion in the tropical Atlantic Ocean. Another example is the spread of the green macroalgae *Caulerpa taxifolia* in the Mediterranean, which has choked out indigenous marine plants and sessile invertebrates.

Conch shells for sale as souvenirs, San Pedro town, Ambergris Caye, Belize.

Use Clean Energy

We should all do our part to reduce carbon emissions. For good suggestions on how to do this, as well as other ways to help save our seas, download this PDF: http://saveourseas.com/content/pdf/ecotips.pdf.

Steer Clear of Traditional Chinese Remedies

The treatments prescribed by traditional Chinese medicine (TCM) include a variety of marine organisms. For example, the trade in seahorses for TCM has almost single-handedly decimated tropical populations. Giant clams, sea cucumbers, sea turtles and sea lions are also revered as miracle cures. The actual medicinal efficacy of these so-called remedies is widely questioned.

References

Allen, G.R. 2000. Indo-Pacific coral-reef fishes as indicators of conservation hotspots. *Proc. 9th Int. Coral Reef Symp. Bali, Indonesia* 2:23–27.

Allen G. R. et al. Rapid Assessment Surveys. *The Nature Conservancy* (find them at http://www.conservation.org)

Arai, M. N. 1997. *A functional biology of Scyphozoa.* Chapman and Hall, London, 317 pp.

Bak R.P.M., M.J.E. Carpay, E.D. De Ruyter van Steveninck. 1984. Densities of the sea urchin *Diadema antillarum* before and after mass mortalities on the coral reefs of Curacao. *Mar. Ecol. Prog. Ser.* 17:105–108.

Brischoux, F. and R. Shine. 2011. Morphological adaptations to marine life in snakes. *J. Morphol.* 272:566–572.

Bryant, D., L. Burke, J. McManus and M. Spalding. 1998. *Reefs at risk.* World Resources Institute. 57 pp.

Carpenter, K.E. And V.G. Springer. 2005. The center of the center of marine shore fish biodiversity: the Philippine Islands. *Env. Biol. Fish.* 72:467–480.

Cervino. J. M., R. L. Hayes, M. Honovich, T.J. Goreau, S. Jones and P. J. Rubec. 2003. Changes in zooxanthellae density, morphology, and mitotic index in hermatypic corals and anemones exposed to cyanide. *Mar. Poll. Bull.* 46:573–586.

Compagno, L.J.V. 1984. *Sharks of the world. FAO Species Catalogue.* FAO Fisheries Synopsis No. 125, vol. 4, part 1 and part 2. Rome: United Nations Development Programme, Food and Agriculture Organization of the United Nations, 655 pp.

Connor, R.C., J. Mann, P.L. Tyack and H. Whitehead. 1998. Social evolution of toothed-whales. *Tree* 13:228–232.

Diaz, M. C. and K. Rützler. 2001. Sponges: an essential components of Caribbean coral reefs. *Bull. Mar. Res.* 69:535–546 .

Duda, T.F. Jr., A.J. Kohn and S.R. Palumbi. 2001. Origins of diverse feeding ecologies within Conus, a genus of venomous marine gastropods. *Biol. J. Linn. Soc.* 73:391–409 .

Erdmann, M.V. 2001. Who's minding the reef? Corruption and enforcement in Indonesia. *SPC Live Fish Info. Bull.* 8:19-20.

Fish Base. www.fishbase.org

Grigg, R.W. And S.J Dollar. 1990. Natural and anthropogenic disturbances on coral reefs. *Coral Reefs,* Elsevier Science Publishers B.V. Amsterdam pp. 439–452.

Hays, G.C. J.D.R. Houghton and A.E. Myers. 2004. Pan-Atlantic leatherback turtle movements. *Nature* 429: 522.

Hoegh-Guldberg, O., *et al.* 2007. Coral reefs under rapid climate change and ocean acidification. *Sci.* 318:1737–1742.

Hughes, T.P., et al. Climate change, human impacts, and resilience of coral reefs. *Sci.* 301:929–933.

Jones, R. J. And O. Hoegh-Guldberg. 1999. Effects of cyanide on coral photosynthesis: implications for identifying the cause of coral bleaching and for assessing the environmental effects of cyanide fishing. *Mar. Ecol. Prog. Ser.* 177:83–91.

Karlson, R.H. 1999. *Dynamics of coral communities.* Kluwer Academic Pub. The Netherlands, 257 pp.

Kathiresan, K. And B.L. Bingham. 2001. *Biology of mangroves and mangrove ecosystems.* Adv. Mar. Biol. 40:81–251.

Mann, J. R.C. Connor, P.L. Tyack and H. Whitehead. 2000. *Cetacean societies: Field studies of dolphins and whales.* Univ. Chicago Press, Chicago, 407 pp.

Marshall, A.D. 2008. *Biology and Population Ecology of Manta birostris in Southern Mozambique.* University of Queensland, PhD Thesis. 306 pp.

Michael, S. W. 1993. *Reef sharks and rays of the world.* Sea Challengers, Monterey CA. 107 pp.

———1998. *Reef fishes.* Microcosm, Shelburne, VT. 624 pp.

NOAA Fisheries Office of Protected Resources. *Marine mammals.* www. nmfs.noaa.gov/pr/species/mammals

Oliver, S.P. , N.E. Hussey, J.R. Turner and A.J. Beckett. 2011. Oceanic sharks clean at coastal seamount. *PLos ONE* 6(3): e14755. doi:10.1371/journal.pone.0014755

Perrin, W.F., B. Wursig, J.G.M. Thewissen. 2008. *Encyclopedia of marine mammals (2nd Edition).* Academic Press, 1352 pp.

Pet-Soede, L. And M. Erdmann. 1998. An overview and comparison of destructive fishing practices in Indonesia. *SPC Live Fish Info. Bull.* 4:28–20–36.

Reef Base. www.reefbase.org

Roberts C. M., C.J. McClean, J.E. N. Veron, J.P. Hawkins, G.R. Allen, D.E. McAllister, C.G. Mittermeier, F.W. Schueler, M. Spalding, F. Wells, C. Vynne, and T. B. Werner. 2002. Marine biodiversity hotspots and conservation priorities for tropical reefs. *Sci.* 295:1280–1284.

Shetty, S. And R. Shine. 2002. Activity patterns of yellow-lipped sea kraits (*Laticauda colubrina*) on a Fijian Island. *Copeia* 2002:77–85.

———The mating system of yellow-lipped sea kraits (*Laticauda colubrina*: Laticaudidae). *Herpetologica* 58:170–180.

Spotila, J. R. 2004. *Sea Turtles: A Complete Guide to Their Biology, Behavior and Conservation.* John Hopkins University Press, 240 pp.

Van Meter, V.B. 1989. *The Florida Manatee.* Florida Power Light Company, 41 pp.

Veron, J.E. N. 2000. *Corals of the World, Vol. 1, 2, 3.* Sea Challengers. Monterey, CA. 1382 pp.

Veron, J.E.N., L.M. Devantier, E. Turak, A.L. Green, S. Kininmonth, M. Stafford-Smith and N. Peterson. 2009. Delineating the coral triangle. *Galaxea* 11:91–100.

Voris, H. K. And H. H. Voris. 1983. Feeding strategies in marine snakes: an analysis of evolutionary, morphological, behavioral and ecological relationships. *Amer. Zool.* 23:411–425.

Ward, P. And R.A. Myers. 2005. Shifts in open-ocean fish communities coinciding with the commencement of commercial fishing. *Ecol.* 86:835–847.

Whitfield, P. E., T. Gardner, S.P. Vives, M.R. Gilligan, W.R. Courtenay, G.C. Ray and J.A. Hare. 2002. Biological invasion of the Indo-Pacific lionfish *Pterois volitans* along the Atlantic coast of North America. *Mar. Ecol. Prog. Ser.* 235:289–297.

Wikelski, M. And F. Trillmich. 1994. Foraging strategies of the Galapagos marine iguana (*Amblyrhynchus cristatus*): adapting behavioral rules to ontogenetic size change. *Behav.* 128: 255–279.

Wilkinson, C. 2004. *Status of coral reefs of the world: 2004. Vol. 2.* Australian Institute of Marine Science, Townsville, Queensland, 557 pp.

Williams, S. 2000. *Artificial reef evaluation with applications to natural marine habitats.* CRC Press, Boca Raton, FL, 251 pp.

Index

Photo Credits

All photos by Brandon Cole except the following:

Gerald Allen: 299 bottom; 385 top; 393 top; 397 top (inset). **Adriana Basques:** 472 right. **Massimo Boyer** / www.kudalaut.eu: 487. **Ken Bondy:** 443 top right. **David Breidenbach:** 205 top. **Marc Chamberlain:** 17 middle left; 136; 188 bottom; 204 bottom; 214 bottom; 221 top; 226 bottom; 228 bottom; 238 top; 254 bottom; 258 top; 341 bottom; 385 bottom; 450 middle right; 450 bottom left; 457 top; 459; 461 middle; 461 bottom; 466 right; 473; 474 middle; 477 top; 480 top right; 481 top; 484 bottom; 490 middle right; 493; 494 top right; 496 middle left; 496 middle right; 512 bottom left; 514 middle left; 514 middle right; 515 top right; 516 top right; 516 middle left; 520; 530 top. **Clay Coleman:** 30 top; 230 top; 355 top; 494 top left. **Mandy Etpison:** 382 bottom; 574 bottom. **Matthew Goddfrey** / Seaturtle.org: 548 bottom. **Nigel Marsh:** 436 bottom left. **Janine Cairns Michael:** 46; 234 bottom; 362 top; 383 bottom; 396 top; 481 bottom; 497 bottom left. **Scott Michael:** 67 top; 67 inset; 69 top; 71 bottom right; 73 top; 75 right; 79 bottom; 83 middle right; 85 bottom right; 87 inset; 87 bottom left; 101 bottom left; 117; 129 bottom right; 153 top right; 154 top left; 155 top right; 160 top left; 172; 181; 188 top left; 188 top right; 189 bottom right; 190; 193 bottom; 197 top; 197 bottom; 198 bottom; 201 bottom; 202 top; 205 bottom; 207 top (main); 209 bottom; 213 top; 214 top; 216 bottom; 218 top; 220 bottom; 228 top; 239 top; 244 bottom; 245 bottom; 253 bottom; 255 top; 256 top; 257 top; 257 bottom; 259 top; 259 bottom; 260 bottom; 261 top; 263 top; 263 bottom; 265 bottom; 268 bottom; 272 top; 272 bottom; 276 top; 282 top; 286 top; 287 top; 298 top; 299 top; 304 bottom; 309 bottom; 314 bottom (inset); 319 top; 321 top; 322 top; 323 top; 325 top; 326 top; 327 top; 327 bottom (main, inset); 328 top (main, inset); 330 bottom; 331 top; 333 top; 334 top; 334 bottom (main, inset); 336 top; 337 top; 339 bottom (main); 340 top; 340 bottom (main, inset); 342 top; 342 bottom; 347 bottom; 348 top; 348 bottom; 350 top; 354 top; 356 top; 357 top; 363 top; 364 bottom; 365 top; 365 bottom; 369 bottom; 373 bottom; 374 top; 374 bottom; 375 top; 376 bottom; 378 top; 386 top (main); 389 top; 389 bottom; 390 top; 391 bottom; 395 top; 398 top; 398 bottom; 401 top; 413 bottom; 423 top; 424 bottom; 428 bottom; 439 top; 439 bottom; 441 top; 477 bottom; 480 bottom right; 491 bottom left; 497 bottom right; 501 bottom; 515 bottom left; 517 bottom; 525 bottom left; 531 bottom; 584 top. **Ross Robertson:** 401 bottom. **Tim Rock:** 37. **Lazaro Ruda** / The Living Sea: 191. **Roger Steene:** 273 top. **Mark Strickland:** 83 top right; 215 top; 216 top; 226 top; 431 top; 474 bottom. **Stuart Westmorland:** 75 top (main); 87 top (main). **Stephen Wong:** 586 bottom. **Lawson Wood:** 352 top; 358 top; 363 bottom. **Photo courtesy of NOAA:** 541.

Queen Triggerfish (*Balistes vetula*)

Brandon Cole is a biologist, wildlife photographer and photojournalist specializing in the marine environment worldwide. His photography has appeared in hundreds of magazines including *GEO*, *National Geographic*, *Newsweek*, *Outside*, *Scientific American* and *Smithsonian*.

Scott Michael is an internationally recognized writer, underwater photographer and researcher specializing in elasmobranchs (sharks, skates and rays) and coral reef fishes. He has been a scientific consultant for *National Geographic Explorer* and the *Discovery Channel*.